D1759209

WITHDRAWN
UST
Libraries

Liberty, Laughter, and Tears

Horace M. Kallen

LIBERTY
LAUGHTER
and TEARS

*Reflections on the Relations of
Comedy and Tragedy to
Human Freedom*

NORTHERN ILLINOIS UNIVERSITY PRESS

De Kalb

All rights reserved. No part of this book may be reproduced in any form without written permission from the publisher, except for brief passages included in a review appearing in a newspaper or magazine.

Copyright © 1968 by Northern Illinois University Press
Library of Congress Catalog Card Number: 68–26268
Manufactured in the United States of America

BH
301
.C7
K3

To
DOROTHY KUHN OKO
and
MILTON RIDVAS KONVITZ

This essay toward Liberty
through Laughter and Tears
is affectionately dedicated

137813

Preface

It is still a convention of our culture that tragedy is nobler than comedy and tears more characteristic of mankind than laughter. Was not man born unto trouble as the sparks fly upward? And is not our sense of this earthly life tragic? Job and Miguel de Unamuno are brothers under the skin of their diverse cultural economies, and the spirit of man is mighty only as he is a man of sorrows. Great art must needs be tragic art; the great poet, painter, musician, or sculptor must be the voice of our tragic sense of life. Compared with tragedy, comedy is deprecated as plebeian, even vulgar; the laughter it elicits diminishes the worth and dignity of him who laughs. Men of great soul, noble men, do not laugh, Aristotle tells us, they only smile. Laughter is for the common herd.

Considerable dissent regarding the role of laughter and tears has entered our cultural tradition from such notable sources as the dramatic dissents of Thomas Hobbes and Friedrich Nietzsche or the consoling ones of Friedrich Schiller and Mark Twain. The writings of these four men alone are exceptions enough to engender a counter rule. The relations between laughter and tears stirred my curiosity while I was yet a youth at college, and I am still curious. One thing I soon noticed was that the "best people" prefer laughter to tears—just like us of the lesser breeds—and give themselves

more freely to the plentiful arts of comedy than the scarcer
ones of tragedy. I came to feel that the distinctions made
much of by philosophers and critics of the dominant tradition were neither those which stand out in mankind's experiences nor those which uncover the vital springs in either
the comic or the tragic. I became possessed by abiding curiosity about them.

Their allure has drawn me, over the years, into excursions
of which this book is a sort of report. It developed without
any overt design, in an order neither quite logical nor quite
chronological. What it reports does not disclose a "system."
If it can be said to advocate a doctrine, it does not propose a
discipline, save as the artists and thinkers (upon whose personal histories it is a series of reflections) communicate something of the sort. Its chapter headings give the themes and
indicate the direction of my reflections after I became convinced that the vital center of man's struggle for his survival
is his freedom. And the book is an endeavor to say what I
came to believe about the nature of human freedom and its
role in the tragic and comic aspects of the human enterprise.
I was myself a little surprised to find how much consideration I have given to figures of the Enlightenment—to the
Englishmen, Jonathan Swift, Alexander Pope, and William
Hogarth; to the Frenchman, François Marie de Voltaire; and
to the American, Benjamin Franklin. Each has seemed to
me, in his irreduceable singularity, a unique example of the
dynamic interplay of laughter and tears in men's struggle
for liberty. Divergent and often opposed as these figures
were (in politics, in the arts, indeed, in almost every dimen-
sion of their civilization), each appealed to reason on behalf
of liberty, and each assumed a sort of championship of
liberty. Each was at once a creation and a creator of the Enlightenment, and the Enlightenment was the commitment
to the mutations of the creeds, the codes, the folkways, and
the mores of what is "modern" in the life of man.

The age of these illuminati is also known as the Age of

Reason, so known because its distinction was to be passionate about reason, as were neither the ages it followed nor the ages which followed it. Its reasons of the heart that, as Pascal avers, the reason as intellect could never know, were a passion for reason as intellect, for that free questioning by the understanding, that daring to know, which could successfully reach into everything except the reasons of the heart which are its spring. That a fruit of this passion was the knowledge which Francis Bacon discovered to be power, is no news. It may be news that another fruit was the always liberating laughter and often liberating tears which so frequently turn out to be by themselves the power in the knowledge which is power.

The more I thought about the actual experiences for which Pascal's "reason of the heart" might be words, the more likely it seemed to me that they are acts of choosing, of deciding, and of commitment for which the word "liberty" usually stands. This, I came to believe, is why liberty is held to be inseparable from life; why each one's life and liberty are held to be unalienable rights; and why the life and liberty anyone struggles for do but name the struggle itself in all its diversifications. Each of us struggles to protect his unalienable rights from the strivings of others to alienate them. Spontaneously, in all innocence, and without malice, we constrain the others of our world in the effort to maintain and enlarge our selves. Mankind's struggle for survival consists of reciprocal endeavors to alienate the unalienable. Only the dissipation of the struggler in the emptiness and impotence of death can annul his struggling; tragedy and comedy, as I now understand them, reside in the paradoxes of this condition. It is a predicament which the arts articulate by means of their own symbolizations; by evoking laughter or tears, the arts reconfirm the unalienability of the unalienable.

On the record, "alienation" remains but one more name for the ongoing warfare between different selves with their different liberties, each fighting for the nurturing instruments of its own existence and growth. Tradition sometimes calls these instruments "values," sometimes "ideals." They signify that which some people prefer and cherish and preserve against the menace of other people's choices to contain, displace, or destroy those precious ideals. Tragedy obtains when a chooser must decide between two ideals which are equally precious to him, but so related that if one is to survive, the other must perish. Comedy obtains when a precious ideal is losing in the struggle with its rejected rival but snatches victory from defeat. Laughter is the victor giving voice; tears are the voice of the defeated in the victory that makes tragedy. Both express the unalienable and its overcoming of alienation. Both symbolize a conservation and enhancement of liberty.

Such is the theme song of the varied reflections which compose into "Liberty, Laughter, and Tears."

As I neither type nor dictate, the translation of my manuscript into a typescript for the use of the printer has been a task made easy by the encouragement of my dear friend and colleague, Dr. Alfred Marrow, and the skill of his secretary, Mrs. Beatrice Peltzer. In the entire process of publication, I have from start to finish had the benefit of the wisdom and patience of another old and dear friend, Professor Rubin Gotesky. These words are but a scant acknowledgement of my debt to these good friends.

HORACE M. KALLEN

Brooklyn, New York

Contents

Liberty, Laughter, and Tears

CHAPTER ONE

Liberty, the First and the Last Thing

EVER AND ANON there comes into fashion a view of the arts which accounts for them as expressions of the singularities of the workmen whose works they are. Poems, paintings, sculptures, musical compositions, dances, and plays are conceived as soliloquies which their makers utter because they must; they no more desire or intend to address anyone else than a spring bubbling or a tree rustling in the wind. For an artist, utterance is held to be consummation and conclusion. What it does, why, and to whom are first and last not his concern. Its consequences are the concern, indeed the creation, of listeners, readers, onlookers who by accident, by wish or by intention, have taken the utterer's utterance into their own experience. Taking it, they translate it, and by their act they convert soliloquy into communication; they endow it with functions and values that its author had not looked to. What the latter feels himself to have uttered and what his audience believes him to have said need possess nothing in common; the meanings of the two may be incommensurable, the different expressions of different persons. For the work in which an artist's labors terminate

[3]

stands to the consumer who first regards it as the starting point of a work his own mind is to accomplish. What this ends up as is little likely to be that from which the artist began. The divergence of meanings is a spontaneous consequence of the difference of means. With it may go praise or misprision of the work whence the divergence started. But, again, the appraisal projects a sentiment of the critic or the public, not the experience which impelled the artist to utterance.

Whatever be the merits of this account of the relations among artist, work of art, and public, its vogue is intermittent. It occurs as an obbligato across the perennial one that all works of art are in their nature ideas which their makers seek to share with others; that they are necessarily communications and that works called soliloquies are uttered only to be overheard. In this view, what an artist tells and what his public learns must be one and the same: the meanings must be sharable and shared; one work differs from another in the measure of such sharing. Excellence, beauty, consummates the range, depth, and clarity of communication. How far and in what way a work arouses delighted contemplation, laughter, or tears, is a measure of its artistry. Enjoying, contemplating, laughing, and crying are modes of men's struggle to live on. And although *homo sapiens*, as distinguished from other mammals, is more commonly signalized a laughing or a rational rather than a crying animal, crying is a survival function whose esthetic exercise all the arts seek to evoke. Whatever his medium, an artist is an artist, less by virtue of *what* he expresses, than by virtue of his mastery over his tools and materials. This mastery is his artistic intelligence, the skill which suffuses creativity with artistry. It is this skill, alike in the romantic and the classic moods of the literary and theatrical arts, which establishes Tragedy as above all the art of tears and, in the great tradition, far higher than its Siamese twin, Comedy, the art of laughter.

True, there are persons who live alone, laugh alone, and

weep alone; persons seeking places where no one shall hear or see them, to spend themselves in utterance, to vent their feelings till no feeling is left. But such persons are not artists, whatever the vehicle of their expression. In the practice of the arts, no such soliloquies are produced. Production there is purposefully disclosure and communication, seeking response. Of course it is also a part of the record that very often responses are not responsive; that artists regularly complain they are unappreciated, misunderstood, and misjudged; that works of art ignored at one time are made objects of excited attention at another; and, conversely, that forgotten works are brought anew into vogue; that works long regarded as important, fall from the center to the fringes of attention, sometimes slowly, sometimes suddenly; that valuation is a Proteus and taste, a philanderer. The ebb, flood, whirling and eddying of the tides of interest are intrinsic to the urgencies of every self's struggle to preserve itself, and the arts are, with all the rest of the human enterprise, changing formations of this struggle.

In the career of the arts, tradition is a consequence of the spontaneities of change—change of vision and working, change of theme, tool, material, or manner. The word "creative" which, when joined to any other term, so exalts what it qualifies, regularly denotes the enduring appearance of new things amid the old; ongoing turns in new directions, bursts of continuing forms into variant formations. These bring inconsistencies, bring conflicts which estheticians and historians of letters and the arts purpose to compose and to interpret as a single natural sequence, flowing from a single everlasting spring of creativity.

The name by which tradition calls this spring is Liberty, Freedom. Some who postulate it, such as Arthur Schopenhauer or Henri Bergson, conceive it as the universal matrix of all creative acts, uniquely at work in men of art and men of faith—Schopenhauer interpreting it as suicidal will, Bergson as self-sustaining *élan vital*. Others predicate Liberty as the singularity of vision which each artist characteristically endeavors to bring to perfect expression by means of his art. Still others predicate it as the energy which gives a person's artistry itself its uniqueness. And there are those who postulate Liberty as intrinsic to the nature of every human being, struggling to live on, pursuing his happiness.

Among those postulants, some urge that living on, pursuing happiness, struggling for survival or self-preservation, are interchangeable expressions for the same doing; for the procession of experience. They appraise every turn of this procession as an event in the ongoing struggle to keep on struggling whereof all men's self-preservation consists. The self thus preserved, they say, is a changing configuration of such events, none identical with any other, each challenging and challenged by some other. Everywhere on the globe now, human beings are fighting, individually and together, for their liberties; in every land and every clime. What one person seeks as Liberty another flees as bondage. Everywhere this one same word, Liberty, signifies a matrix for different, often irreconcilable experiences, first and last the uniqueness wherein each individual is himself and no other.

In the Western world's war of all against all, this uniqueness long was identified as sin—as the "original sin" which the sacerdotal custodians of the gospel of salvation made into the capital on which they charged their usury of sanctions and profits. Suppressions and denials of this uniqueness which is Liberty all receive their meanings through openly or tacitly recognizing it as experienced actuality or experienced ideal. The pursuit of liberty, with its utterances in joy, in laughter and in tears, would collapse into a standstill without that prior liberty of pursuit. Without this prior liberty there could be no pursuit of happiness nor of anything.

The ways in which people pursue liberty are as divergent as the people themselves. Here, for example is a sufficiently representative one, pointed up by Don Miguel Cervantes, among the other psalms of life which the autobiographer of the Knight of the Sorrowful Countenance has provided for posterity. He presents it as a parable under the title of *La Gitana*, anglicized as "The Little Gypsy."

La Gitana is the lovely daughter of a Romany tribe whom a young Castilian noble falls in love with, at first sight, during a show the tribe performs in Madrid. He follows her to the tribal camp beyond the city walls. For her sake he would avert from the life he was bred to and turn a Romany Rye. The tribe's headman instructs him in the import of such a conversion. He expounds "the law of friendship" by which the Romany brotherhood live, and with what works and ways they fulfil their law, so different, so heedless of the townsfolks' mores. According to the latter, the gypsies are thieves and robbers beyond the protection of the law, committers of crimes against property and honor. Nevertheless, love conquers all. The wellborn Castilian youth prays to be accepted into the unlovely gypsy tribe and to be married to the lovely gypsy lass. The tribal fathers stand ready to initiate the lad and marry off the lass. But now the little gypsy puts in her two centavos' worth. "Fine," she tells her suitor. "By their law our lawmakers make me yours and hand me over to you. But that's not for me. By the law of my own will, which is strongest of all, I find that I refuse to become yours except on the conditions that we agreed on before you came here. It's up to you to live with us as one of our own people before you shall live with me as my husband. So you won't lightly repent nor I be fooled because we were in a hurry. If you care to observe these conditions, then, maybe, we shall belong to each other. These fine folks quite well are able to hand over my flesh to you. But not my spirit. My spirit is free. It was born free and it stays free so long as I will it."

Among the Spaniards for whom Don Miguel constructed this parable no woman, gentle or common, owned any rights or freedoms her menfolk had any call to heed. None was a Dulcinea del Toboso. All were, like Dulcinea's original, bondwomen to their fathers, their brothers, their uncles, their lovers, their masters, their husbands. Yet Don Miguel puts in the mouth of the altogether helpless, underage daughter of a tribe of outlaw tramps the ultimate defiance of the strong by the weak. The tribal elders may dispose of her body, never of her soul. That continues invincibly free until it consents to convenant freedom to love.

The parable cannot fail to stir questionings. How, one asks, did its author foresee his readers' response? With better-class anger at the female pariah's polite arrogance? With sympathy for her hapless defiance and futile rebellion in a man's world? With laughter or with tears at her pretension to an independence all society agreed could never be hers? Or with laughter at the male masters whose rule her declaration of indefeasible liberty dissipated into a rule over nothing at all? Cervantes himself had once been as hopelessly without defenses, a slave enduring the hazards of the rope, the fagot, and the stake, crippled and ever-suffering by his unsuccessful struggles to escape to freedom from the Moslem pirates, his owner-masters by *force majeure*. Could the unyielding soul of the Romany maiden have become the public token of his private laughter? A laughter, now, not only at the power it defeats?

But, on the other hand, *was* it a defeated power? True, Don Miguel survived his agonies and his bondage. But he did not of himself win the freedom he so dangerously pursued. His mother at long last was able to ransom him. The freedom that was his going and his goal may have been, like the entire life-plan of his Knight of La Mancha, not reality but illusion invincibly mistaken for reality. And what else but such a vital lie need have been dauntless La Gitana's law of her own free will, "the strongest of all"? If, then, here is irony, if here is a joke, whose is the irony, on whom the joke?

These questions, like Job's, concern human "ultimates"; and among right-thinking people, as is well known, it is *de rigeur* to treat ultimates ironically, certainly to make a joke of them. There is a story of Ernest Renan's about Amiel being displeased, because he, Renan, expressed himself with irony regarding "ultimates." Renan comments: "If philosophy does have a last word, irony is that word. How, indeed can anybody know what the world will end up as? Could not the upshot be a bad farce as readily as the true believer's glory? Which, farce or glory, nobody knows, nobody can ever know. Whichever we choose, we may be making fools of ourselves or being made fools of by others, and we should refuse to be made fools of, let the cost be what it may. So long as we decline to commit ourselves, so long as we keep playing, now with the notion 'life is real, life is earnest,' and again with the notion, 'life's a bad farce,' we insure ourselves against being entirely fooled. Only choosing one of these beliefs and rejecting the other could plunge us into folly. Yes, by ourselves and for ourselves we might indulge in this folly. But we are not entitled to mislead our fellowmen just because we choose to commit ourselves. We must needs be ready to refrain equally from believing and from doubting. We must keep turning now toward faith, again toward scepticism, and never stop at either." Whereon Charles Renouvier, who improved on Kant by confirming Pyrrho, commented that "the ultimate" need not be *what* is chosen, *what* is rejected, but precisely the act itself of choosing or refusing; that hence our last illusion may be that of Renan—the belief that we do not choose and haven't chosen. For to exist is to choose.

As Renouvier saw it, a decision in favor of indecision is still a decision. The decider averts to a *tertium quid* from the alternatives between which he determines not to choose, as Pyrrho averted to ataraxia and probabilities, Kant to faith and practice. The determination itself, at the very least, is the chosen *tertium quid*. It is a commitment; it is what Edward Thorndike called "the confirming reaction"; it discloses man, Thorndike said, as *"imperium in imperio naturæ*

. . . a center of creative force modifying himself more or less to suit himself."

Yet the Renanian uncertainty, which Pyrrho's reverberates, endures. Does the man, modifying himself more or less to suit himself, choose as he must or as he may? Thorndike, like the straightforward man of science he was, gave a due and just report of the "confirming reaction" as he observed it, and in reporting opted against *may* and for *must*. He imaged it liker to a hormone than to the free will most theologians vaticinate about and some physicists postulate or invoke. Its consequences could as well be suicidal as vitalizing. Its operation could drain instead of replenish the personal energies of the chooser. Is not so much that men live by, so much that they live for, just this—an outgrowth and overgrowth which serve no function, or serve a depleting, corrupting, destroying one? A function such as is attributed to all those parasitical survivals for which a common name is "superstition"? Might not liberty, freedom, whether fact or only idea, fail of being even a Pavlovian "reflex of liberty"? Might it not be as such a built-in superstition whose vital lying only drains off the vitality of those who rely on its promptings?

Yes, the same doubts apply in the same way to the determinism which this libertarianism may be masking. When, however, we review the gains of insight and power which the spirit of man has earned by its use of the determinist belief, is it a sufficient vindication of freedom to recall that the same doubts apply to its negation?

The sceptic record, from Pyrrho to Hume to Renan and beyond, attests that the commitment of the sceptic not to choose between alternatives, but instead to hold them together in unchoosing and detached contemplation, signalizes very few personal histories, notably where the alternatives are necessity and freedom. For his self-preservation even as purely a looker-on, the doubter cannot draw a reliable balance between the certainties and securities of determinism and the insecurities and uncertainties of freedom. Are laughter and tears, being expressions of our struggle for survival, more readily understood as necessitated sequences of response to predetermined stimuli than as free decisions, initiated with a confirming reaction? Laughing or crying might well be like breathing, less an action we can take or not as we wish, and more an action we take because we must.

But then, how shall we read "must"? Does it signify powers, activities, dispositions, whose configurations *are* the self we struggle to preserve? Or does it signify ineluctable response conforming the self to an inescapable environment which makes preservation the same as reflex action, conditioned and unconditioned? If the latter, do responses follow in one-one or many-one relations to stimuli? If the relations are many-one, then responses are not ineluctable and environment is not inescapable; then the confirming reaction is a selective decision. "Must" denotes no necessary connexion between an external cause and internal effect; "must" denotes an inward spontaneity of choosing and deciding whose sequences *are* the struggle to go on struggling which discloses our existence.

Nevertheless, scientific accounts of laughing and crying and empiric acts of comedy and tragedy postulate their being automatisms of response which can regularly be touched off by stimuli found or devised for the purpose. Both the constants and the variables recorded of the comic and tragic arts are referred to this postulate. On the record, writers and dramatists are believed to have grown from it a body of knowledge which is power as Bacon meant power, power over men who can laugh and can weep, power packed in knowing and mastering the causes of tears and laughter. The stuff of this power is a recounting of the sequences of cause-effect so sure, so reliable to use again, that the future in this field may be foreseen and predetermined as a precise and singular repetition of the past. In practice this power is a body of knowledge tantamount to a science and art of comedy and tragedy—a science at least as science used to be understood before the institution of the new physics. The doings of the practitioners of these arts, in books and plays, over the radio and in television, should render ridiculous the providence which Alexander Pope gave thanks to for "blindness to the future, kindly given, That each may fill the circle marked by heaven."

Actually, they do not. Practitioners are an anxious folk never quite secure in their power to evoke laughter or bring tears. The knowledge and skill they bet on disclose consequential indeterminacies; they are never sure things. And with this condition, which has been observed since the arts began their careers, the science of our own time manifests a certain congruity. It postulates a process of spontaneous variation, of innovation such as no providence can prevision, no knowledge of the past or vision of the future certainly predict. The process is a shaping of belief and desire, not of certain truth. Basing itself on unprecedented and incommensurable perceptions, it devises new tools and new methods to serve the same old, ongoing purpose of the struggle to live on in an environment where living on and struggling are different terms for the same reality. The purpose is, as everybody knows, in such wise to see into, to disclose, to link up and to channel the energies of the universe and their modes, as shall free us from their fatal necessary connexions and harness them to the service of our struggle to live on. The purpose is so to use determinism as to free ourselves from its determinations: it is a deal in futures, an exertion of faith and hope and an anticipation of charity in a wager that the future will come as one stuff or mode and not another. More often than not we bet that the future will continue the past and prolong the present with little change. Sometimes we even bet on no-change. On occasion we bet that the change will be a break with the past, turning it to nothing; we bet on much, on radical, on revolutionary, change.

Yet the commitment to determinism, which sustains the scientific enterprise, brings to life in its own domain that dilemma of determinism which Charles Renouvier elaborated and William James pointed up. Be it a *Yea-saying* or a *Nay-saying*, a person's act of commitment, his "confirming reaction," originates in him. It enters as an outer force the field of alternatives between which he decides—field of thoughts, field of things, field of thoughts and things commingled. Vis-à-vis any field, his commitment is an undetermined intensive addition, a contingency whose effect is to institute a necessity. Let it be conceived as an ineffably spontaneous reaction of whatever the word "will" is taken to mean; let it be conceived as a motion partly spontaneous, partly determined; let it be conceived as a totally determined culmination of a chain of necessary connexions stretching back to the willer's genes—however it be conceived, its initial relation to the field of its choosings is still tangent, still free. It is a commitment as likely not to happen as to happen. It may continue such: the relation of an onlooker to the scene upon which his wandering eye happens to fall. Should he, however, choose to pass from looking on to entering in, his passage develops as an orchestration wherein his transaction with the chosen aspect of the scene becomes internal. He has diversified and enlarged his attention as spectator into action as participator. His looking-on has matured or burst into working-into and working-over. He has closed off the alternative of his choice from its competitors. Now he first separates it into parts and isolates the parts from one another; then he brings the parts together so as to reproduce the original configuration, if he can, or to create new ones, if he desires and is able to.

Working thus with verbal or mathematical symbols, with laboratory materials or tools, with persons or places, all kept apart or joined together, his personal history—which is his present self—invests the dark void that is the unborn future of anything, with existences already born, grown, or dead, or with unprecedented configurations of them, and with new existences. Within unascertainable bounds he does create, and *ex nihilo*, even to his own surprise. His creations, when they satisfy him, count in his remembrance for reliable determinators of indeterminate prospects. They signalize the liberty which by consummating they terminate. They are now moments of departures for new turns in new directions.

That the scientific enterprise postulates freedom for the scientific inquirer to annul freedom looks like a procedural, if not a substantive, paradox. For the modes and matters of knowing, which we call science, must keep vindicating determinism as science grows. Whatever the context, the method of science is the pursuit of determinism. And the uses of determinism disclose it as mankind's most reliable means of liberating itself from the coercions of the world of necessary connexions which determinism consummates. It is the dynamic of the knowledge that is power. By comparison, however, Liberty is not a means only, but also an end; the means, indeed, which is so supremely its own end; the end which as its own means is the end of ends, the singularity and *haecceitas* of each self struggling to keep on struggling, that is, to preserve itself, to survive. The freely consequential commitment to these uses of determinism seems to be what enables free minds to render free thought systematic and logical and yet to guard this liberty from subjection to the systems they create. Concurrently, it is the sequence of such "confirming reactions" which enables free societies at once to institutionalize liberty and to keep their liberties the sanctions of their institutions. Unfree societies show themselves by comparison to be chronically unstable and to require the *force majeure* of a secret as well as a public police to hold the minds and bodies of their peoples to the authorized line.

In brief, the belief that the experience of liberty is the experience of reality long antedates the philosophic endeavor to falsify it. It is common to libertarians and to determinists and authoritarians alike. But while the former struggle to

diversify and extend, the latter work and scheme to mini-
mize and to contract the liberties of men. Where the former
proclaim that liberty is a self-evident truth, the latter elaborate arguments to prove that it is a disguised error. The first
move to confirm, the second to deny the reality of the freedom
which is experienced. And the deniers could not deny without the continuing freedom to search out and to devise the
means wherewith they strip away the disguise and expose
the error. Be they scientific determinists or theological
predestinarians, their ratiocination assumes a process which
is neither inevitable effects following ineluctable causes, nor
ineluctable conformation to Allah's infallible providence. It
assumes a struggling that resists and eludes and will not
yield, that must be forced to yield and be subdued to the laws
of nature or the will of God. Again, tradition's other name
for this struggling is liberty. Theologians' alternatives for it
are pride, sin, evil; scientists' are contingency, chance, in-
determinancy. To common sense they are the luck or fortune
that bears on our freedoms pervading all that we feel and
think and do, living our lives and earning our livings. This
liberty comes to consciousness as a sometimes happy, sometimes unhappy spontaneity and surprise; or it forms into arts
of twisting, pushing, pulling, vis-à-vis barriers, containments
or compulsions. When we say freedom *from*, freedom
against, freedom *of*, freedom *for*, freedom *to*, the preposi-
tions signify some such walling-up which we strain, work or
fight to break down.

Success would be liberty as such, unqualified, uncompleted, effortless experience. Those who report this experience report the perception of a certain spontaneity of passage, of enjoyment of whatever goes on as it goes on. They
speak of the present moment's being sufficient, ineffable, but
describe it rather as a process of alteration in place than a
transit from one place to another; not a standstill, yet not a
change of place; transition without translocation. As the
liberty eventuates, present sequences become past without

altogether ceasing from the present; while the surprises and innovations of the future come and alter the present without let or hindrance, peacefully. Present, past, and future, reporters indicate, keep suffusing one another in reciprocal diversification and compound into a single, simple propulsion like the color waves of the spectrum flowing together to be the white light simply beaming. They say that persons who have become aware of this seminal liberty at the same time know that it neither has nor needs any sanction for itself. They say that it is of and by itself the one sure sanction and measure of itself and of whatever else becomes experience. They say that it is self-excelling sufficiency and that it is the matrix of ideas of "the Good," "the Beautiful," "the Rational," "the True," and the rest. Many identify it as the mystic's ineffable; many others as the esthetic experience *par excellence.* William James signalized it as "the sentiment of rationality." There seems to be a consensus that the experience is the experience of ongoing diversifications orchestrating to a climax; that its mobility provides the most concrete, the most direct, and the most inward and immediate disclosure of end which is its own means, means which is its own end. Smiles and laughter seem so indigenous in it that literature and the other arts use them more than any alternative human expression to identify gods, sages, and saints with, as well as for Liberty's more immediately human signature.

If the reports on this experience of liberty or freedom are authentic, then the symbols *from, of, against, for, to,* which so largely go with the words and their synonyms, signify first, directions of the spontaneities away from or through or over or under whatever happens to interrupt liberty's diversifying flow. Again, these symbols point up the struggle with the interrupting barriers, and point toward the ways and means of leveling them. Many feel that the doings thence taking shape should not profane the liberty we pursue as a goal by consummating themselves in it. Both mystics and estheticians argue that goal and going are here incommensurable, that the *ways* to seminal liberty cannot participate in the actuality of seminal liberty. True, our attitudes, our preferences, our aversions, unlearned and learned together, do figure as initiations of the ways. True, within their own domain, these are the original nature wherewith we make sense of otherwise ineffably brute blind happenings. Initiates and the learned both appraise the latter as intrusions on our liberties. They delay, they arrest our passage, they stir us to open our eyes, to cock our ears and ready our muscles. We come to an alert. We look, we listen, we explore the scene before and behind, to the right, to the left, and up and down. We "deliberate" its diverse bearings on our transit. We climax deliberation in decision.

To decide, is to conclude regarding both the *what* and the *how* of whatever bars our onward way and the action which shall free the way. The conclusion is a percept whose ideo-motor span links up into a dynamic whole the sequences that compound and feed it. Its components may be symbols only, they may be images or attitudes. They may be objects of sense. When they are images or words or other symbols their resulting configuration with the set of the body toward action presents an ideal.

Our ideals give direction and form to unshaped, spontaneous change. They signalize what we want to become, the future we aspire to grow into. To compose them we choose from past remembrances and present perceptions, we shape them as the condition of our existence and as the feelings, the desires, and the needs with which we encounter it require. We give them the forms of principles and precepts. We commit ourselves to them as articles of faith about ourselves, our worlds, our destinies. We take them for designs of so struggling with the hazards of change and chance wherewith our worlds beset us, that our living-on fulfils faith as fact, subdues change into the unchanging, and chance into certainty. Thus ideals are the themes to which, as we struggle to live on, we orchestrate the transac-

tions between the changing persons we have been, and the
changing manifold of places, persons, and events we struggle
with. Ideals delineate and orchestrate the strategy, they indicate the tactics and the logistic of the war of creating the still
uncreated future life for which other terms are growing up
and growing older.

The orchestration engenders, assembles, maintains, and
alters a person's image of himself which his struggle for
self-preservation strives to preserve. Whatever else be at the
center, his body must *be*, with all its features and functions.
Between it and the varied shifting circumambience of
events, of persons and places and of thoughts and things,
between it and all that the individual's struggling works
over into configurations of his life-space, those configurations establish their ratings. Their center is his "I," the locus
of the choosings whence his values ensue. The life-space is
his "Me"—the locus of the diversities which his choosings
have appraised and ranked and keep reappraising and re-
ranking. "I" and "Me," the choosings and the objects of
choice with their orders and degrees together make up what
we know as "individuality." Thus both he and we appraise a
person's individuality as somehow a whole, and whatever he
says, does, or looks like from moment to moment as somehow segregated expressions of this undivided and consistent
whole. Both of us regard the sequences of his personal history as following from his individuality, and not conversely;
whereas the record of any one's life-story makes evident that
his individuality creates itself via the choosings which are
his "I," as they order and reorder the stuffs of his life-space
or "Me." His individuality is a lifetime of creation of his
life-space as he struggles to live on and not die. Its "Me" is
the content of the values which the elections and rejections
that are his "I" ordain, cherish, strive to enhance or to nullify. We regard the diverse sequences that enter into this
individuality as roles, as careers, and as characters. Should
any alter, then its meaning and importance for the identity of

the struggler alters as well. Some dissipate into the nullity of complete oblivion, others are subordinated, others suppressed, others persist unheeded. Still others impattern conscious endeavors to determine and to illumine the indeterminate dark future coming on. Shapings of remembrance, design and anticipation, effort and hope—these, as we have noted, can and do become ideals. They are the struggler's bet on the future, for good or ill.

Together, the diversifying components of an individual's "Me" team up into his conception of the world, of the world he takes account of. They combine into all the forms and stuffs and ways that make a difference to him. Together they compose his "cosmos" and disclose his "reality," its boundaries a frontier at which the indeterminate and undetermined future infiltrates and challenges and subverts all order and determination. It is at this frontier that he carries on his life-long struggle, projecting his destiny and forming his nature for himself. It is at this frontier that he is truly and uniquely *natura naturans*, to borrow a phrase from Spinoza, but to give it a very different meaning. However much our individual's "realities" may be oriented to his body, in the composition of his image of himself and of his destiny, he assigns his body a variable role. Although he must willy-nilly take it as the dynamic center of reference for his identity and personal history, he may appraise it a good to be cherished, preserved, and served or an instrument to be chastened, altered, used, diminished, alienated to the edge of extinction.

That, since the body is central, such appraisals are self-appraisals should be self-evident. There is no culture in which appraisal and treatment of the body are unambiguous. In all, the body's status shifts. Without losing its primacy (only suicide can effect this) as the seat of values, it gets subdued to secondary and servile roles in the value-system of which it is the matrix and which would dissipate into nothing without it.

It is the moralist's only half-true truism that other persons figure as dominant forces in the cosmos of any person; that they are forces with roles good, bad, beautiful, ugly, comic, tragic. Moralists project this half-true truism whenever they ignore that every "other" exists for every self or "I" as a force and figure in his life-space or "Me." However much personal identities may overlap as Me's, they shut each other out as I's. At the vital center, no two bodies can occupy the same place at the same time or effect the same values in the same transaction. Their indefeasible differences prolong and compound themselves in their perceptions and value-systems. There, other persons can figure solely as contents of this person's value-system, as formations in his cosmos. Their liberty is a presence which confirms or disturbs his own, and he perceives and appraises it according to the manner and consequences of its role in his personal history. The role's force and meaning make themselves as it gets enacted, from its earliest impulsion a unique sequence of movements coming on. First encounters are dark challenges between neighbor and neighbor, wary of each other, acting to define, appraise, anticipate one another, and to verify the foreseeing by its consequences. The perceptions they begin as initiate reciprocal analysis, definition and redefinition. Yet the transactions into which they develop result in products quite different from whatever they are products of.

This last the products do not disclose. They serve only to replace it and for means to handle and to understand what they replace. They are different presences, new perceptions. They are ways of taking the original ones, bets by the perceivers on the tempo and forms of their own enduring self-differentation, spontaneous or stimulated. Of them we shape a cosmos in nature, an order of values in human affairs. Cosmos and order are alike value-systems. Both are insurances we create against anticipated dangers in the sequence of diversifying recipes for stopping, looking, listening, which the sciences and the arts comprehend in their prescriptions, their tests, their experimentations, their inspections, and the like.

We labor to endow these safety-devices with a self-restoring reliability. We strive to keep them as little altered as their vital function permits. We want to have them serve as constants wherewith to guide, to regulate and measure the everlasting diversification of events. The stuff of these constancies is words, numbers, hieroglyphs, ikons, and other symbols. With these we compose those maps of life of ours, lay out our designs for living on. In them, first and last, the singularity of the imaged self—whose enactment our struggle to keep on struggling struggles for—lives and moves and has its being. Of them we shape the self that becomes the self we bet our present selfhood on. Theologians long ago, psychologists more recently, have analyzed the process as a competition of moral ideals, individual and collective at once. They have noted how the competition lets people down into perplexities and doldrums, anxieties and predicaments; how occasions come when no loyalty holds, no vision or value saves. They have noticed that the ensuing experience is sometimes positive, sometimes negative. Sometimes, the cosmos of the "Me" breaks up, its units fall away. Nothing in the value-system, nor the system itself, has any root or role in consciousness. Awareness is Liberty, a process of choosing, deciding, holding on, or letting go. It has no other content. What is usually declared to be content consists of that which consciousness is consciousness of: i.e., consciousness is "the confirming reaction," thus the seat but not the content of value. When it is appreciated as the content of value the psychic distance between seat and content has collapsed. The "I" has contracted into its own "Me"; seat is content, content seat, a spring of self-diversification into no determinate form, no single direction, but an incipiency of multitudinous forms and directions.

As has been noted, some among those who report such experiences call it Liberty, others even *materia prima*, *hulé*, but most call it God. All have much to say about its self-sufficiency, its "absoluteness," its elusiveness. Yet they tell that it differs from all other experiences in that it needs no accounting for, no attribution of causes or consequences. It goes on "because" it goes on, and goes better. It makes no sense; hence, it is either identified with rationality as William James did, or else rationality is irrelevant to it, an impertinence. Pro tanto, its ineffability renders it the standard and measure of all we call rational and the crown of every rationalization. Those to whom the experiential matrix is negative sometimes designate and deprecate it with John Dewey as "free-floating" freedom. Their interest fixes on that which happens after the break-up of a value-system, when we feel rootless, adrift and at a loss, pursuing no goal, following no direction. Then our propulsions go "on the loose," searching, seeking, devising, reaching out to, and withdrawing from, patterns of faith and works, until we have again channelled our struggles in formations shaped to whatever map of life and design for living we decide will inform our going as our goal.

There are many who cannot bear to live on believing each a seat of value with no content, many to whom "free-floating" freedom is anxiety and not ecstasy, to whom its ineffability is a striving to escape from itself to some "positive" content. For such, recovering or constructing a life-plan is once more to make sense of ineffably brute, blind happenings. Yet, not so paradoxically as it seems, the last word of sense is the word which signifies that the experience of "free-floating freedom" is consummation, not nullification. To make sense is to appraise, to qualify an event which is eventuating with a valence of becoming, with a consequential value. To make sense is to measure and to count the happening for its actual and prospective role in the syndromes of our struggle to go on struggling. This is why making sense is an immediate function of perception, the focus of its workings.

Now some happenings only impinge on the perceiver.

They occur tangently, touching perception without drawing it on; the perceiver passes them by. Others work like Goethe's *ewig weibliches;* the perceiver opens up to them, would grasp and hold on to them, absorb himself in them, or them into himself. Those, when they elude or lapse, he pursues and strives to recover or repeat; when they weaken, to strengthen; when they diminish, to enlarge and to intensify. Whatever they are, his response diversifies, and he works to make them last as diversifying. Conversely, his endeavors to diversify them diversifies him. The relation is transactional, a compenetration and orchestration, not an impact. From his locus as seat of values, however, such valences as he has suffused the happenings with are consequences of these endeavors of his; they enter into and alter the configuration of goings and goals of which he has designed his value-system. On occasion they become consummations evincing what his ideals are and how they lead him. They define for him, they disclose to him, so often not without surprise, that which for him is singularly the Beautiful, the Good, the True and the Right. Concurrently, confluences of aversion, evasion, flight, fight, suppression, or annulment set up independent disclosure and definition of the Ugly, the Evil, the False and the Wrong. If these valences are antithetical it is not as contents of values, but as actions and attitudes at the seat of valuation. The systems they compose bespeak the character of the individual or society when and if the latter's struggle to go on struggling renews and supports the system's changeful sameness, ongoingly keeps it going on.

"Spirit" is a common term for value-systems so understood. Speech utters it, works and ways express it. Indeed, they *are* spirit. We appreciate their ongoing alterations as an inward mobility keeping as nearly stable as it can the form it is generating. If the motion stop, the form would collapse and break into bits. There are those who apply the words *feedback, homeostasis,* to this motion.* They seem to intend

---

* Eating and drinking, voiding and excreting are at once the most autonomous and the most aware forms of such motions.

by these words any existence or self which renders itself identically this-and-no-other by sequent identifications of that, and of many, even of every Other with itself, however much the process also keeps diversifying the identity which initiates it. Working and fighting to stay what we are, we render ourselves other than we were as we were. Self-preservation is self-alteration; and, as biography and history are written, the latter repeatedly turns out the more critical activity. Without alteration biography and history are null. As the records read, a person's struggles, or a society's, do so change direction and objective, field and form, whenever the past changes from a present means to a different future into a barrier against differentiation; changes into such an arrest of differentiation that consequences come as sheer self-repetitions, without innovations. Then the struggle to go on struggling devalues the accumulation of experience and the uses of things past. Remembrances lapse into desuetude, or shrink to nothing; or they are absorbed and digested in new visions, new ways of a newer past created by the changing of direction and objective. The changing suffuses the *whats* of existence with untraditional valences. It transvalues old goods into new evils, old beauties into new ugliness, old truths into new errors, old rights into new wrongs. And vice-versa. Seminally at work in the strivings which the process evinces, "free-floating freedom" both initiates and consummates them.*

* There are those who see in the Western world's exemplifications of this process only evil consequences to the "whole man" in his singularity and in his commonality. Truly modern economies, they lament, such as those of the United States, or Great Britain, or Western Germany, with their roots in science and fruits in technologies, consist of gargantuan organizations at war with the wholeness. Whatever they produce, from shoes or shirts to missiles or atom bombs, the processes of production divide and diversify labor in such wise that it takes hundreds of human individuals, each performing a separate and distinct operation, to make goods that only one used to make when performing all the operations by himself alone. Instead of the man, we have now the factory. *That* is the maker, and the men at work in it are but so many factors of its deperson-alized, impersonal, sequence of production. This signifies for them neither the things produced, nor the labor producing them; it signifies only the

weekly wage which follows, yet does not follow *from*, their machine-set motions, as they repeat them without heeding what has gone before, or goes on after, from the start to the close of their working days.

Those motions, skilled or unskilled, are their means of earning their livings and the substance of their lives by day. They are of another order and quality than the activities wherein they live their lives spending what they earn, and which are the substance of their nightlife. If during the factory day men at work are "producers," they are such in an ever narrower, more automatic way, each confined to his separate station at a conveyor. If during the night, they are "consumers," the *what* and *how* of anyone's consumption has no bearing on the *what* and *how* of his production. Daylife and nightlife, labor and leisure, vocation and culture, are disjoined and segregated from one another. They have been dissociated and estranged, deprived of their organic interrelations. Culture does not grow from vocation. It has become the vocation of an authoritarian organization of operatives, who earn their livings by the use of mass media—notably the comic strip, the radio, television, the motion picture, the pulpwood and slick-paper magazine—to produce a "mass culture" for a market of consumers without personal identities, as anonymous as the markets for mass-produced shoes or shirts or cigarettes.

Neither the culture-producing corporations nor the commodity- or tool-producing cartels employ persons. They employ skills, craftsmanships, artisanships, that might soon or late be entirely automated, but are presently not available without the inconvenient troubles of personal beings whose skills or crafts or arts they are. So they accept the trouble and depersonalize it so far as they can by displacing names with numbers and human variability with mechanical repetitions. Thence, persons have come first to look upon their vocations as powers dissociated from their personalities, powers whose meanings and values signify what others are willing to pay; and then, they come to measure themselves and one another by the same standards. Thus the measure and the measurer have ceased to be one and are now two. Western mankind consists in the main of split personalities, in whom the splitting goes on until the individual has segmented the seamless stream of his feeling and doing into a manifold of roles he takes on and leaves off like his clothes, roles which have become separated from his authentic sense of self with its own "true" needs. He is a "mass-man," *in* the culture and its economy but not *of* it, never out of a crowd and always lonely. "Role" and "role-playing" have become significant items in the vocabularies of the psychologists and the social scientists.

The Cassandras of the age, mindless of their Agamemnons, have a word for this newer syndrome of mankind's struggle to keep on struggling. The word is "alienation." It has long enjoyed a vogue among socialists, poets, and novelists, and is by way of becoming a cliché among social scientists. That which it is believed to signify was called to public attention more than a century ago. The viewer-with-alarm was Karl Marx. His word for what alarmed him was *Entfremdung*, which he lifted from Hegel. Among English equivalents, "estrangement" would be closer than "alienation." But "alienation" proved more satisfying to all sorts and conditions of articulate viewers-with-alarm, and it is firmly established in English usage—with the natural diversifications of the original intent. The liking for it may be due in part to its pejorative aura, to the legal use of the word for transferring property, or for causing a transfer—an

Fields whereof the events are all predetermined and foreordained, or a universe of such fields, alike exclude multiva-
lence, shifts of valence and ambivalence; they yoke in law
the contingent and unforeseen. In them, whatever the con-

"alienation"—of affection, with the concommitant replacement of interest
or concern by indifference, by aversion, or even by hatred. When its
aficionados say "alienation," they want their hearers to envisage turning
insiders into outsiders, making strangers or foreigners of them; that is,
aliens never quite to be trusted because they have become, or are, or have
been made different. The differences may range from the minimal degree
of otherness which may distinguish identical twins, to those variations
which are the care of the "alienist."

The record does not show that the multitudes to whom the alienating
élite attribute alienation feel themselves to be "alienated." Their own
images of themselves and of their "true" needs seem to draw for their
shape and color upon the climate of opinion in which they live and move
and have their being, upon the creeds and codes of their ancestral
religions, upon the ways with them of their families, their friends, and
their neighbors; upon the ongoing heroes and perennial symbols of
freedom and success imaged by the public prints—the careers of the long-
lasting characters of the comic strips, the less durable ones of the motion
pictures, T.V., the radio, and of the personal histories of personages in
the news. These, the "common men" compound into the Joneses whom,
aware or unaware, they would like to keep up with—and with their ideals
of what they are not yet and want to become, of what they have not yet
and desire to have. In the course of a personal history, a succession of
actual figures gets taken for symbolic concretions of the invented ones.
Each figures first as an "alienation" from its predecessors, and then works
into a naturalization of its aliency among them.

Each new image presents itself as an emulative role for the individual
to enact. If it continues "alien," he drops it and takes on another. If he
lives into it, the assumed role changes into constitutive function; it becomes the "second nature" which, as Blaise Pascal long ago observed, is
far more definitive of an individual's individuality than the "needs" and
self he started as. Observed thus, the modern human's condition is better
designated "transcendence" than "alienation." It is a striving toward the
future, not a sorrow for the past.

On the record, "alienation" looks less appropriate to the life and labor
of industrial workers than to the way of life of the politicians, publicists,
poets, and novelists who practice and preach it. As an appraisal of the
relation of the modern's institutional economy to the portion of mankind
who sustains it and by it is sustained, "alienation" expresses the felt
hungers and frustrations of those who make the appraisal. It gives voice
to the singularities of their own struggles to live on, a crying out to the
multitudinous others who else, in the nature of things, would pass by the
cryers unheeding. The charge of "alienation" rationalizes the accuser-
élites' challenging, condemning and defying their society's overall indifference to the Joneses *they* crave to surpass; it also sanctions their
manoeuverings to get those emulative ideals accepted and naturalized on
their own terms.

clusion, it is foregone. Experience does not disclose such fields nor imply such a universe. At most they are creations of our struggles to go on struggling. Their self-containments are programs of future closures, not revelations of present terminality. Their wholeness is an altering wholeness, with diminutions, increments and transformations, as their histories show. Only in fields where conclusions are not foregone is there room for strugglers changing their ways, their objects, their instruments, and their surroundings; changing their relations with friends or foes; changing their transactions with facilities and impediments, obstructions and expediters. In sum, only in fields where liberty is both seminal and consequential can such choices and changes occur.

CHAPTER TWO

Beauty, Use, and Liberty

WITHOUT LIBERTY, alternative value-systems could not be envisioned, nor built, nor cherished, nor revised, nor abandoned, nor dissipated. The "faiths," "creeds," "codes," and "ideals," which conform to them local habitations and names, would lack their characteristic fertilities and their hatreds of diversity. Man's seekings and choosings, findings and rejectings, makings and unmakings—the entire unending warfare of all with all which priests, prophets, soldiers, and sages glorify or blacken could not go on happening. This consists of deadly jousts between unreconciled, perhaps irreconcilable liberties. The weapons of the combatants are value-systems. Their smiting power or validity lives in the belief of their true believers. The latter are *true* believers in that they bet their lives, their fortunes, and their sacred honors on their beliefs. They join battle with one another, like Don Quixote for his Dulcinea, in order that they may not doubt this validity in their hearts. Among the commonest words for these embattled beliefs whose validity endures only in their unceasingly renewed validation, are Beauty, Comedy and Tragedy.

Of the three, for reasons already discussed, the primal value is Beauty. The other two diverge from Beauty and return to Beauty. At all times, but particularly in our own

time, societies of men have purported to worship Beauty.
Our own has, perhaps as one consequence of the diffusion of
the scientific point of view and of the spread of the resulting
industrial economy, instituted a self-avowed religion of
Beauty. The cult seems to have taken shape about the middle
of the nineteenth century. Of course, every generation had
its devotees of art and beauty, but none in and for themselves, as their own excuse for being. To earlier ages esthetic values were signs and portents of other, "higher"
values, usually identified with divinity or some like "ultimate," such as the mystic's or metaphysician's One Ineffable.
Works of art had to justify their existence by their uses;
Beauty's function was to reveal truth or goodness or both:
Beauty was but their effulgence. Esthetic objects and values
were utilities—secondary, derivative, and dependent instruments of annunication and revelation, not the realities announced and revealed.

And such they have remained in the dominant tradition of
philosophy. Plato's ethico-esthetic absolutism was not carried over by the divergent schools that grew from his. The
tripartite division was an unequal and invidious one, with
Beauty consistently ancillary to one or both of the others.
Nonetheless, it was assigned a certain metaphysical *aseitas*,
and its role was defined by means of dialectical implication
rather than empirical observation. Not the experience of
their makers and users with works of art, solely the logical
pattern of a metaphysical system of relationships provided
Beauty its status and place. Empirical observations were
plentiful, of course, and some of them acute; but they figured
far more as illustrations of some a priori principle than as
recordings of esthetic experience. Even after Baumgarten
and the Enlightenment's psychologies of taste, the metaphysical presumption debilitated the empirical observations.
Nor is the condition altered by the operations of the psychological laboratories, with their clocking and graphing of
perceptions of shapes, colors, and sounds, their sequences

and configurations. For the laboratory is as isolating as the metaphysician's closet. It treats the esthetic event as if it were an existence *in vacuo*, analogous to a metaphysical absolute, without dynamic bearing on the economy of life and culture wherein artists ply their arts, and beauty and ugliness take place.

For the role of this economy one must look to history and biography. These show works of art and philosophies of beauty as events in the personal histories of individuals and the cultural life of societies. Like all such events, they come to birth by way of responses to specific personal and social relationships signalized in challenges and barriers to the individual and collective propulsions of men's struggles to go on struggling. An artist's response is his endeavor to meet the challenge, to pass beyond the barrier or to raze it, so to alter the relationships as to make them serve, instead of hinder, his own or his group's strivings to live on. As Edna Millay said once upon a time:

> *One way there is of muting in the mind*
> *A little while the ever-clamorous care;*
> *And there was rapture of a decent kind*
> *In making mean and ugly objects fair—*

Works of art are among the more conspicuous of mankind's multitudinous endeavors to unite and overcome the ever-clamorous care, to solve the problem that impels the outcry. Successful, they become meanings in a tradition; failing, they lapse from remembrance and observation, perhaps sometimes to be rediscovered and reappraised, or to perish. The purpose of the artist is not beauty, not ugliness. His purpose is a manifold wherein a few overt motives are to resolve conflicts, to satisfy his patrons, to practice his art, to assuage his tensions, to communicate attitudes, feelings, ideas; to symbolize value-systems, and to win health, wealth, fame, or love.

Nor do an artist's patron and public concern themselves

especially with the beauty or ugliness that metaphysicians argue about and on which critics descant. Television and motion-pictures, paintings, plays, music, stories short or long, poems, or comic strips signify to people as consumers in the same manner as they signify to artists as producers. They occur as events in the consumers' biographies, feeding various wishes or needs, meeting diverse problematical conditions in multiple ways. The ways are not only numerous, they are conflicting. The works of art operate not alone to resolve, to integrate and to liberate; they are as apt, especially if liberators, to generate at the same time new disorders and more problems.

The clash of the schools of art, the quarrels and the tumults of the critics, and the un-unifiable diversities of taste—all attest this plight. There is not a single work of the atelier, the stage, the study, or the platform which has not been appraised beautiful and ugly, tragic and comic, at the same time, or the one at one time and the contrary at another. Certainly beauty and ugliness do not get disclosed as independent essences come down from on high, or up from below; nor as identifiable qualities which can be isolated like a painter's pigments or a poet's words: beauty and ugliness discover themselves as relations in transactions between the things or thoughts to which they are attributed and to those who in good faith make the attributions. On the historical record of letters and the arts, they may be designated external relations that people take on and drop out of as they enter into or pass out of a room.

But beauty and ugliness are relations which cannot be frequently established nor long sustained. The rareness and intermittency of the "esthetic experience" wherein they play the essential role testify to this peculiar transitive immediacy. Beauty may be, indeed, I believe it is, the most original as well as the ultimate of all our values, but it is also the most volatile and transitive. Its recurrence, its fixing and validation are sought through the use of the objects we ascribe it to, and it has often been argued—I once believed this myself—that beauty arises out of use and subsides into use. It has been urged that in the world of plants and animals beauty is consequent to hunger and sexuality, and that it comes to be only as a tool of reproduction, and a channel to plenty. Among the cultures of mankind, works of art seem to figure in the first instance as acts of liberation; canalizing energies, relaxing tensions, molding materials, mastering foes—animate and inanimate, seasonal and perennial—that check, hold back, or confuse the free movement of men struggling to live their lives. Esthetic images develop divergently as accessories to eating, drinking, loving, breeding, or fighting. Their continuing role used to be, and in many respects still is, to incarnate and make visible the powers unseen that mankind imagines and fears and seeks the favor of; and to harness up, through such images, the powers seen. What religion, however abstract and mystical, can do without words and music, pictures, statues, sacred relics, rites and rotes? What can it do without buildings to keep, to say, to sing, and to enact them in? Is it for nothing that so many have described religion as "the conservation of values"?

However, in those cultures where supernaturalist religion, retreating before its innocent alternative, natural science, moves from the center toward the periphery of the human enterprise, art ceases to be a handmaiden of religion and becomes on its own account an institution of the civilization. Its themes become secular, personal, and free; its methods and techniques are taken to be as important as its themes. Letters, the theatre, the graphic and plastic arts take responsibility for the ideas they utter as well as for the symbols with which they utter them. Use ceases to be an acceptable ground for beauty. Despite the ideomotor prolongation of the lapsed past which we call tradition, unforeseen and unforeseeable designs are made objects aiming at beauty. Naturally, these designs are drawn from the conceptions of science and the practices of industry which serve modern mankind as its preeminent weapons of the struggle against foes human and nonhuman, and as its media of self-liberation and self-realization.

They provide the matrix for the unprecedented images and compositions of images which the arts of the day project. And not only do the old arts find new methods, new themes, new forms, from the impressionist to the surrealist, and all the subsequent diversification of the literary and other enterprises. Also, new arts come to birth from the new tools and materials: arts like photography, the silent motion picture and the talkie, each breeding innovations in its turn. The intrinsic allure as well as the competitive rewards of the new arts suck the artistic talent of the world into their service; the new arts awaken new preferences, create new standards, new methods, establishing new fields for beauty and ugliness, transvaluing old ones, and throwing old judgments into embattled confusion. The old arts that live on may do so because they newly enlarge men's liberties. By winning contemporary relevancy and arguing new autonomous meanings, they survive in the new surroundings to give tradition a renewed life and a new direction. Or else they survive because an old mood has not quite lapsed or because they are inculcated by institutional discipline and the coercions of authority.

Sometimes all three influences contribute to their currency, sometimes only one. There are for example, those two much bespoken literary collections—the Sacred Scriptures and the works of Shakespeare. Both have had a variegated history with dramatic changes of status amid the letters of our Western world. Would the Scriptures have retained the rôle they used to play in the minds of Western men, without their sanctification by the persistently powerful ecclesiastical establishments exercising unquestioned authority? Who reads or reverences the Scriptures that doesn't have to, either because he has been habituated to this reading as to his smoking or drinking, or because he believes reading them a

useful activity, protecting his existence and ensuring that he
shall live freely and happily when he is dead? Only he can
read and reverence who has chosen them from alternatives,
freely. Who, among the many who have learned a play or
two of Shakespeare in the schools and who continue to iter-
ate the schoolroom judgment of him, read him or see his
plays acted for any other reason? Who concerns himself
with Homer or Euripides or any of the "classics" for any
other reason?

Some, certainly; but the repristination of these collections
for the sake of such esthetic experience as they might provide depends, not on what they are in themselves, but on
their being fitted into the changing scene; their being rendered relevant to, or escapes from, new enquiries, new struggles, new relations, new purposes. The present argument is
that the esthetic role of these collections depends on the
degree in which their immediate content can be compene-
trated with their instrumental, their consequential values.
Insofar, then, as they can be used to further the strength of
the struggler as he goes on struggling, the old masters attain
a new beauty.

It was earlier said that in cultures turning on science and
not on supernaturalistic religion, use ceases to be an acceptable ground for beauty. But now, when the arts have become
offices of an autonomous and independent institution of our
culture, beauty postulates a use and supervenes upon it. The
relationship was initiated when the dawnmen drew the rein-
deer and the aurochs in the caves of Altamira. If they did so
to utter their hungers and envision their desires, they also did
so to manipulate and control the life-nourishing herds whose
movements meant survival or oblivion. The relationship is
remembered and actualized whenever Australians or Afri-
cans or Indians dance their ancestral dances—as the Hel-
lenes and Hebrews too danced in their time, and some still
dance—in order to ensure a great victory in the war, a great
bag in the hunt, a great crop in the tillage. In due course it

was found that the means did not attain the ends they were means to. But the means survived as ends in themselves. Beauty became a relationship which persons and peoples sought for its own sake. Drawing and dancing and painting and playing and singing were first beautiful actions taken that the actors might usefully eat and drink and love and breed and fight. In many situations they are still such, of course; but more and more it becomes everywhere the case that we usefully eat and drink and love in order that we may more beautifully draw and dance and sign and play-act. Thus, something new is upon us. Beauty is no longer the tool of use, nor is it just a self-sufficient end in itself. Ends and means now freely change places and flow together, each in the other like the years of a life or the tones of a tune, so that in the manifold of a personal existence or a national spirit, one cannot be separated from the other without destroying both. It might almost be said, Beauty initiates and consummates use; use initiates and fulfills itself in Beauty.

Whenever such an action, such a blending and flowing together is experienced, the divergent propulsions of our organs and their energies orchestrate with one another—they have become freely confluent; as subjects, their transaction with the object evoking the action render the two a single, simple value-system of which the experience is the seat, the object the content, while each magnifies the diversifying singularity of the other. Whatever tends to disturb either is for the nonce cut out and shut off in the course of a self-containing passage of means into end. Liberty is experienced in an ongoing perception, an immediate, unmixed stream of consciousness, welling spontaneously up toward a self-compounding climax of envisionment. Judging from the record of such experiences, there is nothing in the world incapable of entering into such syndromes with personality, not any place, not any time, not any circumstance. The person's "Other," his partner—now of his life-space, his "me"—may be simple, complex, concrete, abstract, orderly, disorderly, still, mobile, symmetrical, asymetrical, even chaotic.

Although works of art have been long assigned a foremost, even an exclusive role in this syndrome, their prevailing roles are, as has been observed, directed to other ends. These ends are not that immediate experience of liberty. Rather, are they leadings to it; they are patterned ways toward its attainment, even though the attainment is by no means a foregone conclusion from the ways. The first intention of these ways looks more like freedom *from*, freedom *through*. That confluence of going and goal which is simply liberty is said by estheticians to be what the arts "really" seek, although the record does not confirm them, and although, if the arts do seek it, they do not often find it. But even when they do find it, the arts are not the only finders. Accounts of the esthetic experiences indicate that any event may figure in the untrammelled welling forth of consciousness, in the sequences of perception teaming up into a formation whose first and last moments are simultaneously means and ends, goal, and cumulative ascent toward it.

However else we may speak of beauty, we refer, when we use the word, to the actual relation between the communicants in this transaction. It is, as the record discloses, an external relation; not in the skill of the artist nor the understanding of the critic or connoisseur to command. Beauty is no thing or essence that the one communicant creates, and the other accounts for. All that the most skillful of masters ever creates is an occasion for beauty to happen, somewhat as a chair or a table is an occasion for a man to sit. All that the most learned critic or connoisseur accounts for is the form and history of the occasion and the personal history of its creator seeing and making. Both can, both may or may not, become aware of the beauty-relation consummating their transactions with the masterpiece after it has challenged and engaged their perception. As accounts of the esthetic experience witness, beauty is contingent, beauty is free, beauty happens. Beauty happens freely to any object, any person, in any place, at any time, in any circumstance. Beauty happens and passes. After it happens, simple freedom follows. But where, to what natural event or human creation, and how beauty happens and freedom follows continue tangent outcomes of luck and chance. Every work of art is a bet which its maker or perceiver can lay that beauty will be its outcome, and liberty its consequence. But the history of the arts shows that none is ever a bet on a sure thing.

CHAPTER THREE

Laughter, Tears, and Selfhood

I F THE RECORD may be relied on, what holds of beauty, holds of those relations between persons and persons and between persons and events which we call comic or tragic. Orchestrated formations of dissonance and conflict though they be, neither is ever a bet on a sure thing. The relationships arise contingently and end freely, outside of the arts. Like beauty, they happen and pass over into simple liberty. As happenings they are the raw materials which craftsmen of the arts of comedy and tragedy work over into the drawings, paintings, dances, poems, plays, and novels for aficionados to bet on—to bet, not on their occasioning beauty, but on their evoking laughter or tears. Like beauty, the comic and the tragic come to be in a transaction between a perceiver and something he perceives; they figure as relations in that transaction. What the perceiver perceives is not an orchestration building up to a climax; it is a struggle going on. The comic and tragic relationships supervene within and upon that struggle and confirm the values which survive it. That which they relate may be persons, places, characters, or events. Whatever else they are, they must be "values"—objects from which the perceiver chooses one, to cherish and preserve, or to repudiate and annul, in victory or defeat of the chosen. The climax of the struggle is liberty. The entire event—plot in play or story, design in caricature or comic strip—presents a struggle where victory is freedom *from* an action that engages the free agonist as completely as the less free. For keeping another from his liberty constricts and restrains the keeper's: the doings and sayings of each are but sequences of his pursuit of liberty for his cherished value. Tragedy, however, wins this goal by way of loss or diminution, comedy by way of victory, gain, and enlargement.

Custom marks comedy with laughter, tragedy with tears. Yet neither as spontaneous expressions nor as evocations by the arts do tears signalize only tragedy, nor does laughter signalize comedy alone. One single propulsion may bring both together. Experiences of transactions are reported where both figure in doings or sayings on which beauty supervenes. The tradition persists, nevertheless, which assigns tears to tragedy, laughter to comedy.

The assignment seems so reasonable, so right, that asking *why, what for, how,* looks like seeking the obvious, requiring evidence for the self-evident, treating the familiar like the strange, keeping on testing the infallible for fallibility. In the self's struggle to perceive itself, however, it has been its perennial reconfirmation of the obvious, of the self-evident, of the familiar and the infallible by experience after experience and experiment after experiment, that supports these roles of theirs. Everlastingly putting them to the question reassures the self regarding their function in its struggle to go on struggling. However much, however often, it bets on them, it can never be dead sure it will win.

How then, as tokens of the comic or the tragic spirit, do laughter and tears figure in man's liberty? What is their status among the other psychosomatic propulsions which together orchestrate into the human person? Since each in its

own way brings knowledge which our struggle for survival
must gather and retain if it is to go on struggling, each has
its own significance for our pursuit of liberty. As Darwin
accounted for them, laughter and tears are at bottom organic
functions. Physiologists would list them with other kines-
thetic experiences, such as blushing and paling, sleeping and
dreaming, and so on. They happen amid the multitudinous
diversity of an individual's transactions, both the interor-
ganic ones, which his skin bounds, and those he makes with
one or another item in his surroundings. They become, when
they happen, ideomotor foci of the dynamic interplay between the individual's consciousness and this or that inward
or outer item. They evince appraisals which signalize the
issues with necessities and contingencies that mankind,
struggling for their freedom and existence as human beings,
keep ever joining. They point to the ongoing alterations of
inner stance and outer relations which struggles over these
issues consist of. There is a wide consensus that laughter
and tears punctuate critical moments of an individual's personal history and diverse turning points in his pursuit of
liberty.

Such moments may come in earliest life, and thereafter
come again as sheerly somatic crises; they may come as new
directions in unvisualized, unverbalized experiences of the
body battling to preserve the ever-altering formation which
is its identity *in actu*. Soon or late, a society will cultivate
these primal experiences as independent variables. Abstract-
ing them from their contexts, a culture will devise characteristically diversified visual, verbal, and dramatic skills for
repeating and extending these experiences for the sake of
whatever they yield as they go on, without regard to other
consequences. People seek laughter and tears as modes of
enjoyment and satisfaction, as ends and consummations in
their struggle with fate, with fortune, and with other men's
freedoms. So, they transvalue events into ideals, experiences
into designs for living out their own liberty. One notes what

seems a paradox: as a psychosomatic event, laughter has been more widely studied than tears; but the comic arts which aim at laughter have received less approval than the tragic ones which aim at tears. Tragedy is glorified as the nobler art.

The wise and the smart, no less than the learned, distinguish degrees and varieties of laughter. They note numerous formations of the laughing experience. Practitioners of the comic arts tend to appraise differences of degree as differences of kind. The differences must of course be both audible and visible. But laugh-makers record certain intensities which are visible only, certain others that are adequately known and appreciated through the ear alone. The solely visible is the smile. Its earliest coming is said to be observable in a very young infant, after it has been suckled until it refuses the bottle or the breast, and lies satisfied at ease. The facial expression which sometimes goes with this condition has been called a smile. If a baby regurgitates, the milk's rise in its gullet is said to evoke at times sucking movements which diversify the smile into the beginning of a laugh. Infant smiles have been identified as authentically such on the thirty-ninth day after birth. There is a continuing consensus that infants smile to adults before the end of their third month. From then on the smile's varieties range to the celebrated one with which Dante says Beatrice thrice greeted him, or the one he saw on the Divine Countenance in Paradise, or that Leonardo shaped on the face of Mona Lisa. These smiles are diversely symbolic. In certain orders of polite society they are a checking and inhibition of laughter, its genteel representative. In such societies laughter is regarded as an expression of vulgarity, a yokel's rude and noisy giving voice while his body goes through unseemly shakings and posturings. Ladies and gentlemen must needs maintain an ordered quiet. Good manners forbid laughing, encourage smiling. There is a Buddhist if not a Stoic smile for ataraxia—not for infants, of course. The infant smile is, in the

nature of things, a toothless pulling back of the lips; and as
the teeth come, a baring of incisors with which the feeder
cuts, and the canines with which it tears his food.

At all ages, smiles happen far more often than laughs.
Laughs follow later as the infant grows, though far earlier
than speech follows lallation. We laugh long before we talk
and we cry before we laugh. William Carlos Williams told
me that he first laughed aloud when less than a year old.
Indeed, don't we enter the world with a cry, and don't we use
much the same organs and muscles for all three actions?

The action which is laughing is commonly a sudden action. It may engage only the thorax and voice-box, it may
mobilize the entire body. The forms and degrees of involve-
ment are signalized by different words: giggle, cackle, titter,
chuckle, guffaw, peal, horse-laugh, yowl, belly-laugh, boffo.
We burst into laughter, we hold our sides, have fits of it,
choke with it; we shake like a jelly, we are convulsed with it,
we could laugh on the wrong side of the mouth. Sometimes,
when laughing, we sweat, we lose control of the bladder, we
end up weeping. We could die laughing. Laugh-makers say
of their productions: "it'll have 'em rolling in the aisles";
"it'll kill 'em." A laugh may start and stop with a lift of the
corners of the upper lip, a wrinkling under the eyes while
these moisten and brighten, a slightly sharper intake of
breath, perhaps a very slight outward movement of the
hands followed by breathing out in short quick puffs or
chuckles or gurgles, accompanied by a wider, more expan-
sive movement of the hands. The ascent toward the boffo
consists in throwing back the head as when swallowing
something good, explosions of the breath into louder and
louder sounds of varying pitch, swaying the body back and
forth in both quicker and wider rhythms, perhaps stamping
the feet, one hand pointing toward whatever has occasioned
the laughter, or both waving and slapping together, reaching to anybody near by—friend or stranger—with slaps on
the back, pokes in the ribs, even hugs. The syndrome is

experienced as a single, simple, involuntary movement which often comes to its end in tears and exhaustion.

The motor pattern that forms from the guffaw is defined by convulsions of the muscles of breathing-out, thus cutting-off breathing-in, expanding the chest, moving the diaphragm. In this form of laughter the foremost role is played by the large zygomatic muscle which dominates the muscle group active in laughing. All varieties of laughter—sad, gay, angry, scornful, sardonic, ironic, cynical, joyous—give voice to orchestrations of other muscles such as the risus, the buccinator, the lesser zygomatic. This last is the muscle that raises the nose and lips and shapes the sad expressions which usually go with shedding tears. All these muscles are innervated from the corpus striatum by the thalamus (now by widespread consensus the center for feeling) and by the entire sympathetic nervous system.

That chemicals like the classical "laughing gas," nitrous oxide, hashish, strong drinks in certain measures, and other drugs bring on laughter, early suggested taking laughter as Max Eastman did *—for an instinct, or as some behaviorists speculated, for a built-in, an unconditioned, Pavlovian reflex such as salivation, but an instinct or reflex singular to man.†

---

* See my *Indecency and the Seven Arts*, Chapter X.

† Perhaps the laughing—and the weeping—of "the Wild Boy of Aveyron" has a bearing on this speculation. This boy's story is told by a Doctor Itard, a physician in the south of France during the French Revolution. When picked up in the seventh year of the Revolution, the boy was, Dr. Itard guessed, eight or nine years old. His ways were absolutely animal, but without the natural cleanliness of animals: in that he was unspeakable filthy he was unlike animals. But his interests were exclusively animal interests—the unhumanized wild exercise of his elemental physical functions, yet without the impulse or understanding for the use of any human device to satisfy his needs. He could not "climb a chair to reach for food." He would not and could not play. "No signs had any meaning to him and he passed without apparent reason from profound melancholy into peals of excessive laughter." They named the boy Victor and formed the project of restoring his humanity to him. But his domestication was arduous. Kindness worked out slowly; he kept running away. Over the years, not unexpectedly, Victor became attached to Dr. Itard. When the latter came to see him, Victor, the doctor reports, would hug him and draw him down to sit beside him on the couch. Sometimes he

Observations how a sort of laugh which isn't quite a laugh, a hesitant, uncompleted laugh, ensues upon applying electric current to the larger zygomatic, crystallized speculation into hypothesis. Hypothesis became theory when these observations were joined to others—of idiots laughing, of the laughter of hysterics, epileptics, and the mad. Those laughs often looked like absolute irrelevancies, without relation to any person, situation, or event; unwilled, mysterious, perplexing intrusions into the consciousness of the laughers bringing no enjoyment nor any awareness of something laughable; causing anxiety and apprehension instead. When this blind laughter figured with other symptoms in a syndrome which called for brain surgery, it was generally found that the laughter had been concurrent with one or another of a diversity of lesions in areas ranging "from the limbic system at the cortical level through hypothalamic centers to the bulbar-motor systems." *

Interpret the relations between lesion and laughter as you will; let laughter be an effect of which the lesion is the cause, as the twitching of a frog leg is an effect whereof an electric current is the cause; let laughter be a compensation to the lesion, a counter off-setting its action; let it be a flight from this action, an unorchestrated effort at disengagement from the action. Whichever of these alternatives one chooses, the surgical findings indicate no one sole center for the comic

---

would jump up and laugh and clap or he "places himself opposite me and caresses my knees in his individual way, which is to feel them and to press them vigorously all over for several minutes and sometimes presses his lips to them two or three times." Victor seems also to have become attached to the housekeeper; but she was the occasion of tears. One day he had escaped into the road: "on seeing Mme. Guerin, the housekeeper, he burst into a flood of tears." Were Victor's laughter and tears instinctive? Were they Pavlovian reflexes? Were they functions of the unalienable liberty which the struggle to sustain one's own singularity of living expresses?

* "Involuntary Laughter," Matthew M. Wood, Hendrik I. Svien, and David Daly (in *Proceedings of the Staff Meetings of the Mayo Clinic*, May 14, 1958.) The work would be better entitled "Pathological Laughter" since authentic laughter is also spontaneous and involuntary, but is related to something laughable and is enjoyed.

perception. They suggest that "the sense of humor" obtains in a transaction between the whole self and some other existence; that "absolute" laughter is neither the laughter of the daily life nor of the arts. Yes, the latter comes as suddenly and as "involuntarily" as "absolute" laughter; but its surprise springs from configurations with every sort and condition of human attitude, passion, and experience. Whatever its company, glands become more active, blood vessels dilate, the face flushes, the blood pulses faster through the body, the intake of oxygen mounts. At its optimum, the body laughing is the body heightening its vitality, sensible of well-being; it is a euphoric body. Hence, laughing is recommended as the best exercise for sedentary people; hence, it is employed as a therapeutic technic by certain psychiatrists; hence, there is the cliché, "a laugh a day keeps the doctor away"; and hence, the vogue of the hoary maxim "laugh and grow fat," continuing even into our culture which magnifies the conflict between fatness and health. Perhaps it is not always the case that "a merry heart goes all the way," but we still like to believe it.

At its worst, the body laughing offsets discomfort or pain, and compensates for them; neutralizes or overcomes or liquidates feelings of inadequacy, conflict, containment, frustration, or defeat, until its welfare exhausts it and it collapses, in helpless tears. There is tragic laughter, and we do speak of happy tears and of hapless tears.

Our culture takes tears to betoken every form of unsuccessful struggle. It places them at the opposite pole to laughter, aligns them with polar attitudes and feelings. Even philosophers do take account of their recurrent minglings with laughter.* But the philosophic tradition seems hardly to

---

* Perhaps this inversion is what solemn Herbert Spencer had in mind when he declared that laughter has no role in natural selection, nor in the survival of the fittest; that laughter is naught but a draining of an overcharged nervous tension which, having no organic direction of discharge, finds the easiest; hence, starts at the lips, goes to the respiratory mechanism, arms, legs, spinal column. He called the movements that laughter

have recognized how much more deeply and continuously the two do mingle. Likewise the comic and the tragic arts mingle their lights in certain forms and become "high comedy," "tragi-comedy," arts of "humor." For the most part, however, they take laughter and tears as independent variables in nature and tend to keep them segregated, however diversely, in culture. When tears flow, the muscle chiefly at work is the small zygomatic. It raises our lips and nose for us and in other ways shapes the sad expressions of the tearful face.

Now, our lachrymal glands secrete tears continually. Our eyes must have them to wash away irritations from eyeballs and eyelids; to keep the eyes fitter to do the seeing which Emerson says they were made for, in a world where beauty is its own excuse for being. Strain and tension make for a greater abundance of tears. The flow's excess normally finds its way, through the lachrymal canal or the nasal duct, into the nose. When, for whatever reason, the stream of tears is greater than the canal and duct can channel, they overflow the eyes and run down the cheeks. Then we are said to weep, to cry, to shed tears. The face is said to be bathed in tears. To the tongue or palate, they taste salty, and "salt tears" is an expression in common use. But the first savor of tears is not salt, it is *bitter*, *biting*, *sharp*. The eye, before their overflow, unconscious of their touch and feel, has been rendered sensitive of them. We speak of its "stinging tears," its being "blinded by tears." As usage goes, these experiences are not enough to denote the ocular feel as such, for it varies with the emotions or sentiments that tears come with. Tears flow from pain, from pleasure, from frustration, from rage, from sorrow, from relief, from defeat or from victory, from happiness or from joy. Conventional usage joins tears

---

consists in a luxury and prophesied that laughter would disappear as mankind evolved to the level where it no longer acquired and needed "to spill away" surplus energy. Without surplus, no laughter. Alas for the stage plays that depend on the tired business man!

less to the feelings of release and enlargement than of contraction and confinement. Hence, when the former occurs, it is news. Why else did the press spread large and wide the image of Sugar Ray Robinson weeping when he had won back his middleweight boxing championship by knocking out Bobo Olson?

Tears streaming down his face," read the A.P. report in the New York *Times*, "Sugar Ray Robinson, middleweight king again, was led into his dressing room after his smashing knockout of Bobo Olson tonight.

He looks more like after he exhausted himself against Joey Maxim than a guy who just won the title," said a ring follower.

Big George Gainford, who has been closest to Robinson since Ray started his boxing career, took charge of the Harlem Dandy and elbowed him through the crush of reporters to a table. There Robinson sat down facing the group.

He didn't speak for nearly five minutes as Gainford and others hid him from view, wiping his face, patting his back and getting him out of the emotional strain he obviously was undergoing.

Then Ray spoke quietly over a public address microphone.

"I had to cry," he said. "I just couldn't believe it was all over. This comeback has been a ghost of a thing with me ever since Tiger Jones licked me here [in the Chicago Stadium] nearly a year ago.

Only a few people thought I should continue after that, and to them I owe thanks. But many others said I didn't have a chance, that I should quit for good. It was a very hard thing to swallow and very hard getting ready to continue."

He repeated: "Now I have gotten rid of the ghost."

Tears also flow because of a mote in the eye, and, like Alfred Tennyson's "tears, idle tears," from no known cause at all.

That tears come so readily, so obviously—at least, in our culture—with experiences of insecurity, insufficiency, loss or failure, renders them an easy expression for these and the viable symbol for the syndrome of attitudes and postures they evoke. An easy, viable symbol, yes, but not a necessary one. The notion that tears serve this function of necessity follows from our awareness that laughing is often a liberating alternative to weeping. Byron spoke it: "And if I laugh, 'Tis that I may not weep." Juvenal had his own satirical perception of it: "Laughing is easy, but the wonder is, what store of brine supplied the weeper's eyes?" We may read an explanation of the wonder in Dostoevsky's *The Possessed*. Hear Maria Timofeyevna, the sad simpleton.

But I believe," says I, "that God and nature are all the same thing. And they all shouted with one voice: "You don't say."

The abbess laughed and began whispering with the lady. She called me to her and she patted me, and the lady gave me a silk scarf—would you like me to show it to you? Yes, and the little monk at once began teaching me, and everything he said was so friendly, so gentle, and it seems to me so full of understanding. I just sit there and listen. "Do you understand?" he says. "No," I say, "I haven't understood anything and I'd rather you all left me quite in peace." And about this time an old woman who was doing penance in our midst for her soothsaying whispered to me, leaving the church, "What is the Mother of God, do you think?" And says I, "She's the great Mother, the firm hope of the human race."

"That's right," says she. "The Mother of God is the great Mother Earth, and she offers great joy to men. *And every sorrow of earth and every tear she sheds is a joy to us. Let your tears water the earth at your feet but half an ell deep, and in the same hour, all will make for joy. And never again will you have any worry—any worry at all. That's the prophecy,*" she said.

"And I've kept her words in my heart. *And now, whenever I bow deeply in prayer, I always kiss the earth. I kiss it and weep.* And I tell you, Shatuska, *There is nothing more in those tears, and if you have no worry at all, the tears will come for sheer joy. The tears come of themselves, that's the way of it.* Sometimes I go down to the shore of the lake. On one side is our convent, on the other is our peaky mountain—that's its name, Peaky Mountain. And so *I go up this mountain and turn my face to the East and fall down on the ground and weep and weep—I don't know how long I go on weeping—and then I forget everything and no longer know what's happening.* Then I get up and set off home, and the sun is going down so big and mighty, and beautiful— don't you love looking at the sun, Shatuska? It's a good thing to do, but sad too. And I turn back toward the East and the shadow, the shadow of our mountain, runs like an arrow straight across the lake, and splits this rocky island like this; just as it lies, into two halves; and while it's splitting the island like this, *the sun sets altogether, and everything is suddenly blotted out. Then suddenly all my longing seizes me, and memory comes back to me. I become afraid of the darkness, Shatuska, and weep still more for my little child.*"

I have italicized the words which tell the answer.

Both laughing and weeping seem to be held built-in formations of behavior, responses that we can't help choosing between when an inner condition or an outer occasion presses the pre-formed buttons. Weeping, like laughing, has its characteristic sequence of ideomotor patterns, mounting to a disoriented ecstacy of tears. They start at the streaming eyes in a pale, not-quite-wrinkled face; they go on to the face of sunken features, wrinkled brow, down-drawn mouth, to a body with sob-shaken shoulders, cold skin, clasped hands, pressed-together knees; the torso first swaying back and forth, then rolling as in an epileptic seizure. They start with soundless weeping and go on to the sighs and sobs and ullulations mounting to a frightening lament and finally subsiding into a lassitude of exhaustion.

Like laughing, weeping is considered an unwilled reflex capable of being reshaped into a voluntary, purposeful mode of action. How reshaped, in what situations, into what forms, are, as with laughter, functions of the culture among whose matrices both laughing and weeping sustain their vital roles. To certain peoples of the South Pacific it is *de rigeur* to weep when meeting and not when parting: not to weep is to offend the mores. Among certain Europeans and Americans the power to weep at will is appraised a moral defect and the exercise of it a form of hypocrisy, while laughing at will is another story. If laughter and tears are the unlearned, autonomous, modes of action—which it has been argued that they are—then freedom *from* them, both inwardly and in the world around, could be as significant for survival as freedom *through* them. To laugh when another weeps, to weep when another laughs, may be ways toward greater safety in one's own struggle to be free. A decision not to laugh, not to weep, can serve this safety as vitally as a decision to do either. That oracle of practical wisdom, Lord Chesterfield, had never been heard to laugh "after he had come to the full use of his reason."

Such decisions may also thus serve the neighbor's freedom as well as one's own. For, as the dubbings of radio and video disclose, laughing and weeping are both contagious. Unresisted, they spread. "Laugh and the world laughs with you, weep and you weep alone," expresses a prejudice, not an observation—a prejudice which favors laughing. Its counter is the cliché that "misery loves company." And everybody knows that misery gets company. Everybody can recall the many occasions when another's weeping brought unwanted tears to his own eyes. Lonely weepers may be no less uncommon than lonely laughers. If this be so, the weepers are more rarely commented on. Indeed we are apt to be wary of a stranger laughing to himself; he makes us feel insecure. We'd like to assure ourselves he's not laughing at us. The lonely weeper more commonly awakens a sympathetic concern. But the sympathetic contagion pertains to both laughter and tears. Without it neither the comic arts, from slapstick to high comedy, nor the tragic ones, from soap opera to Shakespearean tragedy, could be anything but soliloquies. All their business is getting their readers and hearers to laugh together as one and to cry as one; and the measure of their success is the scope and frequency of this communion.

Yet it is Western culture which selects laughter as the differentia of *species humanum* and regularly envisions man as *homo ridens*, hardly ever as *homo lacrimans*. Some time ago a psychologist in a midwestern university reported a study of ratios of laughter to tears among the students of his institution. He said that laughing was to weeping as 400 to

1, that the students cried less than once in twenty days, while they laughed oftener than twenty times each day. Women wept three times as often as men and laughed less often. Ninety-eight per cent of the time both sexes were led to laughter by other human beings; eighty to ninety per cent of the time tears came because of "the environment." The chief occasions were class grades and letters—or none— from home. "Dates" ranked tenth as occasions for cheers, their relation to tears was not reported. The learned inquirer opined that the collegiate ratio of laughter to tears might well be representative.

However one person's laughing affects another, its beginnings in any personal history is free, joyous, and generous. The baby-smile of repletion, satisfaction, or welcome diversifies into the laughter of the small child hopping and skipping and jumping and tumbling; spontaneously expending those energies which "play" so diversely enchannels in so many action-patterns. The spontaneous discharge of energies shapes into "play" whenever some give-and-take with somebody else—another child or an adult—gets repeated. Repetition builds a happening into a game. William Carlos Williams told how as a less than one-year-old infant, he watched his father chopping wood: "Each time the axe went wham into the wood, I'd let out a wild cackle of delight." He told of his reaction to a bolt of lightning: "it was so full of laughter that the sense of catastrophe was averted."

Again, repetition may impattern some formation of make-believe. The laugher laughs enacting a role, fully aware of the difference between what he is and what he pretends he is. What he is discloses itself by the constant exercise of his vital functions; what he pretends he is he manifests by behaviors that he takes on and lays off as he does a hat or a coat. His laughing during his play—by himself or with others—is a part of the configuration of his role or game. It lives from his being aware of the distinction between his persistent being and his ephemeral seeming. Its direction and meaning are consequences of this awareness. A small child's laughter is undirected; we might call it "free-floating." It consummates and accompanies the spontaneous flow of its energies via the diverse movements of its limbs and the feel of euphoric vitality which tops off any adequate functioning. The joy of it is closer to flowers blooming or birds singing than human beings playing.* A lone but not a lonely laughter, this of the small child is not *at* anybody nor *with* anybody. It is not the laughter of a victor successful in freeing himself *from* something inimical. It is the utterance of a tiny life when it is at ease, when it is not experiencing constraint or antagonism from an opposed liberty. Constraint and the rest are yet to come, too soon to come, and to engender the perennial powers that the arts of comedy—so much arts of liberation—aim to overcome by means of the complex and purposed laughter which signalizes their success. The laughter of the young child is without cause, without purpose, without goal. It is neither a means nor an end, but simply and delightfully is, and thus is truly free.

---

* Joy, when intense, expresses itself in various purposeless movements such as dancing about, clapping the hands, stamping the feet, jumping up and down, mauling other people, shouting and laughing. "Laughter", writes Darwin (*Expression of the Emotions in Man and Animals*, Chapter VIII) "seems primarily to be the expression of mere joy or happiness." We clearly see this in children at play, who are almost incessantly laughing. With young persons past childhood, when they are in high spirits, there is always much meaningless laughter. The laughter of the gods is described by Homer as the exuberance of celestial joy after their daily banquet. A man smiles—and smiling as we shall see graduates into laughter—at meeting an old friend in the street as he does at any trifling pleasure, such as smelling a sweet perfume. Laura Bridgman, from her blindness and deafness, could not have acquired any expression through imitation, yet when a letter from a beloved friend was communicated to her in gesture language, she "laughed and clapped her hands, and the color mounted in her cheeks. On other occasions she had been seen to stamp for joy."
"Idiots and imbecile persons likewise afford good evidence that laughter and smiling primarily expresses mere happiness and joy." Some philosophers realize laughter thus. So, Spinoza: "Laughter and jest are a kind of joy, and so if they are not excessive, are good." And again, Voltaire: "Laughter always arises from a gaiety of disposition absolutely incompatible with contempt and indignation."

Laughter free in this wise is the initiation and the consummation of the arts which take laughter for roadways to liberty, and are among the surest and easiest openers of such ways. Herman Melville's Ishmael envisions, and in a prose-poem projects, the diverse confrontations and the ultimate transactions of man with his world which the arts of the comic transvalue into the triumphant liberation that laughter consummates. Ishmael is the narrator of Captain Ahab's deadly quest of the White Whale, Moby Dick; he is the chorus in that tragedy. "There are," he writes,

queer times and occasions in this strange, mixed affair we call life when a man takes the whole universe for a vast practical joke, though the wit thereof he but dimly discerns, and more than suspects that the joke is at nobody's expense but his own. However, nothing dispirits, and nothing seems worth while dispiriting. He bolts down all events, all creeds, and beliefs, and persuasions, all hard things visible and invisible, never mind how knobby: as an ostrich of potent digestion gobbles down bullets and gunflints. And as for small difficulties and worryings, prospects of sudden disaster, peril of life and limb; all these, and death itself seem to him only sly, goodnatured hits, and jolly punches in the side bestowed by the unseen and unaccountable old joker. The odd sort of wayward mood I am speaking of, comes over a man only in some time of extreme tribulation; it comes in the very midst of his earnestness, so that what just before might have seemed to him a thing most momentous, now seems but a part of the general joke.

The significant happening in this perception of Ishmael's would be, one takes it, a certain "psychic distance," a detachment such that, however much the battle may engage the laugher, he is above it as well. With laughter, the action has passed into a different field; the moment of laughter is the moment of truth. The laugher has turned from transactions with some or all of the world around, to transactions within his own psychosomatic sovereignty and independence. A human being laughing is a human being disengaged from whatever has been engaging him. His propulsions have with-

drawn inward; action *by* his body has converted into action
in his body—into those singular activities which "laughter"
nominates. These psychosomatic goings-on are, until they
cease, self-sufficient and self-contained. While they last, they
are the man's freedom *from* the constraints he had been
struggling against; they do mount toward that seminal freedom which is both the going and the goal of his innermost
aspiration. *What* he laughs at drops back in his mind; what
he long joyously perceives is now the laughing itself.

Perhaps it is some such autonomous experience that Buridan's Ass chose when his wisdom would not—its jocund
Fathers said, "could not"—choose between the equally at-
tractive bundles of fodder. This most numinous performer in
the circus of philosophical allegory resembles certain abso-
lutists of the tribe that demonstrate how one may eat one's
metaphysical cake and have it too. One should choose between eating and having. By confirming neither, by opting
equally for both, one achieves the lack of both but exalts
lacking to possessing and assimilates hunger to satiety. Buridan's metaphysical Ass also refuses the confirming reaction
to the alternatives before him.* His fellow sages draw conclusions from his refusal: being the creature he is, he must
choose, or starve and die. What is truer to common sense, or
more logical than that a bona fide Ass, to say nothing of a
theological Ass created *ad hoc* and *ex nihilo*, must choose to
be filled and not starve, to live and not die, that he cannot
both hunger and live on? That, hence, the fodders before
him cannot be equal alternatives; that his desire for one must
win over his desire for the other? The syllogisms make of
the Ass a thousand-year object of philosophical laughter and
never the occasion it could as readily serve, for philosophical

* Fit companions for the self-immobilized Ass are the two-headed
giants of the legends. These giants descend from Cain. Their heads are
ever contradicting one another, each Naying the other's Yea, Yeaing the
other's Nay, so that the giant is able to commit himself to nothing; unless,
like Kierkegaard, he could make the abysmal leap from his own ineffable
Yea-Nay, Nay-Yea, to the ineffable Yea of God.

tears. The bearers of the metaphysical tradition seem never to have imagined that this Assinine dilemma could signalize tragedy as aptly as comedy. Nor did Ernest Renan and Charles Renouvier succeed in persuading them from the analogy of their own disputation that the Ass might be meeting the dilemma by choosing the third alternative of hunger, even hunger unto death. So, some living man or woman or some fictional hero might choose to kill himself or to be killed rather than to decide between alternative loves or love and duty, choose desire's poignancy rather than the assuagement of it. And is not the Ass, his symbol and surrogate, likewise entitled to the freedom of deciding between such alternatives? Hear Edna Millay, in one of her moods, telling of her life's "Feast":

> *I drank at every Vine*
> *The last was like the first.*
> *I came upon no wine*
> *So wonderful as thirst.*

> *I gnawed at every root*
> *I ate of every plant*
> *I came upon no fruit*
> *So wonderful as want*

> *Feed the grape and bean*
> *To the vintner and the monger*
> *I will lie down lean*
> *With my thirst and my hunger.*

Laughter or tears, or both together and at once, feed, advance and consummate like choices by a like liberty. Each, in the nature of things, has its own irreduceable singularity which their assimilation in discourse cannot but violate. Otherwise, one could tell how, to his heart, the intent of Edna Millay's feast fulfills itself also in this saying from T. S. Eliot's "Burnt Norton":

The inner freedom from the practical desire
The release from action and suffering, release from the inner
And outer compulsion, yet surrounded
By a grace of sense, a white light still moving
Erhebung, *without motion, concentration*
Without elimination, both a new world
And the old made explicit, understood
In the completion of its partial ecstasy,
The resolution of its partial horror.
Yet the enchainment of its past and future
Woven in the weakness of its changing body,
Protects mankind from heaven and damnation
Which flesh cannot endure.

Eliot, too, can be taken as here intending "liberty" like this, which discloses itself in the self-sufficiencies of laughter or of tears. Maybe his words signify an experience immediately lived. But to this reader, at least, they bespeak rather a conception, a *terminus ad quem* of the dialectician. They certainly stir no image of an experience lived laughing, or lived weeping.

Alas that, however lived, no such experience lasts. It either ceases, or mounts only to fall into that utter defenselessness which terminates both laughing and weeping. Not only may the various moods and phases of the two mingle and suffuse one another; they come, in their ultimate reaches, to the same dead end. At that end, they may vindicate the herders of Buridan's Ass, the antagonists of Renan and Renouvier; at that end, the freed personality has spent itself and has nothing left to live on with. If to live on is to outlive the spending, then it can do so only from a matrix of vegetative passivity. Some hold this to be the perceptual experience which Eliot's "grace of sense, a white light still and moving" signifies. Their argument does not persuade. It is rather an animal recession whence the personality will form again by acts of eating and drinking, doing and undoing, struggling for the freedom to keep on struggling, wherewith it both preserves itself and creates the Self that it preserves. Millay must return to her vintner and monger, Eliot to his inner and outer compulsion of action and suffering. Some speak of such ventures as rebirth, and of the returnee as a "twice-born." Failing return, this freedom of theirs, like the drone's of the beehive, would be the death of them.

But whatever they say about it, they save themselves from this death by their power to deviate from the authentic experience to the singing word, the word that offers itself as surrogate for the event when event fades into the images or ideas of remembering. Then the surrogate is assumed into the original. The word is transvalued into the Word, made flesh and walking on earth, by the immaculate conceptions of the Wordmen. In unpoetic prose, poetry is here a remembrance whose vital function is to save the poet from the death which consummates self-spending liberty.

Perhaps this is the common function of all the arts that have for their theme liberty as the goal and the going of experience. Perhaps they thus serve not artists only, but anybody who has lived out immediacies of this liberty. It is certainly one function of the comic and the tragic arts. Those do renew the spirit of man when laughter and tears are at last used up in defeat and death. Whatever the culture in which these arts are formations, they serve it confirming, nourishing, and exalting the orchestrated struggle to keep on struggling which is our existence—an existence of pursuing to preserve, preserving to pursue the liberties that compose into the federal Self thus laboring for its own laborious continuance.

There is a difference between the enjoyment of laughter and the laughter of enjoyment. There is a difference between the enjoyment of tears and the tears of enjoyment. The laughter and tears of enjoyment are the activities of laughing and weeping. They satisfy and release as they go on; they are the enjoyment. The relation is a sort of self-relation, like the feel of one's skin to one's hand, or the sound of one's heart to one's ears; whereas the enjoyment of laughter or tears is a relation by their means to something other—their object, cause, or occasion. Peoples of all places and times resent, reject, fight against being such objects, causes, or occasions whether by accident or intention. To be laughed *at*, cried *over*, is an experience usually disturbing, sometimes devastating; while laughing or crying *with* anybody, mostly *with* one's own like, is reassuring and may even be strengthening. Hence, often, a person laughed at will strive, by laughing himself, to join the laughers, and thus transvalue the laughable state; a person being cried over may sometimes smile and joke at the weepers—rarely, by choice, will he join the weepers and weep.

In each case the event is an effort to offset, to smooth out, an inner disturbance or to redress an outer imbalance, or both. The saw "Laugh and the world laughs with you; weep and you weep alone" envisages these relationships. Many theories equate the resistance to, or fear of, being laughed at with feelings of inferiority and a sense of belittlement in the resister. They interpret laughing as an act of aggression and an expression of superiority in the laugher. They devise explanations of the comic as some mode of Thomas Hobbes' "sudden glory" consummating a realization of these relationships. Then, by a kind of inferential *ne plus ultra*, to weep becomes human; to laugh becomes, if not divine, then at least inhuman.

Yet everybody wants to laugh, nobody to be laughed at, except when being laughed at is a way of earning a living. Unamuno says somewhere that, to know one is being laughed-at, freely to acquiesce in it, to accept the belittlement it intends, to suffer a fellow man's sadism, yet steadily to follow one's chosen course as Don Quixote followed his, establishes the victim the most heroic of tragic heroes, and gives the most signal expression of all to "the tragic sense of life." If so, it may turn out that laughter signalizes the ultimate tragic choice a person can make. However, the occurrence of such choices seems to be as rare as the choices are ambiguous. In most recorded instances of a victim's laughing *with* his deriders, his laughter is not free and spontaneous nor an enjoyment of laughter. He laughs in order to defend his selfhood, its dignity and worth in his own eyes, from the ignominy which the laughter of his deriders subject it to; his laughter is the self-protective action of his ongoing struggle to live on. He may learn, from using laughter as a weapon, how to use it for its own sake; how to laugh at himself, freely, spontaneously. He *may* learn how, by means of laughter so directed, to generate strength where he feels weak, and a sense of sufficiency where he feels deficient. Humor is appreciated as "the saving sense" when it thus joins one feature of an individual's person or character to some other, preserving the union of else disuniting attitudes and interests. It is in this sense that "laughter is the best medicine."

In most cases, however, the laughed-at is a quality, an existence, an event of the surroundings of him who laughs. The laughed-at is his foe, challenging, holding back, striving with, one or another of the environing items which he cherishes, which he holds a precious component of his value system. In most cases, it is not me, myself that I laugh at; I laugh at him, the foe, the impeder and obstructor. In most cases it is not a good or beauty or truth of mine that I laugh at; I laugh at that which has endangered or degraded or has fought to suppress, enslave, or destroy what I cherish, and has failed. My laughter signalizes its failure and my own liberation.

When or where or with what or how often this happens is contingent. Some items may be but once occasions for my laughter, once and never again. Others may become such repeatedly; others, never. The comic arts labor to create works which will bring laughter to the greatest multitude, the greatest number of times. As the record stands to date, it provides no evidence, despite the disputations of the pundits and pedants of the comic, that comicality is an intrinsic quality of any clash of words or events, of any formation of character or deformation of personality, or of any witticism or plot or situation. Neither does it provide evidence that tragedy is thus intrinsic to any conflict of perceptions or ideas. Comedy and tragedy accrue to clashes and conflicts wherein a laugher's or a weeper's values have been engaged and at last released by victory or defeat—which is a decision of the person's "confirming reaction." Both are a struggle of liberation from engagement, with liberty as the upshot of the struggle. Alone, what the foe does, how he does what he does, to the ideals or values of the laugher or weeper, qualifies him as comic or tragic. The words signify external relations between people, thoughts, or things.

CHAPTER FOUR

Laughter Triumphant: 1

SICK UNTO DEATH, suffering unendurably, yearning daily for death's release, George Santayana wrote his testament and last image of himself:

> *I give back to the earth what the earth gave*
> *All to the furrow, nothing to the grave.*
> *The candle's out. The spirit's vigil spent:*
> *Sight may not follow where the vision went.*
>
> *I leave you but the sound of many a word*
> *In mocking echoes haply overheard,*
> *I sang to Heaven. My exile made me free,*
> *From world to world, from all worlds carried me.*
>
> *Spared by the Furies, for the Fates were kind,*
> *I paced the pillared cloisters of the mind;*
> *All times my present, everywhere my place,*
> *Nor fear, nor hope, nor envy saw my face.*
>
> *Blow what winds would, the ancient truth was mine,*
> *And friendship mellowed in the flush of wine,*
> *And heavenly laughter, shaking from its wings*
> *Atoms of light and tears for mortal things.*

Neither his friends nor his enemies may reconcile themselves to this self-appraisal of the philosophical vindicator of mankind's life of reason. The image hints at a wanderer whose liberty was the comfortable homelessness of a spirit going nowhere, afraid of nothing, desiring nothing, emulating nobody, his words a soliloquy like a bird's song, addressed to no one, and that no one could faithfully repeat; words uttering "the ancient truth," bespeaking a flight of laughter out of light and tears. And the laughter, the laughter is heavenly. Heavenly because perhaps, as the poet resolved it in his youth:

> *Farewell, my burden! No more will I bear*
> *The foolish load of my fond faith's despair.*
> *But trip the idle race with careless feet;*
> *The crown of olive let another bear;*
> *It is my crown to mock the runner's heat*
> *With gentle wonder and with laughter sweet.*

In a way not too apparent, it is the laughter that is heavenly. The poet joins light and liberty, laughter and tears in a vital interplay, with laughter consummating liberty. Only the detailed sequences of the poet's personal history could render clear and distinct the dynamic of this interplay. Without them, the poem is a cryptogram, a symbol signalizing the lifetime of events and experiences from whose rain of light the tears came the understanding which is laughter, the laughter which is liberty.

But when the poet had become a philosopher as well, and full of years, he recalled the past and set down his remembrances for the world to read. He observed: "Now laughter as I have come to see in my old age, is the youthful, innocent side of repentance, of disillusion, of understanding." There had been a time in his life when understanding and disillusion had been without repentance and without laughter. They had been utter tragedy, a desolation even beyond tears. Its signature was his "theological tragedy," Lucifer, now freed of the foolish load of fond faith's despair, lonely and alone on his desolate rock of an island.

Great God, when thy frail son of Galilee
Forsaken on the cross was nigh to death,
Into thy hands he yielded up his breath.
Death's vain forgetting hath no balm for me.
Hereafter, I shall look upon the sun
In sorrow, for my circle is not run,
The circle of mine endless misery.
My pang is greater than a man's could be
Whose father was in heaven and who, forsooth,
Thought he was happy. And I needs must find
A greater, dearer comforter than he.
O truth, O truth, eternal bitter truth,
Be thou my refuge when all else is blind.
Thou art the essence of my lofty mind;
At thy pure wells I will renew my youth.
Thy joyless bosom never was unkind
To him who loved thee; let us now be one.
I have no other friend, I have resigned
All love but thine. My foolish life is done.
But O ye hills that I have known of old,
Unravished of the sun, ye snowy flock
Forever sleeping, take me to your fold
And in your flanks of adamantine rock
Entomb my fiery heart. Over me spread
Your frozen shroud and wreathe me in ice flowers
To watch with you through everlasting hours
And not remember. Lo! I lift my head
Into the void, in scorn of all that live
Through hope and anguish and insensate wars.
For knowing grief, I have forgot to grieve,
And having suffered, without tears receive
The visitations of my kindred stars.

For the philosopher, as against the poet, the laughter of understanding is the self-liberation that mankind, reasoning, achieve when they realize the utter irrationality of the universe whereinto man the reasoner has come, from whatever cause but for no reason, to struggle for his existence. In the Introduction which Mr. Santayana wrote for the one-volume reprint of his *Realms of Being*, he sums up his laughing faith thus:

There is no more bewitching moment in childhood than when the boy, to whom one is shyly propounding some absurdity, suddenly looks up and smiles. The brat has understood. A thin deception was being practiced on him, in the hope that he might not be deceived, but by deriding it might prove that he had attained to man's stature and a man's wit. So with this thin deception practised upon me by nature. The great Sphinx in posing her riddle and looking so threatening and mysterious is secretly hoping that I may laugh. She is not a riddle but a fact; the words she whispers are not oracles, but prattle. Why take her residual silence, which is inevitable, for a challenge or a menace? Her secret is as great a secret to herself as to me. If I perceive it, and laugh, instantly she draws in her claws. A tremor runs through her enigmatical body; and if she were not of stone she would embrace her boyish discoverer, and yield herself to him altogether. It is so simple to exist, to be what one is for no reason, to engulf all questions and answers in the rush of being that sustains them. Henceforth nature and spirit can play together like mother and child, each marvelously pleasant to the other, yet deeply unintelligible; for as she created him she knew not how, merely by smiling in her dreams, so in awaking and smiling back he somehow understands her; at least he is all the understanding she has of herself.

In sum, the mystery of existence is man-made. To accept "the rush of being" is enough, not only for survival, but for shaping the life of reason wherein human survival is an outliving of all things not human. With such acceptance comes the laughter of understanding, the wisdom which *is* wisdom, because mankind becomes wise as well as brave when it has learned to take the menace, the mystery, the dumb absurdity of existence as occasions for laughter. In and of itself, it is neither or both; it becomes the one or the other as a man's "confirming reaction" disposes. The man is the measure of both, as of all else that he measures in order to live on.

Old Democritus has left us another perspective of this response to the dumb nature of things. Santayana writes somewhere that Democritus "delights in the powers of formation inherent in mechanism." Tradition cites him as "the laughing philosopher." He in his time perceived the deep discrepancy between man's conceit of himself and his condition; between the universe of mechanism and man's belief in his own power and goals, as he pursued them sure that they were forever the world's will and purpose, and that his achievements in his own struggle for existence were the precious issues of universal joy and universal sorrow. But the powers of mechanism are a succession of changing patterns in a void, made and unmade by a hurly-burly of unresting atoms. Amid their collisions and repulsions, man's aims and attainments are but so many uncouth jerkings in the atomic beads of being. They are ways of self-deception that ruin, that kill man before his time. To see and understand this, to recognize the brief span and forever narrow limits of human existence, to accept instead of denying and vainly combatting man's estate, renders those who reject and fight it objects of derision. But it also renders laughable the universe which they reject and fight. The cheerful Democritan laugh purports to be a laugh at them both—at the invincible nature of things and at deluded mankind waging its foredoomed war against the invincible nature of things; the laugher frees himself also from the suffering of its coercion and hurt, and he laughs again, his laughter at once his liberation and his liberty.

Such laughter is transcendent. It is beyond words. It is a mystic experience. It is expression which supervenes when words have been used up and serve no longer to utter the events that laughter appraises. It is what one or another Taoist painter labored to signalize on the faces of Taoist sages. It is immanent in the smile of the Buddha; and audible in the voices of some of his disciples. It is the promise in the smile of Erasmus' Dame Folly. It must not be mistaken for the laughter of people laughing when, for whatever cause, words have failed them in ordinary discourse, or when they feel their words deficient or inept. This laughter is the consummatory encoding of a vision of man and the universe, of man's wrestle with the universe and of the condition and quality of his victory—or defeat—in that action. From such an action to the banal experience of being tickled and the concurrent laughter would seem a far cry. Being tickled is by no means a purely tactile experience. Very young children do not respond to tickling. Only around the third year do they break into the characteristic laughing which goes with it. Then, the blind, the deaf, the dumb, the stupid, the idiotic can be tickled, although perhaps not so readily as persons perceiving with all their senses, able to reason, and capable of all of reason's nuances. Then, susceptibility becomes individual. Literally as well as metaphorically, some people can be "tickled to death." The "ticklish situations" which death might terminate are such not only by analogy. They are actually conditions occasioning a somatic uneasiness, acute at certain sensitive spots, as at the ribs, under the arms, at the neck, at the soles of the feet, at the belly muscles, at various erogenous zones; an uneasiness discharging itself in various spasmodic movements of the whole body. The mere sight of a finger pointed at any of these spots may start the movements going. A ticklish person is one with either an initially low threshold of sensibility in those regions of the body, a physical readiness, or one in whom usage has developed ticklishness into a habit of body and mind. What he is sensitive to is not the touch or impingement of some alien thing. What he is sensitive to is the manifold rapid alternations of the thing's impacts and withdrawals, the uncertainty, the indeterminateness, the unexpectedness, the tease of its oncoming. It is this which tickling confronts him with. However delicately pleasurable each actual impingement may be, in configuration with the hiatuses between, it presents a hazard and arouses an apprehension which the confirming reaction usually resolves with laughter, and sometimes with tears. So far as may be, laughter frees him who gets tickled (or slapped) from this apprehension of danger; it relaxes bodily tightness and liquidates the emotion that goes with tightness. Any problem, any state of things, any person, perceived in this way—i.e., any issue unsettled and challenging, any *either-or*—may be and often is, called a "tickler." Whenever challenge mounts to aggression, aggression to assault, tears may first mingle with and then supplant laughter. Tears may come *with* this laughter, or before it, anyhow.

Significantly, forewarning of the victim often seems to deprive tickling of its *either-or* character. Although not "dead sure," it becomes an action with small or no uncertainty or menace; it engenders little apprehension and consequently little laughter—no tears. Perhaps this is why no one seems able, at least in our culture, to tickle himself into laughter. The gratifications from such tickling are like those from touching a sore tooth with the tongue, from scratching an itch, from playing solitaire, and so are its pains and pangs. The ego cannot tickle itself to laughter—or to death. Only somebody or something not itself can, impinging and withdrawing so unpredictably that the victim alternates from uneasiness to eagerness or satisfaction, as when a morsel "tickles" his palate, or a bribe his palm. But again, belief that the other is bent on tickling, that his vocation is to tickle, awakens expectation to be tickled and a readiness on which professional laugh-makers capitalize. Audiences attend to them anticipating laughter and they respond often to weaker stimuli than from other sources.

One might say that both Democritus and Santayana felt man's situation in the universe to be thus "ticklish" and the universe to be a "tickler" in this sense. One might say that their philosophic laughter was at once a nullification of the universal menace and a liberation from the apprehensiveness it ever evokes; that their laughter signalized their accepting the plight of man for what it is, and keeping up their existence of struggle to go on struggling cheerfully, fearlessly, without false hope, and without the illusions which fear and such hope project, institute, and nourish. On the record, the laughing philosophers of history are, as Democritus was, naturalists; or else Erasmus-like, humanists to whom the supernatural was either an episode in nature or an illusion spontaneously woven of human hopes and fears. Even so, not many take laughter for their signature. Some may laugh like the Taoist sages; some, like Epicurus or Lucretius, simply accept the all-pervading *lacrimae rerum*, and endeavor to live on amid them as serenely as they are able. Others, like Spinoza, find the consummation of philosophic liberty not in laughter, but in a reverent discount of tears, an identification of the unlasting Ego with the Everlasting Nature of Things. Spinoza signalizes this identification as the intellectual love of God; that is, beyond the Good and Evil and laughter and tears which qualify mankind.

But who, among the theologians or metaphysicians who image God as an all-powerful force above and beyond nature, as an omnipotent yet personal supernature and nevertheless as good and evil like man, has taken laughter for the symbol of his philosophic faith or been signalized as a laugher? Since Plato, man's estate, man's destiny, stays for these truth-finders an issue rather of tears than of laughter. The Great Deceiver whose deceptions can be exposed and overcome by laughter may be nature or the Devil but must not be nature's God or the Devil's creator, his Father Superior. In the ticklish issue of survival or annihilation, wherewith the latter's dark providence confronts mankind, liberation must be plotted and liberty achieved not as a release of laughter but as a discipline of tears. Save by his unaccountable grace, the struggle with this God must needs be tragedy, not comedy. True, among the Greeks, as Homer's *Iliad* and the plays of both Aristophanes and Euripides make manifest, the struggles with the Olympians and the gods of the earth and her seasons may end up in laughter as well as tears. True, Dante, more faithful to his pagan origins than he knew, calls his version of the Christian drama of salvation the Divine Comedy; it ends happily in Paradise. But there is neither laughter nor liberty in his Paradise any more than in his Hell, nor in any stage of his comedy. Although the Satan of Milton's *Paradise Lost* stands forth as a voice of liberty, he is a voice without laughter, a tragic hero, his eyes bright with unsheddable tears.

We may read in *the Book of Job* how laughter and tears come into play when the spirit of man realizes mankind's struggle for its humanity as a struggle with an uncaring omnipotence. The Book of Job is a book of tears, a naked, ultimate tragedy, which its happy ending only mocks. As literary form in all likelihood it owed something to Greek models. As philosophic expression it is elementally Hebraic. An omnipresent, unjust, uncaring, irresistible power has stripped its hero of all he was and had. His children have been killed. His person has been racked with unbearable pain. His form and features have been made odious with unspeakable sores. At long last he cries out against the heedless injustice visited upon his integrity. The action of the play is the conflict between mankind's illusion about this divine Power, the Power's disillusioning of mankind about itself, and the climax is the Power's confirmation of Job's disillusionment. To Eliphaz, Bildad and Zophar, the spokesmen of illusion, Job is a mighty man, truly a sinner, altogether justly humbled to the dust, a symbol of God Almighty's just judgment, an object of laughter and scorn.

I am as one that is a laughing stock to his neighbor—
I, who called upon God, and he answered!
The just, the perfect man is a laughing stock.
—In the thought of him that is at ease, there is
    contempt for misfortune—
                            . . . .
They that are younger than I have me in derision,
Whose fathers I disdained to set with the dogs of my flock—

The laughers laugh because they see the keening Job who had stood so strong, so rich, so great, and hence so utterly sinless and righteous, shown up by his ruin, his suffering, and his helplessness as a secret sinner. But Job, absolutely sure of his innocence, shouts his anguished protest against God Almighty's injustice, against the tortures which the Almighty inflicts upon him as upon a wicked, sinning man. Job will not yield to the illusion that would have him plead guilty although he is not guilty. Having continued unyielding, having spoken of Almighty God "the thing that is right," the latter nevertheless grants him "twice as much as he had before." Without the prose Prologue and Epilogue, *the Book of Job* is a tragedy; with the Epilogue's happy ending it would, like Dante's divine one, be called a comedy. The divergence of the poetic drama from this prose is so radical that, like the strictly liturgical form which Euripides gave his tragedies, the prose may well have been a protective mask for the tears of disillusion of the essential Joban drama.

By a sort of inverted analogy, yet as I perceive it, a sad ironic congruence, something like the same feeling for the confluence of laughter and tears is communicated by Charlie Chaplin's *The Great Dictator*. Whether the author-actor knew it or not, the problem of the Little Man was again and yet again the problem of Job—the collision of evil prospering and powerful, with goodness starved and impotent and the play upon them of laughter and tears. In *The Great Dictator* Chaplin derides evil, laughs its force down into futility, but without at long last assuming the triumph of goodness, only pleading for it, even though aware that the plea is itself illusion. Its hero is the protean "little fellow" whose story, Chaplin wrote, explaining his ends and means in a letter to the New York *Times*, "I have told and retold all my life." His end is to make comedy of, and thus, for the moment, to liquidate the power over the free human heart of "the tragedy that Hitler is to Europe." His means is an avatar of the Little Fellow, a little Jewish barber who looks so like Hitler that everybody treats him as if he were that mad bombastic concretion of aggression against mankind.

Because of this seeming, the little Jewish barber wins his way through a series of preposterous dangers, the last and greatest being to address the Nazi multitude. His words are an impassioned plea for "a better world"—this, although "a better world" is mankind's perennial illusion, although there is no better world: "There is no promised land for the oppressed people of the world. There is no place over the horizon to which they can go for sanctuary. They must stand, and we must stand."

This is the heart of the matter in the tragedy of Job, too. But the comedy of the Little Barber assuages the tragic apprehension, indeed purges it, with laughter. "There is," said Chaplin (who in this connection wanted to be called Charles and not Charlie), "pathos and great comedy in all human suffering and tragedy. The secret lies in how you approach it. It would be a sad moment if we couldn't laugh now. I've always felt that the nation which can laugh is the nearest to being sane. . . . Laughter is tonic, relief, surcease from pain, healthy and health-giving"—the more true because so little new.

The record does not show whether Henri Bergson had ever heard of *The Great Dictator*. Certainly he had never seen it. Although "the cinematographic instant" serves enlighteningly in his endeavor to bespeak the eluding inwardness of the *élan vital* on which he stakes his philosophic faith, Bergson told his *soi-disant* favorite disciple, who says he converted this faith to Roman Catholicism, that he, Bergson, had never seen a motion picture. His essay on laughter draws for illustration and example mostly on French comedy, and he seems to make it a foregone conclusion that men laugh only at those human failures to adjust which result from the hardenings and mechanizations of men's vital flexibilities. These failures it is the social function of the comic arts to expose, to caricature, to condemn and to correct. On behalf of the ongoing social order, among whose censors and police the comic arts are, really, these arts express and cultivate an anesthesia of heart and a sharpness of mind. They proscribe feeling and compassion; they prescribe detachment and judgment. Instead of the understanding which ensues upon sympathy, they give rein to the critiques of the practical reason. Laughter is the cold, cruel, punitive, depersonalizing expression of this critical judgment, a manifestation of the function of the intelligence. There is, as we shall see, another appraisal of the relation of reason to laughter which is implied by Jonathan Swift in his *Tale of a Tub.* The laugh-maker is the surgeon of the diseases of society, of its delusions, corruptions, and self-deceptions. Reason is his knife "for cutting and opening, and mangling and piercing, offering to demonstrate."

As against this, we may recall a remark by an unidentified nineteenth-century capitalist (quoted in C. Wright Mills' *White Collar*, p. 211): "Laughter, when it is too hearty, weakens the power of the mind. Avoid it." And this we may set beside a saying of Lord Shaftesbury's that the world is a tragedy for those who feel and a comedy for those who think. This again, we may set beside this quatrain in Marquis's *Morals for the Young* and ponder its implication that laughter can also signalize the personal élan rebelling against society, liberating itself from society's overwhelming power and authority, such power and authority as, from the first, children experience in their encounters with grown-ups.

> *Tommy saw his house on fire.*
> *His mother in the flames expire,*
> *His father killed by falling brick,*
> *and Tommy laughed—till he was sick.*

The scholiast doesn't say that Tommy's laughter was an exercise of cold reason and a social corrective. Nor is there on record any indication that Shaftesbury regarded thinking as cruel and heartless.

The record does contain a variation on the Chaplin sentiment, the Bergsonian theme. This variation is played by

persons of sensibility and conscience, who become deeply
distressed by the observation that misfortune is so largely
the occasion for laughter. They are the heirs of Ecclesiastes,
who said of laughter, "It is folly, it is mad; and of mirth,
what doeth it?" Laughter to them is sheer *Schadenfreude*—
Swift's delight—utterly alien to that spontaneous and innocent joy of existence which laughter expresses for others;
utterly alien also to the defiance of misfortune and over-
throw of evil which it signalizes for all others, such as Jesus
of Nazareth. Bossuet, who argued that laughter is of the
devil and devilish, who denounced Molière and denigrated
laughing, believed that Jesus only wept, he never laughed.
Maybe so—Bossuet quotes Scripture for his purpose. But as
the Apostle Luke tells it (6:21–25) Jesus assured satiety
to the hungry and prophesied "hunger to the full, and to
them that laugh now." He said, "Woe, for you shall mourn
and weep." "Blessed," he said, "are those that weep now, for
you shall laugh." Even more such is the Almighty himself,
regarding whose opposers, prophet or psalmist intoned: "He
that sitteth in the Heavens shall laugh: the Lord shall have
them in derision."

All such laughter, sensitive consciences argue, in the contention of the late Heywood Broun, give voice at best only
to fear and stupidity and is but "a coward's livery." People
wear it "who are not truly quick, but actually unimaginative"
people, "who laugh a great deal." Alas, there are so many
evils which "have to be met"—generally, if we laugh at
them, we are laughing at things we are afraid to face and
fight." Indeed "to smile is to be a quitter"—apparently not,
like Hamlet's uncle, a villain. Neither Lincoln nor Mark
Twain were humorous. What, in fact, is there to laugh at,
Broun protested, when we look around the world? Lincoln
Steffens reports a remark of Finley Peter Dunne: ". . .
Dunne told us one day how he and several other humorists
had gone to call on Mark Twain who was, as usual, sick
abed. "And," said Dunne, "we all sat there in that room and

talked about things till we were all crying over life and man, actually weeping."

Heywood Broun was also by vocation a wit and a humorist, sensitively alert to the evils men do to men, and passionate to assuage and end them. For the nonce he, too, was recognizing how inward are tears to the human plight, how inward to all things, not alone those which his daily essays derided. Like Twain and Dunne and the whole line of laugh-makers from Homer and from Aristophanes, he was expressing a sentiment like Bernard Shaw's: "Laughter is at all ages the natural recognition of destruction, confusion, and ruin." And like all of that line of laugh-makers, they came to fame and fortune by the laughs they made purposefully, as makers playing the role of true redeemers from man's ticklish state, as the guides, philosophers and friends, not the foes, of mankind.

CHAPTER FIVE

Laughter Triumphant: 2

AGREED, WE ARE born laughers and weepers as we are born eaters and drinkers. Agreed, that the hungers which crying announces and the satisfactions which laughing celebrates form confluent syndromes in our personal struggles to go on struggling and in our interpersonal transactions as members of communities. Much of what we "naturally" laugh at signalizes the singularity of our personal history. But for most of our lives, this much passes into and out of our experience without fixing attention, without being retained in memory, or becoming recallable. If any item of it does get fixed, held, and becomes recallable, it may also enter into a communal record, and figure as an event in the cyclical rhythm of community ways; it may get installed in the communal rites and rotes, count in the collective formations of utterance and action wherein any ongoing culture lives and moves and has its being. Among these formations the newcomer strives for orchestration; that is, it strives as it can, to maintain its own identity and to move theirs to confirm and support it.

Thus it is that inborn "sense of humor," inborn "tragic sense of life," gets directed toward standards or measures of the comic and the tragic. The latter are in fact contingent to these "senses"; they are productions of nurture, not nature;

we learn them, we don't bring them with us in our genes. *What* we laugh at, *what* we weep over in the long run becomes like *what* we fear, *what* we hope for—a designation of our culture, a value in its economy. We learn to laugh at this and not that, to cry over that and not this as custom and habit. That and this become correct occasions for laughing and crying according to the doctrine and discipline of the cultural order, and the spontaneities of the Self become improprieties which but break into them or cross them. Their roles as tragic or comic get referred to the eternal laws of nature or the ineluctable providence of nature's God. Philosophic interpreters call them manifestations of value-systems the same at all times, in all places. So, they deny or disregard their record, and assign them a role they don't perform. For in religion and the arts, the faces and figures of the tragic and the comic were symbolic masks, signalizing not the living realities beneath, but the treatment of them, with the decision on the treatment a consequence of what the culture believed was the relation of the realities to the actual fortunes of those for whom the rite was performed, the drama enacted.

To writers and actors, priestly or lay, however, it is the maskings, the alterations they effect, which must needs be the realities, for the make-ups signify the measure and judgment of those realities which render them comic or tragic. The masks establish the relations between the event and the laughers. Unless they believed this, the laugh-makers could not well practice their craft. Some perceive their craft as an art of unmasking, a sort of strip-tease, which for the moment frees the unmasked from whatever, by custom or habit, discomforts, weakens, embarrasses, belittles, shames, drives to despair or even to suicide. Such intrinsically tearful predicaments may be countered by their victims with defensive laughter like incredulous Mother Sarah's when she heard the angels of God foretelling that she would give birth (she did give birth to that unhappy token of laughter whom she hence named Isaac), or a laughter like Mercutio's desperate gaiety as he dies from Tybalt's thrust, or like Hamlet's joking at his father's ghost, or the Fool's at Lear's plight. Perhaps the telling instance is that of Wilson de la Roi, a murderer at Alcatraz who, says Warden Duffy, "fought for his life because he said he likes to befuddle the 'mouthpieces.' He kept himself busy drawing florid greeting cards for me and Mrs. Duffy or some friends, or conceiving practical jokes which may or may not have been funny by professional standards, but which certainly amused his companions on the row."

He would send notes to the music department, among other things, and ask them to dedicate numbers to the boys in the row, such as "I Want a Pardon for Daddy," or "I'll be Glad When You're Dead, You Rascal You." These songs invariably got a chuckle along that corridor of gloom, and de la Roi would roar with the rest. "Why, I'm just like a surgeon, warden," he said. "I keep 'em in stitches. Hah-hah."

De la Roi survived the cruel suspense of eleven reprieves, but was finally turned down in October, 1946. I was afraid he might crack when he realized that things weren't funny any more, but was never more wrong.

I was standing by his cell one evening when he was only hours from extinction, and I said, "Bill, are you sure there's nothing more you want done?"

He looked at me gravely, and his voice dropped to a whisper. "Yeah, warden," he said. "I'd like a little bicarb because I'm afraid I'm gonna get gas on my stomach tomorrow."

Before I could recover from the shock, the row guards came to measure him for the new clothes he would wear to his death, and he was still snickering when I turned away and went on to another cell.

Another instance is Tex Thompson. Of him the Warden writes:

Ruthless and violent all his life, Thompson was a good loser nevertheless, and his last request reflected an admirable sense of humor. He had spent all his money—about $100—on his now-useless law books, and just before the end he turned them over to me. "I've learned a lot," he said, "and I'd like to give these to some guy who really needs 'em. Send 'em to my lawyer."

The Warden also quotes a poem by "another jester on the threshold of death":

> *"If I could have my last wish,"*
> *Said the prisoner one day.*
> *As they led him from the death cell*
> *To the chair not far away,*
> *"Please grant me this request, sir,*
> *Ere you tighten up the strap:*
> *Just tell the warden I would love*
> *To hold him on my lap."*

This laughter is akin to Democritus' or Santayana's philosophic laughter. Although there is no escape from the plight, laughing is a release without flight, and thus a victory over it. In laughing, the Self achieves a true psychic distance; it "alienates" the condition from itself and transcends it. "I" detaches from "Me"; for the moment "I" lives on, standing by as a spectator of its own struggles to live on. The detachment is more evident in tragic situations such as Shakespeare's Macbeth's when his lady is dying and Birnam Wood is on the way to Dunsinane, or as his Cleopatra's when she lays the asp to her breast. But it is equally intrinsic to comic ones, although their laughter seems less genuine, more a pretense, than the tears of the other. Some classify such laughter as *Galgenhumor*, Thompson's and de la Roi's easily so, and indeed, Macbeth and Cleopatra could no less authentically laugh down their doom than Mercutio or Lear, had Shakespeare so chosen.

The decision, which—laughter or tears—is ultimately the laugher's, but first the craftsman's. The latter chooses the theme, and it is his craftsmanship which renders it the invitation to the one or the other. For both themes and workmanship he is, within his own culture, the heir of the ages. Tradition, at once continuing and altering products and practices all the way from fertility-rites to advertising, from cave-drawings to comic strips, presents the craftsman with a diverse multitude of materials, media, and methods to choose from. If his craft is laugh-making, however, he succeeds far less because of his knowledge and know-how, than because of the dynamic relevancy of his product to the passions and purposes of his public; because these compenetrate. For laughter and tears never cease to be sudden functions of the actual present, liberations from actually felt bondage. Without this present relevancy, no object, no phrase, no action, however perfect its style, gets laughed at or wept over. It is their unexpected pertinence, their relation, that renders them comic or tragic.

Of itself, no work of art, verbal or other, is either comic or tragic. However it conforms to the canons of the tradition, to Aristotle or Freud, it gets outmoded; or it falls of itself into a different category; or it is presently disregarded altogether. New expressions or things or events come up, are encountered with laughter or tears, pass and perish; long-forgotten ones are recovered and renewed and refurbished to last another term, and pass. All happen into a sort of climate of opinion, a weather of values with an atmosphere peculiar to itself. This the laugh-maker studies as the tear-drawer does not. He assembles instances, catalogs and inspects them for repetitions and precedents, draws generalizations and organizes a recipe book for joke-making and other invitations to laughter. He compounds his studies into a discipline—with teachers and pupils—which might be called a meteorology of humor. The meteorology is a would-be science, all figurings with wise saws and modern instances; its upkeep and elaboration is one of the occupations which distinguish our own time. Broadly, it is a prerequisite to a "comic's" appearance on stage or screen. He comes as either himself, both the producer and the product of the laugh-making, as the product alone, or as the medium through which the product—

nowadays, like most mass-produced productions, the work of many hands—is set to tickle the consumer so that he shall laugh. The commoner word for the tickling is "communication." Another is "transaction."

The comic's look, his stance, his movements, his utterance, separately or together, determine the moment of truth for the laugh-maker—the laughing which decides his success or failure. He seeks to bring it either by making fun of something nowise funny, something disturbing, painful, dangerous, deadly, by having fun with it, or by simply having fun. Having fun is signalized in the laughter of enjoyment—the innocent, free experience of a childlike *joie de vivre*. Making fun is signalized in the enjoyment of laughter; its use as defense, attack, and victory for a cherished good engaged in struggle with a foe that perhaps for this reason only *is* a foe.

Some comedians offer themselves as such, as foes. Their presence is an instant and developing belittlement and defeat of some felt antagonism to the laugher's values. They offer themselves for laughingstocks; to be a laughingstock is their livelihood; they must be perceived instantly as the body of fun. Where a comedian is not such a body, when—however he looks and moves and talks—he is not the tickling communication, but its medium, he is likely to depersonalize himself, to render himself as anonymous and faceless as is compatible with retaining an identity which the public will turn to for laughs. When he is both body and medium, his looks, his clothes, and his actions must distinguish him from the culture's "representative" man. They must caricature the representative. They must distort and unbalance the correct. From the phalluses and masks of the Greek theatre, the cap and bells and bladders of medieval court fools, the motley of renaissance jesters, the garniture of the Punches, the Harlequins, and the Pantaloons, to the contemporary make-ups of the Grimaldis, the Valdos, the Chaplins, to the garbage of the "comics" of the lecture-platforms and television, all are off-center, all are out of tune and out of proportion; they are somehow discomposed. How any looks and what any says manifest no unity. The relation between the person and his funning might be like that between a disc and what is recorded on it save that the very material of the disc is an irrelevancy which could be an intrusion, while the timbre of the comedian's person are essentials of his impersonality. They must be his and no other's. The inexpressiveness of the features must be his "deadpan" or, if he permits himself changes of expression, such as the laugh with which some "comics" signal the conclusion of a joke. They must be very few. The recorded variations range from the painted stereotypes and gibberish of the white-face clown to the solemn, rigidly set features and monotonous style of the monologist or humorous lecturer. The fixedness, the tangency, individual as they may be, are presumed to enable what the comedians say to reach their listeners undistorted by what they are and do. They hold the medium to its function as medium. They desocialize him, segregate him somehow, from the communion which he solicits to laugh or to cry.

Oliver Wendell Holmes—the doctor, not the judge—remarked somewhere that we feel a little superior to every man who makes us laugh. The comic's face, figure and dress serve to heighten and ensure this feeling. High comedy apart—this is formed to mingle tears with laughter—the power of the laugh-makers over the laughers must (like that of Jeeves the Butler) be a hidden power; their own sense of superiority must needs be a secret sense known only to themselves, living in this certainty that they can call forth a laugh at will by their timing, by how they appraise the stretch between impact, realization and response. This is the trade-secret of their laugh-making power. The overt ground is the protruding inferiority of their looks. The court jester and the publicly "allowed fool" must needs have a hump, or bandy legs, or pig-eyes, a proboscis or a button-nose; he must needs have a queer voice, a bark absurdly loud or

sharp, but a toothless bite. Being "allowed" he makes sport
of the mightiest, the holiest, the wealthiest, the wisest, the
most beautiful and pure. But his symbol of power is a bladder—not a spear or a sword. He is "allowed" because he
looks the futility he is assumed to be, and he utters and
enacts the surrealisms he incarnates. Manners are null to
him, codes are rules it is his role to break. For him nothing
follows *from* anything else; logic is an impertinence to life.
His spirit is free and can blow as it listeth—and it listeth to
caricature or parody the mighty and the holy. But it must be
a bondsman's mimicking, most obedient to a master's whim
when most authentically the projection of the fool's will. To
assume a stance of *equal* liberty is to court whippings even to
death. At court, save for his lord's protection, everyone is Ser
Fool's master; and his quips and cranks and wanton wiles
are turned against every hand that by right of status may
beat him down, as hero Ulysses smacked down the cripple
Thersites for his debunking words to the men of might
holding council over their strategy at Troy. Hero, Ulysses
may have been; gentleman, not. Among the princes and
prelates of the medieval courts, he would have lost face.
Among them, plainspoken Thersites would have been
equipped with bells and bladder; none might gainsay him
without degrading himself. His avatar today is the
"dead-pan" comic in conventional dress. It is a far cry from
his ancestral line to the "jester" with sword and spear, literally the fighting man, the man of deeds, the hero of the
Chansons de Geste. Be the "comic" Mark Twain or Artemus
Ward or Finley Dunne or Charlie Chaplin or Will Rogers,
he is still the warrior, still the jester. But his armor is now to
look an "allowed fool," his weapon is still laughter, and he
still fights with it freely for freedom. The oft-quoted lines of
Shakespeare's *As You Like It* (Act II, Sc. 7) tell his tale:
The speaker is the melancholy Jacques, descanting on the
helplessness of the victim before the laughmaker—a helplessness essential to the victim's own honor and dignity,

which forbid he should defend himself against the fool and
his folly.

Jacques: O that I were a fool:
I am ambitious for a motley coat.
Duke Senior: Thou shalt have one.
Jacques: It is my only suit;
Provided that you weed your better judgments
Of all opinion that grows rank in them
That I am wise. I must have liberty
Withal, as large a charter as the wind,
To blow on whom I please; for so fools have;
And they that are most galled with my folly,
They must most laugh. And why, sir, must they so?
The "why" is plain as way to parish church:
He that a fool doth very wisely hit
Doth very foolishly, although he smart,
Not to seem senseless of the bob; if not,
The wise man's folly is anatomized
Even by the squandering glances of the fool.
Invest me in motley; give me leave
To speak my mind, and I will through and through
Cleanse the foul body of the infected world,
If they will patiently receive my medicine.

Jacques here bespeaks the hoary convention of courtly
society that the spring of laughter is a fool in his folly, and
how can any one of gentle blood take folly seriously? How
can anyone treat it as coming from an equal whose hits can
hurt? What other, what better way to defend himself from
the joke than to take it, and also laugh it down? Since the
butt can't lick the laughter, he'd best join it, or else disclose
himself stripped of his worth and power by the very figure of
fudge and nonsense. Maybe this is why churchmen were
forbidden to keep fools, since they were by their calling the
virtues incarnate and even during the Feast of Fools were
presumed to embody them intact. Bernard Shaw—who wore
a motley such as Jacques begged for, in a style all his
own—complained that his jokes were taken for no jokes at

all, meaning that no one was fooled by his motley. Perhaps it was he, also, who admonished his companion: "Let us talk seriously; here comes a fool."—*i.e.*, the joker, perhaps a friend who couldn't—or like Heywood Broun, wouldn't—see the joke, and who must needs be answered according to this folly. Perhaps this joker is Everyman, "so necessarily foolish," as Pascal observed, "that not to be a fool is merely a raised freak of folly."

Such a joker might have been Queen Victoria, royally disclosing, "We are not amused." And in the context of the historic culture of laughter, it might not be too funny to speculate that "amusement" can and does divert princes or presidents, tycoons or führers or commissars—as they muse on affairs of state or problems of profits or games of golf—from the tear-laden hazards and perplexities of their anxious contemplation. One rarely-mentioned commonplace is a mutant of the Aristophanic *komos* and *gamos*—woman and love as "glorified" on the American stage by Florenz Ziegfeld and his annual "follies." The publicly approved, the correct one, is the diverse contingent of laugh-makers producing invitations to laughter. At times the chief himself may be the producer. As Abraham Lincoln had said during a more than usually critical situation in 1864: "Were it not for the occasional vent of humor, I should die." Did not Baudelaire find laughter to be the sign of infinite grandeur and infinite misery? Did not Nietzsche's Zarathustra announce: "I have canonized laughter; higher men, learn to laugh"?

During a decade or so, experiments have persuasively confirmed that the laughter which consummates the venting of humor is inward liberation and victory. Thus Mrs. Nina Bull and her assistants, using hypnosis as an instrument of analysis, set up an experiment designed to bring out in their purity the postural and moodal configurations that answer to the words *disgust, fear, anger, depression, elation, triumph, joy*. Responses to the last three terms—which are terms of "high spirits"—came with changes of facial expression, breathing, and stance. Mrs. Bull reports, "Thus in every case the subject smiled (or laughed out loud), the face becoming broad instead of long. Two of our subjects actually spoke of their smiling as if it were responsible in some way for their happy feeling. More often, however, this feeling was located in the chest which was variously reported as expanded, puffed up, swollen, buoyant, etc., and often connected with 'freer or deeper breathing.'" Subjects reacting to "triumph," Mrs. Bull writes, "looked and felt triumphant. They straightened up and smiled or laughed. Most of them spoke of their chests expanding or breathing deeper, and mentioned a feeling of power. . . ."

But, Mrs. Bull also reports, while the responses to the words *disgust*, *fear*, and *anger* were "well-marked and consistent" strains toward "vomiting in disgust, escape in fear, and hitting out in anger," the response to *depression* "was the slumping posture and heavy facial expression characteristic of the sullen child. The subjects reported pressure on the chest, difficulty in breathing, a feeling of weakness, or slowing down of movement. They also reported a succession of feelings such as self-disgust, desire to cry. . . . The state of depression . . . can probably best be understood as an unconscious communication of distress and helplessness," of a condition of unreadiness, wherein the tendencies toward action which most emotions disclose block one another—until, as quite other studies show, the desire to cry is fulfilled with tears.

CHAPTER SIX

Laughter Triumphant and Erasmus

SUCH THEN IS THE introspective substance of depression and of the "high spirits" which laughers and laugh-makers diversely experience. Such is the mode of satisfaction which sustains the laugh-maker as he manipulates the laugher, and the tearbringer while he works on the weeper, on stage, on screen, or in books and pictures. As introspectively, tears are reported to go with feelings of distress and helplessness, so laughing is reported to go with elation, joy, and triumph. Especially, laughing goes with "a feeling of power" and fits into the achievement of liberation and the experience of liberty. In this experience, there is no question of readiness or unreadiness; tendencies toward action do not block one another, but orchestrate into the freed and free activity of laughing.

Maybe this is why others besides Spinoza had found laughter to be a kind of joy; why, in the face of so many appraisals of the comic by standards of logical consistency and rational necessity, there are very many others that prize it for its disregard of order or the discourse of reason, for its liberation from consistency and necessity. Gelett Burgess (who became a laugh-maker after he was fired as a teacher) said, Dean Swift to the contrary notwithstanding, "that humor is a flight from dull reality and an escape from the doggone rules of reason"; and Bergson, toward the end of his argument to the contrary, hesitantly suggested the same thing. The joker evokes laughter as a fool in his folly; and the gloomy Dean (who believed himself no fool but a sage) expounds how mankind is satisfied only by appearances. Digressing in his *Tale of a Tub*, Swift extols how human happiness resides in ever "being well Deceived," and in "the serene and peaceful state of being a Fool among knaves." If this be the case, might it not be the part of wisdom to recognize Folly as the Muse of Muses and to join the Fool, her consecrated priest, in praising her reverently above Apollo and the heavenly Nine? If this is the case, let be what may the amusements which the Nine perfect in order to beguile the rapt spirit of man still weary with the tears of things; it remains the better part of wisdom to alert his bemused heart to Thalia, the laughter which frees from tears and is a kind of joy. Thalia is a Grace as well as a Muse, the Grace of Good Cheer, the Muse of Comedy and the sister of Mirth, Euphrosyne. We have the detail of such a recognition. It is the paean to Folly which Erasmus essayed.

The Fool whom Jacques aspired to emulate was no creation of Shakespeare's poetic fancy. The Lady Folly and her followers whom Erasmus so aptly celebrated was no invention of his humane imagination. Both were at least as real as Our Lady of Sorrows and her communion of saints. The Fool was not only the singular union of twisted body and simple, rapier-swift mind, whom feudal princes and prelates kept at court for their greater glory and amusement. Shakespeare had projected this Fool in *King Lear*, suited in body, in mind, in his relations with Lear, and in Goneril's reaction to his jibes, altogether as Jacques would have had him. He stands up against the royalties and gentlemen, against all the play's persons but Tom O'Bedlam, as the very spirit of common sense, uttering itself in common prose and common verse, laughing down the amazing doings and more amazing rhetoric of both the good, noble agonists (Cordelia, France, Albany, Kent and Edgar) and the bad (Goneril, Regan, Burgundy, Cornwall, Oswald and Edmund). Lear and Gloucester stand between them, their bones of contention.

The plot proceeds point-counterpoint, from the fantastically naive credulity, the self-deception of both Lear and Gloucester concerning their offsprings' care for them, to their fantastic and pitiful deaths. Many commentators appraise *Lear* as the profoundest, the most tearful of Shakespeare's plays, the most moving of his "tragedies." Yet the plot is such, the rhetoric is such, that a slight variation of movement or posture, a change of rhythm in speaking, an alteration of pitch or accent, could transpose any scene into farce-comedy, and all of *Lear* could be played as such, stirring hilarity as well as *Galgenhumor* and other "serious laughter."

And most of the latter would be aroused by the Fool, even though he disappears suddenly, unexpectedly from the action, with the ending of Lear's out-of-mind dream-trial of Goneril and Regan. Maybe it is of him that Lear cries out, almost at the end of the play, "And my poor fool is hanged!" But there is no way of deciding whether the sick old man means his young Fool or his young daughter (for Cordelia has been hanged), or whether Fool and Daughter have been fused in his fantasy into a single image of loyal love lost to him forever. After Cordelia had been foolishly banished, the Fool had stayed by him, her avatar of integrity and honest devotion. From his unillusioned observations upon the Leary course of events, the old King got a certain release from his developing tensions. He had beaten Goneril's lackey, Oswald, for chiding his Fool, who, in Goneril's presence, called his master a born fool "since he had made his daughters his mother," giving them the rod and pulling down his own breeches! Goneril had railed against the rail-

lery with which "this your all-licensed fool" was taking liberties with her character and her servant. Uncounseled by
Jacques, her railing joined her father and his Fool in one.

Perhaps Shakespeare intended a judgment upon the philosophic quest when he had Lear later take the contrived
mouthings of naked Tom O'Bedlam for philosophy. Lear
saw in the front and figure of this mask of anxious desperation the quintessence of man, "the thing itself . . . poor bare
forked animal," and started to strip himself down to a like
nudity. He addressed poor Tom as "philosopher," "noble
philosopher." He clung to him: "I will keep still with my
philosopher." When he undertook to try his traitor-
daughters, he benched his "sapient sir," the Fool, beside him
(*King Lear*, Act III, Scene 6). A Fool for understanding, a
madman for philosophy, the two together for justice! Did
Shakespeare intend the scene to bring laughter, to bring
tears, or both? We might have the suggestion of an answer if
we could know how the pit and the stalls took it when it was
first played. To the head and heart of a reader, *King Lear*
comes as an orchestration of impulsive misjudgment, of accidents, absurdities, and mock-deliberate choices, weaving together a succession of mishaps, to all of whose victims, good
and evil alike, death comes as freeing and salvation. The
succession makes no sense: "As flies to wanton boys are we
to the gods. They kill us for their sport," says Gloucester;
"Men must endure their going hence, even as their coming
hither," says Edgar, "Ripeness is all." "Vex not his ghost,"
says Kent to Edgar, trying to revive the already dead Lear,
"O let him pass! he hates him/ That would upon the rack of
this tough world, stretch him out longer."

What, then, in this play with its sage Fool and sane
madman, is the course of life but a dance of death? And who
else but the all-licensed Fool has grasped this jointure and is
able with laughter to collapse its tragedy of errors and accidents into liberating comedy? Lear's Fool stands by, the
avatar of human sympathy and unillusioned understanding,

much like the chorus in a play by Euripides or even by Aristophanes! Tom O'Bedlam stands as his complement: a sage Fool and a sane madman, the champions of human freedom from the cruel irrationalities of God and Nature and the pangs and penalties of their own choices and the follies of their own pursuits!

The Fool is the symbol paramount. Often, the symbol signified an actual member of a company of Fools, a guilds-man initiate in the doctrine and discipline of an art of fool-ing, whose patron spirit—naturally not saint—was divine Mère Sotte, Dame Folly, Mother Folly. Her revelation was antiphonal to the revelation of the Holy Church, even though through generations the Church had celebrated the Feast of Fools. In fact, celebrations were officially suppressed by the Council of Basel in 1435, but continued to be bootlegged, and still have a sanctioned residue in the Mardi Gras, the mi-caremes, the carnivals of modern times. With or without priestly sanction, they were the descendents of an immemo-rial tradition, mutations upon fertility rites, upon Dionysian festivals, upon Saturnalia, upon Satyr plays, even upon the Aristophanic farces—all, with the worthies of the Christian Testaments replacing the gods and heroes of pre-Christian antiquity. All were works of the free spirit of man, strug-gling against the cyclical scarcity and hunger imposed by the turns of the year, breaking loose from the routines of the daily life, relaxing the conventions of community, seeking to assure itself satisfaction and survival.

In feudal Europe many a village might have its free com-pany of merry men who enacted the mysteries of the Faith and redressed the Passion of the Lord and the suffering of his saints with burlesques which derided the powers that be, in ways Aristophanes would have appreciated. Among the volunteers were persons of wit and character, often priests. Irked by the hypocrisies of Church and the tyrannies of State, and powerless to condemn and fight them directly, the merrymen joined together in lay companies and did this with laughter. They made up the "joyous societies" of England, the *"enfants sans souci"* and the "Basochiens" and the *"écoliers"* of the schools of France. Pretending to be hopeless fools—all "allowed"—they could, more or less dangerously, make holiday on saints' and other feast days, revenging the folk upon the mighty and holy for their hypocritical abuses by holding them up to derision in speech and song and farcical plots, and showing them up for the fakes they were. In fact, the joyous societies demonstrated the Beatitudes. They gave effect by their make-believe to the deliverances of the Sermon on the Mount, especially on the *"Fête des Fous."* In the character of hopeless fools, the brethren could extend their feast of fools into moral holidays. And if ever-conscious authority suppressed and disbanded them, they could join up again with a new rubric, under a new name, still the laugh-making sons and daughters of "Mother Folly." Like the individual Fools at court, they wore identifying costumes—green and yellow (we see some of them in Breughel the Elder's print, *"Fête des Fous"*)—thus mocking every type of fool, from the wanton and cuckold, the miserly and hopeful, to the gay and the mournful. Their Mother Folly was their providence—a woman prized and dear to many men, born in the heart of the earthly Paradise, 6,500 years old. She it was, not Satan, who induced Adam to eat of the fatal apple. She it was, the Great Mother of fallen man, who in Gringoire's satire on the contest between Medician Pope Julius II and French King Louis XII appears as Mother Church, only to be stripped of her disguise and revealed as old Mére Sotte. By their rites her priesthood of fools brought Everyman surcease of pain, scattered his vexations to the winds, and honestly delighted "le pauvre monde que n'a croix."*

Of course, the spokesmen for the authority which harassed them, lampooned them in their turn. To those the Fool was a fool not because he brought the multitude joyous

---

* *Croix* was the word for a coin as well as a crucifix.

laughter by unmasking the force and fraud of powerholders, but because he did unmask them and thus laid bare his own folly of going against the laws of nature and the grace of God, of refusing authority the obedience that is its right, and thus rendering himself an object of the contemptuous laughter that every dissident from the orthodox creed and code deserves. What is such a one but a weakling to be scorned? What is his whole silly knavish career but a Dance of Death? So, in 1494 German Sebastian Brant's picture-book morality in verse, *Narrenschiff*, the Ship of Fools, held up a mirror to Adam's breed, a *speculum stultorum* and a *summa vitiorum*, wherein they might see what vessels of vice and wrath they are before God and his earthly surrogates. In due course the Ship was sailed in French and English and other European vernacular bottoms—and in the humanist Latin. There is little doubt that it was a precedent for Erasmus' very different *Moriae Encomium sive Stultitiae Laus*, better known as *In Praise of Folly*.

This humanist invitation to laughter was dedicated to Sir Thomas More, on whose name its title is a labored pun. The invitation was first extended in Latin, in the year of grace 1509. It signalizes Erasmus (whom we remember for championing the "humanities" against the pretensions and privileges of the apparent agents of divinity) as a carrier of the tradition of the laughing philosophers. We know that he wrote ironical and satirical dialogues about ancient worthies easily replaceable by equivalent contemporaries. We konw how aware he was of Lucian, whom he had translated jointly with his utopian friend Sir Thomas More. We know how widely he traveled and with what diverse companies he conversed. How likely is it then that there should not have been among them members of this or that Joyous Society? That he should not have attended one or another performance of theirs or enjoyed one of their jolly sermons, say about St. Reason, or St. Onion? Erasmus' praise of folly flows from a deep awareness of how factitious and costumal are the accepted differentiations between man and man; how much they are masquerades designed to enclose the laughter, so near to tears in the nature of things, as the private property of the community's actual and would-be mighty men, who claimed it by right of inheritance from God. It is these claimants whom Erasmus' Lady Folly unmasks, while she points her finger at the honest fools, their dupes, exposing both to laughter. She does it by means of a sermon she preaches on the subject of her immortal self.

Her allocution perplexes. Who is she, the reader asks, Mére Sotte or Hagiasophia? Or are these but two names for an identical goddess, the free man's Muse of Muses? The spirit of Doublethink and the flesh of Doubletalk, whose manifestations are puns and witticisms both common and metaphysical, challenging the reader's mind to choose between them freely, without fear and without illusion? When, a generation or so later, the author's Latin was done over into English, the translator advised that Erasmus delighted in mockery and called things by one name while meaning another. For the reader's enlightenment he provided a gloss to show where Erasmus was making fun. He believed that the *Praise* would bring comfort to "mean men of baser wits and condition." Seeing its ancestry, what could the record testify but that the translator was not mistaken?

For Erasmus' humanism bridged the gap; it reached beyond the humanities, to the miscellany of mankind. He, like the elder Brotherhood of Fools, saw the innocence of Adam's seed betrayed, their liberty stolen, and their mystical integrity of soul compromised by a church and a society nourishing their vicious passions upon humanity's weakness and ignorance. So far as human nature permitted, he wanted to free it from the burden of this folly. That the permission could not reach far, Erasmus knew, for Folly is Janus-headed. If she mothers man's disabilities, she is equally and more, the mother of man's strengths; his life is renewed and more vigorous where she is in apocalypse, with her unrestrained folk-fool as her harbinger. And so she comes now, the very inwardness of liberty, its urges breaking the bonds of prudence and the chains of reason, its positive joy in being alive, so weak yet so intense, so reckless and so self-judging. She is the divine providence of the world: "at first sight of me you all unmask and appear in more lovely colors." Marriage, begetting, birth, and the government of men are her inspiration. She distributes her favors equally without favoritism. If there is neither church nor temple for her worship it is because no place is more sacred to her than any other—her worship is universal.

So look upon Mother Folly here now, sustaining the egotism of poets, artists and scientists, sustaining the powers and privileges of churchmen and politicians that would all collapse once the simple human fool abandoned his reverence of Folly. But can he? Do not Scripture and the humanities alike commend her? Does she not teach her fool-man to love God beyond reason, without reason? What human irrationality does Folly not support, even the hurts and hungers of the senses, even the ambitions and greeds of the servants of other divinities than Mother Folly? Does she not nourish the ambitions and lusts of the money-lenders, the soldiers, the venal judges, the courtiers, the kings, the bishops, the cardinals, and the popes? These are the monopolists of power in the world, so strong that even Folly may not, while she nourishes them, also safely show them up. Join to them the alchemists, the naturalists, the grammarians, the jurists; join, too, the logicians with their fatuous methods and foolish aims, the theologians, the doctors, the scholastics with their egotism and vanities, their misuses of reason, and their moonshine truths.

Especially are the theologians Folly's favorites—all of them, the realists and the nominalists and the Albertists and Thomists and Dunsmen and Occamists, ever intransigent regarding the letter, ever heedless of the spirit of true faith, still disputing over the universal and the particular, splitting hairs over creation, over original sin, over the forms of the incarnation (could the Savior have come as woman, as some other object?), over the attitudes to one another of the three persons of the Trinity. But even more under her providence does Folly hold the monks and the friars, gross, dirty, ignorant drunkards and fornicators, illiterate parroteers of rite and rote, so disgusting that if they were to crusade against the Turks, the Turks would flee rather than face the obscenity.

Yet, with all the evil which men's follies wreak on themselves and one another—the mighty fools enslaving the mightless ones, the cunning fools cheating the simple ones, and mighty, cunning and simple alike fooling themselves through their vanities, lusts and greeds—they are all by nature not evil but good, and Dame Folly is their providence, not their doom. There is no divinity like unto her; none rivals her as the fountain of life and the shaper of destiny. It is the men who most remember her that are best fitted to live on—the simple ones, the very old, the very young, and those who neither worry about the future, nor heed nor fear death. A lesser order of the fit are the men who conduct the world's business. These rely on experience, not on books; on friends, not on learning. Knowing that desire is stronger than "truth," they recognize how much more practicable opinion is than knowledge. Since to be human is to err, can there be tears in error? Isn't error the Self affirming its selfhood? And how can self-affirmation be misery? "For nothing may rightly be called miserable which is in harmony with the springs of its own being—unless, mayhap, some one would hold it a thing to regret that in the nature of things a man can't fly like a bird, or move on all fours like a beast, or thrust with horns like a bull."

So, human beings, each loving himself, generate the self-deceptions and the deceptions of one another which support their struggles to live on! "I pray you, can he love anybody who loves not himself, can he agree with anybody

who cannot agree with himself? Can he please anybody who
bores and pleases not himself?" Mutual flattery is mutual
aid, far more useful in human intercourse than rough, rude
realism. Perhaps this is like the strivings of vermin for their
own survival. True, ultimately mankind's great commotions
likewise provide the stuffs of tragedy. Nevertheless, the
stuffs' reverse side is the mad ecstasy of the spirit which lifts
it, free from all anxiety, to the apex of unreason, to the highest of Folly's high places, to the Ineffable.

"Know Folly, then, Folly our great Mother, the daughter
of Plutus and Youth, born in the Earthly Paradise or the
Fortunate Isles, nursed by Bacchus on Drunkenness, by
Paris on rudeness, known to Cato, Horace, Homer and
Cicero, to Solomon and the Preacher and Jeremiah and Paul,
from whom the Schoolmen picked up something about Her."
But her foremost sponsor is Jesus Christ. Does not Scripture
admonish the race of man to be fools for Christ's sake, and to
suffer fools gladly? So, humans can be simply, devoutly
foolish; meditating upon death they can escape from Self in
the love of God. "Now all these texts that I have alleged, do
they not clearly bear witness that in being fools, mortals are
also godlike? That the Word made flesh is also Wisdom
incarnate in Folly? Farewell, then, clap your hands to show
you are glad. Live without care, be jolly, drink deep, you
trusty servants and solemn votaries of Folly."

In the four and a half centuries since Erasmus thus
publicly praised Folly, there have been added some commentaries upon the tragic, many upon the comic, aspects of
mortal man's struggles to go on struggling. Each voiced a
choice by the commentator, choice of laughter, choice of
tears. Some have laughed in anger, in indignation, in scorn
or in sorrow. Others have wept over the same things for the
same reasons. Tragedies and comedies both have been uttered as acts of aggression, not as communications of insight. When such, they signify the uses to which we put

laughter or tears, not the freedoms we experience in and through them.

That Erasmus, praising Folly, also put them to use is apparent enough. But he used them with a charity, a compassion for which precedents and consequents are rare. Certainly no satirist, no ironist, no humorist, so envisions Folly. She is the surge of Liberty, she could be what Santayana so much later called "the rush of being." But Erasmus discloses her as the perennial wrestle of protean good with protean evil, protean right with protean wrong, confirming victory now to the one and again to the other, but to none forever. I cannot think of another laugh-maker who also appreciates these "values" as formations of the life-struggle which their transit diversely signalizes; or who recognizes that the struggle, since each man persists in it and would not willingly die out of it, should itself be good, not evil. To Erasmus, Dame Folly is *integer vitae*. Because she is this, she serves as a symbol for the nature of things; she enters the humanist pantheon of mythical divinities a figure unto whom no other is like, truly the Muse of Muses, already consuming their ancestral chief, Phoebus Apollo, as Chronos at last would consume Olympian Zeus.

But in calling Folly "our Great Mother," Erasmus spoke more truly than he knew. Homer might have known her in her earlier guise, not the other worthies whom Erasmus lists. In that guise, she was of another derivation than Erasmus assigns her and of another import for man's struggle to live and not die than the Erasmian Christ. In that guise she was the Great Mother who was nobody's daughter, of whom the Olympian gods were but protean diversifications, descendants perhaps, means and media certainly. In that guise she was Mother Nature, the maker and unmaker of all things, the giver of life and laughter, the bringer of death and tears—the Mother Nature of the pagan philosophers modern as well as ancient, but not Christian. The laugh-makers and

tear-bringers of Athens had a truer, simpler sense of her
than the later generations of the Western world; and the
rites and rotes of the Greek religion which became their
comedies and tragedies, were much nearer to the primal
patterns of their strivings to live on and to grow. Aristophanes and Euripides, Aeschylus, Sophocles, and Menander are
their best remembered voices, among so many other forgotten ones. It is not unfitting now also to consider the occasions
and intent of their evocations of laughter and tears.

CHAPTER SEVEN

Laughter and Tears among the Ancient Greeks

SOME YEARS AGO a literary magazine published a poem entitled "Fables of Laughter." The poet discloses how the animals, freed from the constrictions of Noah's Ark at last snug-harbored on Ararat, gamboled and squeaked or roared their release, and how small Ham and Shem, hearing their jubilation, laughed. This never-before-heard unmusical sound disturbed the animals. It stopped them in their play. What could it portend? Alone the serpent had the answer.

> *Laughter that was. The word*
> *One of my race o'erheard*
> *   Back in a Garden dim.*
> *(Man has a secret—wise*
> *Gift of God to him!*
> *   A gift divine!)*
> *And hence these strange, profound*
> *Bubbles of breath and sound*
> *   The man-child's mouth doth give—*
> *   These but the secret's sign!*
> *We play, because we live;*
> *Man laughs, because man dies!*
> *(Thus with his sophistries*
> *The snake, half-wise.)*

The poem echoes and diversifies an immemorial tradition. As the Existentialists mourn in their turn, the human comedy is a dance of death. Some dancers see the Divine Comedy as but an illusory hypostasis of the human one, with human fools forever redistributed in final defeat and final victory according to the loves and hatreds of the comic poet. Heaven alone is a place of no laughter, no tears; a place only of smiling. Triune God, of course, does not even smile. But his Wife and Mother, with her company of angels and saints do. They are the celestial counterpoint to earthly Dame Folly with her Joyous Routs, talking, singing, and dancing up their barriers against death. The latters' fun and games are said to be ongoing variations upon felt but unrecognized collective remembrance of generations of men living together with animals, long, long before they did so in Noah's Ark; of men's reliance on this community for their own existence, of men's appreciation of the turn of the seasons when animals give birth and from it learn the providence of their own human survival.

Totem and taboo signalize this appreciation. It is the begetter of "the holy," the force in magic, the matrix of worship. It is the urge which the rites and rotes of the religions impattern and which at long last disenchants them into the comic and tragic of folkways and mores, and those into the comedy and tragedy of the dramatic and literary arts.

Comedy and tragedy are Greek words. When Plato or Socrates or Aristophanes or Sophocles or Aristotle used them, what they signified still retained much of the seminal rites at the seed time of each year, when celebrants wore erected phalluses, dressed in goatskins, played the goat, and laughed and sang their goat songs, begging and bullying capricious Dionysus in his goatish incarnation to grace their struggles for food with abundance, their struggles for liberty and safety and health with victory. The goat song, then called *tragos oidé*, became the matrix of tragedy. But its uses were the same as the uses of the *komos oidé*, whence grew comedy. Both chanted out the old and chanted in the new seasons. They celebrated nature's alternations and comminglings of death and resurrection, fasts and feastings, defeats and victories. The incantations of both could voice orgy and *askesis*, could pass from an exaltation of revellers to a keening of mourners and back again. In fact, early Greek, like many other ancient tongues, used similar if not the same words for both outcries. However much the two dithyrambs diverged, they gave voice to the one urge, celebrating sacrifice, telling of destruction and death and rebirth and victory, shifting from tears to laughter, from laughter to tears.

But a time came when the forefathers of all the Joyous Societies, the *Satyroi* or Goat-men, achieved an independent role. Aeschylus separated them from the communal rites of tragedy, and even though Euripides brought them formally back, the laughter stayed separated from the tears. Herodotus tells how Arion of Lesbos led a chorus of fifty goat-men chanting the earliest tragi-comic dithyrambs to celebrate the death and rebirth of the goat-god Dionysus. Sixty years later the revellers were wearing Thespis' * masks and filling themselves anew with the spirit of the God who was dead and is alive again, by means of dance and song performed duly and in good order.

Thereby, they also conquered death. Euripides' Bacchae did nothing else. The keeners and wailers (women, of course) the Greeks called *agelastos*—unlaughing. When not Demeter's, Dame Folly could be but Dionysus' avatar; and her son, the Prince of Folly, his surrogate. Laughter, alternately to tears, is the perennial signature of both. It comes to signalize their living presence, able to overcome all foes earthly and unearthly; above all, able to dispel the spell of Death. Laughter's role is felt to be divine. Laughter becomes the god Gelos, helper of men in their sisyphean la-

* Peisistratos gave Thespis a goat for a prize.

bors to bring back life-renewing Spring. The Romans' name for the god was Risus, whom they glorified as *deus sanctissimus et gratissimus.*

We can only speculate whether divine Gelos had a place of his own on Olympus and what dionysian laughter might have meant to Zeus. Nietzsche made his guesses about dionysian tears, and many humanists have bettered his conjectures about the birth and death of tragedy.* But the relationship invites as much conjecture and argument as it ever did. We can agree only that the Zeus and his tribe of whom Homer tells, waged no war with the death which, at last, is the destiny of gods immortal even as of mortals and demigods; that the Olympians used it against mortals for their private ends. Indeed, it might be said that the latter's immortality lived in their not fighting fate, and that not to fight fate was thus their freedom. Immortal to one another, they used their reciprocal indestructibility to fight and cheat and play practical jokes on one another. Homer's Olympians are laughers and provokers of laughter. We are shown a lusting Zeus. We are shown a Hera waging a cold war against her brother and spouse even to the point of seducing him by means of Aphrodite's magic girdle. We are shown the resentment with which the heavenly Patriarch discovers that she has fooled him, so that he threatens to throw her out of Olympus and keep her suspended in the air below. We are told of her jealous quarreling with Aphrodite, the complaisant, smiling, vaporish goddess of love; and with Pallas, the mannish virgin, who can thrash Ares, the god of war. We are shown how these Olympians provoke and trick human beings as readily as they protect and help those who please them. Whatever the gods do, they do irresponsibly and enjoy the doing; they are cruel, Apollo on one occasion tells them, and doers of evil. They are playboys and playgirls, free and irresponsible. Essentially, they don't care about the struggling humans who denounce and scold the gods even as

* Nietzsche said that tragedy died of suicide by the hand of Euripides.

they pray to them. They are the authentic ancestors of the Queen of Heaven and the saints of Carlo Levi's *Eboli*, where Christ did not go. Forbidden by Zeus, who is friendly to Troy, to take sides in the Trojan war, they disobey him and he lets them and laughs even at what they do to each other. He enjoys the sights; and if their brouhaha becomes excessive he takes himself off for a quieter look from Mount Ida.

Homer's Olympians are unaware of tragedy. To them, evil is not authentically evil, since they employ it for their own gratifications; the human tragedy can only make them laugh, and what they do to one another is laugh-making no less. Perhaps this divine condition is the reward—or the penalty—of immortality. We may not agree that its inwardness is of malice, that St. Paul rightly transvalued their pagan godheads into Christian devils. Perhaps their laughter was without malice, as malice manifests itself in human experience. Perhaps it harks back to the innocence of their totemic origins. Then, when human impersonations translated their animalhood into divinity and made of them gods like men, it may also have divested their laughter of its innocence, rendered laughing an expression of *Schadenfreude* such as may have been "the inextinguishable laughter which arose," Homer narrates, "among the blessed gods when they saw Hephaestus bustling about the mansion."

For Hephaestus, although sired by Zeus upon Hera, seems of another race than his fellow Olympians—human, not totemic. Because he sided with his mother during one of her set-tos with her heavenly brother and husband, the divine Patriarch threw him out of Olympus, and thus crippled him. His day-long fall was stopped at the island of Lemnos. Somehow he grew up the sole laborer among his brethren, a craftsman and artist amid nobler godheads, their cup-and-weapon maker, and occasionally their cupbearer. It was in this role that he aroused the inextinguishable laughter of their divinities. But he also freed Zeus from the headaches of reason by splitting open the patriarchal head so that full-panoplied Pallas Athene, goddess of war and wisdom, might come forth. Lame Hephaestus's images show him wearing the *chiton* and *pilos* of the workman and fisherman; they show him the frequent companion of the drunken Dionysus of spring festivals and fertility rites of nature. He continues a comic figure into *The Odyssey*. Then the tale of him turns on his cunning as a net-maker. Phoebus had seen the lame one's lovely wife, Aphrodite, in close dalliance with Ares the fighting man, and reported it—perhaps only for fun with a funny one—to Hephaestus. The latter thereupon wove his net in which he then trapped the embracing pair, displayed them thus to the other Olympians, and demanded that Father Zeus should bring them to trial.

All in all, Hephaestus is a prototype of the perennial laugh-maker as butt, the little fellow who labors, who is clownish and lame and ugly, yet who is, for some not too obscure reason, mated to beauty, to lovely Aphrodite, although in no way the brave who had deserved and won the fair; Hephaestus is a fool, nowise like his elite fellow Olympians, a fighter. When the latter laughed, their laughter voiced the self-confident freedom of the safe and the sure. The biographers of Hephaestus do not record that he ever laughed, only that he was a clever, revengeful craftsman. If he had laughed, it would have been like Pagliacci, the man-clown, who laughs while his heart is breaking; who, as the artist chooses, enacts a hero of comedy, overcoming heartbreak with laughter, or a hero of tragedy, subduing laughter to heartbreak.

For, to repeat, however divergent tragedy and comedy at last become, however much they bespeak a warfare among the passions of mankind, both began—as their rite and rote regularly reminded the Athenian folk—in the same striving to conform the changes and chances which are Nature to the survival of man. Both first imaged Everyman's struggle to free himself alike from the hungers, the thirsts, the propulsions of living and from their extinction in death. Nature's courses are the surroundings of his continuance, so that his personal history is ever a dance of death.

Did the steps of this dance signify élan of life or stasis of death; stasis because no living soul can say "I died" as it can say "I loved," or "I ate and drank"? Was the Feast of Fools one of its many transformations? The record does not disclose only one answer. It tells of "wakes" with their food and drink, their wines, and their funeral-baked meats. It tells of the solemn merry-making that went with the right disposal of the dead—back into Mother Earth, or on a funeral pyre. It tells of the games and dances meant to keep death away from the living as well as to honor the dead, or to propitiate either them or the maleficence which brings death upon living men. It tells how, when dying is so multitudinous and widespread that the ceremonials which render the dead their due break down, the laws of God and men break down; the ritual arts of the comic and the tragic cease to channel the will to live on. It tells how this will becomes a desperate anarchist, takes liberties in every forbidden way, even as do the immortal gods. So the Athenians, during the plague at Athens in the second year of the Peloponnesian War. Thucydides, who had himself been sick with it, says that the Athenians ventured boldly on acts which they had habitually suppressed; that they "were reduced to live for pleasure and enjoy themselves quickly. No one was eager to persevere in the ideals of honor—it was uncertain whether they would be spared to attain the object; present enjoyment and all that contributed to it, was accepted as both honorable and useful. . . . They thought it made no difference whether they worshipped God or not, as they saw all alike perishing; no one expected to live to be brought to trial for his offenses; each felt that a far severer sentence had been already passed upon them all and hung over their heads, and before this fell, it was only reasonable to enjoy life a little." So, each Athenian chose for himself without regard to any other. And later generations of men confronting similar exigencies meet them with similar attitudes.

But the collective desperation on occasion becomes patterned, and the propulsions of life move into their dance of death from a ritual beginning. It was from such a beginning that the thus-named historic Dance of Death received the forms by which tradition envisages it. About a millenium and three-quarters later, in the Christian fourteenth century, a plague swept Christian Europe. It added itself to the already fearsome struggle merely to live on, to get food and drink, to endure or escape cruel oppressions which made the existence of the Christian multitudes. They called this plague the Black Death. They were sure that no one else than Satan could inflict it upon true believers, and that his instruments were Jews and witches whom they must therefore torture and destroy. And they resorted also to the unavailing power of God, his Son, his saints, and his Mother. The people yet on their feet formed diverse processions to churches, to shrines, where they offered prayers for relief. They carried ikons and images. They chanted psalms, they beat themselves with whips, they mortified their flesh, and otherwise devised more ways, speakable and unspeakable, to propitiate the supernatural powers of heaven and of hell.

Often these ways started in festivals, such as the *Johannesfeuer*, that were the ages' own characteristic repristination of a dionysian rout, a *komos oidé* or a *tragos oidé*. The Feast of St. John was a seasonal revel with orgiastic singing and dancing. It could, and did, draw into the common pattern more and more women and men, who on occasion became a jumping, raving, flagellating, blood-sweating, yet not unorderly mob; talking with tongues, telling of visions, prophesying, each dancing the holy dance that St. Vitus had danced. These are the terpsichoreans of the Dance led by a grinning Death which the painters portrayed, the Dance which held so profound yet not astounding an allure for the simple Christian souls. Among them death owned an import

in no way commensurable with its import for the unchris-
tianized Greeks and Romans. The latter accepted it as the
terminus ad quem, the regrettable but natural ending of all
things alive. The former averted from it as an initiation into
the punishment by God for Adam's sin. Francis of Assisi has
no companions in his praise of "sister Bodily Death" among
the other of God's creatures that he praises. Here Martin
Luther is more Christian. Hear him in *Table Talk:* "It were a
light and easy matter for a Christian to suffer and overcome
death if he did not know that it is God's wrath: this is what
makes death bitter to us. But a heathen dies in safety. He
neither sees nor feels that it is God's wrath. He understands
it as the end of nature, and a natural end. The Epicurean says
that it is but to endure one evil hour."

It might be that the Feast of Fools is then the other, the
inner side of the Dance of Death; its obverse, wherein the
immemorial tradition of the urge toward life, and ever more
life, subdues the later anxiety to prevent death. Among the
Greeks certainly, before *komos oidé* diversified into comedy
and *tragos oidé* into tragedy, the urge which the steps of the
dance impatterned was élan, not stasis. A time came, however, when the people of Hellas suffered a "failure of nerve":
fear of death moved men more than joy of life, the tears in
the nature of things shut off the spontaneous laughter of the
spirit of man. Nor Plato, nor Aristotle, can be joined to
Democritus as laughing philosophers. True, they laughed
and discussed laughter, but not as their philosophic faiths.

Let us recall: Plato and Aristophanes knew each other,
were perhaps friends. In Plato's *Symposium*—that remembrance of the talk at a party which the tragic writer
Agathon gave to celebrate his winning the first prize for
tragedy—Plato reports Aristophanes' serious funning, not
unsympathetically. There is at last an almost religious tone
to the discussion of love mortal and love immortal and the
objects of these loves. Toward the end of the *Dialogue*, Plato
represents Socrates as forcing both Aristophanes and Aga-

thon to concede that the genius of comedy is the same with that of tragedy and that the true artist in tragedy is an artist in comedy also. In another dialogue, the *Philebus*, Plato recalls how spectators at a tragedy smile through their tears, and how feelings at a comedy are mixed pleasure and pain. Is it likely that Aristophanes would have gainsaid this? What else were his plays aimed at, if not laughing to naught the tears in the course of Athenian events? True, in the *Thaetetus*, Plato did image his philosopher as a simple and sincere laugher, but he was wary of the comic spirit, and in the *Republic* (Book III) he contended that persons of worth must not be represented as overcome with laughing. Aristotle went this one better—he wouldn't have his great-souled gentlemen laugh at all.

Both philosophers had certain uses for laughter, and Plato's were the same that Aristophanes strove for with his comedies. The dramatist seems to have created those in order to strip and bare, to scorn certain divine and human figures of the common life of his city, to evoke laughter as the means that denudes them of their power and defeats their purposes, thus freeing the city of them. The divinities among his dramatis personæ were both chthonic and Olympian—somehow the choric Clouds of Socrates' heaven show more truly godlike. So do the choric birds of Aristophanes' Cloud Cuckooland. The humans were mostly urbanites and countryfolk of Attica—politicians, peasants, poets, philosophers, women—striving with one another during the ups and downs, until the final down of Athens in the Peloponnesian War. Aristophanes was a realistic believer in the good old ways. He was anxious over the corruptions and stupidities of the democracy and the cruel perfidy of war and empire. He was deeply convinced that peace was necessary and that the new education was perverse. He was eager for the old virtues and anxious that the order of peace might be restored. He believed them to be the *sine qua non* of true liberty.

Over a span of forty mostly war-ridden years Aristophanes made fun of jury courts, heads of state like Cleon, philosophers and teachers like Socrates, tragic poets like Euripides and Aeschylus, gods like Dionysus and Hermes and Zeus. Within the festival permissiveness of the *komos oidé*, he takes liberties with them all, exposing their follies and deriding their pretensions. He masks some of his choruses as wasps, others as frogs, as clouds or as birds. Every mask serves to symbolize a foe whom Aristophanes undertakes to laugh down to defeat or a friend to liberate and bring to victory with laughter. The theme of *The Wasps* is the corruption of the jury courts, the theme of *The Clouds*, the perversion of the new education and the ostensible heresy of the new religion. Aristophanes' perennial hero is the old-style farmer, of whom Charlie Chaplin's "little fellow" is a mutant. His alternates are women, as in *Lysistrata* and *Ecclesiazusae*. They stand and struggle regularly for the good old ways and for peace. Since he-men really care for neither, Aristophanes has women take over on their behalf; and since peace and the good old ways don't get restored among Athenians, they do get re-established in the Cloud Cuckooland of *The Birds*, or in a utopian Athens set up by peaceful, feminine parliamentary revolution. *Ecclesiazusae* brings to mind Plato's *Republic:* its emphasis on community of land and property, its ideal of sexual relations, its establishment of the State as the parent of all children; in the words of the Chorus, addressing the heroine Praxagora, "ideas never practiced, never before suggested, to stir up a shrewd and philosophic mind."

But in *Ecclesiazusae*, the self-discipline of the Platonic guardians becomes a form of fun and games, and the communion of the people a free, merry revel which everybody joins. Plato's is a discipline without release and a communion without joy, certainly without such freedom. But *Ecclesiazusae* could hardly have been a parody of the *Republic*, which, book by book, Plato might have been circulating among his friends or even reading to them. But it hadn't been "published," and the audiences of Athens could not have been aware of any parodying. If men-as-women were funny, women-as-men were, conventionally, even funnier, and thus disarming as well as apt media for Aristophanes' embattled laughter.

By the time Aristotle came to appraise the poet's comic art there was a new Athens and a new climate of opinion. The city had lost the war with Sparta, the Macedonians had taken Athens' imperial pretensions for their own and were by way of making them good. The Hellenic had given way to the Hellenistic state of mind, the cultivation of the citizen-soldier to the market militarism of the mercenary. Civic duty became less compelling than cultural self-realization; the relations between individual lives more meaningful than the economy of nature with its religious management by means of the ceremonies of men. As against Plato's *Republic* comes Aristotle's *Ethics*. As against the comedies of Aristophanes come those of Menander; while in tragedy, Euripides' utterance of personal conflict, set within the framework of the Dionysian rites, takes precedence over all others. Thus, for Aristotle, Aristophanes' comedy only employed a vulgar freedom of speech, and depended too much on foul language and buffoonery—all apt enough for a democracy which enjoys such vulgarisms, such a sadism toward authority, such a taking of liberties with power and excellence as Aristophanes took. Aristotle preferred Menander; so did all the gentlemen of his and later generations. The multitudes have to this day remained appreciators of the Aristophanic ways. The elite, perhaps only publicly, continue to prefer those of Menander.

Our image of Menandrian laugh-making is composed largely from the Latin of Roman Plautus and Terence, supplemented by thousands of quoted Greek bits. Together they make a mosaic which conveys what the authors meant who wrote that this laugh-maker provided "a mirror of human life." But it was only a segment of the human life of the last half of the third pre-Christian century, the age of the Diodachi. Menander was born in 342, before the Christian era, and lived until 290; lived that is, the critical years when Hellenic was being reshaped into Hellenistic culture. He was thus an Athenian of the period when his country's imperialism had ceased to be political and had been made cultural, when the citizen could cease to be also a soldier without losing face, when he could abandon the career of public affairs and absorb himself in satisfactions of a private existence without failing in virtue. When Menander was writing, men's personal histories were no longer shaped by the pooled bet of lives, fortunes, and sacred honor, or by the Periclean glories of a free city of free men. They were shaped by a concern for the amenities of safe and satisfying private personal living. The unintentional definer of this transvaluation had been Isocrates; its missionaries had become Macedonian Alexander and his successors.

Since tragedy was more a religious occasion, ever held closer to its ceremonial and liturgical origins, the sublimation of goals seems to have affected little the figures or forms of tragedy. At the hands of Euripides, those retained their traditional configuration and status. He did bring the choices between the warring passions and purposes of the perennial dramatis personæ nearer to those of the common man; he did moralize their understanding, but they still remained gods and heroes. It was the comic art which signalized the new aspiration and the new ethos. For the spirit of Greek man, this was a liberation. The comic writer could expose naked the passions, the vanities, lusts, greeds, hypocrises, and ambitions, as they weaved the daily lives of respectable, ordinary people into clashing configurations of rivalry and intrigue. The comic muse ruled over an enormously enlarged and diversified region of human existence, beside which the province of tragedy was small indeed. Comedy became genuinely "new," and genuinely an extension of liberty, whereas tragedy retained the *status quo ante*. The "new comedy," with practically no religious import, recovered something of the earlier interpenetration of laughter with tears—recovered it, perhaps, because its writers had learned from Euripides' utterance that the laughter of man is not to be separated from the tears of things. Of all Athenian comic writers, Menander, perhaps the most prolific, had also been the seminal precedent-maker. He was five years old when Plato died, and only twenty at Aristotle's death. His friend among the philosophers was Epicurus, born in the same year but outliving the dramatist by twenty more. Menander, one infers, shared Epicurus' conviction of the tears in things, of the vanity of human hopes and human fears; shared also Epicurus' quest for a way of life freed from the political illusion, from the fear of the gods and the fear of death. It is from one of Menander's plays that we inherit the lines which have become a prime article of the humanist faith: *Homo sum: a me nihil humanum alienum puto*. And his plays—as did the Epicurean wisdom—gave the female of the species humanum something approaching equality with the male. Menander, like Euripides, was much more appreciated after he died than during his lifetime, although unhappily, none of his writings have survived whole, to be restored to the stage as are those of Euripides and other tragic writers. However contrived his plots, his figures and forms had in them something that could appeal everywhere to Everyman's struggle of laughter and tears and could set the laughter free from the tears. In due course, the laughter thus freed became "serious laughter." The expression is George Meredith's. He argued that the conditions for "high comedy" were "a society of cultivated men and women . . . wherein ideas are current and perceptions quick," a society which provides the comic writer with both his themes and his audience. Meredith didn't think that over the ages there were many such writers.

But whatever their number, they stem from Menander.

That he could elicit the laughter rather than the tears in the "follies" of men renders his friendship with Epicurus somewhat strange. For as was generally the case with the philosophers of the age, there was no laughter in Epicurus. Whatever else he had learned from cheerful Democritus, he had not learned laughter. Such laughing philosophers of the time as we read about were ex-slaves of the cynic persuasion like Bion of Borysthemis and Menippus of Gadara (he committed suicide). But the schools of Plato and Aristotle and Zeno were also voices of the failure of nerve; for them as for the school of Epicurus, man's answer to the tears and death in the nature of things could not be laughter. Nor could laughter receive this esoteric role from Pyrrho or from Philo or from Plotinus or their epigones to this day. In the great tradition, the blood-brother of philosophy is tragedy still. However happy the end of man in any philosophic system, his condition before this end is tragic. It is presented as a life of choosings, a warfare of moral ideals. For the philosophic chooser the alternatives are infallibly good and evil, truth and error, right and wrong, reality and appearance. By his act of election, the philosopher-elector commits what he rejects to destruction and death. The pairs may not live on together in the same universe. Ultimately, if one is to survive, the other must perish. This dilemma is also the dilemma of the hero of tragedy. Only, the tragic alternatives, to be tragic, must be good and good, right and right, truth and truth, reality and reality. Mostly, philosophers deny validity to the value they reject because they reject it, to the goods that their arguments defeat because by reducing them to appearance they do so defeat them. The philosophic tradition transvalues the tragedy of life before death into the divine comedy of life after death. The tears, the blood, the sweat of man's earthly condition, and the death which consummates them, are but ineluctable prelude to the happy ending of the after-life. When all is said and done, the latter compensates as ideal for the former as experience.

But authentic tragedy is without compensation. The alternatives rejected are as real and valid as those elected whether they be appraised good or evil. The tragedy is the event that, for either to be chosen, the other must be rejected; for either to survive, the other must perish, and that the outcome follows from the decision of a chooser choosing. Therein is the root, therein is the living spring—the rest is cultivation and fountaining. Custom, repeating and transposing Aristotle's very local and personal anatomies of Greek tragedy, transposes cultivation and fountaining to the spring, to the root. Aristotle sets tragedy in character, in organization of action, in the words and music that go with these and emphatically perhaps, in certain preferred effects upon audiences for which usage gives us the word catharsis. But a composition may have all these yet be no tragedy, may lack all these and be poignant tragedy. That which renders any play or story a tragedy, or a comedy, is not a function of who a dramatist's or a story-teller's characters are, and what they do. It is a function of the valuations he sets upon who they are and what they do. Those are his nuclear choices, which his art utters and would communicate. Plot, story, character, music, word, spectacle, and their rhythms are only his media, not his meaning. Even though to his audience and his critics they become his meaning, his meaning to him is his option between irreconcilable values, each with its ineffable worth. The choice between them is momentous, and momentous because it is a bet freely placed upon a future of consequences whose formation must deny expectation and annul hope. His meaning is the option consummated as its consequence. His meaning is the point of no return where at last no other value survives or can survive. Tradition calls such options acts of free will. But however they be named, and however manifold the unending arguments devised to account for them, they are of the stuff, and at the seat, of liberty.

Not the value chosen, but the consummation of choosings

between values is the theme of tragedy. Hence, some argue that for man, to live is to live tragedy, that tragedy is but another name for the human plight—indeed, Schopenhauer did cultivate some such notion—and that the arts of tragedy develop (Nietzsche so opined) as refinements, as the easements of the plight, as mitigations of it and consolations for it. If true, the opinion may hold the answer to Plato's query, perennially repeated, as by St. Augustine in his *Confessions:* "What is the reason that a spectator desires to be made sad when he beholds doleful and tragical passages which he himself could not suffer to endure?" The answer is that he does "suffer to endure"; that such passages do bespeak the stuff of each man's struggle to go on struggling (remember, we usually call this inveterate and commonplace struggle, struggle for self-preservation, struggle for survival) till the day he dies. In Freud's paradigm of the human person, by the art of tragedy of our id is liberated and gratified via the agonist's misdeeds, while our superego is assuaged by the suffering and death that become his destiny.

What is a man's personal history if not a stream of choices or decisions compenetrating as he struggles on, growing up and growing older? In his body, it is the intervals of incandescent tension between challenge and response as they succeed one another. As his mind, it is the changing formations of his changing awareness, whatever its depth and span. The sense of life is "tragic," is the feel of what is currently signalized "anxiety," "agony," because the alternative rejected is recognized to be as real, as precious, as much to be cherished as the alternative elected. Each choice, each decision extinguishes values no less real than those it creates or nourishes or supports. Each compounds with the others as they pass on to the climax of decision.

Whether the completion of the action, the ending, be "happy" or "unhappy" is irrelevant. The tears in the nature of things are for the killing or dying of what might as rightly live, the killing and dying which are the everlasting penalties of surviving and growing. As Homer's Achilles said to the young disarmed Lycaon, on his knees for his life: "Come my friend, die too; why do you cry like that? Patroclus also died, and he was a much better man than you. Don't you see me, too, a fine big man? My father is a brave man, my mother is a goddess; yet I too have death and fate fast upon me. The day shall come, morning or evening or midday, when someone shall take also my life in battle, with a thrust of the spear or an arrow from the bow."

But that which both the victim and the victor here mourn is not the great extinction, when each shall be as if he had not been. They mourn the death of tragedy, not the extinction of life. They accept existence as tragedy, not tragedy as the extinction of life. They accept existence as tragedy, as the succession of victories and defeats which make up their personal being. In one perspective, this is the theme of Bertrand Russell's *Free Man's Worship*. Once upon a time, contemplating "the blind forces of nature and the all-conquering might of death," Russell, then a youth, celebrated the "eternal truth" that "the supreme and austere beauty of mathematics" disclosed to him. This, together with poetry, enabled him to experience "the sense of being more than man, which is the touchstone of the highest excellence." Herein he found the ultimate Promethean ground, "the firm foundation of unyielding despair, the calm renunciation" upon which he could "burn with a passion for eternal things." This, chants the young Russell, "is emancipation and this is a free man's worship."

Other words for it might be Unamuno's "tragic sense of life." Unamuno expresses the sentiment more in terms of the philosophic tradition, terms ever repugnant to Russell:

And we have arrived at the bottom of the abyss, at the irreconcilable conflict between reason and vital feeling, and now there, I have told you we must accept the conflict as such and live by it. Now . . . to explain how according to my way of feeling and even according to my way of thinking, the despair may be the basis of a vigorous life, of an efficacious activity, of an ethic, of an esthetic, of a religion, and even of logic . . . Let us fight against destiny even though without hope of victory: let us fight quixotically.

That is, for Russell as for Unamuno, to live is to fight on. If tragic climax were death of the agonist, there could be neither philosopher's quixotism. Euripides' Medea could not be tragic, for she departs the scene in triumph; her tragedy is the ultimate choice she makes between the vengeful vindication of her integrity and the lives of her children. Aeschylus' Orestes must decide between the duty of killing his mother to avenge his father and impiety to the memory of his father by letting his mother live. Such for Shakespeare was also Hamlet's option. Sophocles' Antigone rejects the rule of the state and chooses piety to her dead who must be rightly buried. And does not Socrates, for whom life and submission to the law are like goods, choose obedience to law, however unjust, with death and reject disobedience with survival, however desirable? Of course, Socrates consoled himself with arguments for immortality. What does he, what does Russell or Unamuno decide upon? The lesser of two evils? The greater of two goods? "Evil" and "good" proclaim valuations. As actions to choose between, the alternatives are equally before the chooser, neither of itself better or worse than the other. It is the deliberation, the striving which their decisions consummate, that endows them with worth and renders them mutually exclusive. Choosing one is rejecting the other.

In that the chooser knows this, in that he recognizes his option as inwardly momentous, forced, and instant, an existentialist onlooker might describe him as "condemned to be free." But to say "condemned" to be free is only to say "condemned" to exist, "condemned" to be himself, "condemned" to the singularity of selfhood which a man's personal history builds up until he dies. Without a covert preference for unfreedom, for inalterable commitment, it is like saying that a triangle is "condemned" to be a plane figure of three sides and three angles.

For mankind, to be and to be free intend the same struggle to go on struggling; and the choosings which carry it forward are the welling spring of everyone's personal identity. Let the alternatives be what they may; let them be as desirable and precious as the heart can tell—there is no *both-and* for the struggler; there is only *either-or*. By taking one in, he shuts the other out; that is, he enacts tragedy. Compromise may be cowardice; it is also sacrifice, also only an *either* and *or*. "The necessity of rejecting or destroying some things that are beautiful," said George Santayana, "is the deepest curse of existence." Our decisions, says William James, "seem to make nature continous; and in their strange and intense functions of granting consent to one possibility, and withholding it from another, to transform an equivocal and double future into an inalterable and single past."

At this time, James was concerned about the closures which decisions effect, the unifications which are so much their intent. But these are not their sole intent: equivocation and doubleness pertain to them as well. They divide no less radically than they unify. They restore discontinuity to the nature they have rendered continuous, and create it in the nature they have so found. They alter and diversify the past which other decisions appear to have rendered inalterable and single. As the tale of the human enterprise is told, our decisions are moments of our unceasing struggle against the chances and changes amid which we strive till we ourselves cease, moments of our unremitting endeavor to harness the freedoms which ever intrude upon the routines and spontaneities we singularly are, into a team that shall confirm and carry them on, and each moment a diversification of the entire *status quo ante*. The art of tragedy, even as the art of comedy, in or out of the theatre, is such a working-up and stylizing of these confrontations and decisions. It so impatterns their contingencies, that the end is accepted as culminating the beginning; accepted as a climax and not merely a finish. The artist labors to relate the sequences of an actual course of events to one another in such wise, that their configuration shall have reason for its ground, and meaning to the human enterprise for its consequence.

Alas, that by informing events with reason and humanising them with meanings, he should turn the concords and discords whereof the stream of experience composes itself into a sequence of paradoxes! Paradox is a production of order and logic. It is a separation of diversities that otherwise flow together and flow on together or part without meaning and for no reason.

CHAPTER EIGHT

Dr. François Rabelais' Pantagruelism

T HE ERASMIAN interpretation of folly as somehow the universal mother of all things—to him, also of the truly Christian things—was in all likelihood an expression of the humanist's singularity; it could hardly have been a manifestation of the spirit of his innovative, violent, greedy, war-ridden age.

He had a companion in this faith of his. Insofar as it was a laughing faith, there was another who preferred it—and far more boldly, far more copiously, although with a more capricious awareness. This was a younger, greatly admiring contemporary, the doctor François Rabelais, "abstractor of the quintessence." So forceful were this humanist's professions, so abundantly were they demonstrated by his practices, his uninhibited spontaneities of speech and imagery, that people soon began to qualify with his name all disclosures of the undisclosable, all speakings of the unspeakable, all mentionings of the unmentionable. The telling epithet for all that has become, among the learned guardians of our manners and morals, "rabelaisian." And they call the laughter which signalizes the liberties taken by those means "rabelaisian laughter." Customarily, the inventor of the great Gargantua and the good Pantagruel is remembered as a literary purveyor of the obscene and the indecent, a poet of scatology and priapism.

Of course, in its wholeness, his Pentateuch of the Giants, their entourage and their exploits, is nothing of the sort. Rather it is the communication of his philosophic faith by a carrier of Europe's awakening, as avid of experience, of knowledge, and of laughter as any hero of the Renaissance. Accepting them in whatever form life offered them, Rabelais was braver than most in his pursuit of them and more spontaneous and abundant in his enjoyment of them and in his eagerness to impart this enjoyment to other men. Of neither the flesh nor the spirit was anything human alien to him. And the candor with which he bespoke the human and the perspectives of faith and understanding within which he set it, rendered it innocent and free, save to readers agonized by the idea of sin and terrorized by the image of punishment under the sanction of sacerdotal economy and the policings of a sacerdotal censor.

Rabelais' faith and works of laughter seem formations of his personal history, developments and magnifications—not projections, not symbolizations, not allegories. Even though many of his aficionados read them as the latter, they need not so be read. They are not required for understanding what he believed, what he loved, what he hated, and how he uttered his loves in laughter, and with laughter the tears of his hatreds.

Rabelais believed in liberty. Rabelais believed in man's right to knowledge and the free use thereof. His curiosity was insatiable and his information encyclopedic. His scorn and ridicule of those who would put blinkers on the mind's eye and hobbles on the soul's feet suffused all his utterance. His encounters with their animosity and aggression had been lifelong, and his five books were at once an exposure of them and a challenge to them. In France their chief cathedra was the Sorbonne, their prime agents were such provincial parliaments as the Parisian, which so often condemned his books to the flames. His protectors included such princes of church and realm as the brothers du Bellay, Geoffroy d'Estissac, King Francis I of France, and the King's sister, Margaret of Navarre. For their sake, if not for Rabelais' own, Counter-Reformation Popes Clement VII and Paul III indulged him his fractures of monastic rule and his breaches of priestly vows. Although his works were condemned and burned by the Parlements, we do not find them listed in the *Roman Index of Forbidden Books* as we find Erasmus'. Without emulating the style of the pagan "humanities," Rabelais' Pentateuch uses them to measure the most authoritarian expressions of the mediaeval tradition: its ritualistic hypocrisies, its pedantry, its aggressive ignorance and its pretentiousness. Although Rabelais' Pantagruelism bespeaks a piety such as Mére Sotte celebrated, no authenticated charge of heresy seems to have been confirmed against it by the new church of the Society of Jesus, the Holy Office, or the Council of Trent. It makes fun of other humanists' latinities even as its evangelist employs his own to speak new ideas that his French had no words for, and to gallicize them in the speaking. But he was more an aficionado of Greek than of Latin, and his laughing war against the monkish (scarcity) economies of body and mind began over their depriving him of Greek.

For Dr. Rabelais had started his career with a cure of souls; first his own, then his fellow man's. He was Friar Rabelais before he became Dr. Rabelais. His experience as a regular of a Franciscan community—the cordeliers bound to one another by identical vows of obedience, celibacy, and poverty, and keeping them in a Pickwickian sense—drove him to attach himself to a congregation of the rival Benedictines. But these no more satisfied his yearnings than the Franciscans. He left them for the secular priesthood, which vowed only to practice obedience and celibacy and to read its

Breviary every day, and kept its vows with notorious prudence. But he did not serve either of the parishes which were to be his livings. By papal indults he was forgiven all his vows. By the favor of his Greek-loving Bishop he was brought, as the latter's secretary, into contact with the great secular world and its humanists. He travelled all over France and after two or three years ended up in the medical faculty at Montpellier. In due course he earned his baccalaureate in medicine and afterward the doctorate. He lectured on Hippocrates and on Galen and he wrote on the science and art of medicine—a science a little philological and largely rhetorical, an art, in practice, magical. Two hospitals appointed him Doctor, without stipend. He had the luck to dissect human bodies and the common sense to emulate Hippocrates rather than Galen. For cash money he produced almanacs, translations and editions of ancient works, and on occasion even invented some. Wherever he lodged, as at Lyons, he sought the company of other humanists, especially of the Hellenizers among them. His patrons, the du Bellays, attached him to their households as their physician. And he is remembered rather for his medical than for his theological art.

But Pantagruelism is intrinsically both a cure of bodies and a cure of souls, an orchestration of the two, an orchestration in laughter. Its prophet and revelator was of that region of France that had bred both the troubadours of the Courts of Love and the Cathari, and were to breed the *infame* who murdered innocent Calas. His father has been variously identified as an innkeeper, an apothecary, and a vintner, able to provide his son with schooling among such scions of nobility as the du Bellays and the d'Estissacs. The Franciscans had begun to reform the order in 1526, when Rabelais was, at most, twelve years old. It is not clear how he vowed himself into the prison of a monkish rule which prohibited the cultivation of the humanities as a subversion of the soul, which confiscated his hardily-obtained Greek books, which forbade his intercourse with the time's devout Hellenists. Rabelais' own endeavors emulated those of knowledgeable sages like Pico della Mirandola and Erasmus, engaging to orchestrate the wisdom of the ancients (so long under the Pauline ban as foolishness before the Lord), with the spirit of the Gospels. Because the Cordelins condemned and banned this, he discarded their gray habit for the Benedictine black; and because his curiosities were still starved and his insights damned, he resorted to every influence he could reach to wangle his freedom.

He seems never to have forgiven the powers that would have kept his mind on tether. His defense was a laughter that has resounded through the generations. It is such a laughter as the Joyous Societies laughed, as the folk dancing with laughter their dance of death. His legend does not tell that Doctor Rabelais had ever seen such dancing or shared in the merry-makings of a Joyous Company. It tells only that he enjoyed play-acting at Montpellier, that he had taken delight in the Erasmian praise of Folly, that its religion of laughter gave direction and form to his own. The legend also tells that he lived lustily and amply, drank copiously of his *purée de Septembre*, his "true and only Helicon," ate and laughed prodigiously, and wrote of it all with delighted self-approval. His legend tells he was the priestly father of a son who died in boyhood, and another son and a daughter whom Pope Paul III, by order, assumed from bastardy to legitimacy. The doctor's heroes, his villains, his euphemisms and gongorisms and rabelaisisms impart an analogous oversize and multitudinousness.

Whether or not the Five Books of Rabelais are, as readers such as Voltaire opined, allegories of contemporary history, and their personages metaphors for French kings, their counsellors, and their foes, the books move without plot; as Goethe said of his *Faust*, they begin and they end and have no unity. Regarding their production Rabelais wrote: "In the composing of this lordly book, I never lost nor bestowed any more nor any other time than what was appointed to serve me for taking of my bodily refection, that is, whilst I was eating and drinking." He wrote it for the consolation of the sick. He recommended that people suffering from toothache "put the said remedy between two pieces of a cloth made somewhat hot and so apply them to the place that smarteth." Shakespeare, reflecting upon the consolations of philosophy, was less sanguine: "For there was never yet philosopher," he observed in *Much Ado About Nothing*, "who could endure the toothache patiently, however they have writ the style of the gods and make a push at chance and sufferance." And here was Abstractor of the Quintessence, Doctor François Rabelais, gaily writing the style of the gods, making his hilarious push at chance and sufferance, and prescribing it for a poultice to be laid between two somewhat hot cloths on the place that smarteth—a remedy "peerless, incomparable and not to be matched."

His name for his remedy is Pantagruelism, the teachings of his hero, Pantagruel. This name, he says, continues the Greek word *Panta* or "all," with *Gruel*, which "in the Hagarene language doth signify thirsty, inferring thereby that at his birth the whole world was a-dry and thirsty." The *ism* presumably both instils and satisfies the thirst. It is a drink finally compounded in the form of a tall tale about "the inestimable life of the great Gargantua and of the heroic deeds, sayings and marvellous voyages of his son, the good Pantagruel." It is a tale told in five books, at intervals over twenty years, with the second done before the first, and the last unpublished and very probably completed by another hand from the author's notes, years after the author was dead. The first offering told about *The Horrible and Frightful Acts and Prowesses of the Very Renowned Pantagruel, King of the Dipsodes, Son of the Great Gargantua, from the pen of Master Alcofrybas Nasier* (an anagram for Francoys Rabelais). Somewhere the master had gotten hold of a little comic book of the time, telling stories about a couple of giants and their great mare, creations of Wizard Merlin. The male was Grandgousier, the female was Gargamelle, and their one child was Gargantua. When his parents took a purgative which killed them, the orphaned giant went to Paris, performed wonders there (among them, carrying off the bells of Notre Dame), and finally returned to Brittany. Thence Merlin wafted him on a cloud to Britain, where he served King Arthur two hundred years, three months, and four days, after which Morgan Le Fay transferred him to her own domain. This tale of miracles and wonders Rabelais transmuted and retold, diversifying and multiplying the episodes, elaborating them into the four sure and fifth doubtful books of his Pentateuch, using them for symbols, and impregnating them with the intent of his Pantagruelism.

The "ism," Doctor Dom Rabelais tells us, is "a certain Jollity of Mind, pickled in the scorn of Fortune." He makes the point again in the last four lines of the verses he addresses to "most noble and illustrious drinkers, . . . thrice precious pockified blades":

> Good friends, my Readers, who peruse this Book,
> Be not offended, whilst on it you look:
> Denude yourselves of all depraved affection:
> For it contains no badness or infection:
> 'Tis true that it brings forth to you no birth
> Of any value, but in point of mirth:
> Thinking therefore, how sorrow might your mind
> Consume, I could no apter subject find:
> One inch of joy surmounts of grief a span:
> Because to laugh is proper to the man.

For the rabelaisian scene is a sad and suffering scene; rabelaisian society is a sad and suffering society, thirsty, hungry, poor, sick; made up of people at once deceived and self-deceived, playing cruel games on one another by means of their lusts and greeds, their establishments of windy logic and ignorant knowledge, their pretentious verbiage of creed and code. They are ever warring with one another, are united only in devouring the simple and honest. They make their games the crueller when they purport the service of God by feigning that obedience, celibacy, and poverty (poverty of mind even more than poverty of body, such as span all the hungers and insufficiencies of man's plight), both produce and *are* man's highest good. Laughter both defends against these enemies of more abundant life and conquers them. Laughter is at once liberty, and liberator. Man laughing becomes a giant; he becomes greater and mightier than the foes that arouse his laughter. He exceeds in all the enduring goods and greatly multiplies them with new ones. He is Grandgousier. He is Gargantua who is born miraculously from his mother's ear, as the Son of God was conceived miraculously through his Mother's ear. He is Panurge. He is Friar John des Entommeures, "a right monk, if ever there was any, since the monking world monked a monkery"; he defied his Abbot, seceded from his order, and became by brain and by brawn the mightiest champion among the mighty paladins of Gargantua, when the latter was fighting unwilling Grandgousier's war with the bilious Picrochole, King of cake-baking Lerne. He is the living statue of liberty and liberation.

Friar John would accept no reward of land or rule, secular or sacred. "For how shall I be able," said he, "to rule over others, that have not full power and command of myself? . . . Give me leave to found an abbey after my own mind and fancy." So Gargantua gave him all the country of Theleme, there to initiate his religious order and serve it as abbot. He would admit into it both men and women: men comely, personable and well-conditioned, between the ages of twelve and eighteen; women fair, well-featured, of a sweet disposition, between the ages of ten and fifteen. The sexes were to mingle freely, on equal terms; they might marry, be rich, and live in liberty. Their convent would have six tall towers of double porphyry, marble staircases, marble halls, libraries, painted galleries. It would contain nine thousand

apartments hung with tapestries, furnished with embroidered bedding, and gold-framed crystal mirrors. It would be
surrounded by pleasure gardens opening into a park by the
river, and there would be tennis courts, a labryinth, a theatre, a riding-school, swimming pools and an oratory for devotion. There would be an inner court with an alabaster
Fountain of the Graces at the center. There would be shops
for jewellers, tailors, goldsmiths, perfumers. The monks and
nuns of this community would dress as they liked, and
richly. They would live as nature undistorted by monkish
rule, moved them to live—in the spirit of Plato, discoursing
platonic love. For "men and women who are free, well-born,
well-bred, and conversant in honest companies, have naturally an instinct and spur, that prompteth them unto ver-
tuous action and withdraws them from vice, which is called
honor." Upon the great gates of Theleme was inscribed in
verse the rule of eligibility to the Order of Thelemites—who
might enter, who was shut out. For the initiate, "in all their
rule, and the strictest tie of their Order, there was but one
clause to be observed—*Fais ce que voudras*": Do what thou
wilt.

Such then is the establishment and the way of life of the
religious order "contrary to all others" which Friar John
asked Gargantua to institute for him. Rabelais does not,
however, end with the *Fais ce que voudras*. He ends his Book
of Gargantua with a "prophetical riddle" engraved on a
copper plate which was dug up when the foundations of the
Abbey of Theleme were being laid. Among the members of
the Societé des Études Rabelaisiennes there are aficionados
whose labors to rede the prophetical riddle its perpetrator
would deeply appreciate. The issue continues to exercise
un-Rabelaisian wits: Is it a summons to the faith of the
Gospel? Does it mean, as Gargantua says, "The progress
and carrying on of divine truth"? Or is it, as the authorita-
tive Abbot of Theleme suggests, "a description of a set of
tennis in dark obscure terms"? He adds: "After playing,

when the game is done, they (the players) refresh themselves before a clear fire, and change their shirts; and very willingly they make all good cheer, but most merrily those that have gained. And so farewell."

The second book of the Five Books of Rabelais was, let us recall, the first to be written and circulated. Like certain sacred books, it begins by enumerating the ancestors of the line of its hero, the giant Pantagruel, whom his father Gargantua begot "at the age of four hundred fourscore forty and four years," and who was born when all nature was in drouth and all mankind so a-thirst that the Pope and princes of the Church had to order a guard for the holy water. And the babe itself grew in its mother's womb, the very life of the universal thirst, "so wonderfully great and lumpish, he could not possibly come forth into the light of the world without thus suffocating his mother." Pantagruel's birth required his mother's death. This interdependence of life and death places Gargantua in a predicament. He hesitates between weeping the loss of Badebec, his so precious wife, and rejoicing over the gain of Pantagruel, his so wonderful son—"he did cry like a cow, but on a sudden fall alaughing like a calf." But as he hears the litanies and mementos of the priests that carried his wife to be buried another thought strikes him: he himself might sicken and die; then, "by the faith of a gentleman, it were better to cry less and drink more. My wife is dead; well, by God, I shall not raise her again by my crying . . . she is above the sense of our miseries, nor can our calamities reach her. What though she be dead, must we not also die? The same debt which she hath paid hangs over our heads; nature will require it of us, and we must all of us some day taste of the same sauce. Let her pass and then, the Lord preserve the survivors; for I must now cast about to get another wife." And Gargantua directs the midwives to attend Badebec's burial while he rocks his son.

In sum, for the dead, death is the irrevocable end; the

living must needs live on until they too come to their end. This is the nature of things: so let us drink and mate and attend to new life. Let us as we live, accept the dying of our dead for the incident it is in our living. And the nature of things, we read in the twenty-sixth chapter of the fourth book of Rabelais, pulses in sympathy with the life and death of men, especially of heroes who, like a candle, light and delight while aflame, and offend by the stench and smoke that mark the extinction of the flame. Whether they continue to live when they are dead is, Friar John opines in the next chapter, "not a matter of Breviary" but of will to believe; and Pantagruel wills to believe that "all intellectual souls are exempted from Atropos's scissors. They are all immortal. . . ." Then he follows up this assertion with a tale about Thamous, mysteriously commanded to proclaim that "the Great God Pan is dead." And who was Pan? The ancients held him to be the son of Mercury and Penelope; Pantagruel holds him to be "that great Saviour of the faithful . . . shamefully put to death at Jerusalem, by the envy and wickedness of the doctors, priests and monks of the Mosaic Law." He is *Pan* "since he is one *all*. For all that we are, all that we live, all that we have, all that we hope, is him, by him, from him and in him . . . the god Pan," at whose death "the whole fabric of the universe" lamented.

True believers may read in these Rabelaisian envisionings of the place of death in the life of man and nature the terms of the Christian credo; or they may read the Christian terms transvalued and resolved in a Renaissance version of the naturalism and humanism of pagan antiquity. Pantagruel weeps tears large as ostrich eggs as he contemplates the *lacrima rerum* which are the death of Pan. But there is no conclusion in his soul, no commitment of his faith. His personal history remains an insatiable thirst for certainty regarding man's faith, a thirst which is betrayed by all that monks, warriors, women, merchants, and the other exploiters of the free spirit of man offer him for satisfaction, especially the satisfaction of sex and marriage. Spendthrift and bankrupt Panurge, arguing a fable of the bees all his own, decides—Pantagruel having settled his debts—that he must needs take a wife, but fears to be cuckolded. Then is marriage worth the hazard of cuckoldry? Or that worth the hazards of celibacy? How decide? Theology leaves it to God; the law throws dice; medicine says that cuckoldry is intrinsic to the married state. The authorities leave Panurge still at a loss; whereupon Pantagruel persuades him to seek wisdom from a Fool perfect in folly, and the two antiphonally recite the many ways in which men are fools, and compound them in Triboulet, the perfect Fool, for whom Pantagruel sends. The Fool answers Panurge's conundrum with a blow on the shoulders, taps on the nose with his pea-filled hog's bladder, and a shout: "By God, God, mad fool, beware of the monk, Buzancay hornpipe," all the while shaking and wagging his head.

Now this oracle has to be interpreted: Pantagruel learnedly elaborates it as declaring the menace of marriage; Panurge reads it simply as disclosing the joys of wedding a simple shepherdess. So the issue is still in issue, and Panurge petitions Pantagruel to continue their quest for certainty by a pilgrimage to the shrine of the Holy Bottle. Gargantua, appealed to for consent and aid, gives both. He blesses the pilgrims and hopes that Pantagruel might also find a bride for himself on his own. So the latter sets out with his lifelong companions on their long, long voyage to Lanternland and the Oracle of the Holy Bottle, from whose mouth they might drink at last the truth about everything. They add to their supplies for the journey a large stock of the herb, Pantagruelion (from its elaborate description, *cannabis indica*, hemp, whose roles in civilization—Pantagruel created them—range from choking men to death to lifting them out of themselves in ecstasy).

The voyage is a progression from fantastic island to fantastic island, a succession of encounters with one organized deception after another, and a presentation of the illusory personages with the ways and works wherewith they exert their hypocritical rule, and feed their power over the bodies and souls of men. Each organization signifies some ongoing system of exploitation—some actual ruling passion such as the notable Gaster with his rite and rote, whose might Rabelais for the nonce diminishes or even dissipates through his laughing, half-veiled disclosures. None is exempted the indecent exposure: not the papacy with its feasts and fasts, its decretals and its councils; not the calvinists, the lawyers, the gamblers, the money-lenders, the plagiarists, the courtiers; never, of course, the Sorbonne and the monkish orders. If, instead of perceiving the disclosures as half-veiled, we perceive them as frozen—frozen because candor and clarity of expression are dangerous in dominions of organized deception—then, once beyond the reach of the latters' rulers, the disclosing words thaw; they become unfrozen. Some are heard "like drums and fifes, and others like clarions and trumpets, or as the gibberish they truly are." In freedom, words convey what they mean, mean what they convey.

Now the fifth book of Rabelais takes up the tale of the voyage. Pantagruel and his retinue make many other ports. They land first on L'Isle Sonnante, then on the Island of Furred Law Cats, the Island of Apedefts, the Queendom of Whims. Each is a Kingdom of Lies, Evils. The people of L'Isle Sonnante, or Ringing Island, are perverse birds with gray, black, white, and blue-white plumage, different from men only for their cacophonous chanting, kept to it even in their luxurious cages, by the continual tolling of the island's bells—to Rabelais, one recalls, intolerable bells. Their ruler is the unique phoenix-like Pope, Hawk. The Furred Law Cats are horrible and shocking beasts who devour everything, even children, and never leave a wrack of anything behind. Panurge is taken before the Chief Furred Cat, Grippeminault, who tries him with a nonsensical riddle which Panurge answers at last by throwing down a purse of gold, and thus proves himself innocent. The Apedefts are operators of a press that can make everything sweat gold. The Queendom of Whims is also called the Kingdom of Quintessence or Entelechy and the inhabitants are nourished on wind and dream. It is the land of all quackery: philosophical, medical, alchemical, botanical, zoological. By its mumbo-jumbo it ever evades facing up to reality. Pantagruel and his retinue, guests at a royal ball, get away to their ship and their search before the glamors of Entelechy seduce them. They stop at the Island of Odes and the Island of Wooden Shoes (from the footwear of the new order)—is it the Society of Jesus?—of semiquaver Friars who dwell thereon, passing into and out of church by different doors, their processionals headed by an image of Fortune followed by one of Virtue, feeding fat, and singing, chanting, sleeping, waking by the bell. Thence they make Satin Island, overpopulated with fictions, like a tapestry, and inhabited by yea-sayers or yes-men, ancient and modern, acquiring instant knowledge of all things from old Coui-dice Hearsay.

At long last the Pantagruelists reach the harbor of the habitation of authentic learning, Lanternland. There, guided by a "glorious lantern" through underground passages, down Tetradic stairs they go to gates on whose front was an inscription in golden Greek letters *eou oinoi aletheia:* In wine, truth. Now their lantern guide gives them over to Bacbuc, the priestess of the Holy Bottle. Their entire passage is beset with images and marked by symbolic rites and rotes drawn from Greek mythology and Christian fantasy. A similar ritual by Bacbuc opens the gates, which are in fact mechanically controlled. At last the pilgrims are before the shrine of the Holy Bottle. Panurge becomes terrified and shrinks away; Friar John bids him be brave and go on. "I have more than enough courage," replies Panurge. "True, my heart shakes in my boots, but that's because I'm cold." Bacbuc, having advised him to hearken to the Oracle with one ear only, prepares him for the audition of the Word.

Then she has him sit on the ground between two stools, throws into the fountain before him a powder which causes it to bubble up with a buzzing like bees. Soon a Word is heard: *Trinc!* "Come," cries Panurge, "by God I'm just as wise now as I was before. Explain, where's the Book. Find me the chapter! Let's look at this joyous gloss of yours!" To which Bacbuc replies that the Holy Bottle has revealed to him the most joyful, divine and certain Word she herself had ever heard. As gloss on the oracle, she has Panurge drink a bottle. "*Trinc*," she explains, is a word "*panomphee*, celebrated and understood by the entire world . . . here we hold not that laughing but that drinking is the trait which distinguishes the human kind. . . . For you must know, my beloved, that by wine we become divine. . . . *Oinos* is from *vis*—strength, virtue, power; for it is in the power of wine to fill the soul with all truth, learning and philosophy; *In vino veritas!* This, then, is what the Holy Bottle sends you—Be yourself the interpreter of your own endeavors."

"One can't say better," Pantagruel tells Panurge, "I told you as much when we started on this quest." Then they all drank and began to chant Dionysus-inspired poems; they soaked up the wine of knowledge, so Friar John declared, from the Books of the Bottle. *Trinc* was the open sesame to self-liberation and self-fulfilment; the break through the bonds and barriers of authoritarianism, sacerdotal and lay, the avenue to happiness.* "We call happiness," Bacbuc said on taking leave from the Pantagruelists, "not to be receiving and accepting much from others, as it happens the sects of your world decree; but that we are ever giving much to others, enlarging others. . . . To seek wisdom and divine knowledge we need two things: the guidance of heaven and

---

* Compare Fitzgerald's Rubaiyat of Omar Khayyam:

> The Grape that can with Logic absolute
> The Two and Seventy jarring Sects confute;
> The Sovereign Alchemist that in a trice
> Life's leaden metal into Gold transmute.

the companionship of men. We need also the flow of time, which brings to actuality all things possible."

In sum, there are more things in heaven and earth than are dreamt of in any philosophy. Such is the last word of the gloss on the oracle of the Holy Bottle in which the Five Books of Rabelais culminate. What, first and last, can they reveal; what can be their role, if not the perennial ones of which the Dionysian, *komos oidé*, was the earliest? They are, for matter and manner, epic variations upon the comedy-farces of Aristophanes, but inwardly freer, with a limit of heedlessness in savoring the goods of life and thought—even when most wary in laughing down the powers that keep mankind from reaching the goods, or the goods from reaching mankind. As against taking laughter for the *differentia* of *genus humanum*, because, as Rabelais wrote to begin with, "to laugh is proper to the man," the differentia he ends with (even if he died before he could write it) has become drinking: "here we hold not that laughing but drinking is the trait which distinguishes man's humanity."

If we assume that this is the authentic Rabelaisian conclusion and not that of some one else elaborating upon the literary remains of the dead Doctor, then we must conclude that experience and study had taught him that mankind are not laughers by first intention, but by second. By first intention, mankind is a tearful unquenchable thirst, an insatiable curiosity ever bent to quench and sate itself; men laugh as they drink on, or when the thirst confronts drouth, and the drouth be overcome. Pantagruelism is still "a certain jollity of mind, pickled in the scorn of Fortune."

CHAPTER NINE

Pascal, Racine, Molière

O F COURSE, there occurs scorn of fortune without jollity of mind. Such scorn is what renders satire authentically satire: it goes rather with moral indignation, with hatred, with envy, with pride, than with jollity. Its laughter intends more to overcome or destroy its object than as merriment to liberate the laugher. This is the sort of laughter which Blaise Pascal aimed at in his *Provincial Letters*. Like Erasmus, like Rabelais, he wrote to laugh down to impotence the might and aggression of the power-holding churchmen, theologians and certain monastic orders of his time. The theologians were still the doctors of the Sorbonne. But the power of Franciscans, Benedictines and Dominicans had been superseded by the power of the Society of Jesus. Under the pseudonym Louis de Montalto, Pascal composed, in the course of some fourteen months, eighteen letters addressed to an imaginary friend in the provinces who had asked for news of the Sorbonne. His news recited an unworthy attack upon the doctrine of grace formulated and taught among the Jansenists; that being, of course, the one true doctrine of grace for Pascal. The sappers and miners in the attack were the Jesuits who had devised a power-producing logic peculiar to themselves. The letters laid bare the moral and intellectual indecency of that "probabilist" logic with the double-think and double talk called casuistry. The letters undertake to exhibit Jesuitism as scheming to persuade men to forsake the rule of God and submit to the rule of Jesuitry. Pascal wrote them with an irony as subtle as it was luminous and as laughter-evoking as it was subtle. Before the last of the letters was in circulation, Pope Alexander VII had issued his bull condemning Jansenism; and as once Rabelais' butts had charged Rabelais, so now Pascal's charged him with misquotations and falsifications, with appeals to pruriency, with lying about himself and his affiliations, with avowing heresies and ridiculing the Holy.

But Pascal was a man of tears, not laughter. What laughter he had in him did not come free, but as compenetrating his tears. An extraordinarily lucid intellect, with a spontaneous bent for mathematics and the natural sciences, he even devised from his acquaintance with noble gamblers, a theory of probability of his own that might render chances predictable. He himself advocated the ultimate gamble, the oft-invoked "Pascal's wager"—that bet on faith which, if it win, wins you everything; if it lose, loses you nothing—thus the one bet that came to being as nearly a sure thing as any bet could. But Pascal's flesh was not less sensitive than his spirit was strong; his personal history is mostly a history of hurt and pain. He lived in a torment without remission. He reached out after anodynes in philosophy as well as the sciences. He read much in Epictetus, he read much in Montaigne, without receiving assuagement from either, or from any other sage. Neither the dogmas of the church doctors nor the doubts of the humanists and sceptics could free him from the suffering soul and body of imminent death. Death lurked ever just around the corner; of this he was poignantly aware and as poignantly afraid. While "nature confounds the sceptics and reason the dogmatists," misery and knowing how miserable one is, continue one's never-to-be-unburdened portion.

Finally, during a very bad time, Pascal had a religious

experience, a mystic revelation, of which he wrote down incoherent notations beginning with the word *Fire* writ large and alone. The writing was found sewed into his doublet after he died. Some say he used it for an amulet. Its import should be joined to that of the miracle of the Holy Thorn. Pascal had seen with his own eyes, had experienced with his own mind, how an incurably diseased eye of a young girl had been healed by the touch of a thorn which he believed had been a part of his Savior's crown of thorns. The event moved Pascal to turn from the secular pursuits of intellect to the religious contemplation of things holy and divine in the company of the lonely regulars of Port Royal. He devised an emblem for himself—an eye encircled by a crown of thorns, with the legend *scio cui credidi*. He dedicated himself to composing the apology to end all apologies for the Christian drama of salvation; and he read and read, and thought and thought, and made notes and more notes. He died before he could put his notes into the order his art of intellection and expression intended for them. It is from these notes that the perceptive, dull, wise, stodgy, subtle, sound, perverse, and fantastic *Pensées* are culled. Their spring is the *lacrima rerum* of human existence; their burden is that all men naturally hate one another, that they are "necessarily such fools that it would be folly of another kind not to be a fool." But Pascal is not fooling about mankind's folly. It is to him sad and bitter, not gay. The *Pensées* bespeak no laughter. They also tell that man is a hunger which he cannot sate, a thirst he cannot still. He craves a salvation which reason is unable to demonstrate, and which doubt is unable to deny. Man is born unto warfare as the sparks fly upward; no peace can come to him save by a grace reaching in from without and down from above. We know we must die, yet we yearn to live on. Only faith, only the reasons of the heart which the reason cannot know, the reasons of the heart on which we bet our lives, can lift us from the body of this death, this death which, like Eugene O'Neill's iceman, surely cometh: "We are pleased to rest in the society of our own kind, but miserable like us, helpless like us, they will not aid us. We die alone. The final act is bloody, however lovely be the comedy of all that precedes: at last, some one throws earth upon our heads, and then it is forever." But no, not forever: "Know . . . Superb one what a paradox you are yourself. Humble yourself, impotent reason, be silent imbecile nature, and learn from your master your true condition which you do not know. Hearken to God." Alas, the positive deliverances of God's oracle are still, in Pascal's own utterance, the impotence of reason, the imbecility of nature, and the insatiable cravings of the heart of man. Actual man is man tragic, ever having to choose between irreconcilable goods, and unsure of the consequences, whichever decision he makes.

Pascal died in the twentieth year of Louis XIV's seventy-two-year reign as *Roi Soleil*. He was one year younger than Molière and sixteen years older than Racine. He was only thirty-nine when he died. Molière had already been taken up by the Sun King's court and was having his own laughing encounters with the Tartuffes of his world. Jean Racine, twenty-three years old, a Jansenist like Pascal, had come to the verge of the insight that "it is not necessary to have blood and corpses in a tragedy"; that a defeat in a warfare of ideals and values, simply and beautifully presented, suffices—such defeat as love suffered in the warfare of love, honor, and duty which *Bérénice* presents, or in the warfare between love and love which *Andromache* impatterns, or in the warfare between love and hate which *Phèdre* celebrates. There are blood and corpses but they are incidental, not essential to tragedy. The Jansenists of Port Royal could have accepted Racine's ethic, however much they condemned his theatre. But their anxiety over how they would live when they were dead was too deep. Racine had deserted their otherworldly scarcity for Mme. de Montespan's this-worldly abundance; at the last he and his art reconciled them. The libertine compacted into the correct "gentilhomme ordinaire du roi," a husband, father, and true believer who, having died in the odor of his denominational sanctity, was buried at Port Royal. His practice separated laughter from tears as his friend Molière's would not. He could emulate Aristophanes as well as Sophocles, but neither his heart nor his head could accept their mingling and take it for the stuff of his expression as did Molière or, more largely and vitally, Shakespeare.

In Molière, the tradition of the Joyous Societies, of Rabelais, continued—although a bit less authentically. He could be called a Pantagruelist who gave this philosophy of laughter and tears a new turn. By and large, although he prospered, Molière was not a happy man. Bad luck dogged him; his plays bespeak bad luck in health, bad luck in friends, bad luck in love. He seems at first not to have committed himself to drying tears with laughter. There was a time when he emulated Corneille and his heresies; in *Don Garcie*—that forerunner of *Le Misanthrope*—Molière strove to utter the tragedy of defeated love with a Corneilleian rhetoric. But this rhetoric was not for Molière; for him, speech was to nourish the jollity of mind that remolds into laughter the tears of things in the affairs of men. And he did so without rancor; indeed, with a kind of charity which suggests Erasmus more than Rabelais—as he put pity into buffoonery, truth into farce, and decency into satire. Molière had, it seems, learned from Gassendi something of the generosity of Epicurus and the cheerfulness of Democritus. His career inured him to the spurns that patient merit of the unworthy takes, and his dialogue brings into lucid focus and fanciful goods and actual evils wherewith husbands and wives, parents and children, friends and lovers plague one another, and wherewith the fools, the hypocrites, the dupes, the cranks, and the fanatics who people the human comedy deceive one another and themselves only, at last, to be undeceived in the liberating realism of disillusioned laughter.

Even Alceste, that honest man, so blunt, so impatient, so infatuated, so true-seeing, and so scornful of the world and its ways, is not exempted from that freeing laughter when, in the "dark and lonely little corner of his black chagrin," he resolves to flee to "some small secluded nook on earth where one may enjoy the freedom of being an honest man." The Celimenes, the Tartuffes, the Harpagons, the Don Juans, the Armandes and the Messrs. Jourdain who hold sway upon French earth are anything but honest. In Molière's personal history, their likes in his family, at Court, and in the Church, should and would coerce and oppress him (the Jesuits would have prevented the production of Tartuffe altogether; they did succeed in delaying it). They signalized the pickling fortune that his jollity of mind scorned with that "serious laughter" which George Meredith argued is the distinguishing mark of the truly civilized man. It is this laughter which saves Molière from becoming absolutely a misanthrope, like Shakespeare's Timon of Athens. Some sense it in Alceste himself, *le misanthrope*, whose misanthropy is his victory as he smiles at himself, committing to laughter Celimene and her company.

Legend has it that *Le Misanthrope* was a self-portrait; it may well have been. Molière was a sick man (maybe his illnesses were psychosomatic) who was for years busy with the tasks of manager, actor, playwright, and harassed by the escapades of a young wife. He has fun with both the pretentious ignorance and greed of the medicos, and the absurd complaints of the hypochondriac. If his own ailments were actually hypochondriacal, it would have rendered the pain of them more endurable. But the man was hurting nonetheless; his pain was nonetheless pain and he met his responsibilities regardless. One night, in his fifty-first year, he had to go on stage—sick, did he but know it, unto death—in the title role of *Le Malade Imaginaire.* He shouldn't have, but he wouldn't let his fellow players cover. He died, in convulsions, playing the hypochondriac. Curiously, neither death nor the idea of death figures in his vision; he held suicide to be a folly. He saw the entire theory and practice of his art as no "mystery"; its "great rule of rules" is to please. "I should like to know," he wrote, "whether a play which attains this has not followed a good method." For Molière, to please was to overcome tears by laughter.

CHAPTER TEN

Laughter and Tears of the English Enlightenment: Jonathan Swift

FROM MOLIÈRE we now turn to Jonathan Swift, from the France of the Sun King to the England of the Enlightenment. The distance spans a certain subsidence of thirst among the congregation of true believers in the Holy Bottle, the drinkers now becoming collectors and storers, the *uomini universali* becoming recorders and classifiers. Encyclopedias, which had been projects of fantasy with Francis Bacon, became facts of assembled data with the generation of Pierre Bayle and Ephraim Chambers: storing remembrances supersedes learning the unknown. The perennial rout of faking fools and hypocritical pedants gets new recruits such as the learned ladies, the would-be-gentlemen, the charlatans of the learned professions. Their wine of knowledge is unfermented data-juice, undigested and indigestible; not to be consumed, but bottled and displayed in the encyclopedias, so many, so heavy, as only to confuse the mind and overload the heart. Pantagruelian thirst must needs recover the drinker's art. Reflecting upon the pursuit of knowledge and the conduct of the understanding, John Locke suggests that the aggregations of data have become too much; that the wise course is to seek "an increase of the powers and activity of the mind . . . not an enlargement of its possessions." The *how* of learning, instead of the *what* of the learned, is the *Trinc* of life.

Other words for this *how* are *Eclaircissement*, *Aufklärung*, *Enlightenment*. Its spring is assurance that thirsting and drinking are reason *in actu;* are the new reason whose *mechané* inspired Galileo, illumined Spinoza, produced the clear and distinct certainty of Newton's *Principia*, and John Locke's exposition of the ways and works of the human understanding. The Pantagruelists of the new generations believed that this reason could, as the reason of the Schoolmen and the Humanists could not, unmask the faces and undress the masquerades wherewith nature and man-in-nature have kept covering their nakedness ever since Adam and Eve took to cover in Eden. They believed that it could free the human psyche by laying bare the veritable nudities of existence in all their tease and trial. As Kant argued in 1784, when already this avidity was forming itself a different shape, answering the question *Was ist Aufklärung*, it is liberation from an autogenous aboulia; it is courage to use understanding without regard to authority. *Aufklärung* is *sapere audi*, daring to know. Dare to use your understanding freely! This is the motto of Enlightenment. Use it on religion, on politics, on business, on the graphic and plastic arts, on poetry, on the theatre.

Although to some, reason was as Daniel Defoe wrote, a "most serene, most invincible, most illustrious Princess," the "age of reason" was the age of this use, and so, of the Enlightenment. Taking the rule of right reason for the measure of all things renders the most characteristic part of the Illuminati's makings fun-makings; the poems of the Enlightenment became exercises of wit, its stage-play comedies, its stories laughing disclosures of the follies of the breed of Abel and the cruelties and falsities of the breed of Cain, and how futile were the tears of both. The Enlightenment's representative spokesmen, whether men of letters, of the cloth, or the parliaments, were signalized as wits. In the entire national enterprise of the British, but vividly in its arts, the wits give a new turn to the perennial comminglings and confrontations of our struggles to go on struggling, with their laughter and their tears.

Jonathan Swift is usually listed among the leaders of this turn and the voices of the Enlightenment. On the black marble tablet which marks his locus among the dead in Dublin's St. Patrick's Cathedral, he describes himself as such a one, in Latin. "Buried here," the inscription says "where fierce indignation can lacerate his heart no more. Go, traveller—and imitate if you can one who strove his utmost to champion liberty."

But I do not read Swift's record so. His animus is more akin to Pascal's than to Rabelais' or to Molière's. He impresses as a sick soul, a disappointed soul; ultimately, a defeated soul with no laughter in him to reclaim defeat by victory. The laughter he calls upon is laughter such as he would evoke from others to compensate his spirit for the tears of his failures, by levelling a deadly derision upon those he blamed for them and upon their associates, however blameless. Swift's sense of life was tragic, but without the grandeur of style and sentiment which his age attributed to tragedy. It was sordid and bad-tempered. Its sensings drove him to angry reprisals; they neither freed his spirit nor brought it the peace of a noble submission. Nor was the liberation which is laughter for him. His personal history does not point to any inwardness whence might come, or be drawn, the laughter that derides its own *lacrima rerum*. It points only to the satirist art of representing and appraising mankind's plight so as to evoke laughter from others, while raging with bitter unshed and unsheddable tears himself.

For Jonathan Swift was a defeated man, defeated in his career of ambition, in his career of health, and his career of love. "I hate and detest the animal called man," he wrote to Alexander Pope, anent Gulliver, in his fifty-eighth year, "although I heartily love Peter, John, Thomas, and so forth. Upon this great foundation of misanthropy (though not in Timon's manner) the whole building of my travels is erected, and I never will have peace of mind until all honest men are of that opinion." Two years later he volunteered to a woman friend, "Life is a tragedy wherein we sit as spectators awhile, and then act our own part in it." And four years after that he told Pope in a letter, "The common saying of life being a farce is true in every sense but the most important one, for it is a ridiculous tragedy, which is the worst kind of composition." The personal stance of his *Tale of a Tub* and its companion pieces, completed when he was not yet thirty, is no different. Between that initiative of his youth and the consummation of his maturity in *Gulliver*, comes a potpourri of expressions, maliciously designed to get their subjects laughed down to nothingness.

Swift was born in Ireland to a widowed mother. His father had died seven months before. When he was three years old his mother left him to the care of a nurse under the guardianship of a paternal uncle, and returned to live with relatives in England. The uncle discharged his avuncular duties with no more than due correctness. He sent his nephew to school and to college, Trinity in Dublin. There Swift, at the age of seventeen, took the degree of bachelor of arts. His teachers didn't think much of him and he didn't think much of his schooling; he said he had had the education of a dog. He thought even less of his relatives, whom he hated his whole life long. A psychoanalyst might say that he was starved of affection, and faced all mankind as surrogates of the relatives whose indifference turned his unheeded love to hate. The uncle died, an impoverished man, in 1688, the year of John Locke's "glorious revolution," the birthyear

some say, of the Enlightenment. But the event brought neither nourishment for the body, nor light for the mind to
Jonathan Swift, nor to the Protestant people of John Bull's
other island, to say nothing of its Papists. Lacking both
inheritance and prospects in Ireland, twenty-one-year-old
Swift followed his mother to England. There, at Moor Park,
the manor of a connection of hers by marriage, Sir William
Temple (son of the provost of Dublin's Trinity College,
statesman, diplomat, and man of letters, more disgusted
than out of favor with Charles II), had been living in voluntary retirement for almost ten years. He took young Jonathan into his household as a sort of secretary.

The young man quickly came to believe that he was regarded, not the talented mind more than worth his salt that
he knew himself to be, but a mere dependent for whom
favors were being done. He cultivated a grudge, blew hot
and cold on his relationship with Sir William. He had first
thought he might reach fortune and fame as a poet. But the
verse he sent to his distant cousin, John Dryden, brought the
never-forgiven comment: "Cousin Swift, you will never be a
poet," and Swift belittled Dryden's works from then on.
However, he did give up poetry as a career, though not as a
catharsis; instead, he took on religion. In 1695 he was ordained priest, and the Temple connection got him a preben-
dary at Kilroot, Ireland. But after Moor Park, Ireland was
less than ever to Swift's taste, and after a year he returned to
Temple. Part of his service was a defence of the man in his
disputation over ancient and modern letters, which Swift
published some years after as *The Battle of the Books*.

Lady Temple had died in 1694; her husband followed her
five years later. He had remembered Swift in his will, but
not in such wise that the latter could do without a post. The
place Swift wanted was the chaplaincy with the new chief
justice of Ireland, Lord Berkeley. But what he got was a
couple of livings and a prebendship that could jointly bring
him £230 the year. Neither this cure of souls nor cure of

pocket filled the young priest's bill. He went back to England, got himself into the company of Addison, Steele, and other wits and worthies, among whom he was launched on his career of power—writing political pamphlets. He published *The Tale of a Tub*, *The Battle of the Books*, and *The Mechanical Operation of the Spirit* in a single volume. He produced pamphlets on church relations. An especial concern was the equity of Ireland's Episcopalian clergy in first fruits and twentieths (he held, quite rightly, that the cloth of Ireland were no less entitled to Queen Anne's bounty than the cloth of England). But the Whigs in power, on whom he had counted to acknowledge his merits and satisfy his ambitions, remained heedless and uncaring. He returned again to Ireland. When the Tories, who were at all events favorable to the Establishment, displaced the Whigs, he went over to the Tories; he would make those Laodicean Whigs mighty sorry for using him so ill! Swift's prose swiftly brought him standing and influence among the party now in power, and benefits to friends seeking jobs or privileges. He became a companion of politicians, political conspirators, and like-minded writers, a "Brother" to Harley (who later got himself the earldom of Oxford), and to St. John (for whom Harley unforgivably provided only the Viscountship of Bolingbroke).

The last one's Toryism was grounded in a certain scorn, not of fortune, but of mankind. He was authoritarian for their good. Swift said St. John wanted to be known as the Alcibiades or Petronius of his age; nor would an analogy between him and Alcibiades be a forced one, nor a certain sympathy between Swift and him. St. John, to distinguish his Toryism, called himself an Old Whig; he was concerned to restore the Stuarts to the throne, and conspired toward this end both at home and abroad. He might have succeeded if the Pretender, James II, had been willing to exchange submission to the Pope for rule over the English. But he wasn't, and George of Hanover, not James Stuart, succeeded Queen Anne to the English throne.

On "the restoration" of the Stuarts, the hot civil war of Cavalier and Roundhead had become a cold one with hot flashes. The struggle of Parliament against King and of the Protestant against the Papist Idea involved the old power ploys, but employed new strategies and tactics. Charles II had intrigued to nullify the agreement whereby the throne was given back to his line. So Parliament in 1672 retorted with the Test Act which imposed the oath of "allegiance and supremacy" and the rejection of the dogma of transubstantiation. Two years later it enacted Habeas Corpus. In 1677, the law *de haeretico comburendo* was abolished. In 1679, Charles II was urged to name his bastard, the Protestant Duke of Monmouth, heir to his throne and thereby shut out his brother, papist James. Charles refused, had his prime minister, Robert Shaftesbury, charged with treason and jailed. But Shaftesbury escaped to Holland where his friend and counsellor, John Locke, joined him. In 1685, papist James (with his confessor, Father Petre, at his side) ascended the English throne as James II, and fought for it victoriously against the Protestant adherents of Monmouth, and for such enfranchisement of his co-religionists as would once more give them access to place and power. This could not be done without equal liberation for other dissidents; and so in 1687 the first declaration of the liberty of conscience was promulgated, and the following year, the second, to be read in churches.

Thereafter, certain Englishmen, fearful of papist infiltration into the government and the effect on English liberty, invited William of Orange and his Stuart wife, Mary, to come and save their country from papist tyranny: they came. James fled to the protection of the Sun King, and to live on his bounty. John Locke accompanied Shaftesbury back to England. The throning of William and Mary was the English plateau of a revolution which had begun with the struggle of free against authoritarian religion and of parliamentary government against autocratic monarchism. Locke articulated its philosophical rationale in treatises on toleration, on government, and on the human understanding. The record of the Roman Catholic interest being what it was, he could not, in the circumstances, admit its aficionados to the equal liberty that the logic of liberty requires. Eventually, the requirement was satisfied in England's American colonies to which the revolution shifted. Their Declaration of Independence and Constitution consummated "the glorious revolution" in idea. Its consummation as fact is still in process, not alone in England and in the sometime English colonies, but in all free societies, everywhere. For its age, however, and to the Englishmen who were fighting and winning it, the event was truly "the glorious revolution," the vindication and enactment as law of the civil liberties that enlightenment depends on for survival.

The assurance this brought wasn't an easy assurance. Mary and William died, and Anne, daughter of James II and wife of George of Denmark, was crowned Queen of England. In the fifth year of her reign, England and Scotland were united, and Anne became queen of Great Britain. The Whigs were displaced by the Tories, and St. John, now Viscount Bolingbroke, renewed his intrigues for the Pretender and for the papist interest from a place of power.

Bolingbroke was no friend of English liberty. But he devised a political philosophy, which sanctified what we would today call boss-rule, as the defense and safeguard of liberty with a capital L. Liberty, he argued, is a delicate growth, always in danger, especially when a government is a mixed one like the British, where the factions struggle for place and power, and the license and anarchy, intrinsic to the pursuit of private ends, are always threatening the Liberty which would be the goal of public service. This service, vis-à-vis foreign rivals, is to achieve and maintain a balance of power; vis-à-vis domestic factions, it is to enthrone and support a "Patriot King" in the spirit of Old Whiggism and of its incarnation in the emulator of Locke and Machiavelli who was able to imagine such a "standing miracle" as the "panacea" for Britain's ills. By implication, such a king would be like God, a sovereign whose power is limited by his wisdom. The argument seems to have impressed Voltaire, who dedicated his *Brutus* to Bolingbroke; Swift also designated himself an Old Whig, and counted Bolingbroke a good friend—hypocrite, yes, but "hypocrite reversed."

Anne died, George of Hanover was proclaimed King, and Bolingbroke protested his loyalty without avail. He fled in disguise to Paris, insisting he was innocent and continuing to make the cause of the Pretender his own, serving him as secretary. Of course he was attainted by Parliament. An invasion of England and a Declaration to the British people were planned. Bolingbroke advised against the invasion but drafted the Declaration. The Irish priests and the refugees in the Pretender's retinue altered the Declaration and insisted on the invasion. The Pretender dismissed his Alcibiades and the latter had had enough of his liege lord-to-be. He set up a ménage with the Marquise de Villette in Orleans; when Lady Bolingbroke died he married the Marquise. Seven years there he lived the enlightened life of a "gentleman and scholar" who had money, read and wrote philosophy, designed the notions of the human condition to which Alexander Pope gave world-wide significance in the famous *Essay on Man*, entertained all sorts and conditions of visitors (if they could be of use to him), intrigued at George's court for a pardon, even offering Robert Walpole (now in the early years of his long tour of duty as chief of state), to keep him *au courant* regarding relevant matters in France. The exile was allowed to return to England, but not to English politics. So he bought himself that estate at Dawley where he wrote histories and essays, sniped at Walpole under various pseudonyms and again entertained visitors—

Swift and Pope of course, but also Voltaire. He intrigued for the return of the Tories to power, and failing, was off to France again. After three years he returned to England. Although forbidden Parliament, he made himself the actual leader of the opposition to Walpole. The false façade of this opposition was Frederick, Prince of Wales. Its dynamic center was a coterie calling themselves Patriots. It was for this coterie that Bolingbroke composed *The Patriot King*. From it young George is said to have learned his royal duties-to-be. Alexander Pope, to whom Bolingbroke had entrusted a script, together with a couple of other "patriotic" disquisitions, had secretly caused 1500 copies of the essay to be printed, a dastardly deed for which Pope, although dead by that time, must needs be properly punished—improperly and ungratefully according to Pope's friend, admirer and literary executor John Warburton, who was appointed Bishop of Gloucester not long after Bolingbroke died.

Swift's services to the Tory interest were strategic. His being a brother of the Brothers put him in the center of political intrigue and rotten borough bossism. His attacks on such Whig leaders as Marlborough and Wharton got wide reading among the literate. Accused by their defenders of freethinking—he furiously charged that Richard Steele had cast doubt on him "as a Christian and a clergyman" (his vendetta against Steele was ruthless)—he attacked Anthony Collins.* He composed anonymous pamphlets laden with such charges against the Scottish Lords that Parliament found them libels, had their printer and publisher jailed, and offered a reward for the discovery of the author. Swift felt he must get out of reach. For a time even his friends lost contact with him. Finally he returned to Ireland. The Tories had at long last rewarded his services with his Irish deanery. This cure of souls at St. Patrick's imposed living in Ireland, and at the heavy expenses that went with such posts. Swift was

---

* *Mr. Collins' Discourse of Freethinking, put into Plain English, by Way of Abstract, for the Use of the Poor.*

stuck with St. Patrick's. While friends and foes were advanced to bishops, he continued an Irish dean until he died. Although his income was large, he wasn't satisfied. His career of ambition was a career of frustration and defeat for which he revenged himself with satires so unspontaneous, so purposeful, as to stir in readers quite other senses than their sense of humor.

But these satires, the products and residue of his acts of vengeance, are his immortality. In them he succeeds as he could not have, and did not, in the role of churchman or statesman. But it was the mortal act he lived for and in, not its product. That is his immortality, but not the immortality his heart was set upon.

An equal, perhaps on occasion a predominant, component in Swift's syndrome was his career of health. It wasn't as unfortunate as Pope's but his hurt went deeper: early in his striving he began repeating Job's: "Let the day perish wherein I was born and the night in which it was said, There is a man-child conceived." All his life death and dying were on his mind. As he wrote Pope in 1733, "When I was your age, I thought every day of death, but now every minute." His ear troubles hit him in his twenties. With them came fits of dizziness and vertigo, accompanied or followed by vague fears and anxiety. It was not long before he gave signs of hypochondria, resorting for relief even to such nostrums as a clove of garlic dipped in honey to stick in his ear. Against the necessities of constipation and dysentery which beset him, his scatological utterances—some account for them as coprophilic—might have been defenses, liberating catharses. By the time he was composing *Gulliver*, his ailments were at a climax. They absorbed him almost utterly after Stella died—headaches less and less bearable, irritability more and more hair-triggered, temper tantrums of explosive violence. Finally he had to be put under guards for what was called dementia.

Swift knew how his health and faculties were failing, and

he felt their failure, even at his age, as betrayal. "I am now good for nothing," he wrote Oxford, some half dozen years before the ultimate breakdown, "very deaf, very old, and out of favor with those in power. . . . I have a thousand things to say, but I can remember none of them." He lived on—save for unresting pain, pain and anxiety—unalive from the breakdown in his seventy-fifth year to his death in his seventy-eighth year. But the image of Jonathan Swift which Swift cherished—Swift the misanthrope, the scatologist, the derider of *genus humanum*—came to maturity and perished with the completion of *Gulliver* and the death of Stella. By that time "the gloomy dean" had already designed his own memorial visage and settled his accounts with a society that, while denying him his dearest ambitions, granted him a success which was no success to him.

What role sex and love played among these ambitions cannot be surely said. The record suggests that the boy Swift suffered for want of love; that the man Swift came to despise women, feel shame for sex, and, yearning for love, half-feared and fled it. Three women stand out in Swift's career of love. He called them Stella, Varina, Vanessa. Stella was his name for Hester Johnson, whom Swift came to know as a child of eight, when he first joined Sir William Temple's household; rumor had her the nobleman's bastard daughter. Varina was his name for Jane Waring, to whom Swift even proposed marriage, but who would and wouldn't; until, after four years, Swift dropped her sharply, bitterly, resolved never to marry—at least never to marry a young woman. When he returned to Sir William Temple, Hester was a nubile fifteen; in effect, a woman grown, with a heart ready to warm to his perhaps unspoken but manifest wants, and with a head, not alone therefore, apt to recognize in Swift the guide, philosopher, and friend of her life. Beginning as her tutor, he became her lifelong lover—precisely when or how the record does not disclose. His relation to her seems to have been a tether as well as a release. He renamed her Stella. He invented a code—"our language," "our little language"—for their intimate conversation. He wrote her often belittling verses. He kept for her the well-known *Journal to Stella*. He persuaded her to make her home in Ireland, with certain friends of his, among whom she lived; for the most part lonely, insecure, waiting to "drink coffee" with her ever more reluctant, yet surely returning Jonathan. When Swift's "other woman" wrote her, asking bluntly, "Are you Mrs. Swift?" she answered yes (the learned in Swiftiana debate whether she had not been Mrs. Swift some seven years). Many hold that the question was put and answered about the time that Swift had invited Stella to live with him openly and she had declined the invitation. But she did have the "other woman's" query passed on to Swift, who confronted that lady with it, flung it on her table, and flung himself out of her house and life.

This "other woman" Swift addressed as Vanessa. Vanessa was his *nom de coeur* for Esther van Homringe. He had met her in London when she was nineteen and he was forty-one. In three years he became a familiar of the Van Homringe household, used to leaving his gown and periwig there. As the friendship between him and Miss Esther developed toward intimacy, she became his "Miss Essy"; when the intimacy was reached, she became his "Vanessa." "Vanessa" hints at the allegory and conveys the classical overtones which the conventions of the Enlightenment required, but Swift may have constructed it with the *Van* in Van Homringe, and the *Ess* in Miss Essy. He had that way with words, as in the verses he addressed to this lady of his: *Cadenus and Vanessa*. "Cadenus" is Decanus (dean) half-turned around. Cadenus intended these verses for Vanessa's eyes alone. A whole batallion of immortals—Venus, the Muses, the Graces and Cupid—present *old* Cadenus to lovely young Vanessa. The arrows Cupid shoots are books, and Vanessa's heart is pierced at last. The hint in the relationship of a platonic love such as Baldassare Castiglione's mature courtier felt for his beloved lady has for its antiphony hints of the fires—rather damp and smoke-bleared, 'tis true—of youth. Vanessa yearns and burns. She treasures her Jonathan's letters, English letters and French letters, as she cherishes his versified compliments. Her replies are works of loving care; she labors over them before she dare send them to him who was not only her dearest friend but her severest critic as well. She makes copies of them to keep herself. When Swift suffers one of his bouts of illness, she journeys to Dublin to be near him, and to nurse him when he lets her. So does Stella. Vanessa became an invalid on her own account—a consumptive. After hearing Swift was married, her will to live burned out; perhaps in a *saeva indignatio* of her own, for she commanded her executors to publish letters she had from Swift together with *Cadenus and Vanessa*. She did not mention Swift in the new will she made, and a few months after the rupture over Stella's letter, she died June the 3d, 1723. Stella outlived her by five years.

They were five bitter, frustrating years for Stella, and perhaps bitingly frustrating and bitter for Swift. Most of all, he wanted free; he wanted to get away as far as he could get from remembrance of the dead woman who at last turned from him, and the bond with the living woman from whom he kept futilely turning. He began to treat sex as a vileness, the female of the species as a stench.* He worked at *Gulliver*, shaping the *Travels* up into an unconscious and perhaps dimly intended allegory of vengeance for all his frustrations, anxieties, and resentments. Whether in Lilliput or in Brobdignagg, among the Yahoos or the English folk, the female of the species is drawn more deadly than the male. In his *Drapier's Letters*, Swift took the side of the Irish against the English, not because he believed the Irish less

---

* Cf. the verses: *Strephon and Celia.* Strephon peeps and observes his Celia at her ineluctable natural functions. Then,

> *Disgusted Strephon slunk away*
> *Repeating in his amorous fits*
> *"Oh Celia, Celia, Celia shits!"*

capable of chicanery, but because he saw the English exercising it as a privilege of power. The event that *Gulliver* was
an immediate success brought little lift to its author's spirit.
At the time it probably served his readers, as Aristotle says
Greek tragedy served his Greeks, to effect a purgation of
certain emotions, to vent and spend animosities and aggressions from which so much of the age's utterance flows. For
later generations the *Travels* became a succession of stories
that entertain and thrill adolescents, not mature men and
women. But for his contemporaries, and for Swift himself,
they signify a momentous moral judgment. There are those
of a later generation who recognize, in the image of the
Yahoo up a tree bespattering Swift with his excrement, the
author rejecting himself as well as Stella and Vanessa.

When, in 1724, Swift simply had to take to his bed,
Stella, ambiguously welcome, came to nurse him. When,
two years later, she fell under a similar necessity, Swift had
to flee from a newly increasing deafness and giddiness, for
refuge and maybe easement, to England again. Stella wors-
ened; hers became a sickness unto death. Swift couldn't bear
to have her around at the Deanery or to come near her. He is
tortured by the image of her dying. He won't think of Stella
at all; to think of her, to whom he has been so long and so
deeply attached, is to suffer. But in midsummer of 1727
Stella seemed visibly better. Swift publishes a poem to her,
and is filled with anxiety that she might die—or, was the
anxiety a projection of a wish that she should? In October of
that year he is back in Dublin and brings himself to the point
of paying his Stella a visit. But she wants him to acknowledge her as his wife and he turns on his heel and stamps out.
In January, 1728, Stella died—and is buried as "Spinster."

When Stella died, Swift was sixty-one years old. He lived
the seventeen years by which he outlived her ridden by his
symptoms, a man beset by headaches, dizziness, deafness,
tantrums; driven to madness by them. Whatever their cause
(some guess Miniere's disease, others syphilis, still others a

brain tumor), his deep insecurity with its compensating aggressions, its paranoid scatologisms and sadisms, his self-righteous and rationalizing claims for satire, his image of himself as an unrewarded paladin of liberty, go well with the lifelong syndrome. They include his diverse self-dramatizations; among them Cadenus, Bickerstaff, Drapier, Wagstaff, Gulliver, and finally, (in *The Death of Dr. Swift* and *The Life and Character of Dr. Swift**) the image of himself as a configuration of unappreciated excellences. All bespeak scorn born of envy, *saeva indignatio* born of unsuccessful emulation, the satisfactions and release of the *Schadenfreude* which satire procures. Often such expression serves to offset feelings of guilt and shame that the satirist experiences because he fails to live up to certain standards of thought, utterance, or behavior, by which, unwittingly or wittingly, he has come to measure himself. Often the failure is blamed on others who are believed to harass and hinder the satirist as he strives in vain to live up to his own code,

---

* These are verses in Swift's habitual iambic tetrameter. They make out that his friends are sardonically candid about him, that they forget him soon after his demise. They show him ultimately the concretion of honest virtue and courage.

> Fair Liberty was all his cry.
> For her he stood prepared to die:
> For her he boldly stood alone:
> For her he oft exposed his own.
> . . . .
> He gave what little wealth he had
> To build a house for fools and mad;
> And show'd by one satiric touch,
> No nation wanted it so much.
> . . . .
> Our ministers are void of taste
> When such adepts as you, and I
> So long unbishopricked lie by.
> While dunces of the coarsest clay
> That only know to preach and pray,
> Devour the Church's tiddest bits.
> The perquisites of pimps and wits
> And leave us naught but guts and garbage.
> . . . .
> . . . Gulliver divinely shews
> That humankind are all Yahoos.

who so degrade him and cause him to lose face. Jonathan Swift's satire degrades *en revanche* both his peers and his "betters," reducing them to objects of repulsion and laughter. "I know nothing," declared Alexander Pope, almost as near a friend as Swift ever had, "that moves strongly but satire, and those who are ashamed of nothing are so of being ridiculous," while Swift in the role of Gulliver claims that he wrote the *Travels* "for the noblest end, to inform and instruct mankind," to render "man ashamed of his own vices." When the age of reason and sense had opened up into the age of will and sensibility, when enlightenment had matured into the Democratic Revolution, satire was itself revalued into a shameful art, hypocritical, malicious, and cruel; happily powerless long to make the worse appear the better reason. Satire was itself satirized, and its practitioners exposed.*

Considering the gloomy Dean's personal history, his remark that the plight of man is a "ridiculous tragedy" and "the worst kind of composition" signalizes his entire career, a career in which humiliating others by deriding them, by rendering them objects of laughter continues his favorite defense against the tears of his own life. Of course, it does not follow that his expression plays a like role in the experience of his readers and admirers; any more than it follows that rice grown by Chinese coolies in the paddies around Canton upon their own excrement gets its values and meanings from that of which it is a transformation. As Swift himself observed in *The Tale of a Tub*, the consequences of a production are independent of its grounds and occasions. They are even more divergent than the career of a human individual—Swift's say—is from the careers of his parents. This is why it is so difficult livingly to envision an artist's singularity, to read his utterance as a communication from

---

* The trend began at mid-century. See John Brown, *An Essay on Ridicule* (1751); at the farther end is Walter Savage Landor's *A Satire on Satirists* (1836).

him, and not as one's own soliloquy spoken with his words and signified with his images. This is visibly the case with Swift, greatly remembered for *Gulliver*, but hardly anything else beside. And *Gulliver*—except among the learned—continues in the *living* past only as a fantasy of laughable adventure for the young to enjoy, not as the allegory of the human condition for the mature to ponder that it was to Swift, his contempories and comrades.

In every relevant sense, *Gulliver* is Swift's last word concerning man, his institutions, his world, his God, and his destiny. It is the climax of a sequence of expressions which began with *The Battle of Books*, was signally advanced in *The Tale of a Tub*, *The Mechanical Operation of the Spirit*. The volumes of prose and verse that come between consist of reactions to occasions. They project the unexpressed philosophic faith which these documents postulate. In them all we behold Jonathan Swift, a rootless man bereft of love and laughter, a man with only tears in his heart, laboring to dry them and stop his inward shedding of them by means of savage, malicious, rationalized ridicule of persons and principles. This is his inward cry for "fair Liberty." He impresses because he cries in a style that feels so articulately simple, so innocently matter-of-fact, that his allegory looks like history and his fantasy seems reality.

Swift's expression presumes a Real, Good, True and Beautiful entirely absent on the face of it, and indeed denied. Discussing in *The Tale of a Tub* the peculiar contingencies from which the world's "noble writings" derive—"a rainy day, a drunken vigil, a fit of spleen, a course of physic, a sleepy Sunday, an ill run at dice, a long tailor's bill, a beggar's purse, a factious head, a hot sun, a costive diet, want of books, and a just contempt of learning"—he quotes "the words of the famous Troglodyte philosopher" * : " 'Tis certain (said he) some grains of folly are of course annexed, as

---

* It is unsettled whether this sage is a denizen of Plato's cave or a visitor to an actual one at Moor Park called "Mother Ludwell's" which Swift is said to have "described" in verse, Dryden notwithstanding.

part of the composition of human nature, only the choice is left us, whether we please to wear them inlaid or embossed, and we need not go very far to seek how that is usually determined, when we remember it is with human faculties as with liquors, the lightest will be ever at the top.' "

Swift had written this some time in 1696, after he had returned to Temple's household a trained and ordained priest, disappointed in his hopes of place and preferment, and hating the influences he had relied on, but had, like Macbeth's witches, kept the word of promise to his ears and failed it to his hopes. He saw them all as maskers, hiding the most corrupt and falsest of practices behind visages of true and beautiful principles. This is the perception that *The Tale of a Tub* elaborates into a deadpan judgment. But at the same time Swift was composing his *Full and True Account of the Battle Fought between the Ancient and Modern Books in St. James's Library.* His paramount care was to vindicate Sir William Temple in this knight's quarrel with altogether sound critics. But Swift's fantasy dresses the quarrel up into a combat between the classics of antiquity, perfect in their kinds, and the inept fatuities of envious moderns. The latter he presents in the form of a Spider; poisonous, self-seeking, spinning his factitious web of pedantry out of his own entrails. The former he presents as a Bee that gathers wax and honey from all the flowers to produce "the two noblest things which are sweetness and light." The noxious Spider, that "true spirit of controversy," has entangled the innocent Bee in his web. Swift bespeaks sweetness and light for his patron and employer, poison and entrapment for that one's opponents. Of course the Spider is defeated, the Bee is set free: Aristotle hits Bacon and kills Descartes; Virgil gives Dryden his quietus; Homer, Lucan, Horace and Pindar win over their modern rivals. That the creator of sweetness and light is set free hints at a private faith never publicly avowed, a light too piercing and sweet to be looked at, but rendering all visibilities corrupt and sour and dark.

Similar confrontations keep coming up one after another—a manifold variety of them, each with symbols peculiar to itself—in the satirist's long life of woundings and revenges. His personal history is woven of them. In *The Tale of a Tub* they are the coat which their Father wills to his sons Peter the Papist, Martin the Lutheran Episcopalian, Jack the Calvinist; they are the instructions on the wearing of the coat; they are the meanings that each reads into the instructions to suit himself; they are the heirs locking instructions away in a strong box, so that each might follow his own inclinations unhampered by what the instructions so plainly direct. To the heirs, Reality is the garment, not the wearer. Since it is only clothes that man experiences, the clothes are the man: "To instance no more: is not religion a cloak; honesty a pair of shoes worn in the dirt; self-love a surtout; vanity a shirt, and conscience a pair of breeches; which, though a cover for lewdness as well as nastiness, is easily slipt down in the service of both? . . . In most Corporal Beings which have fallen under my cognizance, the Outside hath been infinitely preferable to the In . . . Last week I saw a Woman flay'd, and you will hardly believe how much it altered her person for the worse . . . By all which it is manifest that the outward dress must needs be the soul."

The Tale of a Tub is a philosophic impeachment of all philosophy as laughable pretense, an allegorical degradation of station and power by a balked aspirant to both, an exposure of the emptiness of religious establishments and the hypocrises of their creeds and codes by a churchman who earned his living from them but could not make a life of them. The *Tale* is a fable of hollow men, a parable uncovering the hollowness of all institutions. The word *Tub* signalizes their resounding emptiness. A multitude of meanings come together in it whose initiating image is the reputed whaler's practice of flinging a tub to the whale they are about to harpoon, in order to divert its attention from the harpooners. *Tub* offers neither Leviathan nor any human being nourishment. It resounds because it is empty and they are beglamored by the resonances. War-waging monarchs, metaphysical system-builders, political churchmen and theologians are Tubmen, at once the thumped and the thumpers. They are madmen, the vapors of whose lusts have risen to their brains, effecting "great revolutions in their natural reason." A wide-ranging species of them are the Aeolists, the true believers to whom it has been revealed that Wind or Spirit is the Creator of all things. Like Henry IV and Louis XIV, they expand frustrated sexuality into wars of empire; like Descartes and other philosophers, they blow up their own vapors into systematic knowings of the ineffably unknowable; like the clergy, they profess creeds and impose codes, which derive only from the bodily vapors risen to their brains. Of the three brothers, Jack was the chief prophet of the Aeolist faith.

Disappointed and embittered, young cleric Jonathan, his own vapors rising willy-nilly to the top of his brain, takes revenge on all of them by being the vaporous *fons et origo* of their works and ways. He does it mostly by means of the five "digressions" which bulk so large in the *Tale*. These jet satire against critics, against his time's modern spirit (especially its scientific interests), its Grub Street economy of writing and publishing, and against the support that it provides for the objects of Swift's hate. Peter, Martin, and Jack, the impious and time-serving sons of their loving dead father, are the devisers and inventors of the madness which each digression discloses and interprets. Regularly the clerics emulate the noble wits and Mohawks of the gentlemen-on-the-town. They have lost the feel, if they ever had it, of "common forms, . . . common understanding and common sense are kicked out of doors." But might they not be right; is not fiction stronger than truth; credulity better than curiosity? Isn't self-deception to vision like tickling to the touch? For always the outside is the better side; the inside turns out good for nothing. Happiness, then, must needs be "a perpetual possession of being well deceived . . . the serene, peaceful state of being a fool among knaves."

Swift, no "sacred Aeolist who delivers oracular Belches to his panting disciples," yet hinted that he himself might be a Bedlamite, but, if so, neither a happy one, nor a fool. Although he evaded discovering what he cherished, other than the Dean himself, he made ostentation of his purported hatreds, and from Swift's beginnings, the most hateful was "spirit," a vapor rising from the organs beneath, enveloping the brain, inducing madness, generating Aeolism, nourishing "enthusiasm" with its elaborations into works of science and systems of philosophy and theology, all but rituals of verbiage with no meaning. He diversifies the derision of *The Tale of Tub* in *The Mechanical Operation of the Spirit*.

Ostensibly, Swift is setting a false form of inspiration and utterance against the true one. The true one is that recorded in the New Testament (Acts II-22): the spirit of the Lord enters the souls of men and inspires them to speak with strange tongues. The false one is an upsurge of vapors, an "artificial and mechanick operation," in a Dissenter's own soul, a sort of Cartesian automatism of creed and expression working itself out "when a man's Fancy gets astride on his Reason, is at Cuffs with the Senses, and Common Understanding as well as Common Sense is kickt out of doors." Then a man nor sees nor believes what is, but by coercion or argument conforms what is to what he believes he sees. His "enthusiasm" renders him an inflexible dogmatist of politics, learning, or religion, binds him in "a bigotry of forms." The subjective elaboration cuts him off from that intuitive recognition of the real which is objective insight, and not a soul's laboring of a prejudice. Swift avers that only the Houyhnhnms are possessed of this true Reason. With them Reason is no issue of opinion, "a point problematical as with us, where men can argue with plausibility on both sides of the question; but strikes you with an immediate conviction; as it must need and do where it is not mingled, obscured, or discoloured by passion and interest." The latter but spawn mystical cryptographies; their "inward light" consists of "theological polysyllables and mysterious texts." Those who purport to shine with it cant and spit, hawk and belch, and snuffle as they make out that opacity is depth, darkness is revelation ("it is with writers as with wells which shall pass for wondrous deep upon no more reason than because 'tis wondrous dark").

This working of the Spirit of Unreason, Swift begins by insinuating, makes asses of those it works in and fanatics of those it works on with its pretence of bringing them salvation. But he won't call the former asses, nor the latter fanatics. On the record, one can't say that he appreciated how much he practiced what he preached against. His own pseudonyms, his aliases for his women, his friends and his foes, his allegories, his symbolisms, and his reasonings were all a speaking with tongues (in cheek or out); and if his own afflatus was more divine than that of his Aeolists and mechanical operators, only he could truly appreciate it. Of course, he well knew how much he was their better and what a *lese majesté* their criticism of him was. Years after he learned that Queen Anne had spoken unfavorably of *The Tale of a Tub*, he took his vicarious revenge by having Gulliver gut the apartment of Lilliput's Queen when it was on fire, by emptying his bladder on it. He saved the royal chambers from burning up, but the beneficiary of this act of grace had her benefactor charged as a traitor according to the law of her land.

Gulliver's Travels took a long time from conception to birth. The germ of its idea is said to have been a suggestion to Swift by his fellows of the Scriblerus Club—Arbuthnot, Gay, Parnell, and Pope—that he, as Martin Scriblerus, should go on a journey and report back what he saw. This was around 1713–14, when the Tories were out of power and Swift was becoming his Vanessa's cad. But Queen Anne died, the Tories were out and the Whigs in, and Swift had to retire to his deanery in Dublin and the suggestion was not followed up. Some argue that the vogue of Robinson Crusoe stirred Swift to resume it, and certain of his comments on travellers' tales in circulation after 1719 provide a premise for the argument. Readers can also find in the history of the writing, the order of the books and the publication of *Gulliver's Travels*, some analogies with the history of Gargantua; and an attuned sensibility can experience in the *Travels* a sort of resonance from Rabelais' aim, theme, and thought, although not from his spirit in or out of Bottle. The pundits have it that Lilliput was done first, Brobdingnag and Houyhnhnms with their Yahoos (or the Yahoos with their Houyhnhnms) next; Laputa was last, and least worthy, but was put in third place for publication, so that the Yahooization of (at least English) mankind might stand as the ethical climax of that pilgrim's progress.

The parable of the Houyhnhnms—those true children of nature (as the illuminati of the Enlightenment imagined the child of nature must be), simple, honest, possessed of the horse sense of intuitive reason, living a peaceful, well-ordered life of freedom, learned in all that such a life requires but no more, unafraid of death and unconcerned about dying— brings together so very much that poor Swift was not and yearned to be. It is not beyond his own idea of reason that he made this parable the climax of his fable, because of these compensatory loves of his, and not because of the hatreds which his Yahoos channel. He endows his Surgeon-Captain Gulliver with enough of the commonsense and the intuitive (as against dialectical) reason which he prized, to enable that sociologist to measure and appreciate the values which Swift caricatures to degrade, as well as those which he exalts to the point of caricature. And the endowment goes to a subject of Queen Anne, no less a rational and wonderful Sancho Panza than Robinson Crusoe.

Gulliver makes four major voyages. One ends in a shipwreck, one in an abandonment, one in a capture by pirates, and one in a marooning by mutineers. Each disaster leads to a socio-cultural discovery. Each discovery culminates in a mighty, humorless moral judgment which expresses the decisions of the author rather than the living options of the figures which signify the judgments. The *Travels* is a collocation of abstractions like a medieval morality. With all his remarkably matter-of-fact manner Swift could not make his figures come alive. His play is with sounds (one notes how very much he uses the vowel *u* for comic effect: Gr*u*ltr*u*d, Str*u*ldbr*u*g, L*u*gnagg, Gl*u*mdalaclitch, Lorb*u*lgr*u*d, Gl*u*bd*u*bdrib, Lap*u*ta, Br*u*ndrical, Blef*u*sc*u*, and so on), and perhaps this helps account for the book's present attraction for adolescents in their bull-session phase. Lilliput signalizes the littleness and triviality of what, in Swift's time, men tortured and killed each other for: the fateful animosities of *Tramseckan*, or High Heels, and *Slamecksan*, or Low Heels; the civil war over the interpretation of the prophet Lustrog's teaching in the fifty-fourth chapter of the Laputan Holy Book *Bumidecral*, "That all true believers shall break their eggs at the convenient end"—one party insisting on the Little, the other on the Big End. The Big-Endians were defeated, fled into exile in Blefuscu and there fomented treason against the Little-Endian government of their homeland. Brobdingnag is a sort of paradigm of certain virtues as well as defects of the oversized. Beside the ostensibly calm, sensible sixty-footers of the Court, Gulliver feels himself somewhat a Lilliputian, and passes Lilliputian judgments on the looks and likes of the Brobdingnagian hypertrophy of all things, especially of the females and their propensities. A hypertrophied eagle picks up the ingenious box which royalty had provided him for housing, and drops it into the sea, where it is recovered by the crew of a ship, which is captained by a fellow countryman, a "Mr. Thomas Wilcocks, an honest worthy Shropshire man" who, after a voyage of nine months, brings him home and refuses to take pay for it!

Lilliput and Brobdingnag can less readily be assimilated

to modernity's science fiction than Laputa, the gloomy
Dean's new Atlantis. That sovereign kingdom is Swift's
cryptographic caricature of the new men of science and their
works, which he knew little or nothing of, save that they
challenged the good old Tory order and were to be derided.
Laputa is a Floating or Flying Island. Its motive power is
the attraction and repulsion between the poles of a magnet
and the earth of subject Balnibarbi. Laputa's male inhabitants are abstracted individuals with torticolis who do everything by mathematics, even measuring their clothes. They
are so out of this world that they must have attendants
flapping their ears with bladders when the world requires
their attention. They are no good to their wives, who seek
every means of getting away to more satisfying male company. They are musicologists who every so often stop to hear
the music of the spheres; and they are hag-ridden by fears
and anxieties, for their astronomical lore warns them that
soon or late the sun may fail them. They can't sleep for fear,
and every morning anxiously ask "How's the sun?" Their
counterparts in Lagado, the crumbling capital of incompetent, impoverished Balnibarbi, are the philosophers and
scientists of the Academy of Projectors. These are innova-
tors and planners, bent on replacing the tried and true old
ways and works with ever unachieved improvements, such
as extracting sunbeams from cucumbers; reconverting
human excrement into human nourishment; processing marble into pillows; precisely defining colors, by smell and touch
alone; constructing human housing as the spider his web
and the bee her hive; composing poems by means of accidental combinations of letters produced with a machine; replacing words and symbols with objects; and educating by having the learner chew and swallow the material on which the
subject matter has been written down. There were also de-
signers of perfect societies, projectors of tax-reform, of new
methods of spying and of other political necessities. The
people of Balnibarbi keep rebelling against the sages of La-

puta and the philosophers, inventors, Utopians, and other perverters of commonsense reality who rule over them. But their rulers are also the Joneses they aspire to keep up with, so rebellion never quite comes off. What ho, Einstein, computers and satellites, astronauts and science fiction!

Gulliver-Swift gets bored with Lagado and wangles a side-trip to the island of Glubdubdrib, the homeland of sorcerers and magicians who bring up for him out of the vasty deep, the shades of Hannibal, Alexander, Caesar and Brutus, that he sets over against their scoundrelly opposite numbers of Augustan England. He also gets the wizard to call up Homer and Aristotle, naturally to satisfy an ancient grudge, by showing how mistaken are the commentators on their works, and to have Aristotle predict that Newton and Newtonian physics would be discarded for the errors and frauds they really were.

Gulliver then persuades his hosts to take him to Lugnagg, the homeland of the immortals, the Struldbrugs, who should be the wisest of human beings, since "exempt from [death] that universal calamity of human nature, [they] have their minds free and disengaged without the weight and depression of spirit caused by the continual apprehension of death." But what Gulliver learns revolts him: immortality is misery, senile dementia, dotage, and yearning for the release of death. He wants no part of it.

From Lugnagg, Gulliver, who is loaded with royal gifts, sails without incident to Japan; from Japan, in a Dutch ship to Amsterdam, and thence to England. But after five months with his wife and children, he accepts the captaincy of a merchantman and sets sail again. This time his vehicle to Wonderland was a mutiny and marooning by the mutineers. It is to them that he owes his glamorous sojourn among the Houyhnhnms and his encounters with their Yahoos. His stay in that culture was the longest. In its management of the Yahoo herds, its rule of Houyhnhnm mating and birth control, its readiness for death and its burial rites, he saw the perfection of rationality. In Houyhnhnmland Gulliver became a nature-boy with horse sense; he "enjoyed perfect health of body and tranquillity of mind," since he was here exempt from the schemes, the stratagems, the deceptions and cruelties wherewith the people of the culture he came from struggle with one another for survival. He recognized his inferiority and was grateful to be admitted, a destitute and humble alien of an inferior species, to the company of his equine betters, and to acknowledge without regret their Yahooization of mankind.

For the mankind about which "his Honour, my master" learned from Gulliver was, in the light of the Houyhnhnm horse sense and naturalness, the brutish Yahoo become more corrupt and evil from achieving and using a certain degree of reason. The institutions of this mankind were wickednesses. Its laws served "a confederacy of injustice." Its sex life, like its food and drink, became more diseased as it became more diversified; and the cures of body and soul wherewith it sought recovery from the sicknesses were more disgusting than the sicknesses. Its statesmen and diplomats were embodiments of insolence, lying, and bribery. The education of its peers but perfected them in these perversions of reason and corruptions of sense, and were all too likely to keep their countries at war with one another. A few of the causes of war are "the ambitions of princes; the corruptions of ministers," using war as distraction therefrom; "differences of opinion" such as "whether flesh be bread, or bread be flesh . . . the juice of a certain berry be blood or wine; whether whistling be a vice or a virtue; whether it be better to kiss a post, or throw it into the fire; what is the best colour for a coat, whether black, white, red, or gray; and whether it should be long or short, narrow or wide, dirty or clean; with many more." Wars over difference of opinion, Gulliver tells "His Honour" are the worst; then goes on to enumerate a few other motives of war, and the horror of armament. His Honour comments that the faculty of devising such abominations can't be reason, for the nature of reason renders it impervious to such abuse.

Finally "his Honour's" neighbors and the governing assembly of the Houyhnhnms point out that although Gulliver had become a somewhat equinized Yahoo, he was a Yahoo nevertheless. They therefore proposed to "his Honour, my master" the alternative of either sending this variant to the Yahoo herd, or returning him where he came from. As an equinized Yahoo, he was a danger to the Houyhnhnm economy and style of life. Of course this was Hobson's choice for Gulliver. He just could not join the Yahoos. With the willing aid of the sorrel nag assigned by "his Honour" to look after him, he made a sort of Indian canoe out of skins of Yahoos well-stitched together, provisioned it, bade his master a sad farewell and departed, his ears comforted with the consoling words "*Hnuy illa nyha majali Yahoo*, take care of thyself, gentle Yahoo." After a few misadventures he was picked up by Portuguese sailors, bound hand and foot and brought to their captain, "Pedro de Mendez . . . a very courageous and generous person . . ." who finally got his story from him, somewhat reconciled him to associating with his kind, and persuaded him to return to his wife and family. After five years he could tolerate their Yahoo presence, but he preferred the conversation of horses.

In terms of laughter and tears, Swift's misanthropy is self-explanatory. It is the misanthropy of a defeated man, not of an exploited and betrayed man. As he himself observes, he is no Timon of Athens. His satire runs counterpoint to his disappointments and frustrations in his career of love, his career of ambition, his career of health. Wherever his expectation gets turned to nothing, he frees himself from the void by deriding the persons and powers that create it, even those friendly to his hopes, and the persons and powers that succeed where he fails, such as the men of science and the sciences. A priest of the Church of England, and an officer of the Establishment, Swift was, on occasion, charged with impiety, labeled a latitudinarian, a deist, a freethinker. Richard Steele doubted that he could be a Christian, and Swift pursued Steele ever after. He libelled those he envied, very often anonymously. He hid his meanings behind allegories and parables, and when caught out, he endeavored to shame by deriding honest men who nakedly proclaimed what he was charged with masking. His aptness at the satiric art gratified his itch for place and power. Each aggression released his Ego, for the nonce, from the tensions of his yearnings and frustrations. He would damn, he would vex the world, not divert it. "I am not content with despising it, but I would anger it, if I could with safety." Satire confirmed his existence—"I despise, I deride, therefore I exist"—and established his power. Swift, far more than the author, could speak in Pope's couplets:

> *Yes, I am proud; I must be proud to see*
> *Men not afraid of God, afraid of me;*
> *Safe from the bar, the pulpit or the throne,*
> *Yet touched and shamed by ridicule alone.*

But whether Swift himself was afraid of God, or believed that there was a God to be afraid of, continues to be debated. Since, somehow, deism and freethinking were associated with the Whig interest, Dean Swift, the close friend of Jacobite Bolingbroke, the Tory pamphleteer, had to attack whoever and whatever was in opposition. Anthony Collins was one such. A decent man whom John Locke found congenial, Collins challenged the doctrines of both the Establishment and the Dissent. In 1713 he published a *Discourse on Free Thinking* which argued that only free enquiry could make for sound belief, that the free commitment to Reason takes the mind from revealed to natural religion, from theism to deism; that the free mind needed no middlemen between itself and God. There was a sect of Freethinkers from whose faith and works the Collins argument had developed. Of course the vested interests of both the Establishment and the Dissent attacked the Discourse. Swift produced a tract: *Mr. Collins' Discourse of Freethinking, put into plain English by way of abstract, for the use of the poor.* The animus of the tract was, that inasmuch as all men are fools, freethinking must needs be folly; only, freethinkers are knaves as well, so that Collins' conclusions regarding freedom of thought are worthy only of scorn: "The bulk of mankind is as well qualified for flying as for thinking." Thinking makes denominations, and to have it free is "to give power to the stupid."

One might see Swift as a savage and malicious Hume. Like "le bon David," he held that the established old ways, being established and old, could not but be the right ways, and that whatever the findings of rational enquiry, the conduct of life vindicates itself. Or, one might see Swift, like Pascal, finding authority in the reasons of the heart which Reason could not know. But Swift assigned lusts to the heart, not reasons; his starved heart had no faith in the heart, and the Reason he did have faith in seemed to him to consist either of the rites and rotes of the Establishment or of the creed and code of nature's noble Houyhnhnms. His *Argument to Prove that the Abolishing of Christianity in England May, as things now Stand, be Attended with Some Inconveniences, and perhaps not Produce the Good Effects Proposed Thereby* favors the former, since the enactment of real Christianity could well put an end to the entire material and cultural economy of his England. Maybe the Christianity of the Establishment is only a nominal Christianity. Maybe it is altogether hypocritical and an honest clergy is by no means desirable. But even so, the Establishment embodies the public peace. "I believe it is often with religion as it is with love, which with much dissembling at last grows real." Suppose, then, the Christian mysteries are beyond rational discourse. Why bother to explain them? The ends of peace are served by presenting them: "I am not answerable to God for the doubts that arise in my own breast, since they are the consequence of that reason which He hath planted in me, if I take care to conceal those doubts from others, if I use my best endeavours to subdue them, and if they have no influence on the conduct of my life."

Our Dean propounded this faith in the guise of an unbeliever who was defending the Establishment against the attacks of his own kind for its service to the public peace. He vindicated creed and code on the ground of freedom of thought: for what use is it, he demanded, "if it will not produce freedom of action." He argued from a rule of all or nothing: Either, I affirm, say, the 39 articles, or "I may safely whore and drink and defy the parson." Dostoevsky and certain 20th-century existentialists after him produce like alternatives in the proposition: "If there is no God, everything is permitted." Considering what in his long anxiety-ridden life Swift permitted himself, how might his commitment to the existence of God be appraised? Was the freethinker he pretended to be a disguise put on by a true believer, or was the pretense a disguise put on by a true unbeliever? His tragic rage at his own life and his acquiescence in death and dying provide a clue, even if his bitter appraisal of the human plight should not. As he wrote once from Ireland: "It is time to have done with the world, and I would, if I could, get into a better, before I am called up to the best, and not die here in a rage like a poisoned rat in a hole." But England was no less a poisonous hole to him, and death not an evil but a good: "It is impossible," he wrote," that anything so natural, so necessary, so universal as death should ever have been designed by Providence as an evil to mankind," and he had his noble Houyhnhnms accept it and go to meet it cheerfully as the good it was. He seems without interest in the *where* and *what* of life after death, which continues the overruling concern of the religion he served as priest. Immortality is not in his vocabulary; his image of it is the Struldbrug; and his own death signifies to him but what the survivors will feel and say about him.

Jonathan Swift's themes are in the tradition of Erasmus, Rabelais, Cervantes, Molière. His use of the laughter they dry the tears of life with diverges from theirs. It is another kind of laughter. That "rat in a hole" is no idle figure. He who drew it was a soul entrapped and bound, a suffering soul striving by means of satire to break free. He died striving; but he knew surely what his heart craved, what his mind savagely struggled for. He knew it with that "immediate conviction" of Houyhnhnm reason or horse sense. He wrote it down when he challenged the sincerity of his friends with *On the death of Dr. Swift.* He wrote, "Fair Liberty was all his cry."

CHAPTER ELEVEN

Laughter and Tears of the Enlightenment: Alexander Pope

P ERHAPS AS nearly a friend as Jonathan Swift ever had—other than his Stella and Vanessa—was Alexander Pope, young enough to have been his son (he was born in 1688), and early acknowledged by the wits as the supreme poet of their age of reason. The physical condition of the two satirists had curious analogies; their fortunes and their personal histories were significantly unlike. A sickness, perhaps tuberculosis of the bones, perhaps rickets, deformed Pope's figure into the traditional shape of the court jester. He had a squat, hunch-backed torso and bowlegs so spindly that he would hide their thinness under three pairs of stockings. The never-forgiven King of Dunces-to-be, John Dennis, wrote Pope down in the course of unfavorable comment on his youthful *Pastorals* as a "young, squat, short gentleman"; others referred to him as "the little monster." In his late years he himself said that he looked like a spider. Whether Swift added that, nevertheless, he produced like a bee is not recorded. Nor is there indication how Pope reacted to the accident—his coach overturned in water, and he owed his life to the postillion—which, in 1726, crippled two of his fingers. That was the year his mother died ("a saint expired" he called her, to Jonathan Richardson, the idealizing painter, whom he wanted to paint her dead), and Swift had come to stay with Pope at Twickenham. He was then thirty-eight years old.

Like Swift, Pope suffered head- and belly-aches. Unlike Swift, he would risk both with strong drink and spiced diet. Even more unlike Swift, he was so frail and weak that he needed to keep a servant within call, and could, because all their lives he was the cherished care of his father and mother. Moreover, the Popes were papists, living under the handicaps which England's Glorious Revolutionists had found it necessary to lay upon her Romanists. In the nature of things, segregation and isolation would strengthen the bonds of family and heighten the solidarity of the faithful; rank and station would not divide them as among the privileged. Alexander's father could, without assuming a liberty, show off his dear prodigy among his Romanist betters. The latter could, in their turn, exhibit him and further his prospects among the wits of their acquaintance. They brought their precocious co-religionist to the attentions of Wycherly, Dryden, and Addison, among others.

Pope's delicate health saved him from much bad schooling. (*The Dunciad* pays its ferocious respects to the denizens of Academe), but neither did his tutoring at home advantage him much. His tutors were priests; unless it was the catechism, they passed on to him hardly anything that mattered. What the prodigy learned, he learned by himself, from reading and conversation. In the coffeehouses and clubs Swift and Gay and Arbuthnot became his closest gossips; in the mansions and manors that welcomed him, he matched wits with rich and egregious nobles like Bolingbroke. His knowings were not too precise nor his insights too profound. But his feeling for words and their tonal, if not meaningful relations was, from his earliest years, a feeling for simplicity, clarity, balance and finish, a feeling suggestive somehow of Haydn's or Handel's feeling for musical phrase and form. Besides, Pope had the signal art of translating even uncongenial conceptions into tight, sharp, epigrammatic couplets of Newtonian symmetry.

> *Why did I write? What sin to me unknown*
> *Dipt me in ink, my parents', or my own?*
> *As yet a child, nor yet a fool to fame,*
> *I lisp'd in numbers, for the numbers came.*
> *I left no calling for this idle trade,*
> *No duty broke, no father disobey'd.*
> *The Muse but serv'd to ease some friend, not Wife*
> *To help me through this long disease, my life* . . . .

Pope grew up a ceaselessly self-conscious, self-disciplined cabinet-maker of his numbers; a craftsman, working and reworking their rhyme and reason with a creator's pleasure and a perfectionist's assiduity. "I corrected," he avowed in the *Preface* to an edition of his utterances, published in his twenty-ninth year, "because it is as pleasant to me to correct as to write." Indeed, he corrected and kept correcting everything, including letters to friends, to the day he died, changing words and views as seemed to him at the time best fitted to his image of himself. At thirty, he was an autodidact and a self-made man, with the former's approval of his teacher, and the latter's of his maker. His admirers and detractors both speak of his vanity. It never occurred to them that the self-image he so cherished might somewhat redress the balance of an ineluctable sense of physical inferiority; that his aggressive laughter might for the nonce blank out the cause, and thus lift him from the degradation which the mere presence of a healthier, handsomer, stronger, and outranking figure must needs lay upon a highly sensitive, weak, sick, ugly, but smart little character. Successful in his career of ambition and wealth, not truly defeated in his career of

love, it was from another need than Swift's that Pope proclaimed:

> *Yes, I am proud, I must be proud to see*
> *Men, not afraid of God, afraid of me:*
> *Safe from the bar, the pulpit and the throne,*
> *Yet touched and shamed by ridicule alone.*

His laughter first came innocently, in a spirit of fun more
akin to Erasmus' than Rabelais', and more like Rabelais'
than Swift's. As a youth of twenty-two and already a poet of
repute, he wrote to his friend, Henry Cromwell:

I Resume my old liberty of throwing out myself upon paper to
you, and making what thoughts float uppermost in my head, the
subject of a letter. They are at present upon laughter, which (for
ought I know) may be the cause you might sometimes think me
too remiss a friend, when I was most intirely so! for I am never
so inclin'd to mirth as when I am most pleas'd and most easy,
which is in the company of a friend like yourself.

As the fooling and toying with a mistress is a proof of fond-
ness, not disrespect, so is raillery with a friend. I know there are
prudes in friendship, who expect distance, awe and adoration,
but I know you are not of them; and I for my part am no idol-
worshipper, tho' a Papist. If I were to address Jupiter himself
in a heathen way, I fancy I should be apt to take hold of his knee
in a familiar manner, if not of his beard like Dionysus; I was just
going to say, of his buttons; but I think Jupiter wore none (however I won't be positive to so nice a critic as you, but his robe
might be subnected with a Fibula.) I know some philosophers
define laughter, A recommending ourselves to our own favour, by
comparison with the weakness of another: but I am sure I very
rarely laugh with that view, nor do I believe children have any
such consideration in their heads, when they express their
pleasure this way: I laugh full as innocently as they, for the most
part, and as sillily. There is a difference too betwixt laughing
about a thing, and laughing at a thing: one may find the inferior
man (to make a kind of casuistical distinction) provoked to folly
at the sight or observation of some circumstances of a thing, when
the thing itself appears solemn and august to the superior man,
that is, our judgment and reason. Let an Ambassador speak the

best sense in the world, and deport himself in the most graceful manner before a Prince, yet if the tail of his shirt happen (as I have known it happen to a very wise man) to hang out behind, more people shall laugh at that than attend to the other; till they recollect themselves, and then they will not have a jot the less respect for the minister. I must confess the iniquity of my countenance before you; several muscles of my face sometimes take an impertinent liberty with my judgment, but then my judgment soon rises, and sets all right again about my mouth: and I find I value no man so much, as him in whose sight I have been playing the fool. I cannot be sub persona before a man I love; and not to laugh with honesty, when nature prompts, or folly (which is more a second nature, than anything I know) is but a knavish hypocritical way of making a mask of one's own face.—To conclude, those that are my friends, I laugh with, and those that are not I laugh at; so am merry in company, if ever I am wise, it is all by myself. You take just another course, and to those that are not your friends, are very civil; and to those that are, very endearing and complaisant: thus when you and I meet, there will be the Risus and Blanditiae united together in conversation, as they commonly are in verse. But without laughter on the one side, or compliment on the other.

The Rape of the Lock, which Pope composed the following year, speaks this spirit of raillery; a year later he elaborated and enriched the raillery with the rocaille sylphs and gnomes so congenial to the age. Pope shared with John Gay and John Arbuthnot the composition of a farce, Three Hours after Marriage. Its personae are a medical quack, his playwright niece, his new wife and the rakes, who, disguised as mummy and crocodile, vie to seduce the bride. Whatever be Pope's share in this somewhat belated Restoration piece, it belongs in spirit with The Rape of the Lock. By 1717, when it was produced, Pope had known Swift at least four years, perhaps longer; the first four books of his rhodomantine anglicizing of The Iliad had brought him something of a competence; he had acquired, and with Charles Bridgeman's advice, improved Twickenham; had taken his parents to live there and his father had died there; an edition of his works had been issued. Pope was truly a success as Swift never felt he was, a success that appreciated itself beyond all other successes.

Yet this self-appreciation brought no self-acquiescence. Pope was perversely jealous for his image of Alexander Pope, and would suffer no doubt of it, nor any modification in it. Although his craftsman's conscience recognized sound criticism and acted on it ("I will," he wrote Caryll, "make my enemy do me a kindness when he meant an injury, and so serve instead of a friend."), he hated the critic, and pursued him to the end, with vituperative derision. In his poems friendly raillery is replaced with venomous aggression: laughter is induced in order to sting and maim. He himself is reported to have snickered rather than laughed. What role his insecurity with the ladies Blount had in the change, what role Lady Mary Montagu's derision of his avowal of love, what role his thin skin before the fairest criticism, or what role the example of Swift, are themes for pleasant conjectural punditry. Pope's politics were, of course, Tory. He was a companion and interpreter of Tories—notably the impeached Atterbury and the ostracized, ever-scheming Bolingbroke, who practiced derision as the one relatively safe public weapon against Robert Walpole's long-lasting power in the kingdom. On the record, the most skillful and most considered practitioners of the satirical art of shaming were Tories, writers, and invokers of "reason" such as Swift and Gay and Parnell and Arbuthnot. These became Pope's closest associates. Together they formed a sort of commando of satire; together they encouraged and strengthened and nourished one another in the practice of the cruelties of laughter. Mostly their practice was a hit and run practice—authorships were public secrets of the coffeehouses and clubs, sooner or later avowed. Slander and libel continued punishable, and often scapegoats such as publishers received the punishment, while influence in high places saved the libellers and slanderers. Nor truth nor logic could be a justification. If an author listed among the Dunces was

believed a Whig—"Earless on high stands unabash'd
Defoe," Pope gloated—he might be pilloried and jailed, but
also might be saved as Defoe was by Harley. But this was as
rare as an honest politician; and in due course, Defoe became, perhaps for his own liberty and safety, a double agent.

The commando of satirists called themselves the Scriblerus Club. They made it a sort of residuary legatee of the
Brothers among whom Swift had first exercised his satirism
consequentially. It enabled a venting to one another, against
their Whig rivals for preferment and place, of all their
resentments and jealousies. Their own consensus of feeling
and judgment they incarnated in the effigy of Martinus Scriblerus, son of the learned Cornelius, a projector of a new
scheme of education, wherewith he educated his able son
into an all-knowing pedant of absurd judgment and ab-
surder taste. They set forth the Scriblerian wisdom first in
the *Memoirs of Scriblerus*, ". . . all the false tastes in learning, under the character of a man of capacity enough, that
had dipped into every art and science, but injudiciously in
each." The *Memoirs* were said to have been compounded by
1713, but were not published till 1741. Pope is held to have
been only the claimant, Arbuthnot the actual author of this
satire upon an education consummated in a compendium of
pedantries, drawn from the expression of all the authentic as
well as bogus scholars and critics whom the brethren had
quarrels with. More than a decade after a visit of ailing
Swift's to Twickenham, the Scriblerites published a volume
of *Miscellanies*, its preface signed by the two major members, Pope and Swift. Then came Martinus Scriblerus'
Περι βαθουζ, or the *Art of Making Poetry*, "the Bathos of
the Profound, the Natural Taste of Men, and in particular,
the present age." It was a sort of pre-Duncian *Dunciad*, this
time not naming names, but employing three of four sets of
initials to identify the "genuine ostriches, parrots, por-
poises," who dared disapprove the creations of the Scriblerian fellowship.

Finally came the first version of *The Dunciad*, and without an author by name, although everybody who was anybody knew who the author was. Pope is said to have been unsatisfied with his great epic and to have thrown it on the fire, from whence it was rescued by Swift. The second version, a year after, named names; and to make sure the law could reach neither the author nor the bookseller, the copyright for *The Dunciad* was assigned to the noble lords Bathurst, Burlington, and Oxford. Pope did not claim paternity till 1735, but he kept revising the epic for each new printing and crowning a new King of the Dunces and adding to his subjects with each new grudge.

He dedicates his epic to Swift:

> *O Thou! whatever title please thine ear,*
> *Dean, Draper, Bickerstaff or Gulliver!*
> *Whether thou choose Cervantes' serious air.*
> *Or laugh and shake in Rabelais' easy chair.*
> *Or praise the Court, or magnify Mankind.*
> *Or thy griev'd Country's copper chains unbind;*
> *From thy Boeotia tho' her Pow'r retires,*
> *Mourn not, my* Swift, *at aught our Realm acquires*
> *Here pleas'd behold her mighty wings outspread*
> *To hatch a new Saturnian age of Lead*

The hatcher is the kingdom's Providence; its "Great Mother" is Dulness, who, born a goddess, never dies. Her kingdom is disorder, teeming chaos, where all incompatibles unite and clash.

> *She sees a mob of metaphors advance*
> *Pleased with the madness of the crazy dance;*
> *How Tragedy and Comedy embrace;*
> *How Farce and Epic get a jumbled race;*
> *How Time himself stands still at her command,*
> *Realms shift their place, and Ocean turns to land.*

The crowning is celebrated with games which the Great Mother herself has instituted: games for booksellers, racing

one another after the phantom of a poet; games for poet-
esses; exercises for poets in tickling with dedications, in
vociferating over fustian issues, in diving into the obscene ob-
scurities of party; and exercises for critics:

> *Three college sophs and three pert Templars came*
> *The same their talents and their tastes the same;*
> *Each prompt to query, answer and debate,*
> *And omit with love of Poesy and Prate,*

to sit in patient wakefulness while "two gentle readers" read
them, together with the entire rout of disorder, to sleep "as
verse, or prose, infuse the drowsy God."

These having been brought into the most great peace of
Mother Dulness, the goddess takes the sleeping king with
her to her Temple, pillows his head on her lap, and so
engenders "all the visions [Pope is remembering Swift's
early essays] of wild enthusiasts, projectors, politicians, ina-
moratos, earth builders, and poets." He is mounted on Fancy
and carried to the river Lethe in Elysium whereinto Bavius
dips the dull about to be reborn. The ghost of Settle takes
him to the high place where he can behold what the Empire
of Dulness is, was, and is to become. He sees how forever
this folk must be the dominion of Science and how quickly
her role is checked. He sees the kingdom of Great Britain suc-
cumbed to Dulness, sees the miracle of Dulness which his
own reign brings—as her spirit pervades theatres, court, the
arts, and the sciences.

The docent of the vision is Dante, "the great Father to the
greater Son":

> *"Yet oh, my sons, a father's word attend:*
> *(So may the fates preserve the ears you lend)*
> *'Tis yours a Bacon or a Locke to blame,*
> *A Newton's genius, or a Milton's flame:*
> *But Oh! with One, immortal One dispense:*
> *The source of Newton's Light, of Bacon's Sense.*
> *Content, each Emanation of his fires,*

> *That beam on earth, each Virtue he inspires.*
> *Each Art he prompts, each Charm he can create.*
> *Whate'er he gives, are giv'n for you to hate.*
> *Persist, by all divine in Man unaw'd,*
> *But, 'learn, ye* Dunce, *not to scorn your God.*"

But then this "ray of Reason" is quenched. "Hell rises, Heav'n descends, and dance on earth" hissing gorgons, glaring dragons, ten-horned fiends and giants fight gods, imps, monsters muse, rage, mutter; a fire, a jig, a battle and a ball "breaks out refulgent in

> *a new world to Nature's laws unknown,*
> *. . . . with a heav'n its own.*"

And this world is the creation of the King of Dulness, his crown challenged by other Dullards—and all well-rewarded.

> *While Jones and Boyle's united Labours fall*
> *While Man with sorrow to the grave descends*
> *Gay dies unpensioned with a hundred friends:*
> *Hibernian politics—O Swift, thy fate,*
> *And Pope's, ten years to comment and translate.*"

It is the beginning of the Kingdom of the Dull upon Earth; the end of Order and Science, the gagging of the Muse, the discouragement of the Arts. Mother Dulness makes compromise between her competing devotees, receives the obedience of the schools and universities, the tourists of the Grand Tour [whose spokesman she "endues with the happy quality of Want of Reason]; she ordains the utterly idle as "Virtuosos," and recommends that they should occupy themselves "in the study of Butterflies, Shells, Birds-nests, Mosses"—but should avoid "any useful or extensive views of Nature, or of the Author of Nature." The Minute Philosophers and Freethinkers assure that this will be done. All unite to "make one mighty Dunciad of the land." Mother Dulness invests it:

She comes! she comes! the sable Throne behold
Of night *primeval and of* Chaos *old!*
Before her, Fancy's gilded clouds decay.
And all its varying rainbows die away.
Wit *shoots in vain its momentary fires*
The meteor drops, and in a flash expires.

. . . .

Thus at her felt approach and secret might,
Art *after* Art *goes out, and all is Night.*
See skulking Truth to her old cavern fled,
Mountains of Casuistry heap'd o'er her head!
Philosophy, *that lean'd on Heav'n before,*
Shrinks to her second cause and is no more.
Physic *of* Metaphysic *begs defense,*
And Metaphysic *calls for aid on* Sense!
See Mystery *to* Mathematics *fly!*
In vain! they gaze, turn giddy, rave, and die.
Religion *blushing veils her sacred fires,*
And unawares Morality *expires.*
Nor public Flame, not private *dares to shine;*
Nor human *Spark is left, nor Glimpse* divine
Lo thy dread Empire, Chaos, is restored.
Light dies before thy uncreating word;
Thy hand, great Anarch, lets the curtain fall
And universal Darkness buries All.

Such are the cosmic consequences of differing from Pope, Swift, and company. As Swift wrote in the Preface to his *Battle of the Books:* "Satire is a sort of glass wherein beholders do generally discover everybody's face but their own; which is the chief reason for the kind reception [he might have rightly added, the unstinted giving] it meets in the world, and that so very few are offended with it." That our two satirists differed from one another made no difference in their relations, for their friendship and collaboration followed rather from their common hatreds than from any common loves. Swift lived and died a priest and functionary of the Church of England; Pope, a Papist under the disabilities imposed on his denomination, who in his terminal illness took the sacraments and had Extreme Unction. If Swift held any positive faith, other than that the ways of the Establishment were as rational and right as anything could be, he hid it; the reliable inference which his expression permits is an appraisal of all affirmations as Yahooisms hypocritical, empty, and corrupt, which a liberty-loving spirit must needs reject with the scornful snort of horse-sense, Nay! Pope's beliefs were positive, even though facile and not coherent. He celebrated so much that Swift belittled and parodied, even while echoing Swift. If to Swift's heart and head, whatever is, is wrong; to Pope's, whatever is, is right. With the *Essay on Man* he gave Bolingbroke's incidental and tongue-in-cheek philosophizing so significant a form that it became an expression of the true spirit of enlightenment in epigram. He recognized in the scientific speculation and experimentation that Swift brutally satirized a dignity and worth, a validity—a beauty even—immune to satire. His epitaph for Newton reads:

> *Nature and Nature's laws lay hid in Night*
> *God said, let Newton be! and all was light.*

CHAPTER TWELVE

Laughter and Tears of the Enlightenment: William Hogarth

I F, LIKE SWIFT, Pope made of laughter a weapon of retaliation and assault, it was not entirely because he lacked the capacity to laugh out of well-being, good spirits, and friendliness. We know he could enjoy fun and raillery without rancor. But so much of his recorded funning is rancor-born and seems to have been engendered in an ever-bleeding wound of pride hurt by malice. That he deserved the slings and arrows which his critics bruised and bled him with, he occasionally sensed but could never admit; he could profit by a just criticism, yet regard its author as his ever-unpardonable foe. After *The Rape of the Lock* his funning was no spontaneous enjoyment of a laughable episode: he used it, as humans do, for balm upon hurts which the self suffers from powers beyond the reach of direct retaliation. Even so, that *saeva indignatio* of which Swift boasted, was not the edge of Pope's shaming cuts at his "foes." The laughter he strove to scar them with was, like Swift's, the outward thrust and transformation of an inward weeping over the tears of things in a personal history, inscribing itself on a world where "whatever is, is right." Pope's sense of humor formed as a sisyphean effort to break free of his misery, lest his misery utterly prostrate him. Nevertheless, in its obscured depths, a vestige lived on of that spirit of raillery which young Alexander wrote so warmly about to his friend Henry Cromwell. Pope could now and again deviate into an authentic, even an innocent, cheerfulness. Swift could not.

That Swift could not is manifest in the Dean's verses of compliment to William Hogarth, whom he had never met. Hogarth's political sentiments—in so far as he had any— were far more Whig than Tory. His friends and associates were of the persuasion of Robert Walpole. His preferences in art, in music (although Swift also looked with disfavor on the Italian and German operas which were then fashionable), and in literature were those of the new front of feeling, the new sense of nature. In any battle of the books, he would be on the side of the moderns. In the practice of his own arts of painting and engraving, in the choice of themes, in the conception of design and of its execution, he was an innovator. But the knowing saw in his performance only a kind of satire that made him a brother under the skin of Swift and Pope; and most of his contemporaries so regarded him. By the middle of the third decade of the century of enlightenment, when Hogarth was close to a hearty, healthy, robustious forty and Swift on the edge of a pain-wracked seventy, Swift addressed some doggerel to Hogarth. The latter's "small conversation pieces" (nowadays' word for such is "comic strip") to mention only his larger works, had made him the most talked-of painter in the United Kingdom. Swift was waging a Swiftian war against the Irish House of Commons and wished his butts to be seen as he saw them. He wrote:

How I want thee humerous Hogarth!
Thou, I hear, a pleasant rogue art,
Were but you and I acquainted
Every monster should be painted;
You should try your graving tools
On this odius group of fools,
Draw the beasts as I describe them,
Form their features while I gibe them;
Draw them like, for I assure ye
You will need no car'catura.
Draw them so that we may trace
All the soul in every face.

Of course the painter, not without an appreciation of his own talents which even some of his friends regarded as unduly exalted, was flattered. Who wouldn't be, to have an apostrophe, and in verse, from the mighty Dr. Swift, to be told also that the mighty Doctor was one's "great admirer" and that in the company of Dublin's famous bookmakers, he often drank one's health? Hogarth could not but acknowledge this accolade from greatness with a gift of several engravings.

But the amenities were correct, although pleasurable courtesy, not fraternal communion. Hogarth was indeed "humorous." He did draw his figures "like," as none else could. But he did not perceive them as monsters or beasts or fools. He did not gibe, he did not caricature. He called caricature "that modern fashion" and declared that he had no use for it. But he did perceive all the soul in every face. For he was what Swift was not, a man both compassionate and just, whom the human comedy moved to pity as well as laughter; that is, he was a humorist as our world envisages the humorist. He felt the tears of things and the tears were mingled into his laughter. He could have been, if not a regular of Rabelais' Theleme, at least a lay brother, tactlessly forthright, honestly vain, fond of fun and food, of drink, women, and laughter, enjoying them without pretense or illusion, yet with an aspiration and a faith that struggled against all failure, for fulfillment through works that did not satisfy. Some time during Hogarth's thirty-fifth year, the sculptor Roubillac did a head of him in terra cotta. Twelve or thirteen years later, Hogarth painted his own portrait. With all the difference between the artists and their arts, both the one's sculpture and the other's painting convey a challenging curiosity, at once detached and defiant: each suggests the bare start of a smile at the lips. But the painting communicates a certain settled assurance absent from the sculpture.

In 1732, popular though he was, Hogarth had not yet become the self-made man he portrayed in 1745, the man secure in fame and fortune and highly appreciative of his maker. His self-portrait not only conveys a present satisfaction with a successful past, it also hints at a design for the future. For it is a symbol as well as a representation. The artist appears to have been looking at himself in an oval mirror set on leather-bound volumes of Milton, Swift and Shakespeare. The mirror is partly cut off by a drape, in front of which sits his dog Trump with his somewhat protruding tongue; Trump's expression seems very, very subtly to echo his master's. At Trump's left lies his master's shining palette; a low, curving golden ridge almost crossing the length of it, and underneath the ridge the legend: *The line of grace and beauty.* The empathy of man by dog or dog by man, so struck Hogarth's contemporaries, especially those who disliked him, that they nicknamed him "Painter Pugg," and one lampooned him as dog and man mingled.

The "line of grace and beauty" signified Hogarth's observations and reflections upon his experience as painter and engraver, the reading it led to, and the talk with writers and other craftsmen that followed. Eight years later, he published what he had come to believe as *The Analysis of Beauty.* He was aware that his book might be a challenge and incitement; he made a rhyme:

What!—a book, and by Hogarth!—then twenty to ten,
All he's gained by his pencil, *he'll* lose *by his pen.*
Perhaps, it may be so,—howe'er miss or hit,
He will publish—*here goes—it's double or quit.*

The *Analysis* was his protestation of his artistic faith, his choice of themes, and his rejection of "the historical style" in literature and art which ignored them.* So he just would bet his career on it. To the few who nursed grudges against the author, a book by him was a God-given opportunity to take revenge. To such as honestly believed his practice to be bad and his theory false—as spokesmen for tradition and convention did—his book provided an apt occasion to show up both. In their wake followed the various Grubstreeters of pencil and pen, ever ready to turn an honest penny at no matter whose expense. A high point of insult and derision was a drawing of Hogarth as a human canine or dog-like human on pug's legs with a pug's tail, painting "the lines of grace" of misshapen female nudes.† Hogarth was not immune to the insults of the caricaturists and the gibes of the satirists; he could only console himself with the thought that every action brings its own reaction, so that one's advances cannot but induce their setbacks.

Among the setbacks was a charge that the *Analysis* was not truly all Hogarth (until recently assumed to be true), but exposed by Joseph Burke as an invention elaborated from the fact that Hogarth did talk over his ideas with others whom he considered authorities.

To repeat, the conceptions of the *Analysis of Beauty* are Hogarth's generalizations of his own practice. He uses them

* *The Analysis of Beauty*, with the Rejected Passages from the Mss. and Biographical Fragments, Oxford, 1955.

† This was a work of Paul Sandby, once a fellow-teacher of Hogarth's in St. Martin's Lane School, an art school Sandby wanted very much to see incorporated in a proposed Royal Academy. Hogarth had resisted this proposal with characteristic vigor. Being above all jealous of the artist's independence, he held that an Academy would undermine this, only to bring on a multiplication of paintings such as the world already had too many of, and which "do not perish fast enough to want such a supply."

as means and measures for interpreting every variation of the painter's art. He offers them as statements about configurations he first had made by instinct, then perfected by trial and error, and finally conceptualized and put in words. Among his observations was the visual ground of comic effect as against beautiful ones. The former he saw as all bulges and angles, the latter as smoothly varying and expanding curves. In both he recognized movement: but the first is abrupt, staccato, purposely unordered; and the second fluid, rhythmic in the "invisible rhythm of motion," such as dances and horses communicate. But the second can be either two-dimensional or in depth; and in the first instance its line is the curve of beauty, in the second, it is the serpentine of grace. There are many curving lines, wavy lines, but one and only one line of beauty; one and only one line of grace. Both lines are the artist's abstractions or constructions; they are not nature's. Nature is all light and shade and colors; nature has no lines. Lines are trajectories which movements trace, the eyes pursue, the arts remember, labor to detain and to repeat. Art is action; when excellent, it is dramatic action. For the painter, as for the dramatist, the play's the thing, and the play is a pursuing. "Pursuing," writes Hogarth, "is the business of our lives, and even abstracted from any other view, gives pleasures." And the pleasures are enhanced by the resistances and challenges which the pursuit encounters. This is one reason why men enjoy hunting and fishing; why they prefer to walk a varied road, to follow a serpentine stream, to explore any object in "waving and serpentine lines." The forms of such objects are intricate, their lines lead the eye "a wanton kind of chace," so satisfying that they deserve to be called beautiful.* Movement, action, then, is the dynamic of beauty, and form is functional fitness.

In all, esthetic efficacy is a consequence of "the line of

---

* It might readily follow that the pursuit of happiness really captures it as the happiness of pursuit.

grace and beauty." Humor breaks the line, or renders two or more such lines incompatible. It works with "improper or incompatible excesses" and joins together forms that do not fit one another—for example, "a clown in baby clothes." This "always occasion'd a roar of laughter." Other of Hogarth's examples are the harlequins, scaramouches, Pierrots, Punchinellos of the Italian *commedia dell' Arte*. Each brings its own pattern of linear incompatibilities. Punchinello, for example, is all angles and bulges: his joints are "no better than the hinges of a door"; such, in his own way, is a "rough shock dog," in whom "an inelegant and inamiable figure of a thrown mop" is united to "that of a sensible, friendly animal." (Hogarth puts such a dog in one frame of his "comic strip," *Marriage à la Mode*. He has the dog sniffing at the lace cap which his noble master has absent-mindedly brought in his pocket from a night in a brothel). Such are the church's cherubs, gilded, with ducks' wings under their chins, "supposed to be flying about singing psalms" in a heaven which is "a swarm of these little inconsistent objects." Nevertheless, Hogarth adds, there is "something so agreeable in their form that the eye is reconciled and overlooks the absurdity." The implication is—though Hogarth does not unfold it—that the reconciliation is accomplished by means of the line of beauty. His feeling for this reconciliation, his urge by means of the line to blend the singular and self-sufficient presences he produced into the melodic wholeness of his compositions, is perhaps the most reliable disclosure of his character and ideals. As his "line of beauty" somehow invisibly reconciles laughter and tears and prolongs in art their confluence in men's lives, so it orchestrates the absurdities of both art and life, frees the spirit from the burden of them and turns it from laughter and tears toward beauty. The line of beauty is, thus, one more way to liberty.*

Because of this feeling of his, Hogarth is exempt from the

* See Kallen, *Art and Freedom*, Book I, Ch. II.

satirist's lusts and sadistries. Except for certain shamings of his lifelong rival and foe, the painter Kent, and for his defensive lampooning of the political pamphleteers, Wilkes and Churchill, who had been fellow members of a club he frequented—perhaps even friends—Hogarth did not compose his images of the human condition as projections of his private hatreds, or as broadsides of a personal vendetta. Unlike Swift, he never used the miseries of one society to revenge himself upon another which had failed to satisfy his ambitions. Swift so used the miseries of England's Irish subjects, whom he loved far less than he hated England's ruling Whigs. That Hogarth had the power of satire—his contemporaries of the Age of Reason were unable to see anything else in his expression—his "Burlington Gate" (against Kent), and his counters to Wilkes and Churchill make evident enough. But unlike the age's satirists and caricaturists he could enter into the very spirit of a Cervantes and participate in the faith and feelings of Don Quixote as well as of Sancho. His sense of humor, ever tempering tears by laughter, decided his themes and the organization of his materials. It could well have been the taproot of his artistry,* and the inspiration of his theory of *The Analysis of*

* ". . . I thought both writers and painters had, in the historical style, totally overlooked that *intermediate species of subjects* which may be placed between the sublime and the grotesque. I therefore wished to compose pictures on canvas similar to representations on the stage; and further hope that they will be tried by the same test, and criticised by the same criterion. . . . I mean to speak only of those scenes where the human species are actors, and these, I think have not often been delineated in a way of which they are worth and capable. . . . those subjects that will both entertain and improve the mind bid fair to be of the greatest public utility, and must therefore be entitled to rank in the highest class. If the execution is difficult . . . comedy, in painting as well as writing, ought to be alloted the first place, though the sublime has been opposed to it . . . let the figures in either [my] pictures or prints be considered as players dressed either for the sublime, for genteel comedy or farce, for high or low life. I have endeavored to treat my subjects as a dramatic writer: *my picture is my stage, and men and women my players, who, by means of certain actions and gestures, are to exhibit a dumb-show*."

The "conversation pieces" are the practice which validates the principles. Hogarth scorned the allusory classicism and the other impedimenta

Beauty. An inspection of any one of his drawings, engravings or sets, not only the "conversation pieces," suggests this inspiration. We recognize in each figure a presence encountered in the course of the daily life. If any is "distorted," it has been made so by nature, not by art. The artist's distortions are effected solely by the composition of the picture. The relations of the figures to each other suggest the sequence of the tones in a musical theme.

Hogarth was a natural mimic whose power of mimicry could be channelled through his pencil as well as through his person. He made himself master of his art by dint of a practice aimed at perfecting what he called "the technical memory of forms." He believed this memory to be a necessary condition of rightness of design and truth of representation. It did enable him to combine "the parts of which objects were composed" into the dynamic formations, animate or inanimate, that his imagination envisioned. He rendered them livingly present; and whether as individuals or groups, they are still characters in an action which is confluently one and whole. His compositions are a kind of group dynamics. He brings his figures and forms into active configuration without diminishing their single or collective individualities. He does this by means of his "line of grace and beauty." The "line" signifies an orchestration from the un-ordered manifold of experience into the ordered one of art. When the orchestration does not come about, the formations look centrifugal: their movement is diffluent, their juxtapositions bespeak disorder, they fail to make the sense that the heavenly cherubs make, and could well stir onlookers to laughter. Sometimes, as in "The Entertainment" (the first of the

---

of such pundits as Pope or Swift in letters, or Kent and the other traditionalists in painting, or Burlington and other "connoisseurs" in patronage. However, in letters and on the stage there was a similar shift from "high" to "domestic" tragedy and the sentimental novel. The lives of common men began to be treated as having no less worth than the lives of their "betters". The butt of the Great Tradition was being freed from subjection to the hero; poverty was being brought to moral equality with power and privilege. Hogarth was a vindicator of this equalization.

Election series), the "line" fails Hogarth: the composition looks crowded, its individualities, singular and plural, seem segregate; each absorbed in its own business, whether mending a broken head, politicking at a rectangular or round table, marching with banners labelled *"No Jews," "Liberty," "Marry and Multiply in spite of the Devil."* But it is difficult to decide that Hogarth did not aim to render precisely this gathered heterogeneity which each moment of experience spans, this commingling of the diverse which is the original *comédie humaine.* As intended, a composition's comic effect is the sense of that senselessness. It is the derision which caricaturists pursue, rendering one or another feature out of scale, aborting proportions, making this too large, that too small. Hogarth did not; his sense of humor did not need the violence of caricature to bring laughter's anodyne for tears.

The people of Hogarth's "pieces" are the people of Hogarth's community; more than one person is drawn to the life, their communal roles based on a sort of indecent exposure. But Hogarth's exposures were not the malicious shamings which Swift and Pope practiced on many of the same persons; they were not uncoverings of secret parts. They simply called to mind what nearly everybody lived and saw and knew, but would talk about only in his cups because he had not been taught it was wrong. There was a charity in Hogarth that Swift was utterly without, and Pope almost without. It was perhaps the *humanitas* of the common man, a Yahoo to Swift, a tool with life in it to Pope. Those two were clients and intimates of the rich and the mighty, of the nobility and the gentry, but not Hogarth. His experience with the latter's houses was incidental, his coffeehouse meetings with the known wits accidental. Save once, Hogarth served none of the political ends of his gentlemanly betters. The natural companions of his celebrated Rabelaisian peregrination were his own kind—a couple of fellow painters, a lawyer, a woolens-and-rum merchant. And what hearty,

vulgar fun they had; what a "jocund" time! If Hogarth
became vain and egotistical, it was because of his achievement, not his frustrations. And his achievement was to render his betters as well as his likes together with their pretensions and practices, aware of the ways of life in England's
capital as they were. There, as in all Britain, the multitudes
were poor, hardworking subjects; not citizens. Their standards of living were held at, or below, subsistence by excise
and sales taxes (exacted from them while the landed gentry
and the moneymen went practically free) which paid the
high cost of government, its venalities, its wars, its South
Sea Bubbles, and its subsidies to such profitable corporations
as the British East India Company. Did not Swift, exercising horse sense for his own satisfaction, glorify the states-
manship of this political economy in Ireland, by recommending a diet of their own infants to the starving people? But
among the Roman Catholics of Ireland resistance could take
the form of such conspiratorial companies as the Defenders,
the White Boys, and the Right Boys. Among the commoners
of England, the imbalance of the political economy was
reduced, so far as it might be, by prostitution, beggary,
illegitimacy, smuggling, slow-down, crime, gin, and irony.
Law and order were the cynical rules imposed by the
"haves" on the "have-nots"; were security for property,
privilege and power, not the administration of justice. The
justification of this society could in the faith of its "haves,"
well have been that lamp of sweetness and light, Mandeville's *Fable of the Bees*, which demonstrated to their satisfaction that the public welfare thrives on private ills.

The inference that the second is the soil of the first was
easy and as easily an error. For it is true that the people of
Hogarth's Britain, the Britain of the Glorious Revolution
and the Enlightment, were still the freest, the best fed, and
the strongest of the peoples whose rulers were warring for
the hegemony of Europe and the mastery of the Americas,
India, and Africa. There was, however, little realization

among the enlightened how far and wide enlightenment did *not* reach, and among even the most illumined, how deeply light and the sweetness thereof were a metaphysical compensation, not a social program. Their "nature," her noble "natural man" with his "natural rights" and his "natural religion" signified—in the milieu that was nature and man to Hogarth's perception and imaging, much as his cherubs signified—Newton's paradigm of the order of nature and Locke's order of the mind of man were, beside the Hogarthian panorama, *not* facts of experience but inventions of faith, at once agreeable and absurd. It may be recalled that to Swift, who did not commit himself about cherubs, they were disagreeable and absurd. That panorama was the London of Newgate Prison and Burlington House, Bedlam, Covent Garden, and Old Bailey; of coffee houses for Tories such as Batton's or Will's, for Whigs, such as Child's or King's; of taverns and bagnios, brothels and gambling halls where gentry and commoners passed as ships in the night. That panorama was the procession of the persons of Hogarth's "conversation pieces" and other drawings: Moll Hackabout, Tom Rakewell, Col. Charteris, Justice Gonson, Lord Hervey, "Mothers" Needham, Bentley, and Douglas; murderers and debtors, harlots and madams, noblemen and bruisers; men of God like "the fat pluralist" and his starved curates; policemen, informers, politicians, actors and actresses, workmen, bishops, and beggars.

Hogarth drew them all, whether alone or together, with equal care for the singularity of each. His Nature was the aggregation of singularities; types suggested "monsters of heraldry"; they were not natural. Like Bishop Butler, but without the theologian's prejudice, Hogarth felt that things are what they are, and will be what they will be, so why should we be deceived? He rejected the deception of both the Italianate "connoisseurs" and the caricaturists. People were what they were, lived as they could; they suffered by themselves and hurt one another as they did. But they lived, and they could live better; and he hoped that his art might make them aware at last of how pitiful, how tragic, were their ways of living. What other use does his art bespeak, as we follow the progress to disaster of Moll Hackabout, Tom Rakewell, the profligate young Earl and his naïve bride, the Idle Apprentice? Or as we look at the events of "Four Times of the Day" or *Four Stages of Cruelty?* To perceive the human condition in "Gin Lane," the "Election Series," "Credulity, Superstition and Fanaticism"; to look at the heroine of "The Lady's Last Stake," or at the wife of "*The Distressed Poet*," is to become aware of the tragic aspects of the comedies, and the comic aspects of the tragedies.*

To the "connoisseurs" and critics of his age, however, comedy was comedy and tragedy was tragedy, and never the twain should meet. But life is little more than their meeting; and life, according to Swift, is "a ridiculous tragedy . . . the worst kind of composition." Hogarth reached toward the beauty of this kind of composition. To the generations of critics, who came after the democratic revolution, and responded to Hogarth in the perspectives of the democratic idea, with its self-evident truths that all men are created equal, each one endowed with equal and unalienable rights to life, liberty, and the pursuit of happiness, Hogarths's portrayal of persons, alone and in their companies, seemed a contradiction of these truths, unless their equality were an equality of unworthiness, not of worth. They saw his pieces

---

* "The leading points in these prints," Hogarth writes in his *Four Stages of Cruelty*, "as well as in 'Beer Street' and 'Gin Lane,' were made as obvious as possible, in the hope that their tendency might be seen by men of the lowest rank. Neither minute accuracy of design, nor fine engraving, were deemed necessary, as the latter would render them too expensive for the persons to whom they were intended to be useful. And the fact is, the passions may be more frankly expressed by a strong, bold stroke than by the most delicate engraving. . . . The prints were engraved with the hope of, in some degree, correcting that barbarous treatment of animals, the very sight of which renders the streets of our metropolis so distressing to every feeling mind. If they have had this effect, and checked the progress of cruelty, I am more proud of having been the author than I should be of having painted Raffaele's cartoons."

as caricatures that deride, that make people out to be worse than they really are. It may be that our comtemporary apostles of equal and absolute liberty, the Existentialists, can perceive with what faithful seeing and empathic inwardness the painter sets forth the singularity of his subjects—as Hamlet, dying, bade Horatio set forth his true story.

Portrayals of man's plight alternative to Hogarth's, would be the sentimentalist and the romantic, or the baroque. The former were beginning to put into words the aversion from the "reason" of the wits already manifest during Hogarth's middle period. The latter was the dominant mode of "high" art during Hogarth's entire career. Its incarnation to Hogarth was his lifelong bugaboo, the painter William Kent, and the "connoisseurs" whose tastes Kent satisfied. In part, Hogarth composed his *Analysis of Beauty* to show them up as falsifiers of nature; painters and critics taking their standards from foreign effigies (of course Italian) instead of native fact, and purporting to belittle and scorn the English scene and the English way. In Sir James Thornhill's studio, Kent, as a fellow student and rival, flaunted his having studied in Italy, belittled England as a "Gothick country," and emphasized his Italianate preference by showily patronizing Italian opera. He was nicknamed "The Signior." Lord Burlington made him an intimate; and this rich and powerful nobleman, bon vivant, connoisseur, collector, patron of artists and writers, and amateur architect, even more an Italianate Englishman than Kent, had remodelled a house of his, Kent advising, in the palladian style. Alexander Pope had celebrated the way Burlington spent some of his money in one of his *Moral Essays*, "On the Use of Riches," and of course exalted Burlington and derided Chandos, who had spent his money in other ways. Pope's making fun of Chandos was revenge.

Perhaps Hogarth's cartoon, which he meant should show "the taste of the town" for what it was, also bespeaks revenge. He had decided that he had had enough of the book-

sellers of Grub Street and others, and he undertook to do his
selling for himself. He began with the plate formally labelled "Masquerades and Operas, or Burlington Gate."
Making the palladian façade and central arch of Lord Burlington's Piccadilly house his background, he assembled a
medley of groups and individuals—an Italian soprano, Cuz-
zoni, rakes up the English guineas which Lord Peterborough (a patron of Swift's) throws at her feet; a cockney
harridan is trundling away in a wheelbarrow the discarded
works of Shakespeare, Ben Johnson, Dryden, and Congreve;
a devil and a fool in cap and bells head up a mob, keen after
the Italianate importations and Heidegger's midnight masquerades, and Hogarth places him in a window above, gloat-
ing over the profitable mob. Higher up, William Kent poses
like some Nero; Michaelangelo and Raphael are unhappy
slaves at his feet.

This appraisal of the prevailing taste Hogarth did in
1724. The next year Hogarth had a chance to vent his animus against Kent more particularly and directly. Kent is
best known for his contribution to the characteristic formation of the "English Garden." As a painter in the tradition
which Hogarth challenged, he is hardly worth Hogarth's
scorn, obviously more a personal antagonism than an esthetic judgment. For £60, Kent had done an altarpiece for a
London church, which its parishioners urged the Bishop of
London to get removed. It depicted a heavenly choir—five
seraphs attended by a crowd of cherubs with the Holy Ghost
as the usual dove. Hogarth caricatured it cruelly, and added
injury to insult by his verbal interpretation. Six years later
he repeated "Burlington Gate" with signal changes: there is
now a builder's scaffold; the noble proprietor and *arbiter
elegantiae* is shinning up a ladder, while grotesque little
Pope, in a tie-wig too big for him, is busy on the scaffold
whitewashing the stones of his patron's Gate, the whitewash
bespattering the passers-by beneath, notably Chandos and
Buckingham. The boss over these laborers at the temple of
taste is still William Kent; with palette and pencil in hand

he directs their labors. This time Burlington was so offended as to have the print suppressed.

Hogarth's scorn of Kent and the "connoisseurs" came with his judgment that his butts prostituted the Great Tradition, while pretending to honor and serve it. He believed that the "line of grace and beauty" was the Tradition's living essence. He described it in the Preface to the *Analysis* as "an old acquaintance of painters," who yet could no more account for what it was and how it works than "a day laborer who constantly uses the lever" could account for "that machine as a mechanical power." He invoked the authority of Leonardo and Michelangelo on its behalf. He embodied the latter's advice to a young painter—as reported by Lomazzo in his *Trattato della Arte della Pittura*—to make his figures pyramidal or serpentine, in the symbol (a serpentine S inside a pyramid) which decorates the title-page of the *Analysis*. Hogarth hoped, by stirring up for "the line" the attention it deserves, "to fix the fluctuating ideas of taste," ideas in the context of which the so ancient and obvious truth of "the line" has been a mystery and a puzzle. It needed only such a simple, obvious gesture as Columbus' in standing an egg on end to abolish the mystery and solve the puzzle; and the ticket, which Hogarth issued to the readers who subscribed to the *Analysis*, shows Columbus standing his egg. Nature, which has no lines, is nevertheless the seat and energy of the beauty-breeding line. All existences can generate or evoke it. Contrary to Jonathan Richardson,* none calls for improve-

---

* Richardson, a painter and man of letters of Swift's generation, and author of a guidebook to Italian art, was an exponent of the way of thinking about the arts which based itself on Aristotle's *Poetics*. This conceived art as an imitation perfecting rather than revealing actual nature. It rationalized the taste of the times in the Enlightenment's characteristic metaphysics of nature's perfections that Pope versified. No doubt Hogarth had in mind Richardson's *Art of Criticism*, *Science of a Connoisseur*, and *Theory of Painting*. Their author was also the butt of one of Hogarth's very rare Swift-like caricatures. To show up the pretensions of the connoisseurs, he even participated in counterfeiting prints in the style of Rembrandt, selling them to a pupil of Richardson's as authentic works of the Dutch master's and then exposing the victim as critic at a dinner paid for out of the profits of the forgery.

ment, none needs be rendered better or nobler than they are. That practice, à la Italianate Kent and the "connoisseurs," prostitutes and degrades the arts. Their function is to render "nature unimproved." As Hogarth wrote in a brief account of himself and his ways and works: "I grew so profane as to admire nature beyond the first productions of art . . . that . . . I could not help uttering blasphemous expressions against the divinity even of Raphael Urbino, Correggio, and Michaelangelo."

His blasphemies are graphic, too. In the series, "Marriage à la Mode," he decorates the walls of the Countess' bedroom with oversize Italian paintings, among them an erotic of Correggio's. Early in 1745 the soi-disant blasphemer decided to offer all his available works for sale at auction. To be admitted to the sale, bidders were to show tickets for which Hogarth had composed an epic battle between his own productions and those of the corrupters of the Great Tradition of the Italian renaissance. He entitled the design "The Battle of the Pictures"; in remembrance, perhaps, and in challenge of Swift's *Battle of the Books* published almost half a century before. For the catalogue of an exhibition at the Society of the Arts of Great Britain in May, 1761, where Hogarth showed seven canvases (three portraits, "The Lady's Last Stake," "Calais Gate," "The Entertainment" [from the "Election" series] and "Sigismunda"), he designed a frontispiece and a tailpiece. The latter consists of a winking ape in fashionable dress, watering three pots of withered blooms labelled "exoticks." He derides the tradition among "connoisseurs" that the older a canvas the more important it is, in what he had intended should be another subscription ticket (for his "Sigismunda") "Time Smoking a Picture." We see Father Time, bearded, winged, his scythe at hand, with an oversize varnish pot beside him, darkening a picture by puffing tobacco smoke over it. After James Stuart and Nicholas Revett announced their significant study, *The Antiquities of Athens Measured and De-*

lineated, Hogarth parodied the enterprise with his Five Orders of Periwigs, proposing to do for wigs and hairdressing what the authors had done for the works of the Athenians.

There are those who would trace the phases of Hogarth's stand in the battle of the ancients and the moderns over pictures and books to his hatred of Kent, and would attribute his hatred of Kent to his unsuccessful emulation of Kent as an English heir to the Italian renaissance. A plausible argument could be made, but its premise would at best be a half-truth. Kent succeeded as a painter to fashion, a favorite of the gentry, but not as an original artist with an authentic individuality of his own. Hogarth was, from his beginning, an original with a high capacity for *Einfuhlung*, a capacity for being what he was seeing: as he wrote, "mimickry was remarkable in me." His vision was an interplay of sensory, intellectual, and moral perception, spontaneously mingling its lights with his instinct of workmanship. The line of grace and beauty to him, was the line of their action; at its best, the gradient of excellence in technique and understanding where, aware or unaware, the masters of all the ages shaped their designs. The abstraction of that line, its verbalization, was a slow achievement of Hogarth's. Perhaps it began with the handling of engravers' tools during his apprenticeship; it could well have been reinforced by his contemplation of Sir James Thornhill's frescoes in the dome of St. Paul's Cathedral and the walls of the Painted Hall of Greenwich Palace—the first, symbolic expressions of Christian faith; the second, of pagan freedom; both done with a verve and energy uncommon in English baroque. To young Hogarth, undersized son of a poor schoolmaster and literary hack, nephew of a song writer, apprentice to a silver engraver, confronting day-in-day-out the strugglers and strays of the unkempt places that were his London mostly, these expressions of his teacher and father-in-law-to-be, at the moment England's greatest painter, so grand in manner and rich in historical theme, were invocation to that perduring great tradition they exemplified. Hogarth said of them: they "ran in my head."

But that run was away from the native direction of his vision toward alien forms and alien themes; and that which he saw of those foreign forms and themes in the composition of his contemporaries, he judged a corruption of the art and a degradation of the tradition. He must have felt John Gay's *The Beggar's Opera* to be an effective blow for both. Partly for patrons who wanted prints, partly to scratch some dark inward itch, he engraved five different scenes from it—some of them satires on what had itself been conceived and enacted as a satire. *The Beggar's Opera* was the work of Pope and Swift's fellow Scriblerus, John Gay. Swift had at one time suggested that he write a "Newgate pastoral." After George II and his masterful wife, Caroline, were crowned king and queen of England, Gay, disappointed in his expectations of preferment, translated the idea of a pastoral into the idea of an opera. Musical plays, in the Italian language with Italian singers, fat *castrati* and less fat *cantatrices*, had become so much the fashion in the early decades of the eighteenth century, that German composers (Handel, for example) found it good to write operas to be sung in Italian by Italian singers, even on such a theme as Richard I, King of England. In the opera this hero was *Riccardo Primo Re d' Inghlittera*, and his role was sung by a very famous *castrato*. Gay transposed the noble monarch into a noble highwayman, and the aristocracy of court and field into the whores, fences, pimps, and cozeners of the Newgate scene; English their tongue, tunes from English country dances and English ballads their music, satirical hit after hit at the Whigs in high places, ruling the Kingdom obbligato across the plot. Of course, like all innovations, Gay's opera was resisted, not for its political satire which was *de cove-nance*, but for its form and content and its commentary on the corrupt prevailing taste. Once staged, "Mr. Gay's new

English opera" ran from the end of January through the first week in March, 1728.

It was this commentary, regardless of its Tory prejudices, which suited Hogarth. But among his prints are his own satires upon the Tory satire—where the principals figure as cats and dogs and bull, while an ass is braying. The succession of commentaries on the taste of the age, from *Burlington Gate* on, are diversified championing of the same cause. But deep down, it was Hogarth's heart's desire to stand as the acknowledged English vindicator of the Great Tradition against its English betrayers. *The Analysis of Beauty* was one work of vindication. His "historical" compositions were the others. He tells in his autobiography how temerariously he gave up his so successful metier and "commenced history painter." He commenced, not on commision, nor to sell in the dealers' market, but to make a gift, a gift of "sublime" images from "history" to St. Bartholomew's Hospital. They are canvases, not frescoes, set on the main staircase there. The subject of one is "The Good Samaritan," of the other, "The Pool of Bethesda." The figures are greater than life-size—seven feet high—undersized Hogarth declared proudly. The compositions, as the themes required, contain the sick and suffering as well as the whole and healing, but the latter do not gain from comparison with the former. Neither do the figures of Paul and Felix in the panel "Paul before Felix," nor of Moses and the Egyptian princess in the panel "Moses Brought before Pharaoh's Daughter." The figures which Hogarth painted for the church of St. Mary's Redcliffe in Bristol fell short of that to which Hogarth so deeply aspired—the "sublime" quality he saw in the productions of the Great Tradition. For the Bristol altar-piece, however, Hogarth received a fee of £545, and no one petitioned that it should be removed. It would seem that the themes he himself chose left him cold. Whatever may have been his religion, these themes touched neither his head nor his heart.

Although he undoubtedly had the knowledge and the skill to do so, he did not make these compositions come alive (Fielding said of his figures that they not only seemed to breathe, but also to think) as he did those on which his fame is based.

The contrast becomes poignant when we turn to a painting, not conceived in the categories "history" or the "sublime," which is an achievement in the Great Tradition of Hogarth's desire. This is the portrait of Captain Thomas Coram, a strong, brave, and tender heart, who, having returned to England from Massachusetts Bay Colony, North America, was so stirred by the common sight of abandoned infants living and dead, along walls of London town, that in 1720 he started a campaign to salvage the new-born in a Foundling Hospital. In 1739 the Hospital was at long last granted a Royal Charter of Incorporation. Hogarth, whose love of children and feeling for the actualities of childhood is manifest wherever they figure in his works, was one of Coram's staunchest supporters, and he was listed in the Hospital's charter as a "Governor and Guardian." To signalize its establishment, he painted a portrait of the chief Founder, a commoner of the age and the time. But now Hogarth's whole being was in empathic relation to the theme: Captain Coram is all there now, breathing and thinking; his portrait attains what the painter's sacred compositions fall so short of. The artist said of it that he had painted it with greatest pleasure, and desired that it should be excellent. He gave it to the Hospital as a gift in remembrance of Coram's years of endeavor on behalf of the nameless babes.

The picture of Thomas Coram was done three or four years after the canvases installed at St. Bartholomew's. In the interim Hogarth had worked on the themes and in the style which the tradition calls Hogarthian. After the dozen and more years since the portrait of Captain Coram was painted, there was an analogous reversion. This was the period of, among other "conversation pieces," "Marriage à la Mode," "Industry and Idleness," "Beer Street," "Gin Lane,"

"Calais Gate," "Four Stages of Cruelty." It was when the period was almost half over that Hogarth painted himself, his dog, and his challenging palette which *The Analysis of Beauty* interpreted with such controversial effects eight years later. Only after the publication of *Four Prints of an Election* did the commission to do the Bristol altarpiece turn his attention again to sacred history and the grand style. The year after, 1757, friends got Hogarth appointed "serjeant-painter of all his Majesty's works." The post had been held by his brother-in-law, John Thornhill, until he died, and before that by his father-in-law, Sir James. Hogarth's stipend was £10 a year.

Now in his sixtieth year, Hogarth was at the height of his success. But the divergence between his acknowledged excellence and his emulative ideal was more than he could accept. The worm gnawed; he had to make one more try. Two years later he told his friends that he would undertake a "last oil"—of course, in the grand style of historical painting.

There were two last oils: the first "The Lady's Last Stake" and the second, the much and unjustly abused "Sigismunda." This heroine of a tale of Boccaccio's (retold by John Dryden) was to be so portrayed as to disclose the proclaimed master of only laughter, the master of tears as well. Hogarth would draw tears from the viewers; he would do with vision what actors do with speech. He says he did what he set out to do: "Sigismunda did bring tears to the eyes of women viewing it." The subject was, like "The Lady's Last Stake," Hogarth's own choice. Both canvases were painted as commisions from noble lords with no stipulation regarding theme or composition. Those were for the painter to decide. "Sigismunda" may well have come to Hogarth's mind as the complement of the virtuous young wife, who, having lost her money and jewels to the officer she was gambling with, must choose to stake going to bed with him against winning them back, or losing her valuables but keeping her honor. Is her dilemma tragic? Is it comic? How the onlooker responds to the sight of her deliberating will decide. "Sigismunda," however, has already made her choice and is suffering its consequences. Hogarth meant her to impart deeply the tears of life, its tragic sense—tears without laughter—and he strove, with all his art to this end. Then, before the picture was completed, the noble lord advised him it was too sad to have around, and he didn't want it. After the exhibition of May, 1761, the entire rabble of Grub Street used it as a cat-o-nine-tails against the painter and his philosophy of art. They made a joke of it: the humorist pretending to tragedy could be only farcical; and the wilder and more fantastic their derision, the more vital the painting became to Hogarth's image of himself as artist. Whether or no he felt entirely certain that "Sigismunda" was another apex of "the great style of history painting," he directed his wife (whose features the mourning heroine was said to bear) not to sell it for less than £500. After she died, it was sold for less than £60. A fresh examination of the painting by moderns, with the modern feeling for color and design, and unprejudiced by its history, might bring some justification to Hogarth's regard for this work of his.

But the scorn and derision it was greeted with seems to have wounded him beyond healing. "Sigismunda" became, in fact, his "last oil." His production the few remaining years of his life consisted of defenses of his work and vision against more formidable detractors than he had ever before confronted. One was the same John Wilkes who became a symbol of the successful struggle against government interference with freedom of print and speech which marked the reign of George III. A political opportunist with a face that was itself a caricature, Wilkes was, from 1757, a member of the House of Commons from a rotten borough. Rake, bon vivant and charmer, he boasted he could "talk away" his face in half an hour. He and Hogarth were both members of a Shakespeare Club—they may even have been friends— that met weekly under the presidency of Hogarth's close friend, the actor David Garrick. Wilkes was disappointed in his desire for preferment from the new monarch, and with the elder Pitt joined the monarch's "loyal" Opposition. He launched the Opposition's journal, *The North Briton*, and put his close friend, the renegade but not unfrocked Episcopal priest, Charles Churchill, in charge. The two teamed up against Hogarth.

It could be argued that they entered the war against him unwillingly; that Hogarth asked for it. Certainly, in what concerns freedom of thought and utterance, the three were of the same kidney. But after "Sigismunda," Hogarth felt that he had suffered a setback in public esteem which must be overcome; that he must engrave a plate to win back the lost ground. The theme, he felt, would need to have an instant relevancy, and what could be more instant than the state of the nation and the role of government and Opposition in the country's plight? As it happened, this plight was imperial abroad: Britannia had come to rule the waves; the United Kingdom had become the preponderant power in Europe; most of North America and India had been brought under British rule. But at home, the autocratic propensities of George III and the disposition of the Tory government to gratify them kept the liberty of utterance and conscience, as Thomas Paine well knew, live issues. Where license and libel began and liberty ended depended on who was saying what about whom. For Wilkes and Churchill there was no determinable boundary.

Hogarth, heartsick and angry over the reception of "Sigismunda," afraid of having lost ground and income and desiring to recover both, saw in the ways and works of the Opposition an occasion for a dutiful intervention by the king's serjeant-painter which would restore the artist to his rightful place. In the face of warnings from Wilkes that factional politics was an unworthy field for him, Hogarth produced his first intentionally political cartoon, "The Times." It portrays a city on fire, the blaze spreading toward a great building identified by the sign of the Globe, which is already aflame. Firemen, signifying her Majesty's ministers, are at work with buckets and a fire engine with a leaky hose trying to put the fire out. But William Pitt on stilts keeps it going with a pair of bellows, and a faceless person, from a window of "Temple Coffee House," squeezes the stream from a giant syringe on the firemen below. There are other, secondary symbols, but the prime fable is in the fire.

Wilkes retaliated on behalf of his patrons in number XVII of the *North Briton*. He flayed Hogarth as man and as artist: as man he was envious, vain, greedy, bad-tempered, and intolerant; and as artist he could see only the ignoble aspects of life and admittedly was skilful at portraying them. But when he left this metier he became simply ridiculous. He had left it with "Sigismunda," of which he was so vain-gloriously proud; he had worked hard and long at it—only to produce a dull, unhuman figure. As the *supposed* author of the *Analysis of Beauty*, he has shown that his merits as a writer are as non-existent as the merits of the painter of "Sigismunda."

Wilkes' cat-o'-nine-tails cut Hogarth to the heart. The mob of Grub Street hacks, that sought to better Wilkes' example, he scarcely heeded. But Wilkes had struck to Hogarth's ultimate faith; and hurt as he was, Hogarth slashed back. The opportunity came with the publication of number XLV of the *North Briton* wherein Wilkes committed *lese majesté*. On "general warrants" for the arrest of writers, printers, and publishers of the issue, Wilkes was apprehended and sent to the Tower. Soon after, appearing before the Chief Justice of England, the latter freed him on the ground of immunity as a member of the House of Commons. Whereupon the Commons expelled him, but the Chief Justice then declared general warrants illegal. Hogarth attended on Wilkes' first day in court, sketching his cruel enemy. A few weeks later he issued, at a shilling a print, a too true representation of the concentrated devilish ugliness

of the new champion of Magna Charta *malgré lui*, whose
release by the Court had been greeted with shouts of
"Wilkes and Liberty!" Hogarth had drawn him seated, with
Nos. XVIII and XLV of the *North Briton* at his feet. Wilkes
got into a variety of personal troubles, including a duel (in
which he was wounded) and the publication of the priapic
Essay on Woman. For this and other reasons Wilkes was
outlawed and went abroad, he thought, for life. Two years
after Hogarth's death the House of Commons declared general warrants illegal, but the lords refused to concur. Wilkes
returned home, was elected the following year to the Commons and shortly thereafter was expelled for libelling another
noble lord. At once re-elected, he was again expelled. This
happened three times. He kept coming back, trying to have
the vote against him expunged. It was not until the sixth try,
in 1782, that he succeeded: his rejection was stricken from
the record "as subversive of the rights of electors."

By 1782 Hogarth had been dead a generation. His counter
to Wilkes had greatly angered Charles Churchill, whose
roles were ever being crossed by venereal disease. But in
midsummer of 1763 he had published his *Epistle to William
Hogarth*, repeating in sharper verse the characterization that
Wilkes had made in sharp prose, excoriating his victim for
"Sigismunda," for mixing into politics, ascribing both to
senile dementia. To this Hogarth had retorted with an image
of Churchill. He composed it as he had composed his own
portrait in 1745. Within the oval frame, he put the figure of
a bear in ragged clericals, a pot of beer before him, his hands
on a heavy, fifteen-knobbed club, the knobs numbered Lye 1
to Lye 15. The oval frame rests on *A List of Subscribers to
the North Briton* and *A New Way to Pay Old Debts*, a
comedy by Massinger. In the foreground is Trump, Churchill's *Epistle* under his paws, sending a stream of urine across
the title page. Hogarth labelled the image: *The Bruiser C.
Churchill* (once the Rev'd.) *in the Character of a Russian
Hercules, Regaling himself after having kill'd the Monster*

caricatura *that so Sorely Gall'd his* Virtuous *friend*, the Heaven born *Wilkes*.

For practical purposes this was the last of Hogarth's topical creations. The vendetta lapsed. The vision and the will to utter the vision subsided. Hogarth lived on, remembering, anxious, self-regarding. He kept retouching earlier work, notably his portrayal of himself. In the final one—*William Hogarth*, 1764—he shows himself palette knife in one hand, palette and brushes in the other, unsmiling, strained, before a picture of the Muse of Comedy that he is still painting, for the picture is unfinished. But its painter, so he must be feeling, is finished: he is meditating on *The End of all Things*. He has told his friends that this would be his next undertaking; in terms of a philosophy of existence and value it was also his last. It is the composition known as "The Bathos." It is said that Hogarth designed it to be the tailpiece in his collected prints but he may as well have meant it for the tailpiece of his lifelong struggle to keep struggling on the gradient of his line of grace and beauty, toward the supreme attainment of the great style of history painting. The center of the picture is Father Time, half-seated, half reclining, a too-small wing rigid, against a shattered column, at his feet a print of *The Times* being consumed in the flame of a fallen candle. His eyes are closed, the blade of his scythe is broken, his hourglass is smashed, a clay pipe is falling from his left hand, and *Finis* is in the smoke that issues from his mouth. From his right hand dangles a copy of his will that appoints Chaos his "sole Executor." Before him is a falling signpost marked "The World's End"; the sign is a globe aflame. Behind it is the tumble-down tavern with the leafless branches of a dead tree beyond. Above, the exhausted horses of the Sun God are slipping from the sky, the god himself is fallen back in his chariot. On the earth beneath far off, a man hanging from a gallows, then a withered tree. Around dying Time, a gravestone, a broken bow, a crown, a cracked palette, a broken gun, a cracked bell, and many other suggestions of disillusion and defeat.

Bathos is a Greek word. Its first meaning is depth as the first meaning of *Hupos* is height. But physical height and depth soon get transposed into moral loftiness and meanness, esthetic sublimity and ridiculousness, with their suggestions of tears and laughter. In due course, *Bathos* came to signify any utterance that being flat and empty, turgid, and bombastic would evoke laughter. Hogarth's explanation of this title of his last engraving appears, on the face of it, designed to have the work seen as his last blow at the dealers, connoisseurs, and artists whom all his life he crusaded against as foes of true beauty. *The Bathos or Manner of Sinking, in Sublime Paintings, inscribed to the Dealers in Dark Pictures*, Hogarth's explanation proceeds, is published to deride the "*manner of disgracing ye most Serious Subjects, in many celebrated Old Pictures, by introducing low, absurd, obscene & often profane circumstances into them.* And he reaffirms his esthetic creed with two small figures in the margin of the print—one "*the conic form in wch the Goddess of Beauty was worship^d—at Paphos in ye Island of Cyprus, the other "A Copy of the precise Line of Beauty as it is represented in the 1st explanatory Plate of the Analysis of Beauty . . . .* Had Hogarth read the Scriblerian Περι βαθους, that cynical commentary by Swift, Pope, and Arbuthnot on their own age's "art of making poetry" which has its analogies to Hogarth's anything but cynical judgment on the age's art of making pictures? Was *The Bathos* a recollection of this satire, and perhaps of Pope's *Dunciad* as well? Some think it was, and it may have been. But if they are right, the values Hogarth defended by this means were the inverse of the satirists': they were the integrity of the creative vision, the freedom and independence of the authentic artist as the spokesman of his vision, without penalty and without privilege, as a help to his fellow-man.

The Bathos was issued for sale March 3, 1764. Seven months later Hogarth was dead. Was it an acknowledgment of his own personal failure and disillusion? Was it the reaffirmation of his fighting faith as man and artist confronting failure and disillusion? Whose is the *Bathos?* Whose the *Finis?* Whose are the tears and whose is the last laugh? Certainly in the history of the graphic arts, Hogarth's rivals and foes get their significance far less from what they were and did than from their relation to him. His friend David Garrick wrote the epitaph one can read on the monument his friends erected to him at Church Yard at Chiswick:

> *Farewell, great painter of mankind,*
> *Who reach'd the noblest point of Art;*
> *Whose pictur'd morals charm the mind,*
> *And through the eye correct the heart.*
> *If* genius *fire thee, reader, stay.*
> *If* nature *touch thee, drop a tear;*
> *If neither moves thee, turn away*
> *For* Hogarth's *honoured dust lies here.*

CHAPTER THIRTEEN

Voltaire: Jean Qui Pleure et Qui Rit

THE *HOMO SAP* of the British Isles whom Hogarth portrayed, Pope derided, and Swift lampooned was the same that Voltaire admired for the freedom of his institutions and the decency of his way of life. The Englishmen's Yahoos and dunces were the Frenchman's members of a free society of free men. Among them he counted Pope and Swift, with whom he duly became acquainted, to say nothing of Bolingbroke, whom Voltaire met after the latter's flight to France. It could well be that Voltaire's judgment of England, the land of his first exile, drew less upon how he lived and what he saw and heard there, than upon his experiences in France—the land of his birth from which its rulers kept him exiled most of his eighty-four years. He was only thirty-two when the bosses of his homeland confronted him with an alternative: either exile to England or the Bastille of France. Having already enjoyed the Bastille twice, he chose England. His first sojourn in the royal keep had been required soon after Louis XIV died. The monarch's heir, the dauphin, was only five years old; a vicar was *de rigeur* until the prince might in his turn be crowned king. Philip, duke of

Orleans, received the vicarage. Officially titled Regent, he
initiated a regime that for extravagance and debauchery
improved upon Le Roi Soleil's best example. Resentment
quickly spread and mounted; but only ridicule, not effective
force, could be used to vent it. Young François Marie Arouet was a voice of that catharsis. Apropos of the court's
pretending to economize by selling half the horses in the
Grand Monarque's stables, the youth was heard to say that
dismissing half the asses in the royal court would have been
more economical. Among the verses circulated were stanzas
entitled *Les j'ai vu* and among the things the author claimed
to have seen were tax-exactions and jailings without rhyme
or reason. Young Arouet had the honor of being charged
with writing the verses. The Regent couldn't laugh with the
laughers; "I'll show him something he never has seen" he is
reputed to have threatened. And Arouet, although not the
author, was shown the Bastille. He had a year of confinement there, and it was there that he took the name Voltaire.
He beguiled the time writing plays and poems, among them
the *Henriade*, in which he resumed what he had already
done in his *Epistle to Uranie*, muckraking the Church and its
churchmen. The poem's ostensible theme is the life of King
Henri IV, its covert one is churchly superstition, fanaticism,
intolerance, and covetousness concentrating in the massacre
of St. Bartholomew's Eve. Voltaire dedicated the poem to
the boy Louis XV, urging its hero as the model of kingship.
Naturally, *Henriade* didn't pass the censor. It had to be
secretly printed—and was. When, luckily, the Regent died,
the poem was put on public sale. It became a success in the
salons. Elsewhere it was praised as J. B. Rousseau praised
the *Epistle to Uranie* to the Dutch widow, Mme. de Rupel-
monde: "What terrible profanity!"

Voltaire's second spell in the Bastille followed his alterca-
tion with the powerful and pusillanimous Duc de Rohan. In
the interval, his *Oedipe* had made him famous, his *Artemise*
had failed, he had begun his lasting quarrel with the ex-

priest Desfontaines. His father (whom he had disappointed by refusing the respectable and safe career of the law) had died; and the son had become a conspicuous man-about-town—a frequenter of the court and the salons, a gourmet of the theatre and a composer of fluent verses. At polite gatherings he was entertaining enough to receive the precedence which protocol required for hereditary rank. It was at a soirée of this sort that de Rohan, ignored while Voltaire was surrounded by mostly female admirers, asked with offensive loudness, "*Who* is that young man?" The young man, recognizing the offensive purpose, retorted, "One who bears no great name, but wins respect for the name he bears." For which the inheritor of a great name had the maker of one beaten up, and the latter undertook to vindicate his self-making by repeatedly challenging the former to meet him on the field of honor. Of course, no nobleman could possibly stain his congenital honor by duelling with a commoner; certainly not the brave de Rohan. Since the noble lord's bullies couldn't stop the persistent young poet, their employer procured an always available *lettre de cachet* and got young Voltaire back into the Bastille. By then, the youth had had enough of the Bastille. He managed to get out after a fortnight. Not that he had suffered a bad time in the prison: on the contrary, its governor often invited him to his table, strings of callers brought him books and gossip, and he composed verses. But he wanted his freedom and petitioned to be released and permitted to go to England. The petition was granted and one of the keepers was assigned to accompany the prisoner to Calais and make sure that he did take ship. He landed at Greenwich early in May, 1726.

There is an oft-repeated cliché that Voltaire had gone to England a poet and returned to France a philosopher. As Archibald Ballantyne tells the tale of Voltaire's "Visit to England," the truth is rather that the visit disclosed to him how the liberties of thought and person, enjoyed as privileges among free-thinking clericals and Jesuit-educated aristocrats in the salon of old Ninon de l'Enclos, could be recognized as rights among the noblemen and commoners of England. Voltaire's godfather, the worldly-wise-man, Abbé de Chateauneuf, being a friend of the great *hetaira*, early brought his godson to her (she left the boy a legacy of 2000 francs to buy books). His schooling by the Jesuits of the College de St. Louis le Grand seems not to have been out of harmony with his education at Ninon's. He was a prize scholar who could, at fifteen, nevertheless be welcome at the epicurean suppers of the libertine Temple and its abbé president. Young François Marie's way of life and learning troubled his father. So, his godfather being four years dead, Arouet senior sent his precocious son to serve at the French embassy in the Hague, where the godfather's brother, the Marquis de Chateauneuf, was ambassador. But a change of tutelage and place was no occasion for change of ways. François Marie's entanglement with his Pimpette looked like a much more serious *affaire* than any of his earlier ones. Being sent back to his father made no difference. Arouet père took the drastic step of threatening Arouet fils with *la lettre de cachet*. This was Voltaire's introduction to the Bastille as *idea*. But for the time it stayed only idea. After months of tugging and pulling, father and son were reconciled. Another year, Louis XIV died and events soon made the idea of the Bastille the fact of the Bastille. The line of faith and reason from the French salon of Ninon to the coffee houses, the clubs, and the manors of London's Tories, Whigs and wits is a straight one. There is no article of faith in Voltaire's *English Letters* but has its prelude in the *Epistle to Uranie*.

At the time of his arrival in England, the Frenchman knew no English. On his return to France, three years less than two months later, he declared it troubling to write in French again; he had become "almost accustomed to think in English." This, without flattery, in the dedication of his

Brutus to Bolingbroke, the first act of which he had indeed composed in English prose. Voltaire was living at the time—with interludes away in the great houses like Bolingbroke's, or Peterborough's, or Chesterfield's—with merchant Falkener, his English friend, at Wandsworth, where French refugees were forming a sort of colony. With the help of his titled acquaintances, he got around. He failed to meet Newton alive—the immortal died the following year—but he saw Newton dead, lying in state in Westminster Abbey; and he visited Mrs. Conduit, the immortal's niece and he had many talks with his friend and follower, Clarke. He met George Berkeley and John Gay; he visited Pope and became acquainted with Swift. The former impressed him by his style rather than his ideas; the latter he designated "one of the most extraordinary men England has produced," "a priest and mocked at everything," "Rabelais in his senses." England's stage absorbed the Frenchman but he also sought contact with every sort and condition of Englishman from actors to bishops, noblemen to tradesmen, politicians to boatmen. He was introduced at Court. After eighteen months in the land, he was able to write history and criticism in English, and to translate so peculiarly English a poem as *Hudibras* into French. This, about the same time that Hogarth made twelve engravings to illustrate the epic caricature. The Frenchman also prepared an English edition of *Henriade* which Swift pushed in Ireland; and he wrote his *English Letters*.

Although addressed to his lifelong friend and confidential man of affairs, Theriot, these letters are obviously intended for all France. They are an account of the English conduct of life as the ways and works of a free society of free men. They are the representative articulation of a philosophic faith that their author repeats again and again—each time differently in his plays, his tales, his essays, and his verses. True, his works are not objective; they but exemplify and project Voltaire's own measure of the things of mankind.

His appreciation of "nobles who cultivate literature," his judgments of Shakespeare, of Pope "and other famous poets," and his animadversions on comedy and tragedy can hardly be accepted as in keeping with the philosophy of liberty which he declares guides the English in their ways. "An Englishman who knows France well," he declared, "and a Frenchman who knows England well, are both the better for it." But above all, whereas the French know how to please, the English know how to think: "In this country it is possible to use one's mind freely and nobly, without fear and cringing. If I followed my own inclination, I should stay here, if only to learn how to think." It is the British philosophical outlook, not the British arts and letters that Voltaire would emulate, and indeed he did. Francis Bacon was to him the father of experimental philosophy; John Locke the wisest of human beings; Isaac Newton "he who revealed God to sages." Commenting on Swift's allegorical cryptogram, *A Tale of a Tub*, the Frenchman exclaimed, "How I love English daring! How I love people who say what they think! We only half live if we dare only half think!"

Of course, the outburst expresses Voltaire's antipathy to the rulers of his homeland, not his observation of the land of his refuge. He thinks of English ways—in politics and religion, not the arts—in the context of his French experiences, and the former enable him to reduce the latter to derision. He believed in the unities; that is, the French observance of the Greek theory and practice of them. To this writer of tragedies, Shakespeare's virtues are buried under vices—so he said in his preface to his *Semiramis*—which render the great Elizabethan "the ruin of the English stage." An amazing genius, natural, sublime, endowed with an imagination both powerful and fecund, this Shakespeare was more creative of barbarism, of gross and heavy monstrosities, than of dramas composed duly and in good order.* Withal, as the

* He writes of what in later generations is exalted as the greatest of Shakespeare's tragedies: "Hamlet is a rude piece of barbarity which

writer brought to his countrymen an image of English liberty, so also he brought to his countrymen an image of
Shakespeare, not as reshaped by the Drydens and Popes of
the age, but with a caricature of the same play whose excellence the next generation recognized and glorified. Voltaire's
own generation did not extend to issues of art and letters its
orchestration of liberty with the rule of reason in issues of
religion and government. In arts and letters, reason was
authoritarian. It was libertarian vis-à-vis authority in church
and state.

"The English nation is the only one on earth that has
contrived to regulate the power of kings by resisting them.
By a succession of efforts it finally established this wise
system of government which leaves the prince all-powerful
to do good, but ties his hands if he wants to do ill. . . . It has
taken seas of blood to drown the idol of despotism; but the
English do not think they have bought their laws too
dearly." One effect of these dearly-bought laws is religious
toleration. Here thirty religions live together peacefully and
at ease. Voltaire finds the same sense of freedom and safety
among Unitarians and Quakers, and he thinks the Catholics
of England are much more secure than those of his own
country. "An Englishman being a free man goes to heaven
by the road of his own choice," "you do not see any imbeciles
here who put their souls in the keeping of others." Englishmen, knowing who are the French prelates that call themselves the successors of the Apostles and how they live,
"thank God that they are Protestants. But they [the English-
men] are vile heretics, fit for banning with all devils, as

---

would never be tolerated by the vilest people in France or Italy. The
prince goes mad in the second act and his mistress in the third; and he
kills the father of the mistress, feigning that he is killing a rat. The
mistress throws herself into the river. They dig her grave on the stage,
and the diggers, with skulls in hand, deal out buffoonery worthy only of
themselves, while the prince responds in kind. Hamlet and his mother
and stepfather drink together on the stage. They sing at the table, and
quarrel there, and fight and slay. It is as if the play had been born in the
imagination of a drunken savage."

Master François Rabelais said; that is why I do not mix myself up with their affairs."

Voltaire did not mix himself up with their affairs. But in the Paris of 1734 the devout successors of the Apostles had his book about the English heretics publicly burned in order to protect French orthodoxy from its heretical contamination. It had been published without his consent, his name had been put on the title page, and his "Thoughts about Pascal" had been appended; Jore, the printer and publisher, was taken to the Bastille for issuing a book "scandalous, contrary to religion, to morals and respect for authority." Its author was hunted in Paris and elsewhere, but he eluded the hunters and took asylum in Champagne at Cirey sur-Blanc, an estate belonging to the Marquis du Chatelet.

He had by then been back in France five years. Having returned secretly to take care of some business, he found that he could have his orders of exile annulled, and not only did, but also had his pensions restored. In addition, he made a smart killing at a lottery, worked on his *Charles XII*, and wrote *Brutus* (which the *Comédie* undertook to present, but dropped—not because of "de Rohan trickery" but because actors and management felt it couldn't succeed). Later they revived his *Oedipe*, with Adrienne Lecouvreur in the leading female role. It was during a performance of this play that she collapsed on the stage, and after four days of agony, she died. Voltaire had come to her lodging to help as he could, and it was in his arms that she died. An actress, no priest might shrive her, nor was she admitted to "Christian burial." This burned Voltaire up. Months after, he flared up in the *Poem on the Death of Adrienne Lecouvreur*. Its libertarian heresies made him apt for the Bastille. Although he was supposed to be back in England, actually he was in hiding at Rouen.

The image of dead Lecouvreur, denied the company of her Savior's dead because she was an actress, lived with Voltaire until he too died. He feared the same impiety to his own remains—that they "might be thrown into the gutter like poor Lecouvreur." To the end of his long life he watched to make sure of the rites, but nevertheless had to be sneaked into a Christian grave. In 1791 the National Assembly compelled Louis XVI to have the libertarian's remains transferred to the church of St. Geneviève, since then the Pantheon of France. There his fleshly residue was laid close to those of Mirabeau and Descartes. But soon after the restoration of the Bourbons it was dug up, packed in a sack, and dumped in a pit of quicklime outside Paris. In 1864 it was discovered that Voltaire's tomb had been desecrated and emptied. Fourteen years later Paris celebrated the centenary of his death, against the bitter protests of the Bishop of Orléans and with the fiery praise of Victor Hugo. Their villain-hero's remains suffered the lot he had so much feared, by their very destruction testifying to his words that mankind "will not cease to be persecutors until they have ceased to be absurd."

The lifelong interval which began with his flight to Cirey, Voltaire started as a sort of *vita nuova*, whereof the newness was the role of one woman in it. For the rest, his career of love had been as successful as any could be. He lost some battles but won his war, even in his psychosomatic struggle with his digestive and other organs. His design for living could impattern all the turnovers of his personal history without distortion: no businesslike scheme of getting something for nothing, or much for little, was too unworthy. He wanted fame; he never ceased striving to be counted among playwrights as the peer of dead Racine and Molière and the master of live Crébillon, Piron, and other contemporaries. He wrote, more correctly perhaps, he rewrote, some fifty-eight plays, many as they were being rehearsed. On the whole, this author of such numbers of tragedies and comedies was a self-conscious and facile craftsman, as the age regarded craftsmanship. But his meaning does not reach posterity because of his plays. The generations hear and

cherish him for his tales, his verses, his philosophical treatises, all affirming faith in the liberty of the human spirit, all
sharp and clean and lucid with the laughter that sets free, all
turning to ridicule the prejudice, the privilege, and power
which shackle the natural liberty of *genus humanum*. If he
schemed, with little scruple, for a safe place at court among
the hereditary nobility, if he won and held the affections of a
harem of titled ladies, on occasion even as *amant en titre*, the
affaires were not only *de convenance*, but somehow also
impatterned with his fighting faith in the free mind and the
kind heart. He was undoubtedly very vain, but who, in view
of the record, can say that it was his vanity more than this
faith and its laughter that underlay his image of himself as
the guide, philosopher, and friend of monarchs and enabled
him to endure the frustrations and disappointments of that
society?

Nor can this faith be said to have been lacking in the bold
pretenses to orthodox correctness with which he endeavored
to get seated in an empty chair among the Immortals of
Richelieu's *Académie Française*. He tried several times—the
first around 1735–36. In terms of his recognized successes
—his many new plays, his rewritten *Brutus* (this ran
fifteen nights), his *History of Charles XII*—no one could
have a better claim. But then, he had been guilty of the
philosophical letters about the English. He had done some
worse than impious verses about Jeanne d'Arc which were
being slyly repeated in the salons, and he had revised his
Epistle to Uranie (who meanwhile had entered a nunnery)
and published it under the title *Le Pour et le Contre*. This
cooked Voltaire's goose with the Immortals. Attributing it to
the Abbé Chaulieu (its author even declared that he had
heard the Abbé recite it to the Epicureans of the Temple)
was no help.

And then the impulsive schemer could not resist retorting
to his jealous old rival, the still exiled J. B. Rousseau, with
The Temple of Taste, also published without the *imprima-*

tur of the censor. Rousseau had returned to his angry exaggerations about Voltaire after *Zaire's* great success, and Voltaire hit back. *The Temple of Taste* might have been suggested by Pope's *Dunciad*. It records a dialogue between the author and Cardinal Fleury as they go together to visit the Temple. The story is part prose, part verse; it derides the works and ways of the Parisian world. One by one, the candidates for admission come under the scrutiny of the speakers, notably J. B. Rousseau. Each is gaily, sweetly, rightly, yet devastatingly put in his place. Of course, the Temple became a *succès de scandale*. "In a very short time," Voltaire wrote, "the Temple has became a Cathedral," thus a blasphemous heresy deserving the Bastille, not the *Académie*. Its author had to go into hiding, but with his yen for a seat among the Forty undiminished.

In due course, the ruling powers at Court were displaced by others; Mme. de Pompadour took over the boudoir government of France. This great hetaira appreciated Voltaire's faith and expression, was responsive to his flattery, and not unwilling to advance his interests. On the whole, the disturbed weather of his fortunes became better than fair. His Jansenist brother, dying at sixty, left him a not inconsiderable sum of money; de Pompadour got him appointed historiographer of France, with its tasks of a Laureate; and he also got commissions for plays at fetes. He flattered Pope Benedict XIV as a writer and thinker; in return he was to be addressed by his Holiness as "dear son," and presented two medals with his sacred image. Voltaire asked and received permission to dedicate his *Mahomet* to Christ's vice-regent, and he printed the play together with the letters the two had exchanged. In brief, Voltaire had won the protection of the highest authority in the church. By 1746 another Immortal was dead, another seat empty. Voltaire then did what he believed would win the place for him—averring his literary correctness, his religious orthodoxy, and his cordial appreciation of the Jesuits. He was elected. His salutatory address a couple of weeks later disclosed that neither immortality nor sonship to his holiness had changed the faith or blunted the wit of the new academician.

To avoid the turmoil caused by the *Temple du Goût*, Voltaire had taken refuge in the houses, great and small, of various friends, mostly ladies. Although a fugitive from a *lettre de cachet*, he was busy as ever with his pen. He was still in hiding when Jore, the Rouen printer, put out those notorious letters—"philosophical, political, critical, poetical, heretical and diabolical . . . selling in English in London with great success." The publication made it imperative for their author to get beyond the lawful reach of the *lettre de cachet*. Cirey was as far "beyond" as Voltaire really wanted to go.

The love of his life had come to him. This one and only woman was Gabrielle Emilie de Breteuil, Marquise du Chatelet, the wedded wife and mother of the children of that "bonhomme," her simple Marquis. Voltaire had met the lady first in the company of the young Duc de Richelieu who was her lover *en titre* at the time. She had admired the poet's rather poor new play, *Adelaide du Guesclin*, and in sentimental return he wrote a letter on "Calumny" to defend her reputation from scandalmongers. It was she who offered her husband's somewhat run-down estate at Cirey for a refuge. The intimacy thus begun became sixteen years of a stormy marriage of head and heart. In due course the passionate friendship calmed. Heart subsided into head and habit. By the fourteenth year of her partnership with Voltaire, Mme. du Chatelet, having lived into the dangerous age, fell passionately in love again. Her beloved this time was the Marquis de St. Laurent, a young, handsome, versifying lady's man of an officer of the guard of exiled king Stanislas of Poland, holding migratory court in the quiet little independent duchy of Lorraine. St. Laurent got Voltaire's Emilie with child, a girl who died shortly after birth in the arms of a peasant wet nurse of the village of Cirey, and not long after was joined in the grave by her mother. Unsuspecting, Voltaire had come upon his lady and her swain *in flagrante delicto*. Deeply pained, he was able nevertheless to recognize the reasonableness of his Emilie's protestations that he had long ceased to love her in the flesh, that they were living together all passion spent, that she had to have someone, and whom more acceptably than the charming friend of both, the Marquis de St. Laurent. Something like a *menage à trois* took shape. But first that bonhomme M. du Chatelet was brought home. When he left, he was sure he was the unborn child's only begetter. He returned to his affairs proud and complaisantly tangent as ever to the Cirey household. Star-studying Emilie, wrote Voltaire—now the platonic lover—in some verses he addressed to St. Laurent one day in 1749, had turned from the stars to "those beautiful airs which love repeats and Newton never knew." Had she not told her youthful paramour "I do not even love Newton, only you!"? Nevertheless, she had directed that all her papers should be burned. Only the metaphysics she had worked at with Voltaire was saved from the flames.

"Newton" was a love she shared with Voltaire. Not a little of their life together was given to producing popularizations of the *Principia*, to exposing the fallacies of Fontenelle's *Plurality of Worlds* by opposing the simple Newtonian deistic monism to the sacerdotally-favored dualism of Descartes. They performed for themselves Newtonian experiments; they corrected the errors they found in Algarotti's *Newtonianism for Ladies*, and they composed their *Elements of Newton's Philosophy*. They had made Newton entertaining and this, Voltaire commented, makes Newtonianism available to everybody. In Voltaire's French, the expression was, *Mis à la Portée* to *Tout le Monde*." The censor had forbidden the book; the knowing ones among clericals and Cartesians had attacked it bitterly. Voltaire was saying that it was both being put at everybody's door and being shown the door (mis à la portée) by everybody.

"It is," he observed, "dangerous to be right in things on which the powerholders are wrong."

The exposition of Newton was only one item of Voltaire's day's work at Cirey. Not a little of his time and money—he had acquired a great deal; by 1738 his income amounted to the equivalent of some $25,000 a year—was given to reconstructing the wilderness-ruin Cirey had been when he first found asylum there. And of course, he was ever busy at his plays and poems. He wrote, among other things, his *Death of Caesar* (to show how much he could better Shakespeare's Julius Caesar), *Alzire, The Prodigal Son; Boursouffle*. In part to amuse himself and his Emilie, perhaps more largely to *épater les clercs*, he composed *La Pucelle*, which makes both wild, sly, bold fun of her who is now St. Joan and of her reputed chastity; he composed *Le Mondain*, which defends civilization against primitivism by showing Adam and Eve in the Garden of Eden with interests other than the animal ones of feeding and copulating, and detailing—more à la John Milton than Henry Miller—the modes of both. Civilization is a humanization of animal-like man in the course of which *le superflu* becomes *chose si nécessaire*. Both *La Pucelle* and *Le Mondain* circulated in manuscript among the poet's friends, and *Le Mondain* was the first to be pirated and printed. Authority, as might have been expected, was officially shocked at the image of Adam and Eve copulating in Eden; it condemned the whole poem as a blasphemy. The censor was called upon. Voltaire was warned and sadly he fled Cirey, leaving his sadder, divine Emilie behind. He visited and was enthusiastically welcomed at Brussels, at Antwerp, at Leyden, at Amsterdam. All the while, Emilie implored him to return to her. He gave out that he was going to England, and he returned to Cirey. ". . . Madame du Chatelet is more to me than father, mother or son." But he wrote both a defense of *Le Mondain* and a separate broadside against its critics.

To Cirey came also an emissary of the then Prince Frederick of Prussia, with the prince's picture and philosophical productions. Voltaire and Emilie made a holiday of the visit, and young Kaiserling had cantos of *La Pucelle* and a chapter of *Louis XIV* read to him and witnessed his master's name displayed and praised in fireworks as "the hope of the human race." Kaiserling wanted copies of *La Pucelle* to take to his prince, but this Emilie would not permit. An exchange of letters with the would-be philosopher-king began, with Frederick declaring there was "one God and one Voltaire," and Voltaire talking about "the right divine of kings to govern wrong." When the Prince was crowned Frederick II, Voltaire addressed him as "Your Humanity," not as "Your Majesty," and the latter duly sent him the manuscript of his *Anti-Machiavelli*, to be edited. Mme. du Chatelet became suspicious of the correspondence, jealous of Frederick to the point of hating him; the more so as he always kept luring Voltaire to visit him. Voltaire complied—in transit, one might say, at Moyland, at Ravensberg, at Aix-la-Chapelle— and finally came to take service with him, after Emilie died. He discovered that she was not wrong about the would-be philosopher-king who, on hearing of her death had quipped: "Here lies she who lost her life in giving birth to an unfortunate infant and a treatise on philosophy."

Meanwhile, all their life together Voltaire was a busy, busy man at play as at work. The hospitality at Cirey was unstinted, and included amateur theatricals, charades, and music—as well as readings from the author's works, old and new. The latter kept flowing from his pen—tragedies, divertissements, poems philosophical and theological, amatory and sardonic, and all his production, even the tragedies, laced with denuding yet not ungenerous laughter. Moreover, Emilie had her moods. She could get bored with even the varied routines of Cirey. She had to dress and dance as well as philosophize.

> *Son esprit est très philosophe*
> *Mais son coeur aime les pompeux.*

Voltaire wrote of her early in their intimacy. And her public repute, honor, and role as a great lady became the issue of what is known as the Affaire Desfontaines. This character was an unfrocked priest, who published a journal, *Observations on New Books*. He was charged with an obscenity for which he was sentenced to the stake. Voltaire did not know him, but hearing of the judicial abomination, got out of a sickbed to avert it. He succeeded in having the sentence reduced to banishment from Paris, and he found a friend to provide a refuge for the condemned. The latter wrote his savior a correct "thank you" letter. But his gratitude did not extend to fair criticism of the *English Letters*, and less so of the book on Newton. And when by hook and crook certain complimentary verses which Voltaire addressed to the mathematician Algarotti fell into Desfontaines' hands, he asked permission to publish them. This was some five years after Voltaire's union with the du Chatelets. The verses referred to their happy *menage à trois*, which was common knowledge—often spoken of but never, in decency, to be mentioned in print. The three principals all insisted there be no publication. But publish Desfontaines did, thereby committing an unpardonable breach of honor and decorum. It enraged Voltaire as little else only personal to him could: Emilie was Caesar's wife. An impecunious Chevalier de Menley was paid to append his signature to a piece entitled *Preservatif* which exposes item by item of some two hundred issues of *Observations on New Books*—the illiteracy, ignorance, and ineptness of their writer. Subjoined to the exposure is a letter from M. de Voltaire to the Chevalier de Menley not only detailing the circumstances of Voltaire's intervention on behalf of Desfontaines, but with epigram and caricature specifying the crime punishable with death by fire. Desfontaines hit back with a screed, *Voltaireomanie*. He sent a copy each to Emilie and her man for the Christmas of 1739, and they kept what they read secret from each other until the New Year; then they secured the catharsis of telling and talking it out. Desfontaines had, of course, called Voltaire a liar, and digging up the youthful quarrel with De Rohan, made him out a coward to boot. He claimed that he had gotten the De Rohan story from the poet's friend of many years, Theriot. The *ménage* at Cirey agreed that they must sue for libel. It took almost half of 1739 to assemble witnesses and to get Theriot to speak up. Finally the trial was held, the witnesses were heard, and the libeller was instructed to confess falsehood or be jailed. The magistrate wrote the confession for Desfontaines to sign, as he did, April 4, 1739. The struggle cost Voltaire more than money —almost a nervous breakdown; it left his Emilie with a not-to-be-denied craving for pompous fun and games. So they got away from Cirey for her to enjoy—and for Voltaire to suffer—appreciation and parties in Brussels, and even in Paris.

Voltaire was fifty-five years old when his Emilie died. During his partnership with her he made himself the richest, as well as the best-known and most widely-read man of letters of his generation, not in France alone. He had gotten himself a chair among the Immortals of the *Académie;* had displaced Descartes by Newton; had composed verses and essays that almost always achieved a *succès de scandale*, and tragedies, comedies and other theatrical pieces, many of which were welcomed at Court or produced at the *Comédie*, and which brought even into the royal court the derision with which he fought his never-relinquished fight against the regime of irresponsible power and parasitical privilege. He balked at no means; he could, on occasion be as casuistical as the slyest Jesuit and as comprehensively Tartuffian. The difference between him and them was the ultimate one: that he never concealed his motives or pretended to any other end than some innocent enough personal gain or the advancement of his faith in equal liberty for all mankind, his abominated Jews and infidels included. He deceived no one, least of all the parasites and powerholders whom his masquerades were meant to persuade. Was not so much that he wrote a sort of Aesopian language in which the thing meant was not the thing said, but yet was unmistakably conveyed by the thing said? Was the immunity from *lettres de cachet* which came with a chair among the Forty not worth taking on the role which this presumption to immortality called for? The freedom-loving and saintly mathematician, the Marquis de Condorcet, who pronounced a eulogy and wrote a biography of Voltaire, observed: "Such deceptions did not deceive, while they did protect."

In the societies of privilege and power where Voltaire changed his roles, so that he might the better arouse the laughter which liberates, he perforce lived dangerously even when his safety and well-being seemed assured. On the record, he courted the perils he would escape. He could not give up the releases which derision effected. Those satisfactions were a force in his ambiguous friendship with Frederick of Prussia, who, for a brief interlude, replaced dead Emilie as the foremost figure of the poet's company. Voltaire had tried to fill the interlude with setting up his house in the Rue Traversiere-Saint Honoré and putting his niece, Mme. Denis, in charge; with composing and circulating *Zadig* and the other *Contes* whose unmistakable *double entendre* (social and political—Voltaire never employed *double entendre* on sexual themes) that denuded the pretensions of the powerful and the privileged; and brought into their salons the *je m'en fiche* laughter of true workers at the life of "after me the deluge." He was even direct in the apothegms of *Voice of the Sage and the People.* And, as a matter of course, it all brought him into a jeopardy which even membership in the Academie did not mitigate. So, Frederick again offering fortune, fame, and fun, Voltaire decided that he would go to Italy, but go via Potsdam. As a French "gentleman in ordinary" to his king (Pompadour had wangled the title with its unearned and unearnable increments for him), he had to beg the leave that was given with irritated gladness.

The contrast between Frederick II's welcome at Sans-Souci and Louis XV's farewell at Compiègne lifted up the mourner's heart. He could be his royal friend's starred-and-gartered chamberlain, have a house of his own in Berlin, have his niece, Louise Denis, look after it at the King's expense—four thousand francs a year—and for himself, 20,000 francs a year. After a somewhat hesitating yes, there was a week's long party, with plays, music, and a "carrousel" in which Voltaire's name was on all tongues and his person the cynosure of all eyes. But niece Louise didn't and wouldn't join her uncle. That one began to repeat the role of Plato at the Court of Dionysius. Paris caricatured him as "Voltaire the famous Prussian"; Versailles deprived him of his post of historiographer, but not of "gentleman in ordinary," at 2,000 francs, to the womanizing French king, although he became chamberlain to the otherwise Prussian one at 20,000 francs. His duties rendered him the woman-scorning Prussian's jester, grammarian, ghost, and auditor of the royal flute-playing. There were philosophical symposia of regular supper companions, and visiting firemen, with *Rex contra Mundum* in the disputations. It was not long before Voltaire's anticipated doubts became actual disturbances. Dionysius would have Plato for a servant and yes-man, not for an independent guide and counsellor. The wit and wisdom of sickly, scrawny old Voltaire could not compete with the bodily charm of a handsome young Frenchman whom the poet himself had recommended to the Prussian king long before he found his way to Sans-Souci.

Perhaps it was to drop an anchor to windward that he commissioned a Berlin broker, Hirsch, to buy in Berlin a large amount of certain banknotes issued in Dresden, Saxony, at the Prussian price of half their face value, and to sell them in Saxony at their face value. The scheme developed quarrels. On one occasion Voltaire passed from words to blows. Finally, Voltaire sued Hirsch. There were claims and counter-claims, and no reliable evidence on either side. Voltaire won his case, but old Hirsch died before it was finished. The anti-Semitism of the judgment is visible today; it was an invisible spirit of the laws among Christians, when it was delivered. Voltaire's rage was not all frustrated cupidity; anxiety about the future in Prussia may well have been a spring. Frederick now had a valid excuse for getting rid of his one and only Voltaire; he ordered him out of his kingdom within twenty-four hours but did not press the order. He called the case of Voltaire vs. Hirsch "the affair of a rascal who is trying to cheat a sharper." Voltaire pleaded to be forgiven, first through emissaries, then in person. Finally Frederick wrote: ". . . If you can make up your mind to live like a philosopher, I shall be glad to see you." In due course the king's ghost received in Berlin some other "poems" of Frederick's to improve, one being "The Art of War"; he was also busy about the publication of his *Century of Louis XIV*. This was forbidden reading to the French, gloriously welcomed in England, and pirated in Scotland, Holland, and Prussia. Its author worked at *La Loi Naturelle*, began his *Philosophical Dictionary* and brought his cold war with Maupertuis,* French president of the Berlin Academy, to a hot crisis. His philosopher-king continued to suspect him, and had his correspondence with his niece intercepted and copied. All the while, servants of his household had been copying Voltaire's manuscripts for purposes of their own.

Voltaire's lampoon of Maupertuis, *Akakia*, printed in Potsdam under the general kingly *imprimatur* for the author's works, both angered and amused his philosophical Majesty. He warned Voltaire ". . . if you keep going on with this business, the world will see that if your works deserve statues, your conduct deserves chains." To which Voltaire

* Maupertuis, like Voltaire, was committed to Newton. He got into a dispute with an old friend of Voltaire, the mathematician Koenig (who had spent two years at Cirey), an enthusiastic Leibnitzian. The issue between them was the "principle of least action" which Maupertuis claimed he had discovered. Koenig produced a letter from Leibnitz in support of his refutation of the theory. Maupertuis declared the letter a forgery and had Koenig expelled from the Academy.

responded with artful dodges that decided Frederick to have the entire edition of *Akakia* publicly burned. The Prussian burning was celebrated just before Christmas Eve, 1752, and of course it created everywhere a popular demand for the work that the presses were pushed hard to supply. Voltaire had come to feel that the long overdue end of the beautiful friendship was near. He saw in Frederick's support of the president of his Prussian Academy less a loyal Prussian's refusal to recognize facts than a terminal alienation of the royal affection, not to say favor. He decided that he must truly make a break for his personal liberty. How he judged his position may be seen in a letter to his niece written in December 1752. It included a bit of a little dictionary as "used by kings":

> My friend *means* my slave
> My dear friend *means* I am more than indifferent to you
> *Translate* I will make you happy *into* I'll endure you
>   as long as I have any use for you
> Eat supper with me tonight *means* I'll make fun of you
>   tonight.

So he sent Frederick back his Cross and Ribbon of the Order of Merit together with his chamberlain's key. But Frederick said, no, you're to keep them; and keep them Voltaire, hardly reassured, did. He made known that truly it was not he who had written *Akakia*, but excused himself from joining his philosopher-king at Potsdam on the ground that he was too sick. The King sent him quinine for a cure, but the quinine did not move him. What he needed for his health, he wrote, was a leave of absence; he'd go to Plombiéres in France, to drink the waters. Frederick replied: "Go drink the Moravian waters instead"; but at long last consented to let his Voltaire go: "Monsieur, I wish you a pleasant journey."

So, a scarce three years after his arrival in safety and glory Voltaire fled Prussia in humility and dread, yet with self-respect. He made his libertinist way from German court to German court; by the time he got to Leipzig, he had recovered enough pride, maybe he felt secure enough, to issue an edition of *Akakia* with supplementary chapters. This enraged the philosopher-king: Voltaire would no longer be the philosopher-king's most honored philosopher and flattering ghost-writer. As the latter, Voltaire had in his baggage the poem "Palladium," Frederick's own ribald appraisal of both Christianism and rival monarchs, and he might have the gall to make it public. This time, hence, the honors which the Frenchman had been graced with should be forever revoked; men were broken on the wheel for lesser crimes than his. Frederick's minions caught up with his ghost-writer at Frankfort, and there the writer, under arrest, gave the royal giver back his gifts. After three weeks, the latter let him get out of the German scene. So Voltaire resumed his gay and busy way from German court to court.

He would have returned to France, but was refused permission, lest Frederick take offense. Influence—Pompadour's mostly?—ought nevertheless have opened the frontier to him. But a piratical Dutch publisher issued a version of his *Essai sur les Moeurs*, so badly mutilated that perhaps it caused his reprobation of intellectual and moral tyranny to stick out more than it did in the authentic version (Frederick had a manuscript copy). In consequence, Louis XV told Mme. Pompadour that he didn't want Voltaire back in Paris. The *Essai* also made its author *non grata* in Colmar, which became to him "a town of Hottentots governed by German Jesuits." His public exposure of the difference between the printed and authentic text persuaded neither court nor cloister. He even got a Capuchin to hear his confession, and he took the sacrament (on Easter Day 1754), but to no purpose.* Again he was in danger and had to be on the move. He turned toward Switzerland.

---

* Confessing, taking the sacrament, was something everybody did; doing it also was like dressing for an occasion as everybody else did: ". . . surrounded by barbarians . . . one must imitate their ways of twisting." He sent his Capuchin's convent wine and veal as a token of his penance and absolution.

Switzerland became the scene of Voltaire's most telling labors as a champion of liberty. Geneva's Council of State gave him special permission to live within its territories. He took a house in the city where he met a physician, who also became a close friend, Theodore Tronchin—said to have been a pioneer of the modern way with health and cleanliness. The Geneva publishers, the Brothers Cramer, agreed to print all his writings in a single edition. Finally, another Tronchin, who became Voltaire's lawyer and man of affairs, got him two houses—one at Monrion, the other on a hilltop at the edge of Geneva and near the road to Lyons. Tronchin had to buy both for himself in order to lease them to Voltaire for life.

The hilltop estate became *Les Delices*, and its sixty-one year old tenant-master immediately began to reshape it to his needs and desires. He tore down garden walls that blocked his view across the city to rivers and mountains; he started a garden, and built a hen house; he added guestrooms to Les Delices; he bought horses and carriages; he engaged a bevy of household servants and landworkers; he installed a tame bear and a monkey (he named the latter Luc, and on occasion referred to his philosopher-king as Luc.) He gave parties and had readings of his own plays. And then, as the philosopher's life was falling into a pleasant pattern, came the news that *La Pucelle*—which these many years had been circulating among trusted friends, including royal Luc, in manuscript—had been printed and was being sold in Paris at a louis a copy. Badly divergent as was the pirate version from the authentic *Pucelle*, it was the more indecent, and it contained passages ridiculing even near friends. To offset the impact, Voltaire had hundreds of other copies made with even greater divergences and circulated authentic passages himself so that he might indignantly disclaim authorship. All to no purpose. The Parliament of Paris had the pirated *La Pucelle* burned. The Pope forbade the faithful to read it. The Council of Geneva also had the publication burned, believing that this sentence on a pirated perversion of his own poem would please the poet. The poet proceeded to violate Geneva's statutes against stage plays by setting up a stage and recruiting players among the altogether willing youth of Geneva. The Council warned their guest that he was violating the righteous law of John Calvin, and he, apologizing, took his stage to Monrion in Catholic Lausanne.

Always skirting the edge of danger, Voltaire managed to sustain a life of freedom more abundant. He produced a philosopher's vindication of its goodness in his comment to Genevan Jean-Jacques Rousseau on the latter's brief essay, the *Discourse on the Origin of Inequality among Men*. He called it a "book against the human race." "No one has ever been as witty as you, trying to make brutes of us; reading your book one would like to go on four paws; but as for me, it is sixty years since I lost the habit, and I feel it is impossible for me to get it back." Whatever troubles literature and science may bring their aficionados, he added, they nevertheless feed, comfort and straighten man's heart; one must love them as one loves society or God; whatever be the evils, the superstitions, or the fanaticisms that they evince. Rousseau replied, in sum: Perhaps you're right; we don't agree, but we can appreciate each other and be friends.

Then, about a month later, as if to cap Voltaire's deprecation of Rousseau's natural—thus animal—man, came an unutterable catastrophe in nature itself. This was the earthquake which on All Saints' Day, 1755, destroyed Lisbon, killing some fifteen thousand men, women and children in minutes, and as many more over the hours. Most of the killed were in church. Voltaire did not hear of the horror till weeks later, and what he heard shook him to the marrow of his bones. Over the months his mind kept turning to the earthquake and its import. He recalled Alexander Pope's *Essay on Man*, with its complacent profession: *Whatever is, is right*. Could the unendurable horror of Lisbon be honestly taken for the *right* proclaimed by that once-admired *Essay* of M. Pope? Voltaire's travail of spirit at last gave voice as the *Poem on the Disaster of Lisbon.* What security, it demanded, can man have, what assurance of *right?* Nature everywhere gives the Popean profession the lie. If all be right with God and in God, how wrong all is with man and in man! What does he bring to the divine completeness and perfection but his faults, his regrets, his evils, his ignorance, which the perfect totality lacks? Nature bears them witness, and with them nature refutes Pope's complacent lie.

As usual, Voltaire was evasive about publishing the poem; he had his manuscript copied for circulation among aristocratic and understanding friends: "I do not throw the bread of life to dogs," he told one of them. Of course, the poem was soon in print and for sale in Paris, together with the one on *Natural Law.* And of course, the two were condemned for heresy. Geneva asked Rousseau to refute *The Disaster of Lisbon;* Paris saw the hangman put *Natural Law* to the flames. Some believe that Mme. Pompadour offered to have their author made a cardinal if only he would write to defend instead of to attack the true religion. What she got, if anything, was a couple of paraphrases, one of Ecclesiastes, the other of the Song of Solomon, with notes quite consistent with the *Pucelle,* and meanings authentically Voltairean. Rousseau, responding to his fellow Genevans' petition, wrote Voltaire in defense of Pope's *Whatever is, is right* and in vindication of his own natural man, that if men had not built cities like Lisbon, earthquakes couldn't have hurt them at all so much.

By this time Voltaire had been a guest of the Swiss more than three years. He was in his sixth decade. His three houses (he had added Chene to Les Delices and Monrion), had sheltered gentry and commoners from every land, the gentler sex of the gentry not the least among them. Although he always remembered his Emilie (he had her portrait together with Prussian Frederick's and his own in his bedroom) he had found in Mme. d'Epinay a "Beautiful

Philosopher." The gentle, naive, learned d'Alembert had been his guest five weeks, discussing his projected *Encyclo-pedie* and what it might do to enlighten the peoples of the world. (It was publicly burned in Paris.) His host had joined in the defense of Admiral Byng who, taken for a scapegoat by an incompetent British Ministry, was charged with treason and cowardice because he lost a naval battle at Minorca to Voltaire's patron and friend, the Duc de Riche-lieu; he had also striven to arrange peace between Frederick and Louis XV, amid the ups and downs of the Seven Years' War. (Frederick came out victor at last, but during one of his downs he thought of suicide and there is a letter of Voltaire's arguing against it.) The would-be peace-maker had also striven for permission to return to Paris, but had to content himself with being once again named gentleman-in-ordinary to the French king. Concurrently he had begun to lose his teeth and to change his manner of speech in order to be understood. And all the time he was constructing plays to be privately performed in his own little theatre, was pro-ducing verses and essays, and was completing *Candide*.

But even together, *Les Delices* and Geneva and Monrion in Lausanne could not give Voltaire the feeling of security and freedom he craved. He wanted a title. Perhaps, the hurt he had from de Rohan impelled him, without his knowing it, to seek a title so that he might stand outwardly the equal of the dukes, the duchesses, and other such gentry whose supe-rior he was inwardly sure he was. Whatever produced his itch for a title, to create it Voltaire got a life-lease on neg-lected lands—a whole county, he boasted—a crumbling house, and fields in weeds, but with a title attached. Whoever held the estate would be Lord Count of Tourney, in Burgundy, thus on French soil, yet adjacent to Swiss Berne and close to Swiss Geneva. At the same time, Voltaire acquired Ferney, in Gex, Burgundy, on the north shore of Lake Leman. The location of his new holdings gave the artful dodger from persecution for speaking his mind, a vantage point from which to dodge in the flesh both *lettres de cachet* and *imprimaturs*, both Jesuits and Calvinists. He made a production of taking possession of his two new holdings: entering in a carriage with Mme. Denis, she in jewels and finery, he in crimson velvet with ermine trimmings; having a high mass celebrated at the parish church, with his tenants-to-be extending a noisy welcome. At Tourney the noise was provided by fifes, drums, and cannon from Geneva; the curé made the new Lord Count a speech of welcome. That one took his seigneurial responsibilities very much to heart. He began at once to improve his roads, to remodel and repair his houses—among other things he put in a bathroom with hot and cold water! He put horses and cattle, barns and other farm buildings on his lands. He became an apiarist and breeder of silkworms. And he cultivated with his own hands one field that became known as Voltaire's field.

It was not long before the misery of the French peasant came home to Voltaire. It brought to a slow and steady burn an angry disgust at the scandal that the clergy paid no taxes, the gentry hardly any, while the peasants were subject to the corvée, the taille, the window and the salt tax, fees for religious rites from christening to burial, tithing, and other forms of secular and churchly exaction. At Ferney, he made the priest give back the tithe; he employed the peasants at unheard-of wages on his roads; he built them houses, got the farmers' taxes off their backs and caused the cost of salt per pound to drop. He invited merchants, painters and a doctor to settle in Ferney, and built them houses. The 50 tenants he had when he took possession became 200. For youth he provided a school and instituted Sunday dances. Then he brought disemployed silk-weavers in from Geneva to weave the silk of his worms into stockings for gentlewomen. He gave shelter to watchmakers who had to flee that town, not only providing houses for them but also procuring the raw materials—metals and jewels—which their craft required.

To market their watches, he circulated an advertisement among all foreign ambassadors and solicited the custom of his friends, Frederick of Prussia and Catherine of Russia. To the latter he sent a whopping number, and explained the charges by attributing them to the watchmakers! Catherine replied she could still stand the cost. The egregious Count of Tourney sold his watches everywhere, even in North America and in China. Sometimes the trade brought losses; as when some crowned heads failed to pay, but the now ennobled literary businessman carried on. That, in this new career of his, which gave him greatest satisfaction was his having Romanists and Calvinists live together as good neighbors, enjoying freedom of trade and freedom of conscience; even, when an emergency arose, supplying each other's religious needs: "Is not this better than St. Bartholomew?"

As seigneur of his estate, Voltaire went with Mme. Denis —and later also with Corneille's great-niece Marie, whom he had adopted—regularly to mass every Sunday. But the parish church at Ferney offended his sensibilities and he decided to replace it. He got permission from the not too friendly bishop at Annecy. Demolishing the old structure involved also moving a cross. To the sexy and tricky parish priest, Ancians, whom Voltaire had deprived of his tithe, this seemed a providential occasion to revenge himself on the lord of the manor. He charged that moving the cross was an act of sacrilege and impiety and had the Seigneur up before an ecclesiastical court. To counter the charges Voltaire explored all the provisions of Canon Law, and assembled such a diverse mass of precedents and rules that the court was confused and dropped the case. Meanwhile, his Lordship completed the razing of the old church. He petitioned Pope Benedict for a bull granting him complete power over the construction of the new church and authorizing the celebration of the church's many fete days with work instead of the usual drunkenness. The pope acceded partly to Voltaire's request and sent him besides a piece of the hairshirt of his petitioner's patron saint, Francis of Assisi. It being traditional for the lord of the manor to have a tomb for himself in his church, Voltaire designed one, jutting out from the wall into the open. At first the church was dedicated to *Deo Solo*, to God alone, but after a while his Lordship changed the inscription to *Deo erexit Voltaire* (Voltaire built this unto God).

During the same period, he gave considerable time and money to compel certain Jesuits to disgorge a property that they, in collusion with a councillor of Calvin's Geneva, had embezzled from six poor brothers; he undertook to provide a *dot* for Marie Corneille by getting out an edition of her great-uncle's works, writing a *Commentary* on them, and soliciting subscriptions that in a month assured his adopted niece of an income of fifteen hundred francs a year.

Church-going, church-building *Philosophe ignorante* though he must needs be, Voltaire knew that a philosophy to be a "true philosophy" must be one "which makes the earth fertile and the people happier." Contemplating his role as Lord and Count, he wrote: "I love to plant, I love to build, and so perform the only tasks which gratify old age." And again: "I have done the only sensible thing in my life, to cultivate the soil. He who clears a field renders a better service to mankind than all the scribblers in Europe."

But Voltaire is not remembered for the somewhat Prussian-like philosophy which rendered him a successful utopian of field and workshop. Nor is he remembered for his sharp and often unjustified personal resentment—and the swift wit which employed laughter as a victorious weapon against his many foes. The generations cherish, rather, his philosophic faith of liberty and laughter (with an occasional tear) wherewith he challenged the conscience of the world, and they cherish how, as citizen of the same world, he strove to incarnate faith in fact. His scribblings made him a nemesis of the world's Torquemadas, Tartuffes, pretenders, flatterers, and other fakirs busy burning books, prohibiting such works as the *Encyclopedie* and securing *lettres de cachet* against the free minds of France. He came to think of them all, but singled out the clerics, as *l'infame*, and the latest phase of his ever-diversifying strategy of freedom was *écraser l'infame*. With all his absorption in communal reconstruction on his lands, in the management of his very considerable property and the upkeep of as hospitable a household as any Europe knew, Voltaire was ever composing and staging plays, working out the Aesopian tales—outstanding is, of course, *Candide*—which by exposing power, privilege, and pretence at once derided and exalted human kindness and human freedom, and ever writing letters, closing all with the plea—*écrasez l'infame*.

Among the writings, there was the series, both prose and verse, of *Whens? Whats? Whys? Wherefores? Whos? Wherewiths?* Voltaire exposed and shamed Maupertuis' successor in the French Academy, Le Franc, a nobleman who had once done Pope's "Universal Prayer" into French, but had become a spokesman for *l'infame*, and had maligned the philosophers of the *Encyclopedie* in his inaugural address. As others joined that jolly hazing, Voltaire added to his *Whens* and the rest two plays—*The Poor Devil* and *The Scotch Girl*. In the interim he had given final form to his tears-wringing *Tancred* (which Goethe found satisfying to translate); he had completed his not un-sardonic *History of Peter the Great* (on commission from the Empress Elizabeth of Russia); he had written two pamphlets laying utterly bare the pretenses of Jesuitism, exposing the latter to a ruinous derision. The occasion had been a characteristic attack on both the *Encyclopedie* and Voltaire's *La Loi Naturelle* by the Jesuit Berthier; Voltaire called his replies *The Story of the Sickness, Confession, Death and Resurgence of the Jesuit Berthier* and *The Story of Brother Grasse*. These pieces more than laughed at the type; they laid it bare as *l'infame*, the foe of reason, truth and progress. He protested the illegality of punishing a man (one Covelle) by requiring him to confess to Geneva's Consistory on his knees, to hear his reprimand and beg to be forgiven. He ridiculed a member of the Consistory, one Verret, as a hyprocrite. He intervened on behalf of the commoners of Geneva against the hierarchical political oligarchy and sacerdotal Consistory who held fast to power over that "republic." Having failed, he invited the French to mediate and in verse, *The Civil War in Geneva*, also paid Jean-Jacques the rest of the debt of ridicule he long felt he owed him for *La Lettre sur les Spectacles*. Voltaire had already paid his respects to that passionate idolator of his own invention, the natural man with his natural rights, for persistently inciting the magistrates of Geneva against him with "anonymous" letters making fun of Rousseau's *Nouvelle Heloise*. The bitterly rabelaisian *Civil War in Geneva* not only satirized the oligarchs of Calvin's city; it returned to Vernet and lampooned Rousseau as "that monster of vanity and contradiction, pride and meanness."

By 1769 Geneva's regulation of kneeling to the Consistory was abolished; but the French, failing to negotiate peace between Geneva's "estates," thought to use force; they blockaded the city and quartered troops along the shores of Geneva's lake. The blockade starved Ferney as well as Geneva, and Voltaire had to get his lands and people exempted from that cutting-off.

Meanwhile, our lord of Ferney and Count of Tourney, then seventy-four years old, was again moved "for example's sake" to *faire mes paques*. A priest who was dining with him willingly gave him absolution and on Easter Day he made a production of his churching, including a brief sermon admonishing his flock to be honest and dutiful and praising the curé. Some thought he had returned to the Faith; others that he had made fun of it and degraded the cause of freedom—although the Bishop of Annecy wrote him that he hoped the new communicant's future life would demonstrate that he meant what his act symbolized. His reverence forbade his clergy ever again to administer the sacrament to Voltaire. He also petitioned the king in Paris for a *lettre de cachet* against the jokester, but did not get it. As he wrote d'Alembert, Voltaire, having howled with the wolves and so been by them absolved and fortified in virtue, went on with his war against *l'infame*. He fired at it fusillades of pamphlets in accord with his observation to his fellow-philosopher Damilaville three or four years earlier: "What harm can a book costing a hundred crowns do? Twenty folios will never cause a revolution; it is the little pocket pamphlets of thirty sous that are to be feared."

"But those little pocket pamphlets" and letters signalized a sequence of interventions on behalf of freedom, tolerance and justice to the day Voltaire died. He took up the cause of innocent after innocent: a discarded Protestant wife of a Catholic army officer who wanted to marry another woman; the memory of a man broken on the wheel for a murder another later confessed to; the Montbaillis pair charged with killing their mother—the husband broken on the wheel, the pregnant wife jailed and in irons to await execution after her child was born. Voltaire wrote a short pamphlet about their trial; he appealed to the Chancellor, Marpeou, and the retrial which followed established the innocence of the victims, and liberated the survivor. There was the case of the Irish patriot and Jacobite, General Lally, who as a French officer in India had plotted to drive the English out. He failed and the French in due course tried him—of all things—for selling Pondicherry to the British and for a hundred other crimes and misdemeanors. Lally was beheaded innocently, Voltaire was sure, and said so in his *History of Louis XV*. When Lally's young son asked his help to clear the memory of his father, the seventy-nine year old pamphleteer undertook to review the case directly. He published his findings as *The historical fragments of the history of India and of General Lally*. He persuaded Mme. Du Barry, the first lady of Louis

XVI's court, and she persuaded the king, her lover. General Lally's name and fame were publicly cleared in council by the king himself. Voltaire was then in Paris for the last time, sick unto death, but in glory.

These interventions were, however, quiet incidents, beside the worldwide reverberations of the *affaire Calas*, the case of Sirven, and of sixteen-year-old de la Barre.

The *affaire Calas* is the most moving. Voltaire did not hear of the case until long after innocent Calas had been condemned and abominably maimed. His interest in it was first ambiguous and reluctant, but as the facts came to him interest grew into cause. Calas was a Huguenot merchant living in Toulouse with his wife, three sons and five daughters. One other son, the youngest, was at Nimes. One of the boys at home had been converted to Romanism. Toulouse was a centre of Roman Catholic bigotry which commemorated the revocation of the Edict of Nantes with a public mural and celebrated the Massacre of St. Bartholomew with a two-day feast. Huguenots, for their heresy, were forbidden a variety of occupations. Catholics were forbidden to work for Protestants. They were more greatly assured of salvation by an assemblage of sacred relics, among these a piece of the Virgin's robe and bones of the innocents whom Herod had killed. Monasteries of the Order of Penitence, White, Black and Gray, dominated the town. One October evening in 1761, Calas' oldest son, who seems to have been a manic-depressive, hanged himself. The family found him. Since the law required that a suicide's body should be placed naked and face downward on a tumbril drawn through the streets and then hanged on a gallows, the family feared to have the boy's death reported as suicide. Why, then, did he die? How? Obviously because he wanted to join the church and enter the order of white Penitents. To prevent this, his Huguenot father killed him. That was made the formal and sufficient charge. For against a Huguenot the charge itself was conclusive proof of his guilt. Jean Calas and the members of his family were arrested, separately interrogated and required to confess, while Marc Antoine's body was taken to the great cathedral, and given as ceremonial a burial as the rites of the church could provide. Jean refused to confess, insisting on his innocence, but did concede, as did the other objects of religious justice, that the son and brother had hanged himself. A tribunal of thirteen judges declared Calas guilty by a vote of eight to five. He was first put to the *Question Ordinaire:* his wrists fastened to an iron ring in the wall of the torture chamber, his ankles to a ring on the floor, his body was stretched with ropes until his limbs were dislocated; finally a wooden horse was slid under the lower rope and the inquisitors put the question again, only to hear Calas repeat that he was innocent. So he was put to the *Question Extraordinaire.* Water and more water was forced into his mouth until his body swelled to twice its size. Still, he was innocent. Whereupon, with only a shirt on his back, he was taken in a tumbril to the scaffold, bound to a cross, and the executioner broke each of his limbs into two places with an iron bar. Still, he was innocent. After five hours the executioner strangled him. Calas died, praying for his judges. The latter forced one of the surviving sons into a monastery, where he was terrorized into turning Catholic, but escaped after a time to Geneva. They forced his sisters into different convents and they let his mother go free. The boy at Nîmes escaped France for Geneva.

However the news of the religious-judicial torture and murder of Jean Calas came to Voltaire, it troubled him. He felt that something was obscenely wrong about it. Accounts came to him which started him asking questions. He got in touch with young Donat Calas in Geneva. He hired attorneys. He got friends to investigate the scenes of the events: to interview magistrates, assemble documents. He persuaded his titled friends to use their influence with resistant authorities, who didn't want the dirty waters stirred. He brought Mme. Calas, pauperized by law, to Paris. And he paid all the

costs out of his own pocket. In July of 1762 he published his
Original Documents Concerning Calas. This he followed
with a *Memoir* as by Donat and a *Declaration* as by Peter.
To cap this documentation, he added *The History of Elizabeth Canning and of the Calas*, the first intended to expose
the malicious cruelty and injustice of the second. All these
pamphlets Voltaire had translated and circulated in Germany
and England. He made the *affaire Calas* an international
cause célèbre; to the victim's family crowned heads in England, Poland, Germany made gifts, while the king of France
wanted the case ignored and forgotten. Nevertheless, by
1763, the Council of Paris, with no help from the Parliament in Toulouse, decreed a new trial. But it was almost a
year until the reconsideration of the evidence, upon which
Calas had been condemned, was attained, and he was declared innocent. His family, too, had to be cleared, and they
were therefore formally assembled in the Conciergerie of
Toulouse and finally released as "perfectly innocent." Car-
montil made an engraving of that gathering. This, Voltaire
got his rich and noble acquaintances generously to subscribe
to for the benefit of the widow and her children.

So far as he was concerned, the *affaire Calas* had social
and cultural by-products. Its moral and intellectual import
suffused much of his writing, such as the *Sermon of Fifty*
with its now bitter head-on drive against the ethics of the
Bible and the faith and works of the Christian establishment. Or such as his *Catechism of an Honest Man*, his
Gertrude or the Education of a Daughter, or his *Philosophical Dictionary*. This last was promptly burned in Geneva.
But the paramount consequence of the affaire was the *Treatise on Tolerance*, at first, like so many of his expressions,
not published as his but, forbidden the mails in France and
in Paris, passed on from hand to hand.

The *Philosophical Dictionary* came to figure in the third of
Voltaire's *causes célèbres*. The second was that of the Protestant Sirven family, who lived in Castres, not far from

Toulouse. Their tragedy came up while the *affaire Calas* was
still in process. They were five. Of the three daughters, the
youngest seems to have been feeble-minded. On a day early
in March, 1760, she disappeared and some time later the
Bishop of Castres sent for her father to tell him that she had
asked to join the Church and had been sent to the Convent of
the Black Ladies for instruction. Some seven months later
she reappeared at home, her back a mass of bruises, and
quite mad. Father Sirven protested, moved his family away
to St. Alby nearby. But in a couple of months Elizabeth
disappeared altogether and could not be found. A few weeks
later her body was discovered in a well in St. Alby. Ecclesiastical authorities and their secular arm charged her Protestant parents with killing her in order to keep her from
joining the true faith. With innocent Calas' horrible slaugh-
ter in mind, Sirven and his family fled the neighborhood of
the true believers of Castres and Toulouse. They ultimately
got to Geneva. Tried *in absentia*, the parents were condemned to be hanged, their daughters to stand by and watch
and then leave the land of the true faith forever. Since Pere
and Mére Sirven couldn't be hanged in person, they were
hanged in effigy. In person, Sirven reached a reluctant Voltaire who feared to prejudice the still open case of Calas if he
espoused the cause of the Sirvens. But espouse it he did,
getting for them the excellent lawyer he had engaged for the
Calas, paying the costs, writing memoranda, wangling gifts
of money from the monarchs of Prussia, Russia and Poland,
confronting and defeating the law's delay and the insolence of
office, until some seven years later, the Parliament of Toulouse cleared its victims, the Sirvens.

The cause in which Voltaire's *Philosophical Dictionary*
figured was that of the Chevalier de la Barre. He was one of
three teen-agers who had been charged in Abbeville with
mutilating two crucifixes, one on a bridge, one in a cemetery.
One of the boys fled to Prussia where Frederick made him

an officer in his army. The remaining two were arrested and all three were sentenced, not for mutilating crucifixes, but for impious and blasphemous behavior before the Host, blasphemous remarks about the holy ones—God, the Saints, the Church—and for adoring "profane books." De la Barre and the fugitive were sentenced to have their tongues torn out with hot irons, their right hands cut off, and then to be burned to death on a slow fire. De la Barre, before the burning, was to be put to the Questions Ordinary and Extraordinary, for the names of his fellow criminals. An appeal to the king at Versailles failed. A retrial of the case in Paris confirmed the sentence by a majority of five. Back in Abbeville, the teen-ager was first publicly tortured, then his head was cut off, to the applause of the onlookers, and his still undead body was thrown on the flames, together with Voltaire's *Philosophical Dictionary* and other works of the Enlightenment.

It was those works which brought de la Barre to his Christian end. Like Voltaire, he had been educated by priests whose sacredotal function exercised no restraint upon a taste for the humanities and a sybaritic mode of life. His teachers had been provided by an aunt who was an abbess, who lodged her nephew in her convent and gave him access to the works of the humanists and the philosophers, conspicuously the works of the abominable Voltaire. The latter, hence, disturbed about his own security, went off to Rolle in Vaud. There he wrote *The Death of the Chevalier de la Barre* and to the end of his life he strove to save the memory of de la Barre from the talons of *l'infame*. It was his one failure, even though the horror of the youth's destruction by the men of God resounded through intellectual Europe, and the phrase *écrasez l'infame* became a password for believers in justice and equal liberty. What it signified in Voltaire's way of life may be inferred from the words of a letter he got on New Year's Day, 1765—from his now ailing royal friend,

Frederick of Prussia: "I supposed you'd be so be busy extirpating *l'infame* . . . I didn't dare believe you'd think of
anything else."

But he did also think of something else, something resem-
bling what his imperious friend of Prussia had failed to
maintain at Potsdam, something with a hint of Rabelais'
Abbey of Theleme. He thought that he could get his
fellow-believers to join him in a sort of secular monastery, a
commune of writers and thinkers, a republic of letters, printing press and all. The project was too utopian for the philosophers and poets. The Lord of Ferney and Count of Morny
went back to his estates. When Louis XV died of smallpox,
academician Voltaire eulogized him before the Academy—
ambiguously; except for condemning the general neglect of
vaccination, had he not himself been pitted? Louis XVI's
appointment of Turgot pleased the octogenarian, and the
gift from Frederick, now called the Great, of a porcelain
modelling of his aged features, inscribed *Immortali*, nourished the Voltairean morale as he performed his role of lord
of the manor—vigilant of the business of his multiplying
"children," the watchmakers and weavers; busy with his
letters, his pamphlets, his plays, and his too numerous, too
insistent, and too-long-staying visitors whom he tried not too
successfully to evade by pretending to be sicker than he in
fact was. He spent considerable time in his bed; above which
he had a desk suspended that he could lower or raise as
desired. Out of bed, he went about in red breeches and
embroidered vest, white shoes and stockings on his feet, a
grey wig on his head, and a gold and silver night-cap on the
wig. He even gave young Reine-Philiberte de Varicourt,
whom he had come to cherish so much that he renamed her
Belle-et-Bonne, in marriage to a man old enough to be her
father (a libertine as well as a libertarian, but a marquis, the
Marquis de Villette) in that garb, with the sable pelerine
Catherine of Russia had presented him a decade before, for
added warmth. He began on a couple of new plays, *Irène* and

Agathocle, and as usual kept revising and revising them. His friends, notably the great Condorcet, thought them poor. But the *Comédie* agreed to produce *Irène*, and Voltaire—in spite of the fact that he was still *non grata* to Court and Church—decided to go to Paris, incognito. He was to lodge in Villette's mansion on what was afterward renamed Quai Voltaire.

Of course, the incognito was a quick failure. The five days' journey from Ferney to Paris developed into a triumphal progress; and in Paris all the sorts and conditions of Frenchmen flocked to see and cheer this eighty-four year old "anti-Christ." Amid the tumult and the shouting of these visitations—he had three hundred in one day, among them the composers Gluck and Puccini—he kept revising *Irène*. It was on his mind when Mme. Stecker called; it was on his mind when Benjamin Franklin, who also assisted at his initiation into the Masonic *Loge de Neuf Soeurs* (otherwise the Muses), came with his little grandson to pay his respects. "If I were forty," the anxious playwright told the American sage, "I should settle in your happy country," and laying his hands upon the grandson's head, he pronounced "God and Liberty." He became manifestly weaker with the days, so uncomfortable he couldn't sleep. Sometimes he suffered very great pain. He felt he was done for, and so did his old and most faithful factotum, Protestant Wagnière. The latter suggested that his master write down his real belief; and Voltaire did on a sheet one may see at the Bibliotheque Nationale in Paris. *I die adoring God, loving my friends, not hating my enemies and detesting superstition. February 28, 1778, Voltaire.* When, late in February of 1778, a burst of coughing brought up blood, he sent for the less offensive of the two professional mediators between men and God who had forced his way into the sick man's chamber. This was the Jesuit Gaultier. He heard Voltaire confess; and he requested, and received from him a statement, which Voltaire himself wrote, that he was dying in the Roman Catholic faith to which he was born and that if he had offended the church, he asked both it and God to forgive him. *L'infame* sent Gaultier back with a demand for a more positive commitment—or else no Christian burial.

Meanwhile *Irène* was to have its first night and the prospect so revitalized the author that he was able to receive a deputation from the Academy sent to congratulate him and later one from the Freemasons! He felt well enough to resume revising *Irène* and to rage at the sacrilegious hands who had tampered with his dialogue. One day he called on Turgot. Another, he took his carriage to the Louvre, where all the members of the Academy save the clerical, were gathered to welcome him, to elect him President, to have him listen to a eulogy of Boileau by his friend d'Alembert, which turned out to be a paean to Voltaire.

Finally, for the sixth production of *Irène*, Voltaire went to the *Comédie*. It may be said he stopped his own show. The personal welcome in the theatre consummated the ovation on the streets. First, one of the actors placed a laurel crown on Voltaire's head. He set it on his Belle-et-Bonne but the Prince de Beauvau put it back on the old philosopher's head. It was nearly half an hour before the play could begin, with hardly a sentence that didn't draw bursts of applause. When the performance was over, the curtain was raised again. Center on the stage was a marble head of Voltaire, on which the actor dressed in the robes in which he had been playing the monk in *Irène*, placed a laurel crown. The leading lady recited an ode in honor of the playwright who, delighted but weary beyond telling and moved to tears, was sung and cheered by the multitudes of Paris, all the way home.

The next days, he knew he ought to go back to Ferney but could not make up his mind. He ended by assenting to the solicitation of Mmes. Denis and Villette, who were eager he should buy a home in Paris. But over the days his pains increased; he couldn't sleep, and nothing he tried would give him respite. One day the friend of his youth, the Duc de

Richelieu, suggested laudanum—he himself had been taking it with good effect for gout. Finally Voltaire did take laudanum. It did little to temper the agony, and it was killing him. *L'infame* began to gather round sniffing after the signs of repentance and conversion they required. But Voltaire died at night, May 30, 1778. *L'infame* were certain he died in torment and in fear. The libertarian had witnesses that he died unafraid and peacefully.

To assure Voltaire's remains the decent burial he was so ready to pay for with rites and rotes whose creedal values were to him either hypocritical pretensions or naive illusions, his body was quietly taken to the Abbey at Scellières and there, on June 2, accepted for burial on the strength of the statement handed to Gaultier. The headstone read *Here lies Voltaire*. The interment was accomplished just in time. On June 3 Voltaire's burial in consecrated earth was forbidden, and forbidden, too, was any public notice of his death. As quickly as inevitably word got around. Prussia's great Frederick, now the president of his own Academy, spoke a eulogy of his so fascinating and undependable friend and ghost, in which he denounced the "imbecile priests"; he also had a mass chanted for his friend's soul in the Berlin Roman Catholic Church. Russia's Catherine the Great, who got herself vaccinated on the philosophe's recommendation, averred that Voltaire was "the man to whom I owe all I know and all I am. . . . With his death wit is stripped of honor; he was the divine spirit of gaiety."

When, with the revolutionary nationalization of church properties, those of the Abbey of Scellières also became a possession of the state, Citizen (formerly, Marquis) de Villette got the National Assembly to have Voltaire's remains dug up and transferred to St. Geneviève, that had been transfigured into the Pantheon of the people of France. The transfer was one of those moving colossal rituals which punctuated the French Revolution and signified its pretensions, if not its practices. First, Voltaire's body was brought

in its coffin to Paris, and laid on an altar built upon the ruins
of the Bastille. The next day the coffin was placed at the top
of a magnificent structure on four great bronze wheels, forty
feet high, harnessed to twelve white horses. The structure
was designed by the artist of the Revolution, the versatile
David. On the coffin he had set a full length figure of Voltaire sleeping, a winged Immortality placing on his head a
crown of stars. On the coffin was the inscription: *Poet, philosopher, historian. He gave a great impetus to the human
mind; he prepared us to be free.* The structure itself was
decorated with sentences: *He affirmed the rights of man; he
defended Calas; he inspired toleration.* The procession, said
to have been a hundred thousand strong, after a half dozen
stops—some called them stations like the stations of the
Cross—reached the Pantheon, where Voltaire's remains
were laid in the space prepared, near Descartes and Mirabeau.

But *l'infame* never forgot nor forgave. With the enthrone-
ment of Bourbon Louis XVIII after the destruction of Napo-
leon's empire, Voltaire's tomb—and Rousseau's as well—
was broken open. The bones are believed to have been taken
in a sack to a dump outside the city and there dropped
into a pit of quicklime. In 1864, when Voltaire's heart,
which has been entrusted at his death to Villette, became the
property of the state, his coffin in the Pantheon was opened in
order to restore his heart to the rest of him. The coffin was
found empty. The sole power of *l'infame* which the teacher
of freedom feared had succeeded.

There are some verses of Voltaire's conventionally assigned to 1772. As with so much that he wrote, he kept
changing them, so that it cannot be reliably known whether
the verses belong to his sixty-eighth or seventy-eighth year,
or some year between. He entitled them *Jean Qui Pleure et
Qui Rit* (John—he laughs and he cries):

*Some mornings I see the evils in nature and man
That the very devil runs away from:*

I address Etna, the seas and the coasts, and I say
　　again to tyrants
"You have troubled the world
More than the furies of the waves
And the fires of the volcanoes."
Then, when I behold in their evil bodying
What the portion is of all who see the light,
And that the highest law is that they shall suffer and die,
I cry.

But when, toward evening, with the free spirits
　　And a nice woman beside me,
　　I eat my partridges and I drink the good wine
　　Which the good d'Araude has provided for my table;
When, well removed from fops and sots,
Gaiety, singing, charm and wit
Ornament the between-courses of a delicious supper,
When, without a regret for my own fine days, I applaud
　　a new affair of Cleon and his mistress,
And when the charming friendliness,
That one knot which binds me from the heart, makes me forget
　　I'm old,
And a hundred reborn pleasures warm my spirit,
I laugh.

I see, although from afar, the factions, the cabals
That blow up in Paris, vainly shaken
　　By infernal enmities
While they pour their poisons into society,
And infamous calumny perversely
　　Spreads its darkling scandals;
I am often told about the bleeding north, about a wise and
　　kindly King, persecuted at home,
Unable to find in his royal dwelling the security
Which his own subjects hunt down—hour to hour,
I cry

But if M. Terray would try to pay me back,
If my meadows, my gardens, my woods, grow more beautiful,
If my servants are glad and come to dance in the shade of the
　　trees,
If, sometimes, to relax, I read Ariosto, or even La Pucelle

Ever sly, ever faithful,
Or some other fresh guy whose writings I like,
  I laugh

Life, I must confess is just like that;
Everybody has his tempers which keep leading him from
  disappointments to amusements;
Sure, man is made of a divine matter,
Sure, one day we'll all be glorious spirits
But in this our world of here and now, the soul is something
  mechanical,
Nature alters before our eyes,
And the saddest Heracleitus becomes a Democritus
Whenever his business goes better.

The verses, bald and commonplace in this English, as they are not in Voltaire's French, do express the septuagenarian's enduring appreciation of man's plight, of the role of providence and luck in his days and hours, and of the dynamic relations of liberty, laughter, and tears within that role. It would seem that Voltaire appreciated laughter much as Rabelais did, and that he had a deeper sympathy for tears. He could enjoy laughter for what it is, quite as much as for what it does. Where Rabelais appreciated his gaiety of spirit as a scorn of fortune, Voltaire delighted in the liberty of it without further ado. In this Pope was only a little like him, Swift not at all, nor are there many in the long succession of humanists and laugh-makers that punctuate the history of mankind's cultures. Voltaire speaks of it in one or another preface to a play and in occasional letters. But the directest expression of his sense of what laughter is and means, may be read in his *Philosophical Dictionary:*

That laughter is the sign of joy, as tears are of grief, is doubted by no one that ever laughed. They who seek for metaphysical causes of laughter are not mirthful, while they who are aware that laughter draws the zygomatic muscle backwards towards the ears, are doubtless very learned. Other animals have this muscle as well as ourselves, yet never laugh any more than they shed tears. The stag, to be sure, drops moisture from its eyes when in the extremity of distress, as does a dog dissected alive; but they weep not for their mistresses or friends, as we do. They break not out like us into fits of laughter at the sight of anything droll. Man is the only animal which laughs and weeps.

As we weep only when we are afflicted, and laugh only when we are gay, certain reasoners have pretended that laughter springs from pride, and that we deem ourselves superior to that which we laugh at. It is true that man, who is a risible animal, is also a proud one; but it is not pride which produces laughter. A child who laughs heartily, is not merry because he regards himself as superior to those who excite his mirth; nor, laughing when he is tickled, is he to be held guilty of the mortal sin of pride. I was eleven years old when I read to myself, for the first time, the "Amphitryon" of Molière, and laughed until I nearly fell backward. Was this pride? We are seldom proud when alone. Was it pride which caused the master of the golden ass to laugh when he saw the ass eat his supper? He who laughs is joyful at the moment, and is prompted by no other cause.

It is not all joy which produces laughter: the greatest enjoyments are serious. The pleasures of love, ambition, or avarice make nobody laugh.

Laughter may sometimes extend to convulsions; it is even said that persons may die of laughter. I can scarcely believe it; but certainly there are more who die of grief.

Violent emotions, which sometimes move to tears and sometimes to the appearance of laughter, no doubt distort the muscles of the mouth; this, however, is not genuine laughter, but a convulsion and a pain. The tears may sometimes be genuine, because the object is suffering, but laughter is not. It must have another name, and be called the "risus sardonicus"—sardonic smile.

The malicious smile, the "perfidum ridens" is another thing; being the joy which is excited by the humiliation of another. The grin "cachinnus" is bestowed on those who promise wonders and perform absurdities; it is nearer to hooting than to laughter. Our pride derides the vanity which would impose upon us. They hoot our friend Freron in "The Scotchwoman" rather than laugh at him. I love to speak of friend Freron, as in that case I laugh unequivocally.*

* From the works of Voltaire in twenty-two volumes, published 1901 by the Craftsmen of the St. Hubert Guild, N.Y. Volume VI, Part I, "Philosophical Dictionary," page 58, "Laughter."

The prefaces discuss the uses of laughter by the stage. One remark in the preface to *The Prodigal* supplements what is already quoted. "There are, besides, other characters ridiculous for their admixture of vice, which we love to see well-drawn, although they only give us a laugh; because laughter always arises from a gaiety of disposition, absolutely incompatible with contempt and indignation."

Tears are also a theme of our philosophe's *Philosophical Dictionary*, and he deals with them much in the same way as he deals with laughter. His concern seems to be less with their causes than with their occasions and with their uses—conspicuously, the writer's and playwright's use of them: "Tears," Voltaire writes in the *Dictionary*, "are the mute language of suffering. But why? What connection is there between a sad idea and this limpid, salt liquid, filtered through a little gland at the external corner of the eye, which moistens the conjunctiva and the small lachrymal points, whence it descends into the nose and mouth through the reservoir called the lachrymal sack and its ducts?

Why in women and children, whose organs are part of a frail and delicate network, are tears more easily excited by sorrow than in grown men, whose tissue is firmer?

Did nature wish compassion to be born in us at sight of these tears which soften us, and lead us to help those who shed them? The woman of a savage race is as firmly determined to help the child that cries as would be a woman of the court, and maybe more, because she has fewer distractions and passions. . . .

In the animal body everything has an object without a doubt. The eyes especially bear such evident, such proven, such admirable relation to the rays of light; this mechanism is so divine, that I should be tempted to take for a delirium of burning fever the audacity which denies the final causes of the structure of our eyes.

The use of tears does not seem to have so well determined and striking an object; but it would be beautiful that nature made them flow in order to stir us to pity.

There are women who are accused of weeping when they wish. I am not at all surprised at their talent. A live, sensitive,

tender imagination can fix itself on some object, on some sorrowful memory, and picture it in such dominating colours that they
wring tears from it. It is what happens to many actors, and
principally to actresses, on the stage.

The women who imitate them in their own homes add to this
talent the petty fraud of appearing to weep for their husbands,
whereas in fact they are weeping for their lovers. Their tears are
true, but the object of them is false.

One asks why the same man who has watched the most
atrocious events dry-eyed, who even has committed cold-blooded
crimes, will weep at the theatre at the representation of these
events and crimes? It is that he does not see them with the same
eyes, he sees them with the eyes of the author and the actor. He
is no longer the same man; he was a barbarian, he was agitated
by furious passions when he saw an innocent woman killed, when
he stained himself with his friend's blood. His soul has been all
stormy tumult; now it is tranquil, it is empty; nature returns to
it; he sheds virtuous tears. That is the true merit, the great good
of the theatres; there is achieved what can never be achieved by
the frigid declamation of an orator paid to bore the whole of an
audience for an hour.

David the capitoul, who, without emotion, caused and saw
the death of innocent Calas on the wheel, would have shed tears
at the sight of his own crime in a well-written and well-spoken
tragedy.

It is thus that Pope has said in the prologue to Addison's *Cato:*

> *Tyrants no more their savage nature kept;*
> *And foes to virtue wondered how they wept.*

Voltaire is disposed to take tears more readily for granted
than laughter. If his practice turns more often to laughter, his
theory does not. Both are functions of the spirit of man
struggling to defend its freedom against the compulsions of
fate and the accidents of fortune. But the role of the tears in
his philosophy of life and art is ambiguous. Some will see resemblances to Hume's, whom Voltaire had met when in England and who became also to him "le bon David." He called
himself a "philosophe ignorante," and his sceptical raillery
reached to the very deism that he insisted upon vis-à-vis both
theists and atheists. He came to call metaphysics "the art of

reasoning about that which we do not know," the romancing
of the mind. He spoke of himself as an *"amateur de sagesse,
c'est à dire, la verite."* On the record, he was a man of
religion embattled against its employment by clerics and
cultists to serve their lusts and aggressions; embattled,
hence, against the clerical establishment in all its manifestations. His insistence on churchly rites and rotes, duly and in
good order, for himself, was accordingly no hypocrisy.
Those who performed the rites knew as well as he the whys
and wherefores, knew even that they might be a sceptical
philosopher's Pascalian wager which, if lost, costs nothing
and, if won, wins everything. He found Pascal a "sublime
misanthrope" who treated all mankind as he wrote of the Jesuits, and thought all of them worse than they are. In Voltaire's
view, Christianity doesn't require that cultivation of errors
which is metaphysics or theology, any more than it requires
the myths of Pandora and Prometheus to which the Pascalian metaphysics of human greatness and misery could be
compared. To teach human charity is enough. Religion is
demonstrated as conduct of life; it doesn't make sense to say
that man can't be understood except in terms of an unintelligible mystery. Credulity, not reason, underlies the doctrine
of man's "original sin." In point of fact, our amour-propre is
god-given and is essental for our survival; and the same
giver added religion to his gift so that we, using it, keep our
amour-propre at its proper size. The dual nature which Pascal attributes to man is not a self-contradiction but a diversification. Man is no more contradictory than any other existence. Voltaire agrees with Pascal, that the adamic spirit is
directed entirely futureward, that man's past and present are
but means to his future. But then, he comments, why be sad?
Let us, rather, be glad. Our most precious treasure is the
hope which sweetens the human condition and designs the
future with what is presently satisfaction—even when it
comes to suicide. Why should Pascal condemn Montaigne's
approval of euthanasia? What harm is done if a suffering

human being chooses death over suffering? He spares both himself and society the ills that are his living-on. He saves them from more bitter tears than death brings.

For Immanuel Kant, Voltaire was truly a philosopher, although a philosopher who preaches and rails. It is a commonplace that Newton was to him as to his Emilie, the herald of the Eternal Mind; "a catechist reveals God to children, and a Newton demonstrates him to sages." In fact, the idea of God is a moral necessity even more than a self-evident truth of nature. Voltaire remarked to d'Alembert and Condorcet that if God did not exist it would be necessary to invent him. Necessary, that is, to envision the order of nature as regulating man's struggle for survival, modifying his behavior consequentially with rewards and punishments, but with no promise of heaven or threat of hell; simply emphasizing the satisfactions of reciprocal toleration, the advantages of putting a little gentleness and foresight into the blind quest for fortune, and by the manner of one's own life, helping to make life more bearable for all. This morality is intrinsic to the universal nature of things; and verifies itself as always and everywhere one and the same. The morality prescribed by the dogmas of the clericals is a manifold of inventions by lustful and ambitious men; they drown human life in tears. "The man who says to me, 'Believe as I do, or God will damn you,' will presently say to me, 'Believe as I do, or I will kill you.' And what such men kill for is absurd. Indeed, men will not cease to be persecutors until they've ceased to be absurd." Voltaire's religion, Voltaire once wrote, is "to worship God; to leave each man the liberty to serve him in his own fashion; to love one's neighbors; to enlighten them if one can, pity them when they are in error, to attach no importance to trivial questions which would never have given trouble if no seriousness had been imputed to them. This is my religion which is worth all your systems and all your symbols." Incidentally, his book on Newton was condemned

Now this wisdom of the *amateur de sagesse* came after the earthquake at Lisbon, and was heated to crusading fervor by the cruel machinations of *l'infame*. It was implicit in the ideas of liberty, laughter, and tears which shaped our amateur's art as a writer of tragedies, comedies and satires. Even when, explicitly, he declared how much he was flattered to find that the Pope of *An Essay on Man*, asserting that "from the beginning everything was as it ought to be," confirmed an old observation of his own (Voltaire's): "You are astonished that God made man so limited, so ignorant, so little happy. Why are you not astonished that he did not make him more limited, more ignorant, more unhappy? When a Frenchman and an Englishman think the same thing, they certainly must be right."

L'infame and the disaster of Lisbon showed him that they certainly must be wrong. The first was an evil which could be extirpated, the second a horror which could only be endured. As Voltaire has Candide's Dervish observe to Pangloss: "What does it matter whether there is evil or good? When his Highness sends a ship to Egypt, does he worry about the comfort or discomfort of the rats on the ship?" To Pangloss's "Then what should we do?" the Dervish retorts: "Hold your tongue." The upshot would be that the nature of things had only such care for mankind and its destiny that the record made evident; that in truth these were man's responsibility, not God's; that God's nature consisted of many comings and goings before which man is helpless, which he can only suffer, but cannot and should not justify. For if God's purpose is a mystery and his nature ultimately inscrutable, justice is as self-evident as 2 plus 2 are 4. God is the workman that the laws of Newton's nature imply. A work without such a workman is absurd, but *what* the workman may be *without* the work there is no knowing; nor is there any knowing of the whys and wherefores of the undeniable injustices of the world, be they nature's disasters or man's *infame*.

Men suffer. They can suffer nobly or they can laugh at
suffering. They can defeat the guilty causes of it with laughter. They can also mingle tears into their laughter and
laughter into their tears. The dramatic poet, the satirist,
should be able to evoke all three modes of mankind's encounter with evil. They may produce tragedies, they may produce
comedies, they may produce "crying comedies." Somehow
comedy fits more truly than tragedy, and the dramas that
turn on choices between love and duty or love and love are no
less truly tragic than those which turn on heroic choices such
as duties to one's sovereign or one's people or one's God.
Tears go most aptly with the mighty sentiments which can
be well stated only in the figures and rhythms of verse, and
with the decorum and restrained feeling proper to a great
soul. Voltaire's plays present the tragic choices as involving
commitments to toleration, to public welfare, to horror at
fanaticism and at injustice. Some have no female characters;
all are composed in "the grand style." This language is as
"the language of the gods," and their function is to be
"the school of virtue." By comparison, the Greeks "confused
horror with terror" and the "disgusting and incredible with
the tragic and marvellous," while the English perpetrated
barbarisms of turbulence, fury and fantasy. English tragedies, notably Shakespeare's, are really inflations of mon-
strous farces; of ideas "bizarre et gigantesque" lacking order
and verisimilitude, and composed in a style too imitative of
Hebrew writers and full of Asiatic afflatus. Shakespeare
destroyed the English tragic theatre, and maybe Addison
with his *Cato* has resurrected it. Take Hamlet's soliloquy, as
it is, in the bald blank verse of William Shakespeare Esq,
and compare it with the same soliloquy as it ought to be in
the well-peruked alexandrines of M. de Voltaire:

> *Demeure: il faut choisir, et passer à l'instant*
> *De la vie à la mort, où de l'être au néant.*
> *Dieux cruels! s'il en est, éclairer mon courage.*
> *Faut il veillir courbé dans la main qui m'outrage,*

Supporter où finir mon malheur et mon sort?
Qui suis je? qui m'arrête? et qu'est ce que c'est la mort?
C'est la fin de nos maux, c'est mon unique asile;
Après des long transports, c'est un sommeil tranquille;
On s'endort, et tout meurt. Mais un affreux réveil
Doit succeder peut-être aux douceurs due sommeil.
On nous menace, on dit que cette court vie
Des tourments éternels est aussitôt suivie.
O mort! Moment fatal! Affreuse éternité!
Tout correr à ton seul nom de glace, épouvanté.
Eh! qui pourrait sans toi supporter cette vie,
De nos Prêtres menteurs bénir l'hypocrisie.
D'une indigne maitresse encenser les erreurs.
Romper sous un Ministre, adorer ses hauteurs,
Et mentrer les langueurs de son âme a battue
A des amis ingrats qui detourment la vue?
La mort serait trop douce en ces extremités
Mais la scrupule parle, et nous crie: "Ârretez!"
Il defend a nos mains cet heureux homicide;
Et d'un Héros guerrier fait un Chrétien timide, etc.

Don't think, adds our young *amateur de sagesse*, "I've rendered the English word for word; bad luck to the literal
translator who in giving each word vitiates the sense. It is
that there one can well say that the letter killeth, the spirit
giveth life." Enough said.

English comedy Voltaire found more acceptable than
English tragedy although to appreciate it did require a long
period of naturalization in English culture. Indeed, understanding the comedy of any culture calls for such an accultu-
ration that understanding tragedy can do altogether without.
For tragedy, bringing into play great passions, heroic stupidities consecrated by ancient errors, is universal; its appeal
is to everybody, always and everywhere, the same. But comedy: "I don't much enjoy reading Plautus and Aristophanes.
Why? Because I'm neither a Greek nor a Roman; *bon mots*,
allusions, topicality (*l'apropos*) are all lost on a stranger
. . . good comedy is '*la peinture parlant des ridicules d'un
nation*,' and if you do not know the nation in depth, you'll

hardly be able to appreciate the painting." The comic writer, observed the author of *La Pucelle* in his preface to *L'Échange*, "at his best presents nobility without pretension, without moralizing about it, a morality intrinsic to his subject yet not displayed; he keeps to the simplicities of nature, draws his portraits delicately, and is refined in his fun-making. I wish we might give pleasure without needing to make an audience laugh."

To no small degree the wish conformed to the preferences of the Court and the salons. Their denizens were all amateur actors and were too hoity-toity for public laughter. They did the correct thing by tragedy, but they left that largely to professionals and themselves played comedies almost exclusively and Aristotle-wise, *en amateur*. They also did ballets and operas, the Italian forms of which Voltaire adored. They were to him a fairyland mixture of realism and fantasy, "as bizarre as magnificent." To Denis Diderot opera was an absurd prostitution of the arts. But although a theoretical formalist in his discussion of the place of tears and laughter in comedy and tragedy, Voltaire the practitioner of the dramatist's and satirist's art, could not help knowing better; thus in the preface to *Nanine* he observes, quite simply: "Comedy may be impassioned, may be in transport, or in tears, provided at the same time it makes the good and virtuous smile; but if it were entirely destitute of the *vis comica*, if from beginning to end, it had nothing in it but the serious or melancholy, it would then be a species of writing very faulty and very disagreeable." But where the *vis comica* and the *vis tragica* can be orchestrated, "crying comedy" or tragi-comedy gets perfected into high comedy. This, neither tragedy nor comedy, yet with something of the exaltation of the first and the detachment of the second, calls forth George Meredith's "serious laughter"; it draws cleansing and enlightening tears.

Curiously, it is not any of his dramas that embodies this insight of Voltaire's; it is his prose allegory of the human condition, *Candide*, the brief, most widely-read and best remembered of all Voltaire's expressions. He was a few weeks writing it; in contrast to his lifetime reworking of ten thousand lines and twenty-canto long *Pucelle* which got circulated without getting published, except in pirated editions, until almost the end of the author's long life. Emilie, who read cantos of *La Pucelle* in her bathroom, kept Voltaire from publishing them only to have them stolen and passed on to a piratical printer who published a garbled copy. The salons of Paris cherished it, the Parliament burned it, Frederick in Potsdam had it copied, the synod in Geneva condemned it to the flames. The question why Voltaire kept returning to it is like the question why Goethe kept returning to Faust.

But it is *Candide* which became of enduring public interest, the parallel of Faust. As the expression of its author's matured insight it offers a significant contrast to *Le Mondain*—written in the early years of Voltaire's union with his Emilie, pirated, condemned for blasphemy, and the occasion of the loving couple's flight to Holland. *Le Mondain* portrays the idyllic life of Adam and Eve in the garden of Eden before Eve ate the forbidden apple of knowledge. This life is an unwished immortality of progressively more boring innocence that has nothing save food and fornication to concern itself with. And how much better was life for the descendants of our first parents after the original sin which, if it brought death into the world and all our woe, also brought civilization and all its superfluities (*le superflu, chose si necessaire*). Between *Le Mondain* and *Candide*, Voltaire has attained a new wisdom, on the face of it not unlike that of Rousseau whose errors he had so wisely exposed. *Candide* presents man and his works as they figure under the laws of nature and of nature's God. It shows the basic drives of the human creature, its initial generosities of heart and mind suppressed, exploited, perverted or destroyed by the mere weather of existence, such as the disaster at Lisbon exemplifies, and by the religious, cultural, political, financial and military enterprises that make up civilization. It shows even the utmost sufferer, Dr. Pangloss, asserting in the face of misfortune after misfortune, horror after horror, that the world is the best of all possible worlds, and that, in Pope's phrase, all chance is direction which we cannot see, all partial evil universal good. Each major character is an allegorical symbol: Candide, Cunegonde, James the Anabaptist, Dr. Pangloss, the Jew, the Grand Inquisitor, the Old Woman, Cacambo, Martin, Pococurante, the Dervish. They disclose the ambiguous role of love, war, wealth, faith, art, science and work in the personal histories of men and women struggling to live on in the best of all possible worlds; they embody a gloss on the necessity of the superflous. Pangloss persists in his creed. He argues the world's supreme excellence at all times, on all occasions. Candide responds: "I know very well that we ought to look after our garden." Pangloss answers: "You are right. For when man was placed in the Garden of Eden, he was placed there to cultivate it; which proves that mankind are not created to be idle." But Martin interposes: "Let us work without disputing; work alone is what renders life supportable." And they work "according to their different abilities."

But Pangloss can't be stopped. He keeps repeating to Candide: "All the events in this best of all possible worlds are admirably connected. If a single link in the great chain were omitted, the universal harmony would be destroyed. If you had not been expelled from that beautiful castle with those cruel kicks, because you loved Miss Cunegonde; if you had not been jailed by the Inquisition; if you had not tramped over much of America; if you had not plunged your sword through the Baron, if you had not lost all the sheep you brought from lovely Eldorado, you would not be here today, eating preserved citrons and pistachio nuts." So the supernaturalistic philosopher-theologian.

To which still uncertain, still doubting Candide replies:

"All right, all right. Maybe what you say is true, but we must cultivate our garden."

In sum, work resolves what argument can only keep as an unsolved puzzle. Work is freedom; work is liberation from a life that Martin had summed up as "the distractions of inquietude or the lethargy of disgust." A cheerful and friendly Turk on a neighboring farm confirmed it: "Labor sets us free from three of the greatest evils: boredom, vice and want," and this freedom is all of insight that experience has brought to *Jean qui pleure et qui rit.*

CHAPTER FOURTEEN

Free Man Laughing: Benjamin Franklin

M. DE VOLTAIRE and Dr. Benjamin Franklin met for the first time scarcely six months before the former's death, each aware of the other's work and fame. At once generators and generation of the Enlightenment, their singularities were as outstanding as their common faith in equal liberty, in toleration, and in peace between persons and peoples. Yet Voltaire worked to embody faith in fact by means of *la plaisenterie* with which he disposed of rivals and foes in vision and action; Franklin, by means of projects of conciliation supported by *plaisenterie*. Their laughter diverged as their ways with men and issues diverged.

They came together thrice: first, when the self-made commoner and most-distinguished American that Europe knew arrived with an eight-year old grandson to pay his respects to the seigneur-by-purchase-and-investment French exile and most distinguished European, as the most famous of all Europe's *condottieri* for equal liberty and equal justice among men. That was when Voltaire laid his hands in blessing upon the boy's head, invoking "God and Liberty." To both sages, the God of liberty signified the rational Newto-

nian deity and not the Scriptures' willful All-Father; but
Franklin had reservations in favor of a non-Newtonian God
of will and feeling, because such a God was more compatible
with liberty. He and Voltaire met a second time at the Academy of Science when the French popularizer of Newton was
to hear himself eulogized. That time the two embraced, by
request, "in the French fashion." Their third meeting came
when the French Freemasons of the *Loge de Neuf Soeurs*
(the Nine Muses) inducted Voltaire into their fellowship.
Franklin had become a Freemason long before, had been
several times "master" of the Pennsylvania lodges and once
Grand Master of all the lodges of the British commonwealth: he had been quickly enrolled in the Lodge of the
Nine Sisters; and five years after he had figured among
Voltaire's Masonic godfathers, was elected its "venerable."
The Lodge had chosen him to officiate at the service which, a
few weeks after Voltaire's induction, it held in remembrance
of this most memorable of their confraternity. That time the
American illuminatus and other eulogists laid the laurel
wreaths with which they had been crowned at the foot of
Voltaire's bust.

The record is not clear what mythology, what rite and
rote, were the rule of the Lodge of the Nine Sisters: whether
or not they were the Scottish that had become general among
the French, or something peculiar to that unique fellowship
of the Enlightenment. The faith and works of liberty and
lovingkindness which were the early expressions of the Masonic idea had long been under the church's ban. A papal
bull had denounced the cult as a foe of the *true* faith, whose
authorized spokesman was the Pope alone; and his Holiness
declared Masonry a conspiracy to subvert and destroy the
true faith. Franklin in his way, like Voltaire in his, had
learned to wield laughter as both the shield and sword of
liberty. The two, in common with most of the great agonists
of the Enlightenment, were wits in all senses of that word of
many senses. But Voltaire was essentially a man of letters, a

wordman, and his invocations of laughter were the practice of a superior art; Franklin was essentially a man of affairs and his invocations of laughter were accessory to the working over of matter and the management of men. In 1778, when he and Voltaire first met, he was not only the most persuasive diplomat at the French court, he was an experimental scientist, an inventor, a printer, a journalist, a cartoonist—and incidentally, a ladies' man—and a philosophic author of prose and verse of widespread repute. Eighty-four-year-old Voltaire was already near the end of his life and at the height of his glory as champion of liberty and justice; seventy-two-year-old Franklin still had before him a dozen years of signal endeavor and achievement.

The next year, 1779, the embattled Continental Congress at home changed its emissary's title to Minister Plenipotentiary at the French Court. Already lodging in Passy, he continued there throughout the American war for independence and the negotiation and writing of the peace treaty by which the British conceded it. In 1785, after eight years in France, the minister was permitted to resign his office and return to Philadelphia. Save for the brief and arduous interval between May and October 1776, during which Franklin served as delegate to the Second Continental Congress and on many of its committees (the universally remembered one being that which drafted the Declaration of Independence), he had lived abroad, representing British Colonies of North America during more than a quarter of a century—eighteen years in England, nine in France.

He had lived briefly in England, some thirty years earlier. Already on his own from the age of sixteen, he had, at eighteen, sailed to the mother-country to buy type for a printshop which British Governor Keith of Pennsylvania had offered to help him set up. Only, the Governor no more honored his offer to Franklin than he had to others, and the young colonial needed to find himself a job to earn his bread and have a roof over his head. The printery where he served as a journeyman brought him a diversified acquaintance with writers—among them Mandeville, famous for his *Fable of the Bees*, and Dr. Henry Pemberton, who had known Newton and had helped in that light-bringer's revision of the third edition of his *Principia*. Young Franklin had wanted very much to meet Newton; it was a panache for him to be called, following his legendary kite-flying, "the Newton of electricity." After two years, a friend he had made in London, the Quaker Denham, who became briefly a partner in the young man's Philadelphia printshop, helped him get himself back home, a still undistinguished journeyman printer. When, thirty-three years later, he returned to London, the same undistinguished journeyman printer was greeted as one of the very great men of the age.

His *Autobiography*, written, Franklin says, for counsel to his descendants, presents the formation of his person and power as judiciously as he can appraise it. He began the writing in his sixty-fifth year; perhaps, he suggests not unsardonically, prompted by the vanity which comes to a man who has "gone through life with a considerable share of felicity" and wouldn't mind doing the same again, with some revisions. And he adds, "in many cases it would not be quite absurd if a man were to thank God for his vanity among the comforts of life." However, the demands of living-on and of creating the future arrested his remembering the past when the remembering had covered his personal history only from his birth in 1706 to his founding the Philadelphia Library Company in 1727. He did not resume remembering until 1788, two years before he died. But the *Autobiography* stops at his fifty-second year, 1758, when he was serving Pennsylvania and other British colonies in North America as their agent in London, and was otherwise known as the publisher of *Poor Richard's Almanack* and the author of *The Way to Wealth*, a book that had been quickly translated into many European tongues.

Yet, in 1757, Franklin still had more than a third of a

century of his smiling, freedom-loving, creative and exciting life to live. During those years this tenth son and fifteenth child of a Boston tallow-chandler had educated himself in all the excellences of his time's "gentleman of culture and refinement" without a peer in his homeland; and without the benefit of schooling, he had made himself a propertied man without resort to the morals and manners of business enterprise—a religious man without the churchman's bigotry and superstition, and a leader in civic improvement, intellectual pioneering, and comradely cultivation of the arts and sciences. By training and occupation a printer (he held printing to be "the art preservative of the arts"), an inventor by circumstance and opportunity, who would not patent his stove, his lightning rod, and other inventions, Franklin had already been foregoing the profits of business for the psychic income of scientific public service and private philanthropy. All of his writings communicate a certain cheerful deliberateness, an euphoric matter-of-factness ready to utter itself in kindly laughter, a laughter as nearly unallied to tears as mature laughter can be. His great capacity for indignation was the more telling because it was not savage. If he became truly the most famous American of his age—and one among the very famous of the entire Western world—to whom his people turned with greater confidence than to another for counsel and leadership, it was also the consequence of his insights and his will, not only by accident of fortune. Enlightened Europe took him as his fellow-countrymen took him. The charisma which drew them was entirely unlike that of the charismatic politicians and soldiers of history. The people responded to him as to their understanding and helpful friend and equal, not the authoritarian father who always knows better than the child what is good for him. The maxims of *Poor Richard*, like the counsel of the *Autobiography*, were perceived as recommendations, not commands; the command they exercised became self-command. Franklin was a self-conscious craftsman in the art of the good life or "virtue"; he was to his age the most signal of its self-made men. And it was the age, not himself, that admired and acclaimed this self-made man's maker.

So likewise did later ages, up to the present. For generations the *Autobiography*, all too often bowdlerized, portrayed a Jones that youth everywhere in the West, and particularly in America, might strive to keep up with, or on occasion avert from, as the course of human events changed direction and the climate of opinion changed mood and mode. But the figure of the man making himself, and aware of making himself, doing so in hope without illusion to the day he died, holds firm, as unshaken by the Frankliniana of later scholarship as is an honest and knowledgeable witness who is made to contradict himself by the cross-examination of smart lawyers in a trial at court.

Aversion from the image that Franklin drew is due either to character or fashion. To deprecate his recipes for the making of a self-made man has long been an approved manifestation of a commitment to liberty. Yet the entire Franklinian design for living could be plausibly taken for an existentialist schema, and all his "opportunism" and "utilitarianism" appraised moral implications of a metaphysical liberty struggling to shape up a good life, not inevitably but consequentially. John Adams has left us some indication of the mature form of this striving—he it is who is said to have alluded to the courtesies between Franklin and Voltaire "in the French fashion" as "Solon embracing Sophocles." Among the periwigged, fine-feathered feudal swells of France's courtly society, Franklin moves wigless, soberly dressed like a Philadelphia Friend; but he dines according to their tastes. Even his intellectual peers, such as Voltaire himself obviously, but also as Lavoisier or Turgot or Condorcet, dress more conspicuously although they eat more sparingly.

Dr. Franklin appears to be following the precepts of his own *Bonhomme Richard*, in moderation. At the rented Hotel

Valentinois in Passy he rises late, dictates both personal and public letters while he breakfasts at leisure. Then, till one, he receives this or that avatar of the French Enlightenment—an academician, a fellow-physiocrat, a philosopher, or perhaps a broken queue of women and children. Around one o'clock he takes his midday meal by himself or with a guest. As often as not, he dines out. Then, on occasion in the company of some affectionate and admiring lady, rarely a precieuse, he attends a play. Or else he goes to a meeting of the fraters of the Nine Sisters, or sits in with a session of the Academy. He is the favorite with many ladies, and a few are favorites with him. Helvetius' widow stands out because Franklin kept proposing marriage to her. There was also, perhaps even more special, Mme. Brillon de Juy, whom on occasion he would take on his lap, with whom he played chess while she was in her bath. There was the beauteous Mme. de Chaumont, his landlord's wife and the first of much-admired John Paul Jones's many mistresses. In his ladies' company Dr. Benjamin enjoyed music (he was something on the violin—much less of a something than Thomas Jefferson), visited the theatre, played at chess or checkers, but not apparently any of the Court's games of chance. Sometimes, remembering Hogarth, whom he knew in England, he might draw a caricature or a burlesque of the foes of America. He preferred to discharge his ambassadorial responsibilities through face-to-face talks rather than paperwork.

In England, before Wedderburn so abused him at a hearing by the Privy Council that he became convinced that conciliation—let alone a commonwealth—was out of question, he strove for conciliation. Even thus convinced, he kept striving for peace. He gave immigrant Thomas Paine a letter of recommendation to Americans which started the latter's signal career among the first philosophers of the American Idea. After the skirmishes of Lexington and Concord, Franklin became as firm for war as he had been hopeful for peace. He decided the British to be so intransigent that he ended a harsh, brief letter—a letter he had not the heart to send—to William Strahan, member of Parliament and a friend of thirty years: "You and I were long friends. You are now my enemy and I am yours."

Franklin was sixty-nine years old when he returned to home and war. Yet the people of Pennsylvania chose him to represent them at the Continental Congress; they made him head of their new State's own Constitutional Convention; they sent him to negotiate with Canada. His role at the Continental Congress every schoolchild knows something of; what his share was in the drafting of the Declaration of Independence; and how Congress sent him to France to persuade the ruling powers in that still feudal autocracy to support a new sovereignty which was the antithesis of France in aspiration, faith, political intention, and endeavor. To the King of France, the emissary of the Continental Congress presented himself as the unpretentious citizen of the aspiring republic of free men that he was.

Toward the end of his domicile in Passy, Franklin, for his amusement, set up a press to print and distribute the *Bagatelles* which he wrote to entertain his friends—mainly, the ladies. He had been very readily absorbed into the life and labors of the monarchy's intellectual elite, none of whom, exiled Voltaire excepted, matched his popularity with the French people. He was, for the authority and prestige of his name, appointed to one royal commission investigating the pretensions of mesmerism and to others making geological and meteorological studies. He joined Condorcet before the Academy of Science in supporting a young man's proposal to launch an international scientific journal which should serve as a forum of the free exchange of ideas between scientists and artists everywhere; as *Nouvelles des lettres et des arts*, the journal lived through more-or-less of the decade between the American and the French Revolutions. Franklin had a particular interest in the new experiments with balloons. It was when these were challenged on utilitarian grounds, that this utilitarian and opportunist made the famous retort currently repeated to sanction every variation in theory and practice among the sciences, though significantly not yet among the arts: *Of what use is a baby?*

At last, in 1781, with the casual but vital intervention of Lady Luck, the British in America were defeated and a peace was to be negotiated with Franklin's compatriots. It was foregone that their emissary to the French should be asked to serve as one of their Peace Commissioners. The negotiations dragged on to a slow conclusion. Not until 1785 was Franklin freed to return to his homeland. He had lived and worked abroad nine long years. He returned home laden with honors and overloaded with the pains and pangs of "the gout," that duly he strove to render more endurable by means of a wryly laughing dialogue. Carried to Havre de Grace in the French King's own litter, he brought home with him, together with the stones of his bodily affliction, the King's portrait encircled by some four-hundred diamonds which Louis XVI had given him for a goodbye present. The self-made man was seventy-nine years old; but though he thought to come home and die in peace, he found himself still unfinished and a-making.

For the home-folk did not see him as finished. During the decade or so of his absence in their service, the Confederation had become more than ever an unstable alliance of struggling states. With the pressure of the common foe lifted, the land's tenuous oneness was dissipating into an almost anarchic manyness. The single nation, the lasting One of Many that the authors of the Declaration of Independence had imagined and that the Articles of Confederation had purported to establish, turned out in effect to be scarcely an effective military alliance. It looked as if the thirteen original British colonies had only contracted to join together for the purpose of waging a war for their separate liberation from the authority of a distant politico-military people, of the same stock and culture though it might be. Victory enabled each colony to transvalue itself into an independent sovereignty with all the pretensions, if not the powers, which such sovereignty purports. The liberty to be and to do this was not the liberty which the Declaration of Independence had affirmed as the equally unalienable right of each and every human being. In practice it was but freeing the power-holders of each one of the sovereign states from the preponderant force which prevented their using its sovereign powers as they chose—without regard to the freedom or bondage of the rest of its people, or whether the people of the states lived in them as free citizens of a free society, or of a society of masters and slaves, white or dark-skinned, indentured servants or human chattels. Thomas Jefferson, writing in his *Notes on Virginia* of "my country," referred only to Virginia, not to the twelve other states of the Confederation. Their Many did not then make an indivisible One for him. Rights were not human rights but state rights, rights of thirteen separate and independent sovereignties which, as is ever the wont of such, vied with one another even to the point of war unless confronted by a foe so powerful that they had to unite for defense.

The "equal liberty" of the British colonies from such a foe having been gained, it quickly tended toward an interstate anarchy which alarmed the men who had underwritten with their lives, their fortunes, and their sacred honor their common faith in that free society of equal rights for all human beings which their Declaration of Independence professed; and to vindicate which the states had jointly waged their war for independence. These men feared that their interstate anarchy might well cost the new sovereignties their new-won status; that this secondary and merely incidental liberty might well be forfeited. So, yearning to replace the centrifugal confederation with a more perfect union, they sought one another out. No sooner had Dr. Franklin made his way home than they sought him out. "It seems my Fate constantly to wish for Repose," he had written his friend, the Bishop of St. Asaph in August, 1784, "and never to obtain it." But whom, with more right than the greatest and most famous of all their country's men, could they turn to? Named President of the State of Pennsylvania in 1785, again in 1786, and yet again in 1787, who else but he should be the State's delegate to the very quietly prepared Constitutional Convention of that year. "My country folk," pain-ridden yet smiling Ben Franklin observed, "engrossed the prime of my life . . . have eaten my flesh and now seem resolved to pick my bones."

But he did not deny them. In a gathering of individuals—each with his private "prejudices, passions, local interests, selfish views"—he persevered with his characteristic endeavor to reconcile and to harmonize. The notes which the great James Madison took of the debates in that Convention tell a part of the story; the papers of the Federalist to which he contributed so consequentially tell another part. However reluctantly, a consensus *was* reached, and once again octogenarian Benjamin Franklin made the point that must always be made again when human beings—at once like and irreducibly different from each other, yet need, even if they do not wish to—live together because they are just as irreducibly neighbors, if only as men and women, parents and children. So Dr. Franklin suffered the concession on the slavery which he hated and combatted his whole life long; so he acquiesced in other rules he would rather have done without. So, he told the Convention:

> I confess that there are several parts of this constitution which I do not at present approve, but I am not sure I shall never approve them; for having lived long, I have experienced many instances of being obliged, by better information or fuller consideration, to change opinions . . . which I once thought right, but found to be otherwise. . . .
>
> Thus I consent, sir, to this Constitution because I expect no better, and because I am not sure that it is not the best. The opinions I have had of its errors I sacrifice to the public good;

I have never whispered a syllable of them abroad; within these walls they were born, and here they shall die. If every one of us in returning to our constituents were to report the objections he has had to it, and endeavor to gain partisans in support of them, we might prevent its being generally received.

And in October of the same year he wrote a friend in Europe:

. . . I send you enclos'd the propos'd new Federal Constitution for these States. I was engag'd 4 months of the last summer in the Convention that form'd it. It is now sent by Congress to the several States for their confirmation. If it succeeds I do not see why you might not in Europe carry the Project of good Henry the 4th into Execution, by forming a Federal Union and One Grand Republic of all its different States & Kingdoms; by means of a like convention; for we had many interests to reconcile.

But his hope looked beyond Europe.

"God grant," he wrote, "that not only the love of liberty but a thorough knowledge of the rights of man may pervade all the nations of the earth, so that a philosopher may set his foot anywhere on its surface and say: 'This is my country.' "

The following year the self-made old man, still making himself, led in the endeavor to secure the votes necessary to get the Constitution adopted; it is one of Lady Luck's ironies that he does not figure among the contributors to the Federalist: his activities were elsewhere. That he disapproved of the compromise acquiescing in slavery, as he did of the Congress' excision of the famous paragraphs of the Declaration which denounced it, is emphasized by his accepting in 1789, the presidency of the Abolitionist Society and by a devastating parody which bares the logic of slaveholding for the tissue of fallacies that it systematizes. In the parody the slave-owners are Moslems of Algeria, the slaves, "Christian dogs." The justification repeats the points made by an American congressman vindicating the slave trade to Congress. Franklin published the parable in the *Federal Gazette* of March 23, 1790. Three weeks later he was dead. His loss was mourned by the commoners of the Western world perhaps even more than by its elite. The intent of his faith, the scope of his works, are signalized by Turgot's epitaph: *Eripuit fulmen caelo: sceptrumque tyrannis.*

There obtains among men of letters a petty snobbism regarding the faith and the works of this self-made man who wrenched from heaven its lightning, from tyranny its sceptre. They are the idealists who purport to see in his record only bourgeois materialism, worship of the bitch-goddess Success; in their view, the man himself is but a son of that bitch. This is a self-deception which Poor Richard would have derided in his own way, remembering "the prejudices, pressures, local interests, selfish views" which men incarnate by virtue of "the laws of nature and of nature's God." Their appraisal of the record has alternatives at least as fitting. Who of them, indeed, recognizes the faith, which in fact measures the works of this American agonist of "the Protestant ethic," whom his contemporaries ranked among their times' most genial and most humane of cosmopolitan spirits, as he labored to embody faith in fact? What role had laughter and tears in his emergence "from poverty and obscurity to a state of affluence and some degree of Reputation in the world," and to the ongoing enjoyment of a "considerable share of Felicity"?

This record supplies data for all the images of the man, which the diverse appraisals compose. Each is a fitting together of bits selected *ad hoc;* of items of perception and practice which Franklin may himself have set in the foreground of his personal history, perhaps not aware of the deep hinterland urges for which they were compensations, of which they were harnessings. The compensations and harnessings could be remarked, uttered, reflected upon; the urges could, no more than the submerged force of a snow-

capped iceberg. The utterances could elicit snobbisms such
as that of anti-American Lord Jeffrey who, about half a
generation after Franklin died, sneered at this self-taught
sage and savant upon whom European and American universities had conferred doctorates *honoris causa*, as "the uned-
ucated tradesman of America." They could stir to utterance
such rebellions of the belly and the gonads against the brain
as D. H. Lawrence's, who couldn't stand Benjamin because
"he takes away my wholeness and my dark forest, my freedom." Even when capable of the empathy of a Van Doren or
a Lucas and with as apt a sense of the spirit of the Enlightenment, the image-makers perforce shape the multi-
dimensional Doctor's likeness by each choosing from the
multitudinous or scanty evidences before him, bits which he
unknowingly fits into such patterns as further in bulk the
image-maker's own inward business and desires amid the
persons and places of his own times.

The conventions of creed and code prevailing when
Franklin was born and as he was growing up were formally
Calvinist. To be sure, that there's a divinity which shapes
man's ends, rough-hew them as he may, was commonsense
as well as logic. Although finite and infinitely ignorant,
Homo sapiens can neither see nor foresee his destiny; all of it
exists, pre-established. What is, was; what was, will be. A
person's earthly career and ultimate fate which, as he lives
on from birth to death, seem but a chain of happenings, are
now, at once and all together, the instant and indivisible will
and vision of an "infinite, omnipotent, vain God," "fond of
Commendation and Flattery." Conceive Creator in the manner of the theists or the manner of the deists, by means of
Revelation or by means of Newton's mechanic laws, "judge
from Scripture what is orthodox but . . . from reason what
is Scripture," nevertheless, predestination is man's lot; and
hence—Pope has said it in his way and Dryden in his—
Whatever is, is right. "Though purblind man," Dryden
adds, "sees but a part of the chain, the nearest link, his eyes

not carrying to the equal Beam that poises all above." Why, then, asks the Butler of the *Analogy*, should we be deceived?

Why indeed, year in and year out, is man's struggle to live, his struggle to break the chain he conceives by breaking the link he perceives? Why is it his struggle to make his destiny for himself? Young, very young Ben Franklin, working in his brother's printery, taking on his brother's tasks while the latter is forbidden for a bit of unlicensed (to the Calvinist authorities, licentious) printing, absorbing ideas as he sets types, writing verses and essays that his absorptions bred—young Franklin reflected upon the paradox. He was only nineteen when he issued his *Dissertation on Liberty and Necessity, Pleasure and Pain*. To the thinker, what else could the universe be but an infinitely perfect machine? What else man, but a trivial cog of a gargantuan clockworks, impotent alike to do or to refrain? If, as conscious, man differs from the unconscious stuff of being, he differs only in that he feels pain. Life diverges from the matter of the nature of things as at once such feeling and the striving to abolish it. To live is but to struggle to extinguish the pain with which awareness starts and as which it persists; it is to strain and strive for freedom from this "uneasiness." To experience pleasure is the same as to free oneself from pain; for pleasure *is* the abolition of pain, pain is the absence of pleasure, and each is the equal measure of the other. Abolishing pain is, like "the fall of a heavy body to the ground," inevitable. At any moment, it is man's sole good, with all else evil. Mankind's end is thus one, while the ways to it are many. Young Franklin also had another term for this end—self-love—and argued that to exist aware is not preferable to insensible existence.

As young Franklin grew older, however, experience prevailed over dialectic. With the ongoing increase of his "share of Felicity" by dint of his own labors, he could not but acknowledge that liberty is real, that the experience of it is authentic. But this argument for Liberty did not draw upon the experience of the self-making youth making himself; it drew upon the commonest and most recommended practice of the Calvinist cults. This was the paradoxical practice of prayer. For prayer is a doing which seeks to change the will and vision of the almighty eternal God of foreordination. That men pray is evidence that "all things are not foreordained," let God be what He is. Franklin had concluded so in 1730, and had written a pamphlet to this effect. But as he tells Benjamin Vaughan in a letter written almost half a century later, November 9, 1779, the pamphlet "was never printed, and the manuscript has long been lost." And he sums up: "The great uncertainty I found in metaphysical reasonings disgusted me, and I quitted that kind of reading and study for others more satisfactory."

However, Benjamin Franklin, growing up and growing older, seems never to have doubted that there might be some kind of cosmic providence working as "the laws of Nature and of Nature's God." Its human meaning could not, he felt, be discerned by means of metaphysical or theological disputation; but the uses that man put it to might disclose it. He took for granted Bacon's perception that knowledge is power and that power must needs be power to effect other changes besides the extinction of pain. As he achieved his maturity, he became more and more sensitive to men's will to change, and in his old age he supplemented the beneficence of necessitarian Reason, equating effects and causes, with the like beneficence and even occasional superiority of "instinct," of "enthusiasm," of what Pascal had signalized as the reasons which not the head, but the heart has. Reflecting in his *Autobiography* on how he had himself thought up reasons for satisfying one of his urges, Franklin writes: "So convenient a thing it is to be a reasonable Creature, since it enables one to find or make a Reason for everything one has a mind to do." He wrote in his sixty-second year to the Methodist evangelist, George Whitefield—with whom he had become friendly during the latter's evangel in the colonies—

regarding the terms of his creed: "I *see* with you that our affairs are not well-managed by our rulers here below; I wish I could *believe* with you that they are well-attended to by those above." But human events, he adds, depend on "human prudence or imprudence, as either may happen to be uppermost." He had already observed in his role of Poor Richard Saunders, the seventeenth-century astrologer and almanac-maker, that "experience keeps a dear school but fools will learn in no other," and he had come to Puck's perception of what fools these mortals be, and how troublesome those can be who have wit. In sum, *Homo sapiens*, whether as man of reason or man of feeling and will, is born unto folly as the sparks fly upward. Writing at Passy to the lovable Mme. Brillon (in French, of course), this Poor Richard, without illusions about the female of the species, remarks: "Two like you and me draw opposite conclusions from identical premises. Reason seems to me a blind guide. Instincts are more reliable. Animals together are less rarely mistaken in ages than one man in a month purporting to conduct himself according to Reason. This is why I let my wife's opinion guide me in difficult matters, for I believe that women have a sort of tact much more reliable than our reasonings." One remembers Thomas Jefferson's *Dialogue between the Head and the Heart*, which he addressed to Maria Cosway. Both of these so diverse agonists of the European Enlightenment and the American Idea seem to recognize in the human will and passion a force more potent than mankind's reason to serve its struggle for survival.

And how else indeed could a nature like Ben Franklin's, more than commonly conscious of the *whats*, the *hows*, the *whys* of his own growth and status, appraise the energies at work? He was more sensitive than most to the human craving for absolute certainty and its consequent dogmatism; how aboriginal that is, and how it leads most men "to think themselves in possession of all truth, and whenever others differ from them, it is so far error. . . . But though many private Persons think as highly of their own infallibility as that of their Sect, few express it as naturally as a certain French lady, who in a little dispute with her sister, said: 'But I meet with nobody but myself who is always right.' "

Moreover, is it not very much simpler, very much more convenient to detail the deliberations of reason than to identify the propulsions of feeling, seeing that each has an absoluteness all its own, an absoluteness which only another élan so absolute can counter and perhaps contain? What more natural for a thoughtful young journeyman printer, giving himself the most liberal of liberal educations through working at his job, and so, aware of the supernatural bookkeeping whose balance sheets would determine where and how a person would have to live when he was dead—what more natural, one asks, than to devise a balance sheet of his own for while he is alive, a sheet set to his own experience of the profits and losses of his struggle for self-preservation? Franklin's "prudential algebra" bulks large in the record; it signifies less, much less, in the life. Its role, for any man struggling to keep on struggling, is that of an organ or a tool; and for Franklin, to keep on was explicitly to keep changing one's conditions and one's self. Alike in his often pseudonymous letters to the press, in his bylaws for the many voluntary groups that he formed or counselled, in his reports to committees on which he served, in his personal correspondence and in his public documents, he imparts the sense of melioristic propulsion, an urge to abolish or mitigate pain so as to advance one's own existence and functions in the world. As young Poor Richard he had advised:

> If you would not be forgotten
> As soon as you are dead and rotten
> Either write things worth reading
> Or do things worth writing

After he became alert to our animal urge toward infallibility, he maintained a certain scepticism of the means, and thus

nourished a commitment to a universal toleration. He remarked concerning his own views, as later both John Mill
and William James did concerning all views, "I leave them
to take their chance in the world. If they are *right*, truth and
experience will support them; if wrong, they ought to be
refuted and rejected." His predictions regarding the contri-
butions of science—that is, of the knowledge which is power
over nature—to the freedom and happiness of man, modernity has verified; and even more, perhaps, has it verified the
regret with which he closed one prediction: "O that *moral
science* were in as fair a way to improvement, that men
would cease to be wolves to one another and that human
beings would at length learn what they now improperly call
humanity!"

Franklin's "prudential algebra" might plausibly be interpreted an attempt at "moral science." As it had forerunners
in the philosophico-theological tradition, it also has successors such as Jeremy Bentham's felicific calculus and William James's equation for self-esteem; it now has divergent
elaborations as sociometrics, econometrics and other compu-
tations of this day.

Snobbism takes this algebra as somehow the vital center of
Franklin's philosophic faith; whereas it is no more than the
periphery. The vital center was the collision of urges, the
duel within the will. Franklin's calculus would temper the
spontaneous infallibilities of the colliding urges, whether of
an individual, a church or state, to some sort of reciprocal
accommodation, thus perhaps reshaping the inner impact
from blind clash to orderly competition, from warring absoluteness to maybe pacific relations, so that the survival of the
whole person or society whose drives were colliding may
become more likely. Without deprecating the combative
emulations in men's self-makings, Franklin learned from
experience that men nevertheless could be teamed up, and
that each, while satisfying his own cravings—for example,
by reading and talking—could contribute to satisfying his

teammates. He makes the point in the second *Dialogue between Philocles and Horatio*, when he has Philocles declare that man's good consists "not merely in Action" but in "reasonable Action"—i.e., "the actions which are preservative of the human kind, and naturally tend to produce zeal and unmixed happiness"—hence, "morally good." So at twenty-one he had organized his Junto or Leather-Apron Club whose members were to discuss everything; likewise to "protect the just liberties of the people" and "to love mankind in general, of whatever profession or religion soever; to love truth for truth's sake." All in all, the Junto was a design for self-liberation by means of self-education, and ultimately of all men's self-liberation by this means.

With Franklin as leader, the society sped the establishment of a public library as a tool necessary to this work; it fathered the formation of the now snobbishly elect Philosophical Society that took for its aim to "increase power, convenience and pleasure" by endeavoring to learn the sequences of nature going on rather than speculating about their *how* or *why*. It is not overstatement that Franklin's journalism satisfied a similar motive. So also did the Academy which he helped to establish with a view to education for public service rather than personal salvation; and with a curriculum hence giving greater weight to mechanic arts and engineering than to the classics and theology of the "liberal arts." Franklin, already when a self-making teenager of sixteen, had, over the pseudonym of Mrs. Silence Dogood, ridiculed the uses of theology at Harvard College in one of the more or less humorous Dogood Papers which he was writing for his brother's New England *Courant*. At the Academy, he planned to have scholars busy themselves, especially in reading and writing English as a way to clear and easy style. After some time, convention prevailed over innovation, however, and the traditional order of studies was reestablished.

It is a commonplace that modern pedagogy makes

Franklin's innovations its tradition; that his *Proposals for Promoting Useful Knowledge among the British Planta- tions in America* and his *Proposal Relating to the Education of Youth in Pennsylvania* are more congruous with the scien- tific and industrial, as well as the political revolutions than any of the soi-disant "humanistic" programs. Aficionados of those programs balk at the implications of "useful" as if any knowing, even the most fatuous and fantastic, could be use- less except as it failed to nourish and strengthen the learner's powers for a freer, safer, more abundant life, alive on earth or dead in heaven. Franklin was quite sure of the former. In his view, therefore, good teaching would turn on good actual models, of both pattern and procedure, on which to form character and achieve a style of life, even as they turn good models for forming the character and achieving a style of letters. Good teaching turns also on good counsel, such as Jonathan Swift's *Proposals for Correcting, Improving, and Ascertaining the English Tongue*, which Franklin recom- mended for Class 6 of his English School. Having taught himself to write by means of good models and good counsel, Franklin recommended what he had thus learned—that by means of good models and good counsel, the learner comes to know what he may achieve and what he may become, and how to manage his knowings to advantage as they impattern his powers over himself and over tools and things. "Learn of the skillfull," advises Poor Richard, "he that teaches himself hath a fool for his master."

On the record, the self-made man was counselling contem- poraries and posterity about the stylistic fruits of his first imitating, then emulating, such originals as he read in the King James Bible, in Addison's *Spectator*, in Newton's dis- closures of the articulations of nature, and in the utterances of men at work when they are discussing workmanship. From these he shaped the singularity of his own simple, easy, lucid way with the English tongue in prose and verse. One should write as one speaks, he advised. Unlike Swift, unlike Voltaire (even though some called Franklin the American Voltaire), who did so write, Franklin was by vocation primarily a workman, a do-it-yourself man, while they were primarily wordmen by vocation. Franklin "liked to see good workmen handle their tools," and was a maker and improver of his own. (His words first signified his seeings and doings and are words for images and ideas usually by second intention.) Swift's words and Voltaire's words usually mean images, ideas, other words first, and persons and things last.

One might say that, for the men of letters that Swift and Voltaire were, function was determined by form and their evocation of laughter or tears depended on their word-man art. Per contra for Franklin, the man of affairs, form was shaped by function, and his evocation of laughter or tears depended on the uses it would serve for him. How a thing—or a person—should look or sound or feel its present worth, would depend on what it was doing and how it was doing it. "Nothing" Franklin once declared," is good or beautiful but as it is useful. Yet all things have a utility under particular circumstances. Thus, poetry, painting, music and the stage as their embodiment are all necessary and proper gratifications of a refined state of society, but objectionable at an earlier period, since their cultivation would make a taste for their enjoyment precede its means."

In a letter to Lord Kames (June 2, 1765), re his lordship's *Elements of Criticism*, Franklin wishes the author had "demonstrated that the pleasure which artists feel in hearing much of that [music] composed in the modern taste is not the natural pleasure arising from melody or harmony of sounds, but of the same kind with the pleasure we feel on seeing the surprising feats of tumblers and rope-dancers, who execute difficult things." For this was Franklin's own opinion. Non-musicians, he goes on, whose faces he had watched on purpose, gave "no sign of pleasure . . . during the performance of a great part that was admired by the performers themselves, while a plain old *Scottish tune* which they disdained, and could scarcely be prevailed upon to play, gave manifest and general delight." After a discussion of the esthetic of music, and contingently of form and color, Franklin concludes: "The connoisseurs of modern music will say I have no taste, but I can not help adding that I believe our ancestors, in hearing a good song, distinctly articulated, sung to one of those tunes and accompanied by the harp, felt more real pleasure than is communicated by the generality of modern operas, exclusive of that arising from the scenery and dancing. . . . Whoever has heard James Oswald play [the old tunes] on his violincello will be less inclined to dispute this with me. I have more than once seen tears of pleasure in the eyes of his auditors; and yet, I think, even *his* playing those tunes would please more, if he gave them less modern ornament." This in the days when Bach and Hayden and Handel were "modern." * Franklin did not say whether the fiddle he could play, or the "armonica" he invented, was designed for simple Scottish tunes only; nor is there any record of a reaction of his to the compositions which Mozart and Beethoven are said to have written for it.

Holding education to be the means of means, it is not surprising that as Poor Richard he declares that a schoolmaster is worth a dozen poets, but there is no record of his having appraised either writers or performers of music by the same measure or of his relating pleasure in music to laughter as he has to tears.

Condorcet said of Franklin and Voltaire that "both had often made use of the arm of *la plaisenterie* which corrects human foolishness [*folie*] and teaches us to regard perversity as a more calamitous foolishness." But however one may account for it, Voltaire the tragic poet, who valued his trage-

---

* In an undated letter on the same theme to his brother Peter, Ben writes: "A modern song . . . neglects all the proprieties and beauties of common speech, and in their place introduces its *defects* and *absurdities* as so many graces." He illustrates with a song from "the ever famous Handel's 'Judas Maccabeus.' "

dies far above his *plaisenteries*, had a profounder human if
not a profounder philosophical sense of *lacrimae rerum* than
Franklin. This may have been due to the differences in their
education as well as in their temperaments. Franklin's definition of man's plight as a necessary equation of pain and
pleasure, with pleasure only the negation of pain, in a foreordained personal history, was a youthful conclusion which he
abandoned not long after he came to it, and seems not to
have returned to. For whatever reasons, besides the fact that
men pray believing that prayer can and does change the
course of human events, he became persuaded of the reality
of liberty and lived on, its champion and organizer, to the
day he died. But there is no indication that he came to
appreciate pleasure as something positive, or how together
with pain it gives direction and shape to man's struggle to
go on struggling. Modern psychology renders an error
Franklin's belief—a not infrequent one in the history of
philosophy—that pain alone is the original stuff of awareness, that pleasure is always pain's diminution and extin-
guishment. His life work and his prudential algebra ensue,
but animated by a fighting faith in equal liberty. "All men
are by nature equal," Poor Richard asserts, "but they differ
greatly in the sequel." Men's struggle to preserve themselves
is their struggle to eliminate pain and suffering, thus by
learning their own ways and nature's, to overcome the causes
and occasions of pain and so make progress toward ever
greater liberty, security, peace and abundance with the
pleasure they are means to. "If you would thrive," counsels
Poor Richard, "first contrive, and then strive." To contrive is
to produce innovations, discoveries, inventions, the uses of
which can not be guaranteed in advance any more than a
baby's. These works of man develop consequentially, one
leading to another; if any fails to develop, it soon or late
becomes extinct.

The same thing holds for the arts that evoke tears or
laughter: like the baby, an evocation must occur before it

can come to consequences which approve or condemn it. Individuals can be constitutional laughers, like Potts, or constitutional weepers like Parsons. Potts and Parsons were friends of Franklin's, members of the Junto. Potts was a poor man, Parsons, well-to-do. Franklin referred to them in one of his parables: "The happiness of life rather depends on internals than externals," he wrote, ". . . Parsons in his prosperity always fretting, Potts in the midst of his poverty, ever laughing. . . . There is such a thing as a happy or an unhappy consitution." Parsons, the unhappy rich man, owned the means of overcoming the pain of original nature, but couldn't use it to any effect; Potts, the ever-laughing poor man, drew means enough from his very lacks. Poor Richard remarks, "we build the ladder as we rise," and in any man's rise to "happiness," his own propensities are the vital building materials. Franklin, if not Parsons, could experience the pleasure of tears: having read Thomson's *Seasons*, he wrote to Strahan before he broke with him, "That charming Poet has brought more Tears of Pleasure into my Eyes than all I ever read before."

However, save regarding the postulate that pain is the prime stuff of experience, Franklin's ideas about the relations of liberty, tears, and laughter turn more on the overcoming of pain, and the role therein of laughter than of tears. His sense of humor seems consistently to dissipate any tragic sense of life he may have experienced. He gave moral, far more than esthetic weight, to funning for the fun of it, as might be expected from what is called his utilitarianism. When, as a boy only seventeen, he took on his brother's editorial responsibility for the then *New England Courant*, he wrote a preface defining his editorial policy. Among other things, he said: "Long has the Press groaned in bringing forth a hateful, but numerous Brood of Party Pamphlets, malicious scribbles, and Billingsgate Ribaldry. The Rancour and Bitterness it has unhappily infused in man's minds, and to what a Degree it has soured and leven'd the Tempers of

Persons formerly esteemed some of the most sweet and affa-
ble, is too well known here, to need any further Proof or
Representation of the latter.

"No generous and impartial Person can then blame the
present Undertaking, which is designed purely for the Di-
version and Merriment of the Reader. Pieces of Pleasantry
and Mirth have a secret charm in them to allay the Heats
and Tumours of our Spirits, and to make a man forget his
restless Resentments. They have a strange Power to turn the
harsh Disorder of the Soul and to reduce us to a serene and
placid State of Mind."

There is no evidence that Franklin ever changed this
youthful view, nor would he have needed to. For those
"pieces" are not *ad hoc*, but incidental and diversionary.
They are items of the comic art, and the catharsis they
induce is not a release from the causes of the pain men suffer
but such a drainage of the original stuff of consciousness as
converts it to the pleasure of laughter. One might guess that
the twenty-five years of Poor Richard's aphorisms, original
and quoted both, effected a good deal of such drainage for
Richard's creator even when serving, like *The Busy Body*,
ad hoc purposes. *The Busy Body* titles a series of feuilletons,
which Franklin, at twenty-two, wrote with a comrade of his
Junto for the *American Weekly Mercury*. The second of the
series states Franklin's lifelong view of the indecencies of
laughing-at instead of *laughing-with* others. He had himself
had a disposition to *laugh-at*, and his father had warned him
against this "too much inclination to lampooning and libelling." He begins his essay by quoting Pope's couplet:

> *All fools still have an itching to decide.*
> *And fain would be upon the laughing side.*

One such fool of a "witty gentleman" is Ridentius, who
makes fun of some other person's way of dressing, facial
expressions, bodily defects, in order to "put him to the
blush." "If such a fellow," says Franklin, "makes laughing

the sole end and purpose of his life, if it is necessary to his constitution, or if he has a great desire of growing suddenly fat, let him eat; let him give public notice where any dull, stupid rogue may get a quart of four-penny for being laughed at; but it is barbarously unhandsome, when friends meet . . . that one should be the butt of the company, and four men made merry at the cost of the fifth." Franklin's foil to Ridentius is "the good-natured, gay Eugenius, who never spoke yet but with a design to divert and please . . . takes more delight in applying the wit of his friends than in being admired himself; [and] makes use of some ingenious artifice to turn the edge of ridicule [if anyone is hurt] another way, choosing rather to make himself a public jest than be at the pain of seeing his friend in confusion." "Among the tribe of laughter," Franklin says in conclusion, "I reckon the petty gentlemen that wrote satires, and carry them about in their pockets, reading them themselves in all company they happen into; taking an advantage of the ill taste of the town to make themselves famous for a pack of paltry, low, nonsense for which they deserve to be kicked rather than admired by all who have the least tincture of politeness. . . . I expect they will be squibbing at the Busy-Body himself. However, the only favour he begs of them is this, that if they cannot control their overbearing itch of scribbling, let him be attacked in downright biting lyrics for there is no satire he dreads half so much as an attempt toward a panegyric."

Poor Richard declares somewhere that "he makes a foe who makes a jest." Perhaps he should have said he *has* a foe who makes a jest, for when jesting is not simple gaiety and mirth, or sadist pleasure, it is defense against felt enmity, personal or communal. Those phases of Franklin's jesting which receive attention are the latter. They are his "satyrizings," his defenses against public evils. Withal, his sincere *ad hoc* intention is to change, by evoking laughter, the ways of a mankind that he purports to understand without illusion, without the bitterness of disillusion and with sympathy. Parton calls him, first and last, a "humorist," and invites the inference that Franklin's was that laughter which George Meredith declares to be the prime intent of his comic spirit, the spirit that laughs down all passions, all purposes and principles which pretend to claims upon reality with nothing real to draw upon, with no power or knowledge or skill to give them the reality they pretend to and do not have. So Franklin's "satyr" laughed down the claims of priestcraft and the logic of theology; the tergiversations of politicians and the stupidities of the better people, all pretending to one or another form of power although they had none, and by their pretensions serving only to diversify the pains and prevent the pleasures of man's struggle to go on struggling. Whenever Franklin felt it was to the purpose, he evoked laughter by showing them up, by laying bare their empti- ness. He did this with a dead-pan phrasing of which the denuding effect is perceived before it is realized, and then is realized with a shock. An instance is the seemingly innocent question which made the literal-minded Father-to-be of Our Country burst into hilarious laughter. Franklin asked it in response to an English "gentleman's" complaint that it was unfair for the Yankees at Concord and Lexington to shoot at British soldiers from behind walls. "Why," said Franklin, "didn't those walls have two sides?"

On occasion he took up beliefs, attitudes, happenings as they appeared and uncovered their inherent absurdities by developing their implications to their ultimate conclusions in some nonsensical bigness or nonsensical littleness. Tradition often calls these techniques hoaxes. But hoaxes are malicious deceptions or practical jokes, and Franklin's sequences could fool nobody not so prejudiced or so ignorant as to ask to be fooled by images and rationalizations such as whales pur- suing codfish into the Great Lakes and up and over Niagara Falls. Or by any of the following: the Moslem argument justifying commerce in Christian slaves; the Count de Schaumbergh's letter to the commander of the Hessian troops in North America about handling his troops so that the per capita total for all the soldiers killed might be sufficient to pay the expenses of the royal pleasures; the edict of the King of Prussia—Voltaire's own Frederick—annexing Britain on the ground that the original settlers of the island kingdom were of Germanic blood, and ordaining for the new dominions the rules which the British government had imposed on the American colonies; the comment on the British use of Indians during the War for Independence, in the form of a letter from Captain Gerrish of the New England militia giving an account of the booty his force had captured— booty including eight packages of scalps which Indians had taken from the heads of Virginians, New Yorkers, New Jerseyites and Pennsylvanians and sent by the scalpers, with an invoice, as a gift to Col. Haldimand, Governor of Canada, in order that he should transmit it to his Majesty in England. This last invention, set forth so matter-of-factly, is an atrocity-story which wartime feeling could take for true, and thus a hoax, more consistent with Swift's *saeva indignatio* than with Franklin's disillusioned humor. But Ben's indignation is for the British, not the "Senekas." In a Pamphlet of *Remarks on the Savages of North America* he wrote: "We call them savages because they are different," and he implies that their way of life achieves qualities of sincerity, innocence, and reasonableness such as Voltaire attributes to that child of nature, the Huron of his tale by this name.

On the whole, Franklin's parables and anecdotes were no more hoaxes than his cartoons. They were more complex and less readily interpretable parables; the logic of their metaphor consisted in applying existing relationships to imagined terms; but to terms imagined as interchangeable with the real ones as their relations were identical. Parton also called Franklin the first American caricaturist. His reproductions of the sage's "caricatures" however, in his *Caricature and Other Comic Art*, present rather graphic statements of ideas and situations than distortions of human or non-human actualities. The well-remembered one of a serpent in sections, with New England the head, South Carolina the tail, the remainder of the thirteen colonies the middle, and the warning, *Join or Die*, beneath, is representative. When Franklin had the idea that Britain and her colonies might form a single self-governing commonwealth, his symbol for the actual relations between them was a female torso with its arms and legs scattered around.

His "satyrs" of religion and professional religionists had more bite. It is said that he early had learned Butler's *Hudibras* by heart and quoted it to suit any occasion. He had made his appraisal of the preponderant doctrines and disciplines of the denominations while still in his teens and it persisted with no vital change to the end of his life. This is the image of the *Temple of Theology* in Silence Dogood's *Dream*. Those busy in the Temple had to work hard and suffer, yet their numbers were great. The dreamer wondered why, until she "spy'd *Pecunia* behind a curtain, beckoning them with her hand." Except "the ambitious and fradulent contrivances of Plagius," she saw "nothing (else) worth mentioning." Clericus, who woke her, easily interpreted her entire dream as "a lively representation of Harvard College." In another paper, Silence also offers her readers "A Receipt to Make a New England Funeral Elegy," which she had from the hands of her "Reverend Husband." It gives directions how dishonestly to speak well of the dead. Franklin says he never doubted the teachings he holds to be essentials of all religions, however diverse: belief in a deity at once creator and providence; belief in man's immortality, in rewards for virtue and penalties for vice—as, of course he himself conceives virtue, vice, rewards and penalties, and hence altogether as issues of thisworldly conduct and consequences. He replied to Whitefield, when the latter characteristically thanked him for a favor: "Don't let me be mistaken: it was not for Christ's sake but for your sake." For his own and his posterity's sake he rewrote the Lord's prayer, made up a "little liturgy . . . entitled *Articles of Belief and Acts of Religion*," and after a time "went no more to the public Assemblies." But his God is best satisfied by the conjoint practice of his thirteen thisworldly virtues to which, he informs his posterity, he "ow'd the constant felicity of his life down to his 79th year in which this is written." The vital thing, he reflects, is not the perfection of virtue, but the practice which might achieve perfection. He had started with only twelve virtues but added the thirteenth, humility, because somebody had accused him of the vice of pride; and while his prescription for attaining humility was: "Imitate Jesus and Socrates," his execution was distinctly Socratic. Moreover, he reflects that pride is the toughest of our natural passions, and that if he could achieve perfect humility, he would probably take pride in his humility.

Whether Franklin enjoyed his "constant Felicity" because he satisfied his Deity, or satisfied his Deity by enjoying constant Felicity he does not say. His mode of enjoyment is the cultivation of an art, the *Art of Virtue*, "as properly an art as painting, navigation or architecture," and an art which any person of any religion can practice. He never got around to writing down for everybody's use, as he had meant to, a *Way to Virtue*. But he did weave together from maxims in his almanac a *Way to Wealth*. Some describe this way, à la Max Weber, as a compendium of "the Protestant ethic." But it takes a certain eccentricity of comprehension to diversify those convictions of the changing fortunes of experience in plain peoples' daily lives into the consequences of a specific creed and code. Actually, they were what Franklin called them, "gleanings he had made of the Sense of all Ages and Nations." Father Abraham's impatterning of these gleanings comes to the climax as Candide's: "It is necessary to cultivate our garden."

One might say that Franklin identifies this laborious, life-saving stress and striving with the spending of time, but not time as money, rather, time as life. "Dost thou love life, then do not squander time, for that's the stuff that life is made of." Then, "if time be of all things the most precious, wasting time must be the greatest prodigality. Lost time is never found again." Nor can there ever be too much of it, or enough of it, since "time enough always proves little enough." Merely to hope for better times, hence, is to live on air, promise-crammed. We make times better if we bestir ourselves; "one Today is worth two Tomorrows"; "Diligence is the mother of Good Luck; God gives all things to Industry." In a later idiom—the survival we struggle for is the struggle for survival itself; the self for whose preservation we strive is the striving itself. Thus, "wasting time" is the struggler's own, or another's, appraisal of that which time is being spent on, and how; one man's waste can well count for another man's thrift; the spendthrift may well be the saver accumulating his own peculiar treasure of experience, once his spending is realized as self-fulfillment.

Was not Franklin's own career such a spending? A transvaluation of the pain at the springs of his personal history, by means of humorous reasonings such as he utters in the fables of *The Whistle*, *The Handsome and Deformed Leg*, the *Dialogue between Franklin and the Gout?* In terms of earning and saving, did he not spend at least half his long life violating the Protestant ethic—this self-made man who had freed himself from the necessity of earning his bread in order to busy himself in the liberties of exercising his spirit? Workman Ben Franklin made himself the gentleman of leisure who wasted his time practicing political wisdom, pioneering in science, and cultivating letters and the arts, all even more for their intrinsic satisfactoriness than for their consequential uses. Who among the born gentlemen of leisure of his age ever had half his fun or "felicity"?

First and last, it is this time-binding intrinsic satisfactoriness which, as time passes, measures and assigns their values to persons and places and thoughts and things for this reputed Oliver Optic of the Enlightenment. At nineteen he could argue with an irrefutable logic that "since it is supposed that God the Maker of the Universe is infinitely wise, good and powerful," all his makings are equal in his sight, and life is not preferable to insensibility—a conclusion which brings *genus humanum* "down to Equality with the beasts of the Field! . . . with the meanest part of the creation! . . . hurts man's Pride and degrades the Species!" At twenty-four he could argue that inasmuch as prayer exists, liberty must be real and mankind are not altogether effects of causes they cannot control; at least in part men are the makers of their own happiness or misery; nor does the one balance out the other in a sort of Newtonian equation. At seventy-three or seventy-four, ill-at-ease and lamed with age, yet with no imbalance of his "constant felicity" from such practicing of the art of virtue that he could do, and with some eight years of intense activity still before him, Franklin reverts to the abandoned philosophic ultimacies of his youth. *The Ephemera* utters one mood of his reversion. He wrote it at Passy, in the form of a letter, probably to Mme. Brillon. Some verses from the *Prologue to the Book of Job*—of all his books of the Bible—together with a commentary, *The Leveé*, channel another mood.

The Ephemera are insects whose "successive . . . generations . . . are bred and expire the same day." Franklin finds them spending their time, "seemingly as regardless of the shortness of life as if they had been sure of living a month." He overhears the soliloquy of a lonely oldster of theirs who, although he has outlived his own generation, knows well enough that soon he too must die. So he asks himself: What's the use of living? Of all my deeds? And what will be to me the lasting fame my friends promise me when I'm dead? What good will anything be when the entire world comes to its end "and be buried in universal ruin?" And what is now left to a senescent self, save the solid pleasure of recalling he spent "a long life in meaning well, the companionship of a few good lady Ephemerae and now and then a kind smile and a tune from the ever-amiable *Brillante*?"

From the Book of Job, Franklin offers, ostensibly as a sample of a long over-due translation, "a few verses of the first chapter:

Verse 6. And it being levee day in heaven, all God's nobility came to court, to present themselves before him; and Satan also appeared in the circle, as one of ministry.

7. And God said to Satan, You have been some time absent; where were you? And Satan answered I have been at my country seat, and in different places visiting my friends.

8. And God said, Well, what think you of Lord Job? You see he is my best friend, a perfectly honest man, full of respect for me, and avoiding everything that might offend me.

9. And Satan answered, Does your Majesty imagine that his conduct is the effect of mere personal attachment and affection?

10. Have you not protected him and heapt your benefits upon him, till he is grown enormously rich?

11. Try him:—only withdraw your favor, turn him out of his places, and withold his pensions, and you will soon find him in the opposition. . . .

Commenting on the celestial *levée*, Franklin suggests that the author of Job modelled it on terrestial levees of "the eastern monarchs of the age that he lived in." "Since," he adds, "the Book of Job is called by divines a sacred poem, and with the rest of the Holy Scriptures, is understood to be written for our instruction," what is the instruction, when you see Deity itself giving "way to calumny, permitting the destruction of the best of subjects?" Beware, therefore, of trusting any one man with the government of your State, "even with limited powers, lest sooner or later he sap and destroy those limits and render himself absolute." In short, inasmuch as absolutism in heaven leads to ultimate injustice, what else can it lead to on earth?

Together with the *Ephemera*, Franklin's sample from Job and his satirical discussion of Satan and his influence at

the Almighty's *levée* have a religio-philosophical import
which seems to sustain the working hypotheses of his personal history: however long be art and however brief the
life-time of the oldest of persons, the pleasure and pain, the
laughter and tears thereof are functions of the liberty with
which he can keep reforming pain into pleasure, tears into
laughter. The reformation is the reasoned practice of the art
of virtue which is the art of life, and sustaining it renders life
a life of reason, whatever the liver's business and desires
may be. So consequential an artist of life had Franklin made
himself in this way, that jealous, cantankerous John Adams
could report the self-made man's reputation to have been
"more universal than that of Leibnitz or Newton, Frederick
or Voltaire, and his character more beloved and esteemed
than any or all of them."

CHAPTER FIFTEEN

Destiny and Joie de Vivre: Mark Twain

Toward the middle of the road of his life—the aficionados set the year as 1870, more or less—Mark Twain published a brief essay entitled *The Late Benjamin Franklin*. This was the year of his marriage to his never-to-be-enough-cherished Livy, daughter of a coal baron of Elmira, New York. With the support of his father-in-law-to-be, he had become editor and part owner of the Buffalo, New York *Express*, and had a stake in a literary venture baptised *The Galaxy*. The comment on Franklin appeared in *The Galaxy*—an appraisal ambivalent, but not balanced. If Twain's remembrance was reliable, the genial doctor's autobiography provided Clemens père with the Jones he wanted his sons to live up to. At least, Franklin's name earned enough distinction for the Clemenses to have brother Orion identify his printery as the Ben Franklin Book and Job Office, and to emulate Ben's diet. Brother Sam says that he doesn't want to detract from the late Benjamin Franklin's record and fame, but not withstanding, attributes to him "a malevolence toward boys without parallel in history," and denounces him for rules of conduct which would suppress the spontaneities of boyish nature; rules which are for all times "an affliction to millions of boys . . . whose fathers had read Franklin's pernicious biography. His maxims were full of animosity toward boys." They imply, our humorist complained, that discipline and doctrine can "make a Franklin of every father's fool," which is just not so. Defending nature's boys against this falsehood, Twain took up his pen "to snub those pretentious maxims of his . . . worked up out of truisms that had become wearisome platitudes as early as the dispersion from Babel." Although his own father had died when he was twelve, Sam too, as a child "had to do everything just as Franklin, in the solemn hope that I would be a Franklin some day. And here I am."

Nor, on the record, did Sam fail to share the hope. He made many summaries of his personal history with its diversified careers of failure. One, in *Roughing It*, tells that he has clerked in a grocery, studied law, worked for a blacksmith, for a bookseller, for a druggist and finally, took to printing only, alas, to find himself a "slow compositor . . . I had made myself a tolerable printer, under the impression that I would be another Franklin, but somehow had missed the connection thus far." But at eighteen, wandering east, visiting Philadelphia, he sought out Franklin's grave.

So young Sam made a different kind of connection. He gives Franklin a stance akin to his own. He suggests that the sage had himself been a nature boy, only making believe to follow his own rules; that his true aim had been to gratify his boyish impulses. Maybe the hope imputed to papa was not so too, too illusory. For certainly, in its externals, Twain's career was not so unlike Franklin's as he implied. Both men were "self-made"; both evinced a certain curiosity about their Roundhead forbears and a not unprideful discussion of them. Both had considerable appreciation of themselves as makers, although Twain's purported to be more deprecatory than that of his ostensibly rejected Jones. Twain, too, was taken from school at the age of twelve and put to work in a printshop. Him, too, a Calvinist Providence impelled to get himself the measles as the initiation of his entire career; afterwards, it made him the editor of the home newspaper and a writer of prose and verse. He, too, equipped with the printer's good loose trade to earn his living by, left home to wander in search of fortune. Runaway Franklin wandered to New York, to Philadelphia, to London, and back to Philadelphia and the printshop; Clemens wandered to St. Louis, to New York, to Philadelphia, and back to his riparian Mississippi land again. Franklin undertook to make his fortune by becoming a master printer, Clemens by working at his craft off and on, and dreaming get-rich-quick schemes, including some enterprise (it is said, a slave empire) on the banks of the river Amazon, to which he got no nearer than New Orleans at the mouth of the Mississippi. That river's flow was to Clemens what the tides and winds of the Atlantic had been to Franklin.

Both reported, each according to his business and desires, how they felt and what they saw; Franklin, the man of affairs, scientifically curious about the practical import of natural phenomena; Clemens, the romantic ephebus who beheld in a pilot on a Mississippi riverboat not only a glamorous Jones to live up to, nor only the earner of a greater wage than any he had ever been paid, but also, the master of an empirical science more glamorous and challenging than that which made the river so safe when he returned to write his book about it.

Like Franklin, Clemens had a penchant for machinery; but machinery as signifying patents and speculative investments promising fortune; to Franklin machines signified improvements in the conditions of human living—he patented nothing, not even the stove Twain was querulous about, nor his lightning-rod, nor his musical instrument.

Both sage and ephebus had a deep concern for the ends and means of government, and both, still in their young manhood, participated in governing—Franklin, as a free male seeking and choosing a public duty, Clemens as an opportunist, needing to earn his living. More and more, Clemens discovered that he could more abundantly fulfil himself as a laughter-evoking writer and a lecturer able to exercise only a critic's and commentator's competency even in his own business; and to the day he died he gained large fortunes in this role, to lose them in his business ventures and to recoup them and pay his creditors to the last penny by perfecting the roles. Franklin gave up business in his forties and fulfilled himself as statesman, man of science and of letters, concerned to enact his faith in the equal liberty of all men into the institutions of a free society. He and Twain both became autodidacts loaded with academic honors, native and foreign. Both spent many years in foreign lands, Franklin mostly in England and France, Twain in almost all of Europe, for his wife's health and his own; and in his role of reporter and humorist he traveled the entire world.

The personal histories of both disclose them deeply sensitive to *lacrimae rerum* and concerned to dry the tears. Both had recourse to laughter. But Franklin thought of laughter very much as a means to redirect the energies of men toward a greater felicity. Twain's laughter changed from a jollity of spirit into a tear-like overcoming of imaginary helplessness and perhaps occasionally actual despair.

Beneath these likenesses live differences so utter that the resemblances seem forced. The vital center of Twain's caricature of Franklin is the recognition, perhaps mistaken, that Franklins are born, not made—plausible enough for anybody, and especially so for a person still making himself, and making himself at a phase of his striving when his frustrations figure in his sense of his selfhood far more largely than his achievements, which seem but a gift of Providence while the frustrations seem a product of ambition. There was an inwardness to Sam's frustrations besides which Ben's were superficial: "A boy's life is not all comedy, much of the tragic enters into it," Sam observes; and it enters both as the evils of the world around with its knifings, killings and hangings, and as the horrid dreams, the nightmare of a troubled conscience which, Sam continues, "I knew as inventions of Providence to beguile me to a better life. My repentance was very real, very earnest, and after each tragedy they happened every night for a long time. But as a rule they could not stand the daylight. They faded out and shied away and disappeared in the splendor of the sun. They were the creatures of fear and darkness and they could not live out of their own place. The day gave me cheer and peace and at night I repented again. In all my boyhood I am not sure that I ever tried to live a better life in the daytime—or wanted to. In my age I should never think of wishing to do such a thing. But in my age as in my youth night brings me many a deep remorse. I realize that from the cradle up I had been like the rest of the race—never quite the same at night . . . for months I was pure as driven snow. At night."

But although the splendor of the sun obscured the deep dark of the night, it was there under the sunshine, and the nightmares and the fear of them were there, haunting his days with their tragedy and impelling him to the pseudo-fatalism of his philosophic faith and the defiant laughter which perennially qualified it. As printer and journalist, as editor, as reporter, as river-pilot and would-be miner of gold and silver, as political secretary, as overseas traveler, and as Sam Clemens becoming Mark Twain the humorist, giving lectures and writing essays and stories, Sam had, man and boy, hewed his ends rough and hewed them fine, with Providence shaping them, he felt, without regard to his hewings, sometimes to his benefit, and always to its own dark unheeding will. His *Weltanschauung* seemed a creation of this feeling, and he was convinced that it had been, again and again and again, tested and confirmed by each crisis of the struggle by which he made himself the person whom he intended his autobiography to truly unveil. For this naked self-disclosure he began, while in Florence, to write down his recollections as they came or were occasioned. Remembering went on and built up into "a systemless system" of free associations. The rememberer was then sixty-two years old. After a while he stopped, not to resume until he was sixty-seven, but then dictating his memories to the man who was to become an intimate friend and chosen biographer. Purposing that the history of himself should be as veracious as he could make it, Mark Twain undertook to write and talk as "from the grave." It was in this role of ghost without inhibitions that he observed: "It isn't so astonishing the things that I can remember, as the number of things I can remember that aren't so."

Franklin also began his autobiography in his sixties, during a more or less idle interlude in England—he was sixty-five. He also had dropped it, but didn't resume it till eighteen years later, and then didn't carry the story very far. But he reviewed his personal history because he felt he had enjoyed a life good enough to be worth reliving, with some changes; and since living life over again was impossible, he did the next best thing—remembering it and writing down what he remembered on the chance that his memories might be of some use to his descendents. Although he had enjoyed a good life "with the blessing of God," the Blesser was the kind of God who, in the words of one of Poor Richard's maxims, "helps those who help themselves"; self-help was the *conditio sine qua non.* As we have seen, Franklin had transvalued liberty from a human illusion to a vital experience; Calvinist foreordination or Newtonian mechanism from an eternal providence or a universal law of nature into a force amenable to human manipulation—if only by prayer. Twain, the more successfully he made decisions and achieved goals with the means he devised, the more bitterly he argued mechanical necessity. His art of humorist by

tongue and pen brought him fame even in the groves of
Academe, and fortune sufficient to render his business gam-
bles only incidental wild oats. After Oxford had awarded
him his first honorary degree he remarked that hitherto
Academia had ignored him altogether, although "for a generation as widely celebrated a literary person as America had
ever produced, and I am also privately aware that in my
peculiar line I have stood at the head of my guild during all
that time, but I shall get my strength back now."

Then a laughing-sad sage of seventy-two, Twain had
come to this lonely eminence because laughter was alive in
him and he was able more successfully than the rest of his
guild to move his readers and hearers to laughter. He knew
that laughter was alive in him; but in his appraisal of himself and his experience he gave his sense of humor the role of
anodyne to his tragic sense of life. His world-wide delighted
public found the laughter sufficient unto itself—its own justification and not ever to be sufficiently rewarded with cash
and kudos. Even Twain's intimates had assured one another
and their own publics that he was an earnest moralist, no
mere funny man. His lifelong friend and literary counsellor,
W. D. Howells, who laughed at his pose on "the damned
human race," also spoke of the "fury" underneath the "fun"
which won Twain such a miscellany of friends. "Emerson,
Longfellow, Lowell, Holmes," Howells wrote, "I knew them
all and the rest of your sages, poets, seers, critics, humorists;
they were like one another and like other literary men; but
Clemens was sole, incomparable, the Lincoln of our literature."

The implication is that Mark Twain had achieved, as is
the wont of the rare bona fide humorists, a deeply felt, even if
not luminously articulated, philosophy of life. Maybe he
had, maybe he hadn't. If he hadn't it would be because he
had not livingly diverged from the dynamics of the creed
and code which in his childhood had designed the world and
ordered its happenings for him as good and evil, right and

wrong. He had simply transposed Christian orthodoxies of Hannibal, Missouri, concerning man, his world and his destiny into godless Newtonian and Darwinian terms. In those terms he restated original sin, inevitable yet unwon and unmerited good fortune and bad, ordained by a necessarily implacable, all powerful Divinity, whom to placate and cajole "the damned human race" had devised their comforting supernaturalism, organized their churches, trained their power-and-gold greedy priesthoods, and resorted to all the other nostrums and chicaneries wherewith mankind build their barriers against death—death, the one and only good which that omnipotent and uncaring nature *sive* omnipotent and loving God, has assured to every living thing.

It is upon this utterly commonplace and ineffably tragic universe all tears, that philosopher Mark Twain would direct the laughter of his public, who nevertheless are, as he sees them, beyond salvation even by laughter. His poet's eye, in fine frenzy rolling from times recent to times past, from his gauchely utopian American river to the panoplied but miserable castles and palaces of Europe and Asia, to the befouled sacred places of the Holy Land, endows the thus transvalued conventions of the ancestral faith with habitations and names. It provides the humorist with concrete immediate symbols of what it is his urge to laugh down. It enables him, as artist and thinker, to entertain even when he means only to edify, even when he doesn't want to entertain. Twain once remarked that his role was to teach. But save by a peculiar elite, his jocund debunking of the damned human race—its "moral sense," its God and His Word, its destiny, as he was indoctrinated in those by the Christians, his elders—is experienced as a joke and not as a debunking. For all the urgency of Twain's tragic sense of life, of his realization of the tears of things, his expression imparts a sort of matter-of-fact *joie de vivre*. The zest and zeal of it stir a realization of how greatly and how diversely human reality is human imagination in action, human fantasy in performance. Twain was himself intermittently sensible of this. A person's "real life" he wrote anent his plan for his autobiography "is in his head and is known to none but himself. All day long and every day the mill of his brain is grinding, and his thoughts, not those other things, are his history. His acts and words are merely the visible thin crust of his world, with its scattered snow summits, and its vacant wastes of water—and they are so trifling a part of his bulk, a mere skin enveloping it! The mass of him is hidden: it and its volcanic fires that toss and boil, and never rest, night nor day. These are his life, and they are not written and cannot be written." And in *The Mysterious Stranger* he suggests—a theme we shall return to—through the mouth of the Stranger, that this turbulence is a dream-work of a thought, *solo ipse*, "the only existent thought . . . the inextinguishable, indestructible." Revealed to himself by the Stranger, the solipsist is now free. He may "dream other thoughts and better."

Now it is such ineffable turbulent dreaming that the great writer opens his characteristic door to, even when the dreamer-author believes that they who enter through it are also part of his dream; even if he only dreams that he craves to commune with his creations and strives thus to make his soliloquy a veritable communication. Once and again, Twain opened a door. And although he would not have conceded this—in that he was such an opener of doors, he was disclosing a conception of value and existence which defined the human enterprise for what it is: the tumult and the shouting of lusts and hungers and rages, creating their own assuagements of fact where they could, of fantasy where they could not, in a circumambience which destroys them as heedlessly and helplessly as it creates them.

Twain struggled to keep up this existence and its values for all he was worth. He lived them, materially and spiritually, to the utmost of his resources of zest and zeal and regret. He did not commit the suicide which would be the conclusion of that bugaboo of little philosophic minds, consistency; and he would have regretted the world's belief that he had, when, after his Livy's death, he almost fell from his chair: "The fall would have killed me; in my bereaved circumstance the world would have been sure it was suicide." Once, much later, he broke out to his Fidus Achates, Paine, "Why can't a man die when he's had his tragedy? I ought to have died long ago." On another occasion he said: "I've been thinking it out—if I live two years more I will put an end to it all. I will kill myself . . . I am so tired of the eternal round. . . . The country home I need is a cemetery." But he lived for some years yet in country homes where he could hold levees and smoke and work in bed; where he could wear white suits, play billiards, curse and swear freely and happily; where he could cultivate the friendship of small girls and bask in the affectionate admiration of the lords and commons of the damned human race from all walks of life.

He was concerned to live well, even lavishly, while he lived; and to provide, by means of his expression, for an immortality of remembrance when dead. Hence, the autobiography; hence, the safekeeping of his little daughter Susy's story of papa's life; hence, the official biography arranged for while he was still abundantly alive; hence, when his daughter Jean died suddenly, without forewarning, on Christmas Eve, 1909, he responded to death—his philosophic creed signalizes it as God's best gift to man—by putting in words on paper his inner turmoil of deprivation and remembrance, as this flared to utterance from the time he was told that his youngest and epileptic child was dead, to the time of her burial the next day in Elmira, four hundred miles away. He said: "Now Jean is in her grave. In her grave—if I can believe it. God rest her sweet spirit." And on the following day, he told Albert Paine, who had become a member of his household: "I have finished it. Read it. I can form no opinion of it myself. If you think it worthy—some day—at the proper time—it can end my autobiography. It is the final chapter."

In a sense it was a sealing of such immortality as poets and artists can provide for themselves and for others, insofar as they can incarnate their images and signs and symbols in such materials as outlast their persons. Then later generations may, as they are directed or happen or choose, take up those residues to contemplate or to decipher. Twain was very mindful of his immortality, he had a care for every item of his expression; much of it he saved for working over while he was alive, much else for his posterity and aficionados to treasure for publication after he was dead; and some was "not to be exposed to any eye until the edition of AD 2406." He was afraid of self-deceived mankind's reaction to the last, but with less reason that he thought. As to the rest, the record justified his care. Time has not diminished his public. Moreover, it has joined to the other carriers of the torch of his immortality a diversified company of critics and literatuses, from the groves of Academe and from those congregations of the faithful, who are not without sympathy toward the heretical religion for which, Twain said, his inheritors would be "burnt alive if they venture to print it this side of 2406 A.D."

There is a trope which images every human production as the formation of a child from conception to birth; an event in a personal history where birth consummates a sequence of urges, occasions, decisions and endurances singular to itself. Soon the creation, again like the child, discloses a separate identity independent of its creator and his ways, with a career and fortune all its own. Biographers and historians may explore the creation in order to account for its creator; critics, connoisseurs and the rest of mankind do not need to—they take the creation as it comes to them, enclosed in a frame or between the covers of the book. For them it exists in and by itself; they value it, not for its antecedents but for its consequences to themselves. These last they compound into merits or demerits wherewith they measure its role in the culture of their times. Its place in the personal history of its creator is to his public a tangent condition, only to him central, and maybe to the historian of his life and labors. And it need not be central to him. Many artists and thinkers become, after a work is completed, as detached and separate from it as the reader or critic who has not yet read or heard or viewed it; the makers become able to perceive and judge that work with a like unconcern.

This seems not to have been Mark Twain's relation to his creations. With few exceptions his works figure not only as events in his personal history, but as the recordings of this history. They are autobiography, at times costumed, but always with the soul of the man himself, nakedly visible through the costume, laughing, weeping, and laughing again. He is there "in person," in his books as in his platform appearances. The presence there has composed itself of many roles, and its projector's occasional self-appraisals show him often uncertain which perdures, which passes, dominates, recedes. Having completed *Following the Equator* while mourning for his Susie, lecturing and writing for money to pay off his creditors, Mark commented to Howells: "I don't mean that I am miserable; no, worse than that, indifferent. Indifferent to nearly everything but work. I like that; I enjoy it—stick to it. I do it without purpose and without ambition, merely for the love of it. Indeed, I am a mud-image, it puzzles me to know what it is in me that writes & has comedy fancies & finds pleasure in phrasing them. It is the law of our nature, of course, or it wouldn't happen, the thing in me that forgets the presence of the mud-image goes its own way wholly unconscious of it and apparently of no kinship with it."

Some critics have read the concurrence, alternations, and conflicts of Mark's roles as an "ordeal," others have seen their configurations as a fountain spurting from a single source. The comprehensive image projects the figure of a man with a gambling lust for life and zestful of it; a man tense, explosive, given to moral indignation and voicing it in caricature-like exaggerations of thoughts and traits and things; a man eager to be appreciated and praised especially by as such of the rich, the famous, and the blue-blooded whom he quite innocently took for his Joneses; a man who held grudges, yet made friends with all sorts and conditions of the race he damned, and was concerned for such friends his whole life long to the point of sentimentality.* No one could be surer than Mark Twain of his own merits and deserts or more humbly dubious about them. His Livy intuitively name the ever-dominating inwardness of him. She called him "Youth" from the first day of the thirty-five years of their life together.

Youth's wooing and winning of Livy, set off romantically by the sight of a miniature in her brother's possession, became also a moment in his career of ambition as his career of love, and the two remained confluent to the end. He won her father and her brother before he won her. The miniature-owner came only reluctantly to agree that Sam was a fit husband for his sister. In fact, Sam became the most uxorious of husbands, nevertheless the most irreverently reverent, treating his darling with the combination of submissiveness, defiance, and teasing that he had learned to use toward his mother. Indeed, in her own relations to him Livy was mother as well as wife, the dearest friend and severest critic who insisted that he suit his speech and his manners, his ideas and his dress to the mores of the Elmira, New York which set her style and measure of gentility. She incarnated a Jones whom he strove, with not too frequent lapses, to surpass. Neither her family's fortune nor her share of it tempered his passionate urge to the success he speculated and schemed and wrote and lectured for—the success of

---

* G. W. Allen quotes William James, who first met Twain in Florence: ". . . a fine, soft-fibred little fellow, with the perversest twang and drawl, but very human and good. I should think one might grow very fond of him." A second meeting happened in New York, more than a generation later, when James found him "only good for monologue, in his old age, or for dialogue at best, but he's a dear little genius all the same." (*William James*, 1967.)

supporting her in a life much more magnificent than she had been accustomed to. "I was," Youth wrote in 1874, "a mighty rough, coarse, unpromising subject when Livy took charge of me four years ago and I may still be to the rest of the world, but not to Livy. She has made a very creditable job of me." Like Yankee Hank Morgan in King Arthur's court (Its author said of this work: "It will be to English nobility and royalty what Don Quixote was to ancient chivalry."), Livy was "the Boss." Youth's other and mostly literary mentor, William Dean Howells, speaks of Livy's "wonderful tact with a man who was, and in some respects wished to be, the most outrageous creature that ever breathed."

And Youth complained that his outrages could be condoned by "no excuse, no palliation or argument." Livy's "How could you, Youth!" spoken as only she could speak it, could bring Sir Husband up short. He says he was "always catching it," and he was as regularly purging himself of those outrageous urges behind her back and out of her sight and hearing. One such purge was the "Fireside Conversation in the Time of Queen Elizabeth" that he purported to emulate Rabelais with, and did delight his buddy, the Rev. Joseph Twichell and his friend, the Honorable John Hay. The latter, moreover, contrived to get the conversation privately printed while refusing the would-be printer the imprimatur. But before Livy's face or within her hearing, her adoring mate scarcely ever failed to assume the Parsifalian role that would meet his Livy's requirements: "Livy wouldn't have it, so I gave it up."

Her day-to-day role of wife-*cum*-mother in Mark's personal history may have been supplemented by something like Beatrice's in Dante's. When Youth wrote the diaries of Adam and of Eve, such actualities that he projected were his own and Livy's. Apart from his sense of her, he seems unable to shape a real presence of the female of the species—how unable his stories make manifest—and such spurts of *élan vital* as he succeeds enlivening any with, seem whispered memories of the Livy of his devotion. His female villains are puppets, but his heroines—Eve, Joan of Arc, Marjorie Fleming, all the scions of the sex who figure in his fiction, figure like genteel shadows of Livy, Livy realized, Livy remembered. Eve and Joan are Livy's disguises. Those "personal recollections" of the virginal St. Joan—so utterly other than Voltaire's *Pucelle*—that Twain *knew* was the best of his books, the recollections he took twelve years to prepare and write, enjoying seven times the pleasure he had from any other of his productions—he dedicated to his "literary adviser and editor" to celebrate the twenty-fifth anniversary of her Youth's career under her gracious providence. He made believe that he was Joan's childhood friend and eventual secretary, writing her life after her martyrdom; and at the same time, the translator of that personal history "Jean Francois Alden." He would make-believe, a letter told Livy and Susy, because "I shall never be accepted seriously over my own signature. People always want to laugh over what I write and are disappointed if they don't find a joke in it. This is to be a serious book. It means more to me than anything I have ever undertaken. I shall write it anonymously."

It was an anonymity which fooled no one. Its author could not keep his signature out of it. He could not refrain from inviting laughter in this most carefully worked and purposefully tragic of all his expression. Nor could he let the narrative itself disclose his virginal Saint's transcendent virtues, Christian and military. He kept pointing out the virtues, in grieving commentary. But he also gives accounts of Joan's Paladin; of the innocence of Stomach and the duplicity of Head; of Joan's uncle, trying to ride a bull to a funeral and what disturbed bees happened to do about it, and of what that fable teaches. And he writes of these with a gusto not communicated by this epic of the "only entirely unselfish person whose name has a place in profane history—the noble child, the most innocent, the most lovely, the most adorable, the ages have produced."

Unlike Dr. Samuel Johnson's contemporary at college, who abandoned philosophy because cheerfulness was always breaking through, Mark Twain pursued philosophy because cheerfulness was always breaking in. What would the Adam he was have become without his Eve, the Adam who asserted that temperament "was the first command the Deity ever issued to a human being on this planet"—the only command Adam was never able to disobey. It said, "Be weak, be water, be characterless, be cheaply persuadable." The later command to let the fruit alone was certainly disobeyed. Not by Adam himself, but by his temperament which he did not create and had no authority over. For the temperament is the man; the thing tucked out with clothes and named Man is merely its shadow, nothing more. The temperament, then, is the Old Adam contributing no material to the making of Eve. Presumably it was to a ribaldry all her own that the first Satan appealed when persuading Adam's better half not to let the fruit alone, thus making sure of the Shadow tucked out with clothes. Mark Twain does not say. His toast, *To the ladies*, at a banquet in Washington five years after his marriage, does hint at a full awareness of the Old Adam in Eve and her daughters. But he clearly would have us believe that, beside the sensitive good sense and correct ethic of Olivia Clemens-Adam's-Rib, Samuel-Clemens-Adam was weak, was watery, was characterless, and cheaply persuadable; that, so far as he could be saved from the penalties of his temperament, her woman's grace saved him.

Of course, Youth had other providences for whose watchfulness he was ever so grateful—notably, William Dean Howells, Henry H. Rogers, though probably not the more companionable man of God, Joe Twichell. The first watched tactfully over Mark's ways with the tales he told and the words he told them in; the second watched knowingly over the money Mark made and the ways he spent it. Both loved and had joy in the laughing Youth of him, and guarded him against himself. But beside his Livy, these friends were mere men, and even as he knew himself dependent on them, he knew himself as good as they, if not better. But this charismatic ex-river pilot, ex-miner, and now journalist, lecturer, author of *The Jumping Frog* and *The Innocents Abroad*, knew himself the inveterate dependent upon Livy; the bad boy always needing her perduring maternal understanding and forgiveness. Perhaps his love of this delicate valetudinarian had a touch of guilt in it; she was so of another world that love could never be enough to make up for the hurts it sometimes not unwittingly brought: "Her death was the disaster of my life." Involved with this sense of Livy was also the memory of their child, premature Langdon, who died soon after Susie was born, and for whose death the proud and doting father willy-nilly felt responsible. Love and the guilt which love so often breeds! Could they have been the deeper springs of laughing Youth's realization of the tears of things and of laughter and of death as their anodyne?

Youth does not rationalize Langdon's death as he later did Susy's and Livy's and Jean's. Bitterly mourning, he nevertheless argued that not to exist was better than to exist; that death is God's sole boon to life. The providence which he prized and the comforts which he enjoyed as impersonal effects of the laws of an indifferent nature, he interpreted as sadistic malice when he conceived them in terms of gifts of grace from the hand of his mother's God. As the joking, romancing, teasing boy Sam Clemens grew into the laughter-evoking humorist Mark Twain, this sense of providence eased the Peter Pan of his "temperament" without freeing it from the guilt of the original sin of being what he was, doing what he did, feeling as he felt, speaking as he spoke, and of the pride and pleasure he continued to experience in all that, and in how greatly and widely the damned human race appreciated it, and him; appreciated both because, in fact, the standards by which he condemned them were their own standards, and the laughter he drew from them brought them relief from the charges of cowardice, cruelty, vanity, hypocrisy, lust, greed, dishonesty, obscenity, and self-deception that he brought against them.

These qualities are after all, Mark observed, damned man's *imitatio Dei*, even though Satan, touring the human world, writes in the eighth of his *Letters from Earth* that the species "hasn't a single written law, in the Bible or out of it, which has any but just one purpose and intention—*to limit or defeat a law of God.*" And the heavenly tourist concludes his letter:

> "I will tell you a pleasant tale which has in it a touch of pathos. A man got religion, and asked the priest what he must do to be worthy of his new estate. The priest said, "Imitate our Father in Heaven, learn to be like him." The man studied his Bible diligently and thoroughly and understandingly, and then with prayers for heavenly guidance instituted his imitations. He tricked his wife into falling downstairs, and she broke her back and became a paralytic for life; he betrayed his brother into the hands of a sharper, who robbed him of his all and landed him in the almshouse; he inoculated one son with hookworms, another with the sleeping sickness, another with gonorrhea; he furnished one daughter with scarlet fever and ushered her into her teens deaf, dumb, and blind for life; and after helping a rascal seduce the remaining one, he closed his doors against her and she died in a brothel cursing him. Then he reported to the priest, who said that *that* was no way to imitate his Father in Heaven. The convert asked wherein he had failed, but the priest changed the subject and inquired what kind of weather he was having, up his way."

Withal, Youth the humorist, who made himself heavenly Satan's medium, was able once to observe that "pessimism is only the name that men of weak nerves give to wisdom," and during his later years wisdom became something, if not the same as laughter, then a near kin to it. Even where he arranged to damn without laughter, "as from the grave" (that vital center of honesty where "there is free speech and

no harm to the family"), whence Mark Twain intended to
sound off in *Letters from Earth*, he could not keep the laughter out; he could not keep out that primal challenging mockery of a fun-loving boy reworked into a weapon of righteousness, wielded by a warrior for moral ideals. But more and
more the laugh-evoker's satires came accompanied by psalms
of praise for the role laughter holds in the tear-laden record
of the damned human race.

For the damned human race is given to hoaxes and fables
and allegories such as are so abundant in Youth's personal
history and in his spoken and written thoughts. Perhaps the
race are damned because they do know and reverence—as its
self-proclaimed laughter-evoking judge did—the good and
the right, and because they pretend them to be absolute and
universal and eternal, all the while that their struggles to go
on struggling keep debunking their pretenses. Those, at
once self-deceiving and deceivers, could be an homage which
evil and wrong render to the good and right, which enslave-
ment renders to the freedom that it is the damnation of
human nature at once to exalt, to destroy, and not ever to
forget, but laughingly to keep hungering for and recalling,
and so to assuage the sorrow and dry the tears of mankind's
struggle to live on. The damned human race is the race of
make-believe. "Earn a character if you can," advises
Pudd'nhead Wilson, reminding one of Pascal, "and if you
can't, assume one." Everyman is an "extraordinary twin,"
one body for two "temperaments." Col. Sellars, not a little an
alter ego for his philosophizing progenitor, is their signature. Mankind are histrions all, ever play-acting, for real
even more than for fun, ever striving toward a future in
which they shall be what they would seem, as in Captain
Stormfield's heaven, and never succeeding. Yet some do succeed, becoming what they are not yet, at least in a dream,
like Hank Morgan, the Yankee Americanizer of King Arthur's Court, so full of goodwill toward the damned human
race, and by his American faith and works striving to free

them from the bondage of their medievalism, and scheming
to deceive his people in order to help them. Some need not
dream. Like those avatars of good will and faith, Livy, Joan,
unique Huck Finn, they seem what they are, deceive neither
themselves nor any other, and suffer at the hands of those to
whom they are devoted: Livy, at the hands of her dear,
remorseful Youth; Joan, at those of her conscienceless Dauphin; Huck, at those of his admired and trusted friend, Tom
Sawyer.

Tom, indeed, is the urge to make-believe enfleshed in a
local habitation and a name. Huck suffers all an existentialist's anxieties of conscience over the conflict between his
commitment to Nigger Jim's struggle for freedom and his
Dixie-bred ethic of the sacredness of property rights in
human beings with black skins. Tom, on the other hand, has
known from the beginning that Jim's dead owner has willed
him his freedom, that he is free by law and in fact. But Tom
deceives Jim, he deceives Huck. Tom pretends that Jim is
still a slave so that he might stage a fictional conspiracy of
liberation replete with sharp hurts and tragic dangers for his
friends; so that he might stage a poignant practical joke on
his trusting friends, delighting in his own mumbo-jumbo.
Although Tom's hoax is fertile of evil, it is not as such evil in
Tom's make-believe. Tom knows that it can't be incompatible with Jim's freedom, since Jim is already free. There is no
malice in Tom's deception; he designs it innocently, for the
fun and the glory of it.

To pretend that Jim is bond, to plan and enact his liberation, has been to make-believe for the sake of the excitement,
the joys, the releasing laughter of making believe. Of course,
it could have come to grief, could have ended in tears instead
of laughter. An actual hoax of Mark Twain's own did come
to bitter grief, instead of evoking from his victims and his
audience together, the delighted laughter which was his aim.
But his mime was met with a shocked and oppressive silence. For years the shame and remorse of his failure kept

the deflated artist in laughter, who had been so pleased with his invention and so sure of its power, pondering the failure's why and how.

The occasion had been the dinner which the *Atlantic Monthly* was giving in honor of the poet John Greenleaf Whittier's seventieth birthday. All the New England Olympians were there, and Youth was sure that his rendering of the chief divinities, Emerson, Holmes and Longfellow as drunken Western tramps speaking the Olympians' tongues would bring roars of laughter. But neither his victims nor their fellow-diners even cracked a smile. To the latter, the laugh-seeking incongruities seemed blasphemous irreverence: Howells, the host of the evening and humorist Twain's friend and sponsor, could only gasp. "I shall never be as dead as I was then," his Livy's Youth recalled, more than a quarter of a century later, still questing the how and why of that forgiven but never-forgotten defeat. Finally, he decided it was due to some indecision in himself, to a sort of unsureness and timidity in the telling of his tale: "You can't be successfully funny if you show you are afraid of it." The role must be played as if the truth. Mark decided finally that his farce *was* good fun, that if he had the same chance, he's do it all again, "and melt them till they'd run all over the stage."

Somewhere Youth remarks that at twenty-seven, life was a fairy-tale to him. Years later he wrote: "When I was 43 and John Hay 41, he said life was a tragedy after 40. I disputed him. Three years ago, he asked me to testify again: I counted my graves and there was nothing for me to say."

But he had a great deal to say, time and again, about death and dying, and as anything but tragedy, and about other things so momentous in his consciousness that he irresistibly resaid them again and again. Those themes compound into the tragedy of the damned human race and Twain's resaying it into the humor with which he uncovered and laughed down the tragedy, with the laughter which transvalues tragedy into comedy. "Everything human is pathetic," he remarks as Pudd'nhead Wilson (Susy had died the year before) : "The secret source of Humor is not joy but sorrow. There is no Humor in heaven." Mankind's doom is to spend their lives in a vale of tears which the unafraid may counter with laughter. Saint Joan's champion ruminates on the pathos which both her father and uncle saw in Uncle Loxart's failure to get to a funeral in time by riding a bull and angering bees: ". . . Yes, both those old people thought that the tale was pathetic; whereas to my mind it was purely ridiculous and not in any way valuable to any one. . . . And as for history, it does not resemble history, for the office of history is to furnish serious and important facts that *teach;* whereas this strange and useless event teaches nothing; nothing that I can see, except not to ride a bull to a funeral, and surely no reflecting person needs to be taught that." Further, if ridicule is evoked by futility or failure, it also evokes them. "There is no character, however good and pure," reflects Pudd'nhead Wilson, "but can be destroyed by ridicule, however poor and witless. Observe the ass for instance: his character is about perfect, he is the choicest spirit among all the humbler animals. Yet see what ridicule has brought him to. Instead of feeling complimented when we are called an ass, we are left in doubt."

Mark Twain is not concerned with the fact that it is the man, not his ass who is degraded by the ridicule. The latter, like Buridan's, continues untouched. So would the man be, if he were not a snob who would not be an ass, however choice, however enviable. A man like St. Francis or an Asiatic saint convinced of Karma or the fabulist of the Golden Ass, might regard the ass a beloved brother or an unknown uncle, or a secret sage and prophet. Youth's philosophic creed bred no ambivalences in Youth's cosmos; good was good and bad was bad, right was right and wrong was wrong, always and everywhere. They might share the same flesh like "these extraordinary twins," still everywhere and always the bad and the wrong reduce the world to a weeping from which only laughter can free it, and only death put an end to. It is illusion, Youth wrote at sixty-seven, with Susy dead and Livy bedridden, to take Fame, Love, Riches, and Pleasure as true boons of life. Pleasure consumes life in waste and mockery, Love is overpaid in grief and desolation, Fame is followed by envy and by detraction, calumny, hate, persecution, derision, and finally, by "pity which is the funeral of Fame." Wealth buys power, deference, respect, esteem, worship and ends up in sickness and hunger: "Pleasure, Love, Fame, Riches are but temporary disguises for lasting realities—Pain, Grief, Shame, Poverty." The genuine boon to life, the inestimable one that terminates forever the betrayals that are life's stuff, is the last one man thinks to choose— Death, whose sole remaining alternative is "the wanton insult of Old Age."

Satan writes from Earth to his correspondents in heaven: "Life was not a valuable gift, but death was. Life was a feverdream—the heaviest curse devisable by divine ingenuity, but death was sweet, death was gentle, death was kind, death healed the bruised spirit and the broken heart and gave them rest and forgetfulness; death was man's best friend: when man could endure life no longer death came and set him free." Recalling the day that Jean died, her father writes, "she has been enriched with the most precious gift of all—that gift which makes all other gifts mean and poor—death. I have never wanted any released friend of mine restored to life since I reached manhood." Susy, Livy, Henry Rogers, came to mind. Of the latter his grateful friend wrote: "There were tears of sorrow in my eyes—for *me*, not for him. He had suffered no loss. All the fortunes he had ever made were poverty compared to this one."

In his parable of the five boons of life, Youth, resenting old age, did not join laughter to death as its anodyne for the pain and burden of living. Laughter's spontaneities, their Edenic innocence, were too central in his "temperament"; he could no more help making and enjoying fun than he could help breathing or talking. Nor, as he saw it toward the end of his life, could God. The humorist's biographer reports a conversation during which his hero called humor "one of the chief attributes of God." So many plants and animals look funny and have funny traits that they must be God their Maker's jokes—and added, "humor is mankind's greatest blessing." Later, the humorist adds, with the words he puts in the mouth of his most unhumorous character, the Mysterious Stranger, the character who keeps laughing at all the evils humans weep over, laughing without evoking human laughter: that mankind "have a mongrel perception of humor, nothing more: a multitude see the comic side of a thousand low-grade and trivial things—broad incongruities, mainly grotesques, absurdities, evokers of the horselaugh: the ten thousand highgrade comicalities which exist in the world are sealed from their dull vision. Will a day come when the race will detect the funniness of these juvenilities and laugh at them—and by laughing destroy them?"

The question spans the spiritual stretch between the original innocence of the infant's first laugh, to laughter's acquired survival function in men's struggle to stay alive and grow. For first, the joke and the joy of humor come up like divine grace, tangent to all logic, impervious to rhyme and reason, useless and absurd as that miraculous October morning of which Youth chants in the "Double-Barrelled Detective Story":

that crisp and spicy morning in early October. The lilacs and laburnums, lit with the glory-fires of autumn, hung burning and flashing in the upper air, a fairy bridge provided by kind nature for the wingless wild things that have their homes in the treetops and would visit together; the larch and the pomegranate flung the purple and yellow flames in brilliant broad splashes along the slanting sweep of woodland, the sensuous fragrance of innumerable deciduous flowers rose upon the swooning atmosphere; far in the empty sky a solitary oesophagus slept upon motionless wing; everywhere brooded stillness, serenity, the peace of God.

After such senseless joy follows the harnessing-up of those serendipities and disciplining them to the uses of survival. This had become Youth's art and mystery, and he had long been a master of it. He had learned that in and out of civilization, laughter, first the voice of joy in simply being alive, ineluctably becomes employed as a weapon of defense and offense, which every man somehow wields in his struggle to live on, to grow up and grow older; that, short of death, man's liberator and liberty can be, has been, and continues to be, laughter. Power, money, persuasion, supplication, persecution—the Mysterious Stranger, Satan alias Philip Traum, concludes: "these can lift at a colossal humbug—push it a little—weaken it a little, century by century, but only laughter can blow it to rags and atoms at a blast. Against the assault of laughter, nothing can stand."

Automatically one asks: Not even death? And one must answer: Not for Mark Twain, not for Livy's Youth. As he sees it, laughter is at best but the peer of death, and like the rest of life redeemed from existence by death. Such is the plight of the damned human race.

> *We laugh and laugh*
> *Then cry and cry*
> *Then feebler laugh*
> *Then die.*

For a fatalist who purported to be sure that "the future is absolutely fixed like the past," Mark Twain lived out his life in successful efforts to unfix it, and give it shapes nearer his heart's desires. His reformations assumed and practiced the liberty his head damned. What he challenged and debunked was rather the value-system of a fundamentalist supernaturalism than the actual experiences, spiritual and physical, of the life more abundant—so abundant as to include osteopathy, telepathy, Christian Science, and other forms of mind cure. He set, over against the metaphysic of ends and means implied by the fundamentalist credo on selected authority from the Bible, another one, which with a more cogent logic translated man-the-end-of-all-creation into man-the-means-to-nourish-and-shelter the infinite microbe race. Why, the humorist bitterly demands, should mankind believe themselves so precious to Omnipotent Good God that His Goodness punishes an original sin of which they were never guilty?

His answer recalls the Dervish replying to Pangloss in *Candide*. And his gusto, so much more puritanical than Voltaire's, recalls Voltaire. He speaks with absurd violence, in his comment to his intimate friend, the Rev. Joseph Twichell, on Calvinist Jonathan Edwards' *Freedom of the Will* which denies man's freedom but proclaims unfree man's foreordained responsibility to the just and good God. He calls Edwards "a drunken lunatic," his book "all insane debauch," because, after arguing so much that was consonant with certain chapters of Youth's own "suppressed Gospel," that theologian "suddenly flees the logical task and . . . makes man and not those exterior forces responsible to God. . . . It is frank insanity." Youth agrees with "the resplendent mind gone mad," that man is moved by impulses he doesn't create and that each such impulse "infallibly chooses," from alternatives before it, "the one which for the moment is most pleasing to itself."

As if impulses were selves apart from and independent of the personal self whose impulses they are! Humorist Youth's "Gospel" repeats the notion. In that dialogue between Age and Youth, Age argues that man's equipment enables free choice but not free will. All the generations of the damned human race have ever for their ends self-approval, self-satisfaction; to attain them they may employ conformity or rebellion as a means; they may repent or they may gloat, but true altruism is out of their human reach. "There is a Moral Sense," Twain wrote elsewhere, "and an Immoral Sense. History shows that the Moral Sense enables us to perceive morality and how to avoid it; and that the Immoral Sense

enables us to perceive immorality and how to enjoy it."
(What a logic for a Reinhold Niebuhr to improve upon!) But
by and large, each human individual gets moralized by the
world around only so far as its ways and works do not violate
his original nature, his original sin, his "temperament."
Hence, Age advises Youth, an individual's optimal means to
a good life is to keep striving "toward a summit where you
will find your chiefest pleasure in conduct which, while con-
tenting you, will be sure to confer benefits upon your neighbor and the community."

This sounds like an ethic of the banal, a rechewing of a
perennial, much-chewed rag. But to its prophet, it was so
momentous, so exciting, so inviting of the penalities and
pangs of heresy, that he would keep it dark until long after
he was dead. He felt no conflict between this creed and his
performing urges, his declaring himself "a revolutionist by
birth, reading and principles . . . always in the tide of the
revolutionists because there never was a revolution unless
there were some oppressive and intolerable conditions
against which to revolute." And he "revoluted" so much, so
variously and so eloquently, that one newspaper would have
him run for president or at least, senator. To this he replied
that his "natural trade" was teaching, his role in the damned
human race to be a "professional moralist," worthy of a chair
in the College of the City of New York. Only, his art of
professional moralist was the art of satire, and he avowed
that the one he preferred in his heart was that of the sheer
funny man evoking laughter for laughter's sake, the laughter of enjoyment rather than the laughter of attack and
defense. There was more money in it as well as more fun.
The record is obscure on how our humorist's credo related to
the actualities of automatic choosings, and to the supreme
goods of death and laughter. It is clear that Mark Twain
was a superlative husband and father, a good friend, a good
neighbor, and an insistent champion of liberty and righteousness, living the life more abundant to the very end,

making the damned human race laugh. It is clear that he wanted the race to remember and cherish him as a master of the mystery of comic art—the art of evoking laughter, even though apes and jackasses also laugh, and men are unique only in blushing.

The dynamic of his singularly American mystery, Youth opines, is: "To bring incongruities and absurdities together in a wandering and sometimes purposeless way, and seem innocently unaware that they are absurdities." They can, he believed—although he did not argue it—evoke tears as readily as laughter; he remarks of "those Extraordinary Twins" that "the story itself changed from a farce into a tragedy while I was going along with it—a most embarrassing circumstance." He calls his *Library of Humor* "a cemetery of forgotten names—forgotten because Humorists of the 'mere' sort can not survive. Humor is only a fragrance, a decoration. Often it is only a wild trick of speech or spelling, as in the case of Ward and Billings and Naseby and the 'Disbanded Volunteer,' and presently the fashion passes and the fame along with it. There are those who say a novel should be a work of art solely and you mustn't preach in it or teach in it. That may be true as regards novels but it is not true as regards humor. Humor must not professedly teach . . . preach, but it must do both if it is to live forever. By forever I mean 30 years. With all its preaching it is not likely to outlive so long a term as that. The very things it preaches about and which are novelties when it preaches about them can cease to be novelties and become commonplaces in 30 years.

"I have always preached. . . . If the humor came of its own accord and uninvited, I have allowed it a place in my sermon, but I was not writing the sermon for the sake of the humor. I should have written the sermon just the same, whether the humor asked for admission or not."

So writes the author of *The Jumping Frog*, the discoverer of the solitary oesophagus sleeping upon motionless wing far in the empty sky, the designer of the tramps playing roles as Emerson, Longfellow and Holmes, when he sees himself as the author of *The Man Who Corrupted Hadleyburg*, of the *Letters from Earth*, of *The Mysterious Stranger*. But it could be the case—and one is disposed to believe it was—that, in Mark Twain's practice of the humorist's art, spontaneity was regularly the life harnessed to method and contrivance. The latter were, of course, celebrated, and so skillful that the animating propulsions were not suspected. Howells writes of his friend on the lecture-platform that he was "The most consummate public performer I ever saw . . . a great and finished actor," producing "carefully studied effects." In *How to Tell a Story*, Youth sums up what he had learned as he went up and down and to and fro on the earth, lecturing. It is recognition without its shock to discover that here is one more adept of the Jester's art, sort of disclosing his mystery. Our Jester may come to the rostrum with a manuscript or a book in his hand, but he speaks always deadpan, poker-faced, with the effect of improvisation: "Written things are not for speech; their form is literary: they are stiff and inflexible, and will not lend themselves to happy and effective delivery with the tongue—where their purpose is merely to entertain not instruct; they have to be limbered up, broken up, colloquialized, and turned into common forms of unpremeditated talk—otherwise they will bore the house, not entertain it." Twain speaks of the voice, its tone, its pitch, and particularly of the role of pausing: "I used to play with the pause as other children play with a toy." (Was "other children" intended, purposeful, or a happenstance?) On the platform, the function of the pause is as critical as that of a rest in a musical sequence. The pause comes just before "a nub, a point, a snapper," is "in a carefully casual way" dropped into a wandering monologue seemingly headed for nowhere, with the missile so utterly a non-sequitur as to bring on the hoped-for belly-laughs.

First and last, Mark Twain wrote as he spoke. That was

the other side of his mystery which it cost him great pains to perfect. In his writings as in his speeches he undertakes to bring "incongruities and absurdities together in a wandering and sometimes purposeless way, seemingly unaware that they are absurdities." It is this studied effect of unstudied communication that gives substance and body to his fantasies, rendering them somehow extensions of the actualities one lives among.

Also *The Mysterious Stranger* is such a personal history, even though it can hardly be said to fit its author's idea of how he and other Americans practice the jester's art. *The Mysterious Stranger* was published some six years after Twain had died. He is said to have worked it over several times and to have brought it to its present form a couple of years after Livy had received what her inconsolable Youth called life's most precious boon. It could be that he was stopped by illness from completing it to his satisfaction. For he was a sick man growing sicker while he was writing it, tortured by seizures of angina, asking for death but not requiring it, rebounding into his life more abundant whenever his loving God withdrew his hand from his challenger's heart. However poignant the suffering, Mark Twain knew, as he observed, reflecting upon his loss of Jean, that he could not help being happy again: "My temperament has never allowed my spirits to remain depressed long at a time." Withal, his biographer reminds us that "he lived curiously apart from the actualities of life"; he felt presence—dead Jean's for instance—heard voices, dreamed dreams (how long, how full, during a single moment of waking time a life in a dream could be!). He reasoned that such experiences could be solely works of the imagination but he felt and told of them with a convincing realism. Still, the ever best gift to life was death: "I have never greatly envied anyone but the dead. I always envy the dead."

Such now are the motifs for *The Mysterious Stranger*, which suggests all the aspects of Twain's humor as an imag-

inative meditation upon his "temperament" and upon the
valuations of his struggle to keep on struggling that consummated his experience. All, that is, save the actualities of the
innocent laughter so signal of his "temperament." The
young Stranger is his creator's avatar, Satan the angel who
is the nephew of Satan the Devil, and his earthly name is
Philip Traum. His generous uncle is "in business in the trop-
ics . . . very well off . . . has a monopoly. . . . [He is] a
gentleman, some even call him a Prince out of compliment,
but he is not bigoted; to him personal merit is everything,
rank nothing." Nephew Satan has come visiting mankind.
Like the Yankee in King Arthur's Court, he comes from
another world, a figure in a costumed fable confronting two
value-systems: one exemplified by the beliefs and behaviors
of the damned human race, the other by the presence, the
attitudes, the words and the deeds of the Stranger. The time
is 1590. The place is an Austrian village, Eseldorf, where
the manners and morals of Hannibal, Missouri, are seen
without disguise. The spokesmen for the damned human
race are three boys to whom Satan-Philip Traum makes his
relevation. One, Theodor, evinces some of the honest and
simple perplexity of Huck Finn: it is he who tells the tale of
the Mysterious Stranger, who comes always laughing, although his guileless and charmed audience of three boys are
as little able to laugh with him as his creator's own audience
were during the latter's allocution at John Greenleaf Whittier's birthday party.

Philip Traum might be said to be a Tom Sawyer, able
instantly to create whatever is wished for, *ex nihilo*. He
makes facts of fantasies. In his presence, to wish is to have.
Being an angel, he is, even as the animals, untainted by the
Moral Sense, by illusions of Right and Wrong. He destroys
as he creates, with an imputed gaiety of spirit, an insouci-
ance which in no way masks the Twainian moral fervor, the
passion for righteousness that Twain assuaged by Traum's
creation. An immortal "of the aristocracy of the Imperish-

ables," the creation is a beautiful, life-enhancing youthful presence whose nearness brings a "most cheery and tingling freshening sensation." "You know that kind of quiver that trembles around through you when you are seeing something so strange and enchanting and wonderful that it is just a fearful joy to look at it; and you know how you gaze, and your lips turn dry and your breath comes short, but you wouldn't be anywhere else, not for the world." To behold the Dream-Stranger and to hear "the fatal music of his voice," is the peak of experience, with laughter bubbling up. "He made us forget everything; we could only listen to him and love him and be his slaves, to do with us as he would. He made us drunk with the joy of being with him and of looking into the heaven of his eyes, and of feeling the ecstasy that thrilled in our veins from the touch of his hand—ecstasy . . . a thing that will not go into words; it feels like music and we can not tell about music so that another person can get the feel of it." And the boys experience this presence, seeing it where no one else did, feeling it and responding to it also where it was invisible to them, too. Its disclosures of the human predicaments, present and past, on occasion made them feel "secretly ashamed of being human."

The Stranger had made himself known as both the judge and liberator of the damned human race, "laughing in the most unfeeling way" at all that its stupid, foolish generations continue to hold for true, all they keep hoping for, all they fear and regret, all they take pride in, all their self-limitations by means of time and space, all the mounting misery and unhappiness that their boasted progress in civilization consists of. He keeps laughing and laughing; his unkind laugh "made a person sick to hear him." Yet, he also stops to remark: "But after all, it is not ridiculous; there is a sort of pathos about it when one remembers how few are your days, how childish your pomps, and what shadows you are." He anticipates Thomas Hobbes' observation that man's brief life is a brutish, mean, and nasty war of all against all;

and divulges that he is able to free, and by freeing, to save, their race from this necessary and inescapable condition. But not by breaking the chain of ineluctable connexion in which every link, however mankind appraise it, is "of one size and importance"—he can free and save only by adding another link.

Theodor comments: Man, therefore, is "a prisoner for life and cannot get free." To which the Stranger replies: "No, of himself he cannot get away from the consequences of his first childish act, but I can free him." His intervention can free and save the damned human race by speeding the peace which is death, thus eliminating years of suffering; it can render the conventionally sane conventionally insane, thus replacing a tragic unhappiness by a comically self-confident happiness, for "only the mad can be happy"—that is, the human mad; Philip Traum, neutral and heedless regarding all the values he perceives as human, is both sane and happy.

And he can set man free by teaching him to use the power of laughter. The multitude, he says, have only the rudiments of this power, only "a mongrel perception of humor, nothing more." They but see the comic side of a thousand low-grade and trivial things—broad incongruities mainly, grotesqueness, absurdities, evokers of the horselaugh. "The ten thousand high-grade comicalities which exist in the world are sealed from their dull vision. Will the day come when the race will detect the funniness of these juvenilities and laugh at them and by laughing at them destroy them? For your race, in its poverty has unquestionably one really effective weapon—laughter. As a race do you ever use it at all? No; you lack sense and the courage."

In due course Angel Satan began to get bored. His enlightenment of Theodor came at longer intervals. Finally, he appeared to say goodbye and to disclose the gladdening ultimate truth—that there is no Otherworld, and that the life of this one is only a vision, a dream; that "nothing exists; all is a dream." Nothing exists save empty space and the individual. You, the individual, are "but a thought," "by its nature inextinguishable, indestructible." Like all the universe, Satan's self is also the individual's dream, "creature of his imagination"; man's world and his God are but a nightmare of incongruities which only the madman [alone the happy one?] could dream up; incongruities to be annihilated as they had been created. Creator and annihiliator are one and the same: the singular *thought*, vagrant, useless, homeless, "wandering forlorn among the empty eternities."

Now, then, what price death and laughter? Would it not seem that on reflection, Mark Twain's laughing at Maya was quenched in tears and the tears quenched in the bitter nirvana of weeping without tears—such a weeping as perhaps Santayana's Lucifer once wept? On reflection! Still, the essential *life* was the laughter, and it is his laughter on which Mark Twain's immortality lives.

The Mysterious Stranger is the guise, then, of Livy's *Youth*, Ma Clemens' *Sam*, Everyman's *Mark Twain*, as we take leave of him. He has stripped himself down to his essence, an "inextinguishable and indestructible 'Thought' wandering forlorn among the empty eternities," dead yet imperishable, "vagrant, useless, homeless," a unique particle of free-floating freedom, weeping his laughter, laughing his tears. Soon or late the Dreamer dreams afresh the irresistible allure of his Mysterious Stranger, and behold, he is returned, in all his satanic heavenliness. This time his gift is the consummate gratification of a long lasting dream of earthly Mark Twain's—that he and Miguel Cervantes were of the same brotherhood, that he had achieved with *Yankee in King Arthur's Court* for the British of his own time what Don Miguel had achieved for the Europeans of his, with *Don Quixote:* they had laughed down the illusions of caste and rank and freed the people. But the glamorous Stranger's good tidings must needs have its satanic twist: not Hank Morgan, but Tom Sawyer is the fantastic avatar; and Mark's kinship with Don Miguel is a trope of a philosopher of the life of reason who, toward his laughing conclusion about life, had come to read Huckleberry Finn and to draw Tom Sawyer in the likeness of Quixote. The philosopher was octogenarian George Santayana, in whose vision the life of reason had become the liberation of the human spirit as a cosmic laughter: a laughter which turns on reason's recognizing how blind is the almighty which at once creates, destroys and cares not, nor can care. Unrecognized, it keeps the life of reason a life of tears; recognized, reason exposes it for the visionless force it is. Reason's life, then, becomes a life of laughter, of heavenly laughter shaking from its wings atoms of light and tears for mortal things.

CHAPTER SIXTEEN

As of the Present Age

S HORT, HOWEVER, of that terminal transvaluation of Santayana's reason, and meaning as well, are formations of the human psyche and goals of the human enterprise.
Non-human existence receives them whenever human beings
define and appraise them for human bearings. We encounter
them, a flow of diversities now clashing, now congruent,
which our laws of logic keep ever segregating, ordering, di-
verting, and redirecting, while the diversities overflow and
swamp our exclusions of "the excluded middle," our repudia-
tions of "contradiction," and our other quests for certainty and
inalterable identity. As every so often the Mississippi pours
over and reduces to swamp and quicksand the levees that
have been built up to channel and contain its streamings, so
existence extinguishes logic. But the peoples who live on and
from the river bet their lives on their levees, and so all
mankind bet their lives on reason and meaning.

Tragedy and comedy are among the levees of the human
spirit. They are arts which contain, which channel, which
overcome the abominations that our struggles to go on struggling find or create, abominations which pertain no less to
the freedom, to the spontaneity, at the core of our human
singularities, than to the heroisms and generosities of our
personal integrity choosing, ordering, ever and again choos-

ing and ordering, and thereby rendering the event a comedy
or a tragedy. So, the self-same senseless stony nature which
breeds and slays us is to Santayana the occasion of laughter;
to Mark Twain, to Thomas Hardy, to Bertrand Russell, to
Unamuno, the condition of tears. It is "Hap" as Hardy calls
it, and man's plight is a tragedy because it is bad hap and
bad hap not inevitably, only arbitrarily; it might as readily
have been good hap. Hardy repristinates Job:

> *If but some vengeful god would call to me*
> *From up the sky and laugh: "Thou suffering thing,*
> *Know that thy sorrow is my ecstasy.*
> *That thy love's loss is my hate's profiting!*
> *Then would I bear it, clench myself, and die,*
> *Steeled by the sense of ire unmerited:*
> *Half-eased in that a Powerfuller than I*
> *Had willed and meted out the tears I shed.*

> *But not so. How arrives it joy lies slain,*
> *And why unblooms the best hope ever sown?*
> *—Crass Casualty obstructs the sun and rain,*
> *And dicing Time for gladness casts a moan . . .*
> *These purblind Doomsters had as readily strown*
> *Blisses about my pilgrimage as pain.*

John Milton did envision the vengeful God and how Lucifer his avatar, stood up to him, accepting the tragedy which
his struggle for his essential singularity chose and sustained.
What other import can these soliloquies of Lucifer's convey*?

> *Hail, horrors, hail*
> *Infernal world! and thou, profoundest Hell*
> *Receive thy new possessor—one who brings*
> *A mind not to be changed by place or time.*
> *The mind is its own place, and in itself*
> *Can make a Heaven of Hell, a Hell of Heaven.*
> *What matter where, if I be still the same.*
> *And what I should be, all but less than he*
> *Whom thunder hath made great? Here at least*

* *Paradise Lost*, I, 250–64.

We shall be free: The Almighty hath not built
Here for his envy, will not drive us hence.
Here we may reign secure—and in my choice,
To reign is worth ambition, though in Hell:
Better to reign in Hell than serve in Heaven.

. . . .
                    Yet all his good proved ill in me
And wrought but malice. . . .
Hadst thou the same free will and power to stand?
Thou hadst. Whom hast thou then, or what, to accuse?
But Heaven's free love dealt equally to all?
Be then his love accursed, since, love or hate,
To me alike it deals eternal woe.
Nay, cursed be thou; since against His thy will
Chose freely what it now so justly rues.
Me miserable! Which way shall I fly
Infinite wrath and infinite despair?
Which way I fly is Hell; myself am Hell.
[Submit? Never.]——Ease we recant
Vows made in pain are violent and void. . . .
This knows my Punisher: therefore as far
From granting He as I from begging, Peace.

. . . . All good to me is lost,
Evil, be thou my good: by thee at least
Divided empire with Heaven's King I hold.

If defeated Lucifer incarnated will for Milton, he incarnated reason for Santayana. He symbolized for both an option to defy Omnipotence and to suffer the earthly consequences which transvalue human tragedy into divine comedy. Santayana's Lucifer does not transvalue; it is through and through heavenly tragedy. Its climax is Lucifer as Reason's self, sitting lonely and alone upon his barren rock, invoking "eternal bitter truth" to be the refuge that no other being has eyes to see, bidding welcome to the cold comfort of its "joyless bosom":

Lo. I lift my head
Into the void, in scorn of all that live
Through hope and anguish and insensate woes.

For knowing grief, I have forgot to grieve,
And having suffered, without tears receive
The visitations of my kindred stars.

An alternative version of Lucifer is Faust's alter ego, the Goetheian Mephistopheles. This one symbolizes neither human will nor human reason; rather, he stands for the contingency that besets and mocks them both, for that ultimate impishness which attends the course of human events. The peer as well as the rival and servant of all-powerful divinity, Mephisto is Hardy's "crass casualty" strewing for Faust "blisses" and not pain, to the end that Faust might lose his bet, and be swallowed up in the Mephistophelian nothingness. And as tradition tells, and as Mephisto appraises Faust's magical career of lust and power, he has lost his bet. The consummation of Faust's earthly life is tragedy, the utter blank of death capping the lesser emptiness of desires fulfilled (Mephisto is the fulfiller), which compose into Faust's personal history. For Mephisto, Faust is a comic figure of self-deluded futility; his struggle to go on struggling is foredoomed to come to nothing; his earthly tragedy is Mephisto's unearthly comedy.

Mephisto
No joy could sate him, and suffice no bliss!
To catch but shifting shapes was his endeavor:
The latest, poorest, emptiest moment—this,—
He wished to hold it fast forever,
Me he resisted in such vigorous wise,
But Time is lord,
The clock stands still—
Chorus
Stands still! Silent as midnight now!
The index falls.
Mephisto
It falls: and it is finished here!
Chorus
'Tis past!
Mephisto
If past, then why?
Past and pure Naught, complete monotony!

> *What good for us, this endlessly creating—*
> *What is created then annihilating?*
> *'And now 'tis past!" Why read a page so twisted?*
> *'Tis just the same as if it ne'er existed*
> *Yet goes in circles round as if it had, however:*
> *'I'd rather choose, instead, the Void, forever.*

But eighty-year-old Goethe could not have it so. He must needs provide his dead hero with an afterlife and a heavenly career which transvalues the earthly tragedy into a divine comedy. Whether he knew it or not, doing so confirmed what his friend and fellow-poet, Friedrich Schiller, argued concerning the relations of the comic and tragic (in *Ueber naive und sentimentale Dichtung*). Schiller was a libertarian writer of tragedies. Nevertheless he contended that the end of "comedy" was higher than that of tragedy; that where the end is attained, tragedy becomes superfluous. For comedy frees the human spirit from "passion," it enables man to envision himself and his world clearly and serenely, to recognize that chance is more influential than destiny, and rather to laugh at life's inconsequentialities than to rage or weep at its wickednesses. Such seeing is man's supreme goal. It is the authentic happy ending.

The record contains another signal expression of this appraisal of the human plight. It comes later than Schiller's, in the last decades of the nineteenth century. The appraisal is made by the remarkable W. S. Gilbert. Among the laughmakers of the Victorian era he stands out, much as both Aristophanes and Menander stood out in their time. He was as prolific as they; the record credits him with some ninety pieces for the stage, apart from his verses (*Bab Ballads*), short stories, and a novel or two. He could draw, he could compose tunes, he could parody the masters, such as Shakespeare. (He had the same feeling about Shakespeare's verbiage as William James.) He could make fun of the Olympian gods, as in "Thespis or the Gods Grown Old," or in "Pygmalion and Galatea." But what lives on and is regularly restaged, not only in Great Britain and the United States, are the works he produced in collaboration with Sir Arthur Sullivan. The Gilbert and Sullivan operas have a life not unlike the plays of Shakespeare. Thirteen of them are well-known; one or two others, like *Utopia Limited*, deserve to be. First and last, the themes are like those of Aristophanes. They denude and laugh down evils of the juries, the courts, the clergy, the aristocracy, the military, the woman's movement, the democratisms—indeed, almost all the pretensions, injustices, and prejudices of Gilbert's Victorian world. But they do this in a manner not unlike Menander's. The poet's touch is light, his laughter deep yet not sardonic. His plots, and the role of the Chorus in them, seem somehow concordant with Hellenic invention. Sullivan's music carries the sentiment and the action, but they are in no way dependent on it. The poet's attitude toward death and laughter gets its definite expression in *The Yeomen of the Guard*, which he preferred above all his works. The vehicle of his appraisal of death is Col. Fairfax, soon to be executed, but of course, farcically saved and married. The vehicle of his appraisal of laughter is Jack Point, "a strolling jester," who of course gets the worst of it. To hear this Jack is to think of Shakespeare, of Jacques, and of the Fools of the tradition. To hear Fairfax is to think of how death is appraised by Hamlet (which incidentally, Gilbert parodied), and by Kent in King Lear. Hark to Fairfax, comforting his would-be comforters:

> **Lieutenant.** *Halt! Colonel Fairfax, my old friend, we meet but sadly.*
> **Fairfax.** *Sir, I greet you with all good-will; and I thank you for the zealous care with which you have guarded me from the pestilent dangers which threaten human life outside. In this happy little community, Death, when he comes, doth so in punctual and business-like fashion; and, like a courtly gentleman, giveth due notice of his advent, that one may not be taken unawares.*
> **Lieutenant.** *Sir, you bear this bravely, as a brave man should.*
> **Fairfax.** *Why, sir, it is no light boon to die swiftly and surely at a given hour and in a given fashion! Truth to tell, I would*

gladly have my life; but if that may not be, I have the next thing to it, which is death. Believe me, sir, my lot is not so much amiss!

Take my word for it, it is easier to die well than to live well—for, in sooth, I have tried both.

BALLAD—Fairfax.

Is life a boon?
If so, it must befall
That Death, whene'er he call,
Must call too soon.
Though fourscore years he give,
Yet one would pray to live
Another moon!
What kind of plaint have I,
Who perish in July?
I might have had to die,
Perchance in June!
Is life a thorn?
Then count it not a whit!
Man is well done with it:
Soon as he's born
He should all means essay
To put the plague away;
And I, war-worn,
Poor captured fugitive
My life most gladly give—
I might have had to live
Another morn!

And now hear Point disclosing, with some lingering echoes from Shakespeare's *As You Like It*, the plight and role of the jester:

Lieutenant. *I have a vacancy for such an one. Tell me, what*
Point. *Aye, sir, and, like some of my jests, out of place.*

Lieutenant. *I have a vacancy for such an one. Tell me, what are your qualifications for such a post?*

Point. *Marry, sir, I have a pretty wit. I can rhyme you extempore; I can convulse you with quip and conundrum; I have the lighter philosophies at my tongue's tip; I can be merry, wise, quaint, grim, and sardonic, one by one, or all at once; I have a pretty turn for anecdote; I know all the jests—ancient and modern—past, present, and to come; I can riddle you from dawn*

of day to set of sun, and, if that content you not, well on to mid-
night and the small hours. Oh, sir, a pretty wit, I warrant you—
a pretty, pretty wit!

Recitative and Song—Point

I've jibe and joke
>   *and quip and crank*
For lowly folk
>   *and men of rank*
I ply my craft
>   *and know no fear*
But aim my shaft
>   *at prince or peer.*
At peer or prince—at prince or peer,
I aim my shaft and know no fear!
I've wisdom from the East and from the West,
>   *That's subject to no academic rule;*
You may find it in the jeering of a jest,
>   *Or distil it from the folly of a fool.*
I can teach you with a quip, if I've a mind;
>   *I can trick you into learning with a laugh;*
Oh winnow all my folly, and you'll find
>   *A grain or two of truth among the chaff!*

I can set a braggart quailing with a quip.
>   *The upstart I can wither with a whim:*
He may wear a merry laugh upon his lip,
>   *But his laughter has an echo that is grim!*
When they're offered to the world in merry guise,
>   *Unpleasant truths are swallowed with a will—*
For he who'd make his fellow-creatures wise
>   *Should always gild the philosophic pill!*

Lieutenant. *And how came you to leave your last employ?*

Point. *Why, sir, it was in this wise. My Lord was the Arch-*
bishop of Canterbury, and it was considered that one of my jokes
was unsuited to his Grace's family circle. In truth I ventured to
ask a poor riddle, sir—Wherein lay the difference between His
Grace and poor Jack Point? His Grace was pleased to give it up,
sir. And thereupon I told him that whereas His Grace was paid
$10,000 a year for being good, poor Jack Point was good for
nothing. 'Twas but a harmless jest, but it offended His Grace,
who whipped me and set me in the stocks for a scurril rogue, and

so, we parted. I had as lief not take post again with the dignified clergy.

In another scene Wilfred Shadbolt, the dour head-jailer and assistant tormentor, fooled by his lady love and depressed, wants to change his vocation and asks Point to teach him how to be a jester:

Wilfred. *Aye, it's well for thee to laugh. Thou hast a good post, and hast cause to be merry.*
Point (bitterly). *Cause? Have we not all cause? Is not the world a big butt of humour, into which all who will may drive a gimlet? See, I am a salaried wit; and is there aught in nature more ridiculous? A poor, dull, heartbroken man, who must needs be merry, or he will be whipped; who must rejoice, lest he starve; who must jest you, jibe you, quip you, crank you, wrack you, riddle you, from hour to hour, from day to day, from year to year, lest he dwindle, perish, starve, pine, and die! Why, when there's naught else to laugh at, I laugh at myself till I ache for it!*

. . . . .

SONG—Point.
Oh! a private buffoon is a light-hearted loon,
* If you listen to popular rumour;*
From the morn to the night he' so joyous and bright,
And he bubbles with wit and good humour!
He's so quaint and so terse, both in prose and in verse;
* Yet though people forgive his transgression,*
There are one or two rules that all family fools
Must observe, if they love their profession.
*   There are one or two rules*
*   Half a dozen, may be*
*   That all family fools,*
*   Of whate'er degree,*
*   Must observe, if they love their profession.*

If you wish to succeed as a jester, you'll need
* To consider such person's auricular:*
What is all right for B would quite scandalize C
* (For C is so very particular);*
And D may be dull, and E's very thick skull
* Is as empty of brains as a ladle;*

While F is F sharp, and will cry with a carp,
   That he's known your best joke from his cradle!
When your humour they flout,
     You can't let yourself go;
And it does put you out
     When a person says, "Oh,
I have known that old joke from my cradle!"

If your master is surly, from getting up early
   (And tempers are short in the morning),
An inopportune joke is enough to provoke
   Him to give you, at once, a month's warning.
Then if you refrain, he is at you again,
   For he likes to get value for money;
He'll ask then and there, with an insolent stare,
   "If you know that you're paid to be funny?"

     It adds to the tasks
       Of a merryman's place
     When your principal asks,
       With a scowl on his face,
   If you know that you're paid to be funny?

Comes a Bishop, maybe, or a solemn D.D.—
   Oh, beware of his anger provoking!
Better not pull his hair—don't stick pins in his chair;
   He don't understand practical joking.
If the jests that you crack have an orthodox smack,
   You may get a bland smile from these sages;
But should they, by chance, be imported from France,
   Half-a-crown is stopped out of your wages!
     It's a general rule,
       Though your zeal it may quench,
     If the family fool
       Tells a joke that's too French,
     Half-a-crown is stopped out of his wages
Though your head it may rack with a bilious attack,
   And your senses with toothache you're losing,
Don't be mopy and flat—they don't fine you for that,
   If you're properly quaint and amusing!
Though your wife ran away with a soldier that day,
   And took with her your trifle of money;

Bless your heart, they don't mind—they're exceedingly kind—
They don't blame you—as long as you're funny!
  It's a comfort to feel
    If your partner should flit,
  Though you suffer a deal,
    They don't mind a bit—
They don't blame you—so long as you're funny!

That Gilbert's appreciation of death and laughter are antiphonal to Goethe's need not be further argued, even though the plot of *Faust* can be found as comic as the plot of the *Yeoman of the Guard* or of *Lear*. It is a question for the Goethe initiates whether Faust's happy ending was achieved when, under the lure of the Eternal Feminine, he began his afterlife as a celestial schoolmaster (to a school of boys who died so young that they died innocent) among the saints and angels of the Christian heaven.

For the authentic spirit of laughter, the happy ending is, of course, an event of the here-and-now, not of the hereafter, and the happiness is laughter over-ruling whatever rule holds sway over the liberties of man, cuts them off and shuts them in. Witness Cardinal Pedro Segura y Saenz, prince of the Roman Catholic establishment in Spain, indicting the age because the free men of Spain derided his person and the pretensions of his creed and power: "The universal aspiration of the present time may be summed up in one magical word—which has succeeded in seducing people—liberty. The worst type of liberty is proclaimed as representing a positive achievement of our times. This is true of freedom of thought, learning and the press . . . actually liberties of perdition, whose origin is a poisoned font giving birth to the greatest evils of the world." And what can be more a liberty of perdition than laughter? To laugh at any power is to make obscenely free with it, to take a hated liberty, to deflate and empty it of rule; and this is within the ability of the most hapless and powerless. Thus the spread of liberty is advanced as the spread of laughter, and perhaps it is for this reason, more than any other, that fear-supported power is itself afraid of nothing so much as laughter. On the record, there is no despot, no authoritarian, who does not work at turning laughter aside, suppressing it, or punishing it. The princes of state and church maintain a police force of the spirit, with censors, inquisitions, indices of forbidden books, and programs of thought-control wherein a major purpose is the protection of the holders of authority from derision. *Lese majesté* is an ancestral crime, from which, in American motion pictures, priests and politicians and other depositaries of authority have been defended by means of a "production code" devised by a Jesuit priest and long administered under lay Roman Catholic direction. During the golden days of Hitler, the Nazis conducted joke courts (*cf.* Edith Roper and Clara Leser: *Skeleton of Justice*) among whose duties was trying and punishing the Füehrer's subjects for naming horses and dogs Adolf. Telling a joke could be, as Hermann Goering admonished the Academy of German Law, an "act against the will of the Füehrer, or an act against the Nazi *Weltanschauung*, the Nazi idea of the State, or the National Socialist Government." It could be followed by arrest and imprisonment without trial or hearing, or by trial and something worse.

In their way until very recently countries behind the Iron Curtain appear to improve upon this justice. They not only labor to defend their personal and ideological sacred cows against the laughter which frees the psyche from that sanctified domination, they also prescribe what shall be laughed at, how it shall be laughed at and assume to indoctrinate comic artists in their cult's revealed orthodoxies concerning the arts of comedy. Thus at one time Communist clowns— other than those that perform, like the late Vishinsky, the recent Khrushchev, on the political stage—might neither wear Prince Albert coats nor employ slapstick. Their clowning had always to be based on Lenino-Stalinist principles and show up the bourgeoisie. For the clown, Communist clowning thus is no laughing matter. In 1948 an analogous requirement was made of the Soviet's journal of humor, *Krokodil*, by the Central Committee of the Communist Party. *Krokodil's* cartoons, stories and jokes had failed to toe the party's line. So *Krokodil's* editorial staff was shifted and its policy altered. The Central Committee decreed that *Krokodil's* duty was: "By the weapon of satire, to expose the thieves of public property, grafters, bureaucreats, boastful snobs, subservient individuals and rottenness; to react to an international event promptly and to subject to criticism the bourgeois culture of the West, showing its ideological insignificance and decay." This was how it was directed to battle "with the vestiges of capitalism in the consciousness of the people." Since Soviet subjects are still prisoners in their own country, the actual models for their satirists can be only their fellow countrymen and the actual "vestiges of capitalism," after almost two generations under Communists, can be only the Communist way of life. If *Krokodil* laughs these down, it is Communist persons and doings that it laughs down. If it Either way the party censorship must needs surely to purge poor *Krokodil* again and again and again.

For the power that laughter deflates to futility must be presently felt if the freedom which laughter vindicates is to be presently achieved. The comic spirit works as an on-the-spot spirit. It does not react to the psychologically remote or the morally unrelated. There are no irrelevant jokes. If an irrelevancy appears to be an occasion of laughter and not merely a trick with thoughts or things, the laughter has brought the irrelevant to instant relevancy. So far as I have been able to learn, no Soviet "theoretician" has yet integrated the directives of actual Communist authority with the doctrines of proto-Communist Karl Marx. To the latter, comedy was the terminal phase of a dialectic of form. He argued that Aeschylus' *Prometheus Bound* had wounded the Olympians unto death, and that Lucian's treatment of them in his *Dialogues* had killed them once again with laughter. He asserted that this dialectic of history has a purpose: for mankind to separate itself from its past "joyously." A miraculous purpose certainly, but not beyond the mysterious ways by which the dialectic of matter moves its wonders to perform.

To the right-thinking Marxist it does not matter that mankind is its past and cannot separate itself therefrom either joyously or sadly; it does not matter that, to the laugher, "past" and "future" signify present conditions too strong for his own strength to fight as such, and hence, to be cut down to size with laughter; it does not matter that among the jesters of the world no "dialectic" or "history" is as such in play. We need only consider how in Africa, "the savage hits back" with derision at his civilized white betters.* Better, we

---

* See Julius Lips: *The Savage Hits Back* (1937):

"Europe's loss of prestige will be so tremendous that Africa will become a focus of perpetual unrest for the white world and what distant issues that unrest may have defies prediction. The White God of the earlier centuries, who had the power to keep the black man in fear and terror, has proved himself puny and impotent. The black man, who is now just as inclined to limitless presumption as he was centuries ago to submission, is convinced of his own power and greatness, and will lead himself and the rest of humanity into new phases of development, which can be foreseen by neither the white man nor his dark-skinned brother, who now suddenly imagines that he knows the 'open sesame' to the mighty problems of power this earth presents.

"Whether it was this idea of the black man's awakening and his anticipated triumph over the white races, whose secret he had guessed that inspired the Loango artist to his creation, we do not know (Fig. 2, Trocadero Museum, Paris). . . . But . . . we have here before us the plastic work of a black artist far ahead of his day, and on the base of the model might well be inscribed, *The Savage Hits Back*.

"The central figure is that of a negro who has disdained giving his body the outward attributes of the white man, a negro without hat or umbrella—things which he knows to be ridiculous. His body is painted as it was painted thousands of years ago, his face is tattooed, his front teeth filed in native fashion. He stands ready to attack with a weapon in his right hand. This weapon is not the white man's once-adored rifle, it is the native's ancient lance, forged of iron melted in African blast furnaces . . . which had been in use before the white man had fathomed the secret of metal alloys. On his body this savage wears the container of the sacred magic medicine, and his lower limbs are clothed with an apron of native material. His left hand is holding the upper part of a European rifle, but it is not ready for firing. Its butt is resting on the black man's

may consider the attitudes of the Negro in the United States, until practically the turn of the century one of the several avatars of the jester in this white man's sweet land of liberty. Brought to its shores as a chattel slave, his ancestral ways of life prohibited, his original religion outlawed and persecuted, not often admitted to baptism and the salvation of Christ except as he renounced liberty as an ideal and a hope; admonished, as by Cotton Mather, to cultivate patience and be content with the condition that God had ordained for him; bred by Virginia gentlemen for the market like an animal; at long last emancipated but not truly liberated, the American Negro's laughter became the most effective weapon of his spontaneous as well as his reflective struggle to recover his God-given unalienable rights. His formal role as jester continued into the 20th century, and if he did not play it himself, it was played for him by white comedians in black-face make-up (now hardly ever to be seen).

First projected as Jim Crow, the jesting became the vocation of the variegated "end men" of the now obsolete Messrs. Tambo and Bones of the minstrel shows. These shows were long as popular in Europe, especially among the British, as in the United States. Their comedy was developed in dialogue between the presiding genius, called Interlocutor, and the comics called end-men. The Interlocutor was usually a large, tall, resplendent, unblacked white with a booming voice. His part was that of straight man or feeder to the end-men who used him for a butt. The end-men were made

---

foot. . . . It is a subordinate reserve arm but it is no longer a firearm of magic power. And there, in European dress, stands a small figure between the black man's legs, a figure seeking protection."

But, for its content, Julius Lips might more aptly have called his book "The Savage Laughs Back." As Bronislaw Malinowski observed in his Introduction, the book is "anthropology . . . defined as the art and craft in the sense of humor," an inquiry "into the vision of white humanity as held by the native . . . analysis of the white man from the point of view of the coloured races," the "tangible plastic" expression of native opinion of the white world with its strips and trade-goods, its God and its missionaries, its officials, its teachers, physicians, lawyers, explorers and its women and chieftains, deriding all.

up as Negroes whose prototype was the original Jim Crow.
The stage Jim Crow was the creation of a New Yorker, Thomas Dartmouth Rice. This actor, somewhere between his
twentieth and twenty-third year, for the first time in stage
history gave a black-face performance that used Negro physical and psychological attributes as the sole vehicle of laughter. Rice had noticed, somewhere in his trouping, an old
Negro with a hunched-up right shoulder, a left leg bent stiffly
at the knee, limping painfully as he went about his work, his
movements timed to a mournful chant without much sense
whose stanzas he marked by a queer jump, landing with his
"heel-a-rickin'." This old Negro was the original Jim Crow.

Rice multiplied the verses, diversified the nonsense, and
shaped a chorus to the jump.

> *Fust on de heel tap, den on de toe*
> *Ebery time I wheel about, I jump Jim Crow*
> *Wheel about and turn about and do jis so*
> *And ebery time I wheel about I jump Jim Crow*

Very quickly, Jim Crow became the American mutant of
the European fool and jester, the warrior who liberated people, whatever their color, from bondage and oppression of
every kind by this power of laughter. As end-man in the
minstrel show, his stupidity, his bombast, his fantastic
grammar and strange pronunciations that were attached to
his dark color and distorted form, contrasted so sharply with
the booming splendor of the white Interlocutor, that he became the little David slinging his deadly pebbles of pun and
parody against all the Goliaths of white manners and morals
from patriotism to piety. Galbreath, in his biography of one
of the great "minstrels," Daniel Decatur Emmett, cites a
stump-speech or sermon by an ostensibly Negro dominie,
preaching on a text "found" in "de inside ob Job whar Paul
draw'd him a pistol on 'Fessians lebenteenth chapter, an' no
'ticklar verse: "bressed am dem dat espects nuttin' kaze dey
aint a-gwine to git nuttin'."

Here is the climax of the sermon:

I sees a great many heah dis ebenin' dat cares no moa what 'comes of darr souls dan I does myseff. Suppose, frinstance, dat yoa eat yoa full ob possam fat an' hominy; yoa go to bed, an' in de mornin' yoa wake up an' find yourseff dead! Whar yoa speck yoa gwine to? Yoa keep gwine down, down, down, till de bottam falls out! What 'comes ob ye den? You see de debble 'comein' down de hill on a rassle-jack, wid a ear like a backer leaf an' a tail like a cornstalk; out of de mouff comes pitchforks an' lightnin', an' him tail smoke like a tar kill! Whar is you now? No time for 'pentin'; de debble kotch ye, shoa! but bress de lam! he habn't kotch dis child yet! What's gwine to 'come ob ye on de great gittin'-up day? Maby yoa tink you hold on to my coat-tail; but I'm gwine to fool yoa bad on dat 'casion, kaze I'm gwine to wear my coon-skin jacket! Yoa crawl, up de hill on yoa han's an' 'nees, yoa fall down again, wallup! . . . den you's call'd a bacslider. Dar's de brimstone, de grindstone, de millstone, de blue stone, an eb'ry udder kind o'stone de debble's got to tie 'round' yoa neck, to sink ye in de nebber-lastin' gulf ob bottom-less ruin. Yoa call for a cup of cold water an' de debble say "No!" . . . Den yoa weep an' wail an' smash out yoa teef out. Den wake up, sinners, an' let de daybroke in on ye!

My fren's, I neider preach for de lob ob de lam', de good ob yoa souls, nor de fear ob de debble; but, if you got any ole shoe, ole coat, ole hat, jiss pass 'em 'round' dis way, an' I'll light upon 'em like a racoon upon a green cornstalk. It's no use passin' 'round de plate for "Bressed am dem dat 'specks nuttin' kaze dey ain't a-gwine to git nuttin'."

And so, in the tradition of Erasmus and Rabelais, the Negro in his turn mobilizes the comic spirit to lift from the heart of man the burden of oppression whether by persons, institutions, or ideas, and cuts him loose to come upright in the freedom of laughter. By laughing down insuperable power it enables all sorts and conditions of men to overcome the fear of power and to set their minds free. Listen to Botkin, summarizing the tone and temper of the simple ex-slaves whose stories he gathered: "The talk is canny talk, full of shrewd meanings and sly humor. The stories have the unaffected sincerity of honest folk plus the reticence of those

whom cruelty has made wary and whom oppression has
taught the art of evasion and irony as a compromise between
submission and revolt. The mood is exemplified by the remark of the Negro preacher, "*Our* people de best, of co'se;
but de white man been dealing wit' yo' so long some of yo'
gettin' real tricky." Or by the reply of a Negro citizen of
Little Rock, Arkansas when a reporter asked him: "What
were you doing while the Faubus National Guard were sur-
rounding the high school?" "We were praying for rain." A
similar quality may be discerned in the folk-humor of European Jews and in the jokes reported as having been current
among the peoples of Franco Spain, Mussolini Italy, Hitler
Germany, Mao China and the Soviet Empire.

But as times move from the evasion and irony of compromise to the laughter of rebellion, whether the Ghandi-like or
the Ghana-like, the laughter acquires a new rhythm and new
tone disclosed perhaps by the opening prayer of a Negro
minister in the ineffable Eastland's Mississippi: "Oh Lawd,"
he prayed, "give Thy servant de eye of de eagle and de
wisdom of de owl; connect his soul wid de gospel telephone
in de central skies; luminate his brow wid de sun of heaben;
pizen his mind wid love for de people; turpentine his imagination, grease his lips with possum oil; loosen his tongue wid
de sledge hammer of Thy power; 'lectrify his brain wid de
lightin' of de word; put 'petual motion in his ahms; fill him
plum full of de dynamite of Thy glory; 'noint him all over
wid de kerosene oil of Thy salvation, and set him on fire.
Amen."

Does not this record somehow strengthen the conclusion
that Goethe's friend and collaborator Friedrich Schiller
reached when he decided that comedy is higher than tragedy, which it is so doubtful that Goethe agreed to? The
Goethe pundits may, of course, gainsay the notion that the
old poet's "mature" judgment is recorded rather in Mephisto's observation that human existence is, as human, tragic

existence, more tears than laughter, with laughter but a
barrier against tears. To Schiller and Mephisto, tragedy was
the human condition; comedy, man's self-liberation from this
condition. The observation presages the modern one that our
time's uses of the word "tragedy" disclose. Today "tragedy"
is used to denote any and every ill that happens and that
flesh is heir to. Less commonly, the word is nowadays used
to signify the deeper aspects of man's global plight: namely,
that all human existence is a sequence of choosings which
compound, as they occur, into personal histories and as personal histories compound again into the cultural commu-
nions which are the ways of life and "value-systems" which
the yea-sayings and nay-sayings of the choosers at once create and disclose. Or again, "tragedy" is used to point up
nay-sayings only; rejections, denials, losses, destructions and
the sufferings and sorrows which signalize them as the prevailing weather of existence. Modernly, "tragedy" intends
more the material which artists work over than the
works which their labors create. Our newsmen use "tragedy" as a synonym for disasters and calamities which befall
human beings—and even animals—whom they consider
friends or whom they do not regard as rivals or foes. But
friend or foe, there is not today one item of a man's plight
which an artist might not transvalue into an artistic formation of a tragic actuality. Recall Gorki's play, *"Nachtasyl."*
Read Bartolomeo Vanzetti, at long last accepting the judicial
murder he had been fighting against because he came to
envision it as vindicating the values he cherished:

"If it had not been for these thing," Vanzetti wrote, "I
might have live out my life, talking at street corners to
scorning men. I might have die, unmarked, unknown, a
failure. Now we are not a failure. This is our career and our
triumph. Never in our full life can we hope to do such work
for tolerance, for joostice, for man's onderstanding of man,
as now we do by an accident. Our words—our lives—our

pains—nothing! The taking of our lives—lives of a good shoemaker and a poor fish peddler—all! That last moment belong to us—that agony is our triumph!"

It requires no great effort of the imagination to translate the good shoemaker's appraisal of his doom into divine comedy, into a drama consummating his sadness, his suffering, his failure in a death which is his triumph over his enemies, and so the "meaning" of his life. Had the victim's perception of his plight held laughter as well as tears, his insight could readily have been joined to Santayana's. But it holds no laughter, the agony is the triumph; Vanzetti's sense of his life is tragic only. Tragic likewise is Max Anderson's version of Vanzetti's plight, in his play, *Winterset*. But how divergent the confrontations, how ultimately incommensurable the choices, what different tragedies! Had Vanzetti not signalized his recognition in his letter, could his personal sense of triumphant death have received any immortality in Anderson's utterance? Now, which shall live on, which will be extinguished in the stream of the Great Tradition? Will Anderson be to Vanzetti as Shakespeare to Geoffry of Monmouth, or as Geoffery of Monmouth to Shakespeare? Or will they figure as peers, different and equal, each with his proper excellence?

Modern feeling points to the latter: the tragic sense of life, whether or not articulated in words and images, is modern mankind's common sense of its own plight; perhaps it is all mankind's, in all times and places. The distinctions which the generations make are distinctions between uniquely diversifying appreciations of the ongoing experience. Their choices are choices between communications. The theme of the communications is self-renewing. But as between the living man and the poet who takes this man's experience for his theme, the advantage is usually the poet's. More commonly than we know, poetic vision keeps suffusing prosaic events and assuming into tragedy the most senseless, the most brutal hap of some hapless career; thence, we trans-

port the word "tragedy," quite unaware, from the values of
poetic discourse to all the untoward encounters of personal
history. The transport suggests an enlightenment of the in-
stinctual dark struggle not to cease struggling, to live on and
not die. It suggests a general recognition that to cease struggling, to die, can be and often is as precious and desirable as
its alternative; that brute death is as precious a value as
sheer life. Since when either is, the other can not be, the
victory of death in a struggle for existence aware of itself,
can be signalized by laughter even as by tears. To die can
be as meaningful as deathlessness, whatever a person
chooses to die for: love, honor, possessions, country, God,
peace, power, truth, right, justice, revenge—or the annihilation of them all. Survivors glorify or curse such choices and
translate the choosers into heroes and saints or devils and
sinners and even gods; Jesus of Nazareth, assumed into the
only-begotten son of God is a best-known instance of such
translation. How much Dostoevsky makes of him, and of
similar but undeified choosers!

But there continues an unacknowledged awareness that
causes die with their champions, so that it is traditional for
sacerdotal and political powerholders to give it effect by
extirpating the champions. They confront the true believers
with the alternative: *Your cause or your life.** The tragic

---

* We might recall the utterances of Montenegrin Milovan Djilas, a
fallen prince of Jugoslav communism. When jailed by his peers, he remembers his family, his country and their story as they are refracted by
his personal history. He set down his memoirs in a book, *Land without
Justice*. Writing of one battle, he says: "The grandeur of this battle lay
in the expression of an undying and inexplicable heroism and sacrifice,
which held that it was easier to die than to submit to shame—for in
death there is neither defeat nor shame." Writing of the choice his father
made between Montenegrin sovereignty and Jugoslav unification, he
remarks that his father, believing in the sovereignty, elected the unification and comments: "Choosing between conviction and a better life,
most, including Father, decided in favor of the latter. Must it be so? Is
this not a deliberate rejection of something that is peculiar to man alone,
free thought, that which is most human in man?" One is reminded of
Mill's appraisal of the man freely choosing slavery and of Renouvier's
exposition of what a free choice of determinism implies.

ones prefer suffering and dying for their causes to living on as deserters from them. The cause gives the true believer's existence all the meaning it can have. For its name's sake he sustains the ultimate abominations of man's inhumanity to man. It becomes his integrity, and he holds fast to it, knowing that he will die. So, in *The Last of the Just*, when Hitler's heroes, bravely busy gathering the household goods of the non-resistant Levys for their fiery oblation to the Nazi race, demand their books above all, the patriarch Mordecai takes his "insane" martyr's stand: "For a thousand years, ha, the Christians have been trying to kill us everyday, ha-ha-ha! And every day we managed it somehow, my lambs. Do you know why? *Because we never give up our books. Never, never, never.* We prefer to give up our lives. We'll give you our lives, ha-ha!" The pogrom passes on, without taking either books or lives. But the feeling is intimate that the book lives on only if the man who bets his life on it lives on; the cause lives but in and through its devotees. So Mordecai invokes his book to assure him that he will continue to live when he is dead, in order that he may continue to cherish and adore the book. Indeed, whatever be the cause, anxiety that the cause should survive and win generates an intense yearning that its champions shall surely live on, likewise when they are dead.

For this yearning, laughter is not consummation but occasion, incidental satisfaction. It arises as the free man's resistance to suffering, to dehumanization, as a passing reaffirmation of his humanity, as a moment of triumph in the deepest pit of other men's cruelties. Victor Frankl, a notable survivor of Auschwitz and Dachau, tells how in those abominations human lives were stripped down to an existence which no animal, but only humans could support and which only humans could inflict on other humans. Men of good will tend to appraise this existence as sheer tragedy, indeed abominable beyond tragedy. For the Nazi malice broke personality down to the sheerest animal urges of fear and hunger, with their helpless schemes and stratagems of survival, their progressive disillusion, until at the pit of despair, the sudden upsurge of liberating laughter: "Unexpectedly most of us were overcome by a grim sense of humor. We knew we had nothing to lose except our so ridiculously naked lives. . . . Humor was another of the soul's weapons in the fight for self-preservation. It is well-known that humor more than anything else in the human make-up can afford an aloofness and an ability to rise above any situation, if only for a few seconds. . . . The attempt to develop a sense of humor and see things in a humorous light is some kind of trick (*sic*!) learned while mastering the art of living . . . even in a concentration camp, although suffering is omnipresent."

Here humor once again appears as man's vindication of his own integrity, his overcoming of the utmost cruelties of his unmerited suffering, overcoming the utterly evil malice working his destruction by stripping his existence of all vision, all purpose, wherewith it could design a future growth singular to itself. Here laughter acts as both the liberation and the liberty at the very core of the enslaved victim's being: it affirms the value which only killing the laugher can extinguish but not ever deny. Unhappily the affirmation is here only transitory. It must be ever renewed, and the laugher must live on that he may keep renewing it—live on also, after he has gone to his death. So, for most sufferers, laughter is not enough; they yearn for an existence without suffering, without tears, even though without laughter. To those whose faith declares the certainty of such an after-life, laughter can well be an impertinence, a blasphemy, while death, though still an evil, must be an illusion. To those whose faith denies this certainty as self-delusion, the spirit of laughter can be the Holy One of their salvation.

CHAPTER SEVENTEEN

Liberty of the Tortured Life: Dostoevsky

Broadly, the recognized voices of that denial of death used to be the philosophers, rationalizing the dogmas of the priests of the world. Today, however, "the afterlife" is an ambiguous concern of theologians and morticians; liberty is a bugaboo of philosophies with "science" for their exclusive theme, or of pseudo-philosophies lumped together as "analysis"; or else it signifies the sentence that existentialists say, is laid upon mankind on its way to the death which is life's foregone conclusion. There is little or no place for free philosophic laughter in any of their disputatious revelations.

Yet, on the record, the ruling passion of philosophers —and of poets—is deathlessness. Their preoccupation with death and its extinction is far more poignant, far more assiduous than that of the unpriestly multitudes. Not many are recorded who accept dying as intrinsic to living, with worths for the living as momentous as any other. The moments of truth which are moments of laughter when death is achieved, or merely happens, are rare indeed in man's recorded utterance, and more rarely prized. Since Socrates, whatever place philosophers gave laughter in their scheme of things, the foremost place was death's. The anxious attention of every true believer was directed to it. All antiquity's paramount concern became to assuage the fear of death, to annul death as prospect and as event. The role of reason and faith became to dissipate death from substance to shadow. The Epicureans, holding it substance, were treated as betrayers of mankind. Lucian, who in the second century of the Christian era, performed the functions of Aristophanes by the methods of Plato among the enlightened folk of this entire world, accomplished nothing against that world's anxiety about death, although he turned to laughter its unreason, its dogmatisms, it credulities and fears. Like Mario in Santayana's *Last Puritan*, he postulated that "the absurdity of things is woven into them so inexhaustibly that we never tire of the drollery we have once really perceived."

Until well into modernity, the assurance that, in truth, death is not was the mightier magic of the Christian drama of salvation; it was why this drama's plot and action could be appreciated and presented as divine comedy. However poets designed it or theologians argued it, whatever its places and times and persons, whatever its dialogue, Death continued the foremost figure of the piece; it was the villain of course, more villainous than the Devil; it was evil, ugly, mean, low, calling the tune to which all life irresistibly danced. Let the dance be as devout, as God-fearing or as riotous and orgiastic as the dancers could make it, they were Death's fools, dancing themselves into its immortal keep whence only the risen Christ can deliver them.

The learned have devised many ways of accounting for the Renaissance; but what else could be the creativity, the new abundance and new mirth which signalized it, if not the event that in the ongoing dance of death, the joy of life had come to prevail over the fear of death? What else does Erasmus' *Praise of Folly* utter, Rabelais' *Abbey of Theleme* envision? The new struggle of these passions for mastery is,

in persons and peoples alike, the turn of action which diverts
Western culture into its modern ways. Through the eighteenth and the nineteenth centuries, joy of life was by much
the winner over fear of death. Those, the cognoscenti tell us,
are the centuries of enlightenment and liberation, of enterprise, of innovation, of the brave heart and the perceptive
mind striking out at their own risk to build the economies of
science, the arts, and the industries upon which our twentieth century is an inconceivably new and great variation.
With all the counts against them, they are centuries of enfranchisement and democratization, of a forward movement
from economies of scarcity to economies of abundance in all
things, with the good and the satisfying outweighing the
bad and frustrating.

The configuration of the new faith and works receives
signification in characteristic symbols: Liberty, Enlightenment, Equality, Fraternity, Progress, Happiness. Everywhere now, as in the West, mankind freely bet their lives on
designs for living which these symbols signalize, knowing
that their new bet is far from the same thing that their old
wager—that wager of Pascal—was declared to be. Their
works of utility and beauty multiplied, and diversified as
they multiplied, with their wagers; and Marx notwithstanding, laughter, too, came into great new abundance; the arts
of comedy came into a scope, a dignity, and a richness
beyond the most prolific of the earlier times. Nonetheless,
the most honored voices among poets and philosophers still
were those that chanted the ancient incantations and
reargued the ancient arguments against unwelcome Death.
How many existentialists can be counted who would join
Byron in holding—he wrote this in a journal of his—that
"the great object is sensation—to feel that we exist, even
though in pain. It is this 'craving void' which drives us to
gaming—to battle—to travel—to intemperate but keenly
felt pursuits of any description, whose principal attraction is
the agitation inseparable from their accomplishment." And

of the poets and philosophers whose expression prolongs the Great Tradition, how few could challenge Tolstoi's observation that "if a man learned to think, no matter what he may think about, he is always thinking of his own death. All philosophies are like that. And what truth can there be, if there is death?"

Walt Whitman, who wrote "When lilacs last in the dooryard bloomed," had an answer; Mark Twain had an answer, and perhaps it was to the effect that there could be no truth if death were truly not. The vogue of Omar Kháyyám's *Rubaiyat* carries no more weight as witness than the sinking of Algernon Swinburne's remarkable poems below the horizon of Western attention.

Above that horizon, almost from his beginnings, and in his maturity high above it, was Tolstoi's countryman, Fyodor Dostoevsky. Perhaps, as we have seen, even more voluble than his great contemporary, he was like him more deeply concerned to disclose a faith than to tell a story. The Dostoevsky pundits tend to take his *dramatis personae* for symbols and his tales, especially those of the last twenty of his sixty troubled years, for allegories regarding human nature and human destiny. Of course—as with all mankind—both are functions of the writer's personal history and his interpersonal relations; of course they signify, in the order of their succession, his changing sense of the chronic predicament and recurrent crises that his biographers must take account of. Dostoevsky, not exceptionally among the notables of *genus humanum*, suffered epileptic seizures, and the feel of them affected both his outlook on life and his expression of it. The awareness plays obbligato across his schooling, military and humane; his service as an army officer; his resigning from the military to take up a career of authorship; his appreciation—not unparallel to Karl Marx's—of Balzac; his developing sympathy, so like and so different from Tolstoi's, with the *muzhik's* psyche and the *muzhik's* faith and works; his concurrent participation in an endeavor of student-comrades to design a reform of his country's feudal-autocratic political economy, according to the vision and aspiration of such social philosophers of post-Revolution France as François Fourier, whom Karl Marx, mocking them, called "utopian."

It was foregone that these student-comrades should be spied upon and jailed. In the eyes of Tsarist authority they were cultivating heresy and designing disloyalty; justice required a punishment to fit the crime—which, to authority, was treason. And for treason it was that the group was tried, found guilty, and sentenced to be shot. In due course they were led to the place of execution, lined up before a firing squad, and heard the order "Fire!" But there was no volley. The trial had been serious, the sentence a deception, the preliminaries of the execution an unspeakable practical joke that could be described as a tragic instance of Immanuel Kant's idea of what every joke is—but this one, more than any a piece of sadist *Galgenhumor*, devised with the purpose of signalizing for its victims both the justice and the mercy of the Little Father and his agents. (It is a jest even Orwell's Big Brother has not improved upon.) In place of the shots that should kill, an official gave voice to the true sentence. It was banishment to hard labor in Siberia.

This sudden inversion of fortune—was it tragedy? was it comedy?—from an expectation of instant death back to the unceasing struggle, now to be more than ever hard and bitter, to struggle on, to stay alive, could not have failed to be seminal, perhaps of their entire lives. All the more so for Dostoevsky, he being the man he was. During the stretch of anticipation, between the order to fire and the volley that did not follow, all the years of his life could gather up in a single refusal of the certainty of instant death. An enduring consequence of the experience was a worsening of his epilepsy. And there are hints of the role of that terrible moment of truth also in his *living* past, in the diversity of experiences whose confluences consummated into his personal history and were the formative energies of his going on *now* as a man alive and aware. There is a sentence in *Crime and Punishment*—certainly Mark Twain never read it—which suggests such a poignant actuality of remembrance: "Where is it I have read that some one condemned to death says or thinks an hour before his death, that if he had to live on some high rock, on such a narrow ledge that he'd only room to stand, and the ocean, everlasting darkness, everlasting solitude, everlasting tempest around him, if he had to remain standing in a square yard of space all his life, a thousand years, eternity, it were better to live so than to die at once! Only to live, to live and live. Life, whatever it may be!"

From his twenty-seventh to his thirty-second year, Dostoevsky lived a prisoner in Tomsk. Then he was sent to Siberia as a private in the Little Father's army, ostensibly no longer a prisoner. The following year, the masters of his fate gave him back his officer's rank, but required him to stay on in Siberia in the army four years more. It was not until 1859 that his liberation was extended to include living in Moscow or St. Petersburg, and even traveling abroad. During the interval, he had taken a wife and had begun to write again. Save for his epilepsy—and this had become more critical—he was no longer the spirit that had faced the firing squad expecting "to die at once." This spirit had indeed died and had been born again. The twice-born Dostoevsky who came back into the freer world brought with him a new revelation and a new gospel. For the preaching of these the changes and chances of his subsequent personal history supply diverse images and divergent confirmations but shape up no alteration of intent. All his expression impresses as on-going disclosure of this new gospel.

The Nowhere that Dostoevsky brings news from is an ikon of Holy Russia, holy like Holy Church elsewhere, and the God-bearing Quixote among the profaner lands of the earth. Its original is the all-suffering Russian *muzhik*, so anxious, so anguished and so sure, in his simple faith that Christ the God-Man is his salvation; the *muzhik*, the might of whose certainty stands impregnably against the logic of the reasoners and the determinism and materialism of the scientists—he denies as folly their claim that the world ends and man's life comes to nothing in death. For life, Dostoevsky's revelation discloses, is everlasting. However unlaughing, however fear-ridden, however horrible, it shall not, *must not* end. In men's personal histories, let cause and consequence be said to come as the sayers choose. But the innermost core of each is nevertheless a vital freedom singular to himself and ever responsible for the ongoing consequences of its choosings and decidings, wherein a man may "prove himself worthy of his sufferings." Not to be so worthy, Dostoevsky wrote, was the one and only thing he dreaded. Balzac was wrong: not *comédie humaine* but *tragédie humaine* denotes the absurd plight of mankind. The most telling symbol of this plight is Don Quixote—"of all the beautiful figures in Christian literature, Don Quixote is the most complete. Don Quixote, however, is beautiful because he is at the same time absurd."

In a later generation, the Don's countryman, Miguel Unamuno, perhaps unread in Dostoevsky, preaching his own "tragic sense of life," invokes their common symbol more absolutely and comprehensively than the Russian. He could do so because he discoursed in concepts and not in images, in reasonings and rhetoric and not in parables. It is better, Unamuno argued, to suffer the mortal struggle never to die, to be immortal, to keep awareness everlasting, and therewith to endure the anxiety and the anguish that are organic to it; it is better to strive on, suffering, loving, hoping, than to cease to be and "rest in peace." And the highest symbolic concretion of this excellence is the Knight of La Mancha. He is a tragic figure that to Unamuno embodies the soul of the Spanish people as to Dostoevsky he embodies the Russians'. Tragic, because laughter achieves the consummation, the ultimate turn of the screw of tragedy in mankind's plight, and Don Quixote is its most telling disclosure and symbol: "The human, the intrahuman tragedy is the tragedy of Don Quixote, whose face was daubed with soap in order that he might make sport for the servants of dukes and for dukes themselves, as servile as their servants. 'Behold the mad-man,' they would have said. And the comic, the irrational tragedy is the tragedy of suffering caused by ridicule and contempt." But that absurd martyrdom is at the same time "the greatest height of heroism . . . to know how to face ridicule . . . to make oneself ridiculous and not shrink from ridicule." At this height, man has attained his ultimate of tragedy, the tragedy of laughing at himself, of becoming ever more aware of his own comicality. This height is for the tragic sense of life its point of no return: who reaches it may die of laughter at himself. And might not this be Don Quix-ote's case? At least he stayed alive conscious of his own comicality, Dostoevsky said. Heywood Broun could have said Amen; but what would Mark Twain have said? What did he say, he who saw in Dulcinea's champion, but not in his squire, the analogue of his own Hank Morgan?

However, not many readers of Cervantes' tale see in its hero what Unamuno and Dostoevsky see. Their making a symbol of the Don, particularly such a symbol as they do make, seems an idiosyncracy of their own, most doubtfully consistent with his creator's design. If what the learned say is true, knighthood's flower had faded and become dust of castles and keeps, by the time Cervantes made it an occasion for laughter with a touch of tears, or for tears with an overtone of laughter. A reading occasionally induces both and what prevails is a transaction of the reader's with the writer's images. Those set forth Don Quixote as, in his actual being, a true believer; his invincible faith has reacted to the reality beneath the appearances—to the knightly hel-met which is the reality within a shaving bowl, to the noble Rosinante that is the reality within a spavined, sway-backed drafthorse; to the Queen of Love and Beauty who is the real lady within the figure of a peasant servant-girl. And so on. For all true believers, their faith is a revelation of the reality ever beneath and beyond. Such was Quixote's; but alas, no common faith, only one singular to himself, impervious to communization. Although what it shaped for his eyes to see is to him no less real than the windmills and the peasant girls as such were to the infidels, the last did not share his insight, nor could he persuade them of it. To them, his faith was a challenge and denial of theirs, which they laughed down, while theirs has no like impact on his. His defeats but confirm his beliefs. It is when others treat these beliefs as no challenge, and pretend, only pretend, to see as he sees and believe as he believes, when they respond to his belief with their make-believe, using it to make a mock of him, that he recognizes a genuine alternative, a veritable challenge, and realizes that he must choose which is appearance, which reality.

It is this option, forced upon him by events, which incarnates the sad knight's tragedy, rendering his world a place with no room for both "reality" and "chivalry." The Russian people had such an option between Dostoevsky's Christianism and Lenin's Communism, whichever is dubbed reality, whichever appearance; the Spanish people had it when faced with the alternative: republic or oligarchy. Neither, however, were left free to choose: authoritarianism was imposed on both by *force majeure*. They have yet to be brought away from their submission as the Knight of the Sorrowful Countenance was brought away from his "delusion." He appraises his plight: "God pardon you, my friends, for you have robbed me of the sweetest existence and most delightful vision any human being ever enjoyed. Now I positively know that the pleasures of life pass like a shadow and a dream." Perhaps the peoples of Russia and the peoples of Spain have this yet to say to the freer peoples of the world. Should this turn out to be so, it is them that God will not have pardoned, not the killers of their unwarranted dream.

However this turn out, Unamuno uses Don Quixote as the cryptogram of quite another meaning than Cervantes': Dostoevsky interprets the sad Knight's consummation of absurdity in beauty with quite another frame of philosophic reference. Dostoevsky's analogue for Cervantes' hero might well be his innocent pure fool, Prince Myshkin, whose epileptic ecstasies suggest Plato's *anamnesis* and Socrates' trances. Like Wagner's *reiner Thor*, the Prince walks a stranger through a believing world whose energies are not Love but Force and Fraud; he walks, ever opting for that lovely one he so darkly recalls; he walks, living tragedy. No less a concretion of the *tragédie humaine*, this saint is the criminal, Raskolnikov, like a Dostoevsky-ized Achilles remorselessly bent on his private ends, whatever the gods may will or the laws of men command. At last, having become most concerned over the import of his options, he confronts a new choice—to accept or not to accept the uttermost responsibility for the liberty he had so ruthlessly taken, and by accepting, to vindicate and confirm the liberty. Accepting is an act of faith by which the new believer is released from the self-isolation of his criminality into fellowship and communion with other men, in Christ and through Christ; accepting signalizes the togetherness which Holy Russia has been sent by God to disclose and to teach to mankind.

Mutatis mutandis, today's no less holy successor of Holy Russia holds to a like Gospel; her Communist hierarchs have only changed the creed and the symbols of their dictated communion, they hold fast to the functions. For Dostoevsky the symbol was Christ; the creed, a mystical marriage of Slavic Christianism with Russian nationalism. The Dostoevskyan singularity grows from his employing the one as the figure and force of liberty and responsibility; the other as the disclosure and exaltation of the human tragedy.

Two parables within the one epical parable of *The Broth-ers Karamazov*—the last and ripest of Dostoevsky's expres-sions—bring this singularity to the point of no return. One is a "poem" which Ivan, the intellectual among the brothers, reads to Alyosha, the brother who is a monk and a saint. Ivan is the unbeliever and rebel who insists that if there were a God, he would be answerable to man for man's tragic condition. Alyosha is sure that there is a God and that man is answerable to him. The name of the poem is *The Grand Inquisitor*. The second parable is a "dream," a nightmare perfection of *Galgenhumor*, which Ivan, delirious, experi-ences and cannot distinguish from waking reality. The name of the dream is *The Devil*.

In the "poem," the symbolic protagonists are the Grand Inquisitor and Christ-Jesus the God-Man or Man-God. Commentators refer to the former as the ikon of the Roman Catholic establishment, with its pretorian guard of Jesuits, at the time of Dostoevsky's writing, notorious for their hatred of liberty, their push for power, their alliance to political authoritarianism with its police-methods, and their unyielding aggression against democratic movements. None seems to have interpreted the image of the Christ as any-thing but the symbol of love and liberty. The poem tells that Christ has returned to earth and, welcomed by the multitudes, is exercising his lovingkindness in their midst. As he so moves among them, the Grand Inquisitor comes upon him. That one—an old, old man, Prince Cardinal of his church, sovereign over all men's souls, claiming to be the surrogate of the God-Man declared to have founded this Church—sees its founder raising a young girl from the dead. He orders the miraculous healer arrested. The multi-tudes whom the latter had come again to serve, see and do not protest. For this compliance the Grand Inquisitor blesses them, and they humbly receive the blessing.

Comes midnight, the Prince Cardinal of Christ's Church

visits the prisoner in his dungeon. He addresses him: "Thou, whoever thou art, tomorrow I will burn thee and the people will turn on thee. For thou hast come to hinder us." Hinder, because the God-Man is the spirit of liberty, and the foe of authority. Authority must needs wage war against liberty in the souls of men with its sole weapons, "food" and "happiness." For this mess of pottage the multitudes ever pay with their liberty. The rebel generations that defended it were defeated, as they had to be, because this was very Christ's unrescindable will. That foregone conclusion to rebellion had been foreseen as the temptings of Christ in the wilderness. There, that eternal Denier, Satan, that wise and mighty spirit of negation, of self-destruction, that demon of non-existence thrice tempted God's only-begotten Son; and these temptings infolded mankind's entire future. For there the spirit that ever denies, urged upon yea-saying Christ that his pledge of liberty was an empty pledge; that the sons of Adam cannot understand liberty; that they continue anxious, afraid; that to them "nothing is more insupportable than liberty"; that it is bread they want more than anything. Change stones into bread, then for the bread's sake, they will believe you, and obey you and follow you. Bread can and does buy obedience. What, now, does your liberty buy?

We, providing bread, gain and hold power and banish liberty, so that they, the weak, live on, not for themselves but for us the strong and great. In return, we look after them. Although "they are rebellious and sinful, they will, in the end, have learned to obey. . . . We fool them . . . we will continue to fool them, in thy name." And our deception, we being forced to it, will be our agony. "So long as man stays free, he struggles for nothing so incessantly, with so much pain as to find as quickly as he can, some one to worship, a one beyond dispute, whom all can together worship as one." This is why, before Christ came, mankind fought one another, each for the imperium of his separate oneness. Their

Christ preferred liberty in the place of empire. He exalted liberty to unprecedented greatness, he lodged it with the "free love" of Christ and called to men: Choose!

Choosing is a "fearful burden," as the history of Christianity makes clear. Sin and suffering are intrinsic to liberty, are ways on which men must travel in order to find themselves. But men cannot take the responsibility of these ways. They are less than he, Christ, believes they are, so the Grand Inquisitor informs his Divine Prisoner, and are guilty of their own deficiency. If they are not, then permit man "the quiet, humble happiness fitted to his own nature (such happiness as ants attain in an anthill, chickens in a chicken coop). It is bread man must have, not liberty; miracles, not faith; empire that will diminish suffering. Now Christ rejects these devilish alternatives of the Tempter; he insists on liberty. Therefore the Grand Inquisitor must needs reject Christ: "Didst thou forget that men prefer peace and even death to liberty of choice in the knowledge of good and evil? Nothing could seduce a man more than his liberty of conscience, nor is anything a greater cause of his suffering. . . . Didst thou not know that man would reject even thy image and thy truth if they weigh him down with the fearful burden of free choice?" Men are still children, humble, weak, pitiful. They crowd into the churches, awestruck and afraid, "quick to shed tears like women and children." "But they will be just as prompt at a sign from us to pass to laughter and rejoicing, to happy mirth and childish songs." We whom they heed, however, remain always unhappy. For we have been laboring at Satan's side these eight hundred years, performing miracles, perpetrating mysteries, in payment for the kingdom of all the earth.

"Know that I fear thee not, know that . . . I too blessed the liberty wherewith thou hadst blessed mankind; that I too had striven to stand among the chosen, among the strong and powerful. But I woke from that dream; I would not serve madness. I returned to join the ranks of those who have corrected thy works. I abandoned the proud and went back to the humble for the sake of the happiness of the humble. . . . I repeat: Tomorrow wilt thou see the obedient flock hasten at the first sign from me to heap up hot coals around the pile on which I will burn thee because thou camest to hinder us. If any one has ever deserved our fires, it is thou. Tomorrow I will burn thee. *Dixi.*"

And the God-Man continues silent throughout the long harangue. When it ends, he kisses his priestly executioner.

That is, the laughers are only fooled; but the laugh-makers, the deceivers, they, it is, who suffer. Ivan comments: "It is no great moral blessedness to attain perfection and liberty, if at the same time one has become convinced that millions of God's creatures have been created as a mockery, that they never will be capable of using their 'liberty.' " Alyosha replies: "Your Inquisitor does not believe in God. You believe that the Devil's advice is best for the feeble, unruly, incomplete, empirical creatures who are men, created in jest'." In sum, mankind's existence is a practical joke of its creator, who made them free, and suffering as, and because, free; and hence, searching and seeking for a swap: liberty in return for a mess of pottage. So, mankind's comedy is tragedy. Quixote is his paradigm and the Dance of Death his road of life.

Ivan's nightmare is another trope presenting the Dostoevskyan gospel. Ivan dreams that he is being visited by a member of the landed gentry, fiftyish, not rich, "a poor relation." He cannot believe that the apparition is real, and proofs cannot change a will-not-to-believe into a will-to-believe. He tells the visitor "You are myself, only with a different face." To which the latter retorts: *"Satanas sum et nihil humanum a me alienum puto* (not even human rheumatism) . . . I was predestined to deny, yet I am truly good-hearted and nowise disposed to negating." Only, negating is a necessity: "Nothing but hosannas do not suffice for the business of living. Yet men, with all their indisputable intelligence, do take the farce of existence as something serious, and this is their tragedy. . . . To suffer is to live. . . . Nothing need be destroyed—only the idea of God in man, to make of this world a heaven. . . . But when?" "But what about me" cries Ivan, "I suffer, just the same, I don't live." Satanas doesn't know what the good God might be, or might do—there is no law for God: "It keeps the world going that I desire good and do evil." (Note that Goethe's Denier, Mephisto, keeps the world going by desiring evil and achieving good.) "How many souls have had to be ruined and how many honorable reputations destroyed for the sake of that righteous man, Job, over whom they made such a fool of me in the old days. Yes, till the secret is revealed, there are two sorts of truth for me—one, their truth yonder, which I know nothing about so far, and the other my own. There is no knowing which will turn out better. . . ."

Thus Dostoevsky takes Job's tragedy as a joke on the adversary and a divine comedy. For him, so much a man of tears, laughter suffuses tears, but obbligato. For such men of laughter as Mark Twain, tears are the import of the laughter; if not its spring. So, likewise, of liberty: for the Dostoevskys of the damned human race, *lacrima rerum* are downpourings of mankind's ineffable liberty, its mirth and laughter rewards of its subjection to preponderant power; for the race's Twains, mirth and laughter are liberations from such power to whose inescapable coercions man owes all his sins, sorrows and sufferings. But the most welcome liberator is ever-feared, ever-evaded Death, while for the Dostoevskys, life, life the most tragic, the most insufferable, is better than no life at all. Within the bounds of these divergencies, *genus humanum* keeps turning its kaleidoscope of liberty, laughter, and tears.

Index